Political Opposition
and Foreign Policy in
Comparative Perspective

Political Opposition and Foreign Policy in Comparative Perspective

Joe D. Hagan

Lynne Rienner Publishers ▪ Boulder & London

Published in the United States of America in 1993 by
Lynne Rienner Publishers, Inc.
1800 30th Street, Boulder, Colorado 80301

and in the United Kingdom by
Lynne Rienner Publishers, Inc.
3 Henrietta Street, Covent Garden, London WC2E 8LU

Library of Congress Cataloging-in-Publication Data
Hagan, Joe D.
    Political opposition and foreign policy in comparative perspective
    Joe D. Hagan.
      p. cm.
    Includes bibliographical references and index.
    ISBN 1-55587-027-9 (alk. paper)
    1. International relations—Research. 2. Opposition (Political
science) I. Title.
    JX1291.H334 1993
    327—dc20   93-15853
                                          CIP

British Cataloguing in Publication Data
A Cataloguing in Publication record for this book
is available from the British Library.

To the memory of my father,
Benjamin F. Hagan, Jr.

Contents

Charts, Tables, and Figures

Charts

Tables

Figures

Preface

This book reports on an extensive examination into the cross-national relationship of domestic politics to foreign policy. It is premised on the widely argued theoretical idea that domestic political phenomena—in this case, patterns of political opposition—broadly condition (but do not alone determine) how governments cope with the demands and constraints of the international system. Although grounded on a synthesis of the various strands of theory and research on this topic, the thrust of this book's research is largely conceptual and empirical, with a focus on political opposition. Its overarching concern is that comparative, cross-national, empirical research, which includes newer analyses on war proneness as well as some on foreign policy change, has failed to capture the complexity of domestic political phenomena that is theorized to account for foreign policy patterns. Most of this research infers the existence of domestic constraints from the basic structure of national political systems, assuming that leaders in some politics (e.g., established democracies) face opposition while their counterparts in others (e.g., authoritarian and less developed systems) operate free of such constraints. Furthermore, to the extent that actual political opposition has been considered across varied political systems, the focus has been mostly on the most extreme forms of political instability, e.g., revolutions, societal turmoil, and other forms of domestic conflict.

Drawing upon both the major theoretical works and analytic case studies of foreign policy decisionmaking in non-U.S. settings, the contention here is that domestic political constraints are far more pervasive and variable than suggested by structural notions of domestic politics. This is true in several respects: (1) political opposition may exist in any type of political system although in a variety of forms, (2) it is by no means automatic that major levels of opposition occur in democratic systems (or in any other type of system), and (3) the pattern of political opposition may vary significantly across time without changes in a nation's political structures. It would also be premature to assume that the most relevant opposition in a political system usually takes the form of extreme instability and mass unrest. Rather, as consistently demonstrated by non-U.S. cases, the more typical pattern of opposition is relatively mainstream, organized political groups operating within various governmental institutions, whose influence may vary across a variety of political conditions. While not dismissing the periodic significance of episodes of extreme turmoil and revolution, the focus of this volume is on these more regular patterns of political opposition.

The purpose of this book is, then, to develop and illustrate the conceptual and empirical materials necessary for executing comparative, cross-national analyses of regular domestic opposition patterns as they relate to foreign policy. This includes a sequence of three tasks. The first is the conceptualization of opposition actors at different levels of the political system in a manner that captures some of the complexity in the theoretical literature and the insights of area specialists. Of particular concern is to tap "equivalent" levels of constraints involving different types of opposition actors across institutionally diverse political systems. The second task is to develop procedures for directly measuring patterns of political opposition in a way appropriate for cross-national analysis. The challenge here is that subtle aspects of the strength and intensity of opposition be measured in a way that is not so detailed that it does not preclude the realistic collection of extensive cross-national data. The final task is to implement the scheme. An opposition data set for the regimes of diverse political systems of a sample of thirty-eight nations is constructed. This data is then employed in a preliminary, largely exploratory analysis of the association between opposition and several basic dimensions of foreign policy: commitment, independence, and aspects of conflict behavior. Although somewhat tentative, the findings provide some clear clues as to how varied domestic political phenomena interact to influence foreign policy.

This kind of research, especially in its initial stages, is not without risks. Not only has this first attempt at systematic data collection and analysis been a very open-ended exercise, but the scope of the effort is restricted in certain ways that should be clear to the reader from the beginning. One risk is that this research, given the broad, comparative manner in which it is cast, might be interpreted as offering a comprehensive explanation of foreign policy. Not only must political explanations be seen in the context of wider international and societal influences (with domestic politics usually taking a supplementary role), but the opposition focus taken here is not intended to incorporate the full array of political phenomena relevant to understanding domestic constraints on leaders. Although regular, organized political opposition is captured, various kinds of more fluid political constraints (particularly, nongovernmental groups and public opinion) are beyond the scope of this study, and possibly defy incorporation into the kind of general scheme developed here. Also, relevant literature on state-society relations, as well as that on domestic instability and turmoil, will have to be incorporated at a later time.

Other risks stem from the fact that this subject matter spans the fields of comparative politics and international relations, and it may well be that attempting to bridge these fields does not fully satisfy the concerns of either. My treatment of political opposition and its foreign policy effects is grounded less in general comparative politics theory and more in case study research and theoretical work by country and area specialists on foreign policymaking in various non-U.S. settings. The conceptualizations in this book should therefore not be viewed as a summary of comparative politics theory; rather, although consistent with basic themes in that literature, these efforts are more an integration of the non-U.S. decisionmaking literature. As to the concerns of international relations, I have resisted the temptation to extend (and prolong) this project to focus on the important research into the domestic political roots of more complex foreign policy phenomena such as restructuring, cooperation, and war proneness. At this stage, my concern has been to link opposition to foreign policy behaviors most direct-ly associated with political outcomes of the decisionmaking process. Clearly, a subsequent task will be to extend the research here to analyses of foreign policies that drive the dynamics of international change, complex interdependence, and the outbreak of interstate war. I would hope that some might see the relevance of this book's concepts, research design, and find-ings to these broader concerns in international relations.

This book is the outcome of an ongoing interest in how domestic polit-ical systems shape what nations do in international affairs. Given that this is my first book, I want to express my gratitude to those who have had the most enduring influence on my research. My interest and training in this topic date back to my years as an undergraduate at Drew University and, in particular, to memorable courses in international relations and comparative politics from Professors David Cowell, Barbara Salmore, and Douglas Simon. Perhaps to her dismay, the ideas Barbara and her husband, Stephen Salmore, outlined in an early manuscript on political regimes and foreign policy have never left me. As a graduate student I had the good fortune to study under Maurice East from the moment I arrived at the University of Kentucky. Mickey framed my entire approach to the study of foreign policy and guided the development of my serious independent interest in regimes and domestic politics as they relate to foreign policy. Mickey was for me an exceptionally devoted graduate professor and mentor, and I look back warmly to the hours late into the night at his house being aggressively tutored in the comparative approach to foreign policy. In recent years, my richest collaboration has been with Charles and Margaret Hermann at Ohio State University's Mershon Center, where we have been working on a pro-ject on decision units and foreign policy. Although separate from this book's research, my work on political explanations of foreign policy has benefited greatly from the many intense and imaginative theoretical discussions on the third floor of the center.

A few other individuals also deserve mention for their specific input into this project. Lynne Rienner has been extremely patient, to say the least, through the life of this long project, and I am most grateful to her and also my editor, Gia Hamilton. Vincent Davis at the University of Kentucky socialized me to the virtues of case study research in the development of decisionmaking theory. My new colleague at West Virginia University, Bob Duval, read much of the manuscript and pointed out problems in the statistical analysis, while also reassuring me that its relatively simple techniques were not inappropriate for the objectives of this book. This project, particularly the recognition of its place in the larger context of international relations, is better because of my conversations with Jerel Rosati on the foreign policy restructuring project. Michael McGinnis, as a discussant on a panel at ISA several years ago, cogently critiqued several features of this project in its original formulation. The many interactions with the case authors in the "decision units and foreign policy" volume and the members of "Stockholm comparative foreign policy" working group have provided numerous theoretical insights into non-U.S. settings. Finally, I am grateful for the support provided by Alan Hammock, my department chair, and for funding from the Office of the Dean of WVU's Eberly College of Arts and Sciences.

I owe many thanks to other good friends and family who have sustained me through this long venture. Chris and Jen Carney and the Milams—Mike, Eileen, Dylan, and David—helped my family and me settle in Wyoming and were an essential part of our good years in Laramie. With our move to West Virginia we have grown comfortable quickly, thanks in large part to a supportive department and a network of new family friends, such as the Duvals, the Millers, and all the parents and children at Jeanne's day care. My mother, Elizabeth Hagan, has to have by now set a record of sorts for the longest sustained enthusiasm for a single book. I'm always grateful for her interest.

My deepest debts are to my wife, Jeanne, and our four children—Allyson, Rebecca, Michael, and Katelyn. Jeanne holds all of us together and without her love and support this sustained effort would never have been possible. My life is greatly enriched by the mix of demands and supports of *my* domestic settings, and although this project has to have been quite foreign to my family at times, I thank them for never opposing it.

This book is dedicated to the memory of my father, Benjamin F. Hagan, Jr. Like the Vietnam War, Huey Long, and Cohasset life, he surely would have put this project into proper perspective long ago. That has been missed.

—*J. D. H.*

1

Introduction: The Problem of Domestic Politics in Comparative Foreign Policy Research

The importance of domestic political influences is widely acknowledged throughout the analytic literature on foreign policy. Political explanations are an important element in efforts to account for such diverse phenomena as the origins of war (Levy, 1988; Vasquez, 1987), crisis decisionmaking (Lebow, 1981; Snyder and Deising, 1977), international cooperation (Putnam, 1988), foreign policy change (Holsti, 1982; Goldmann, 1988; Hermann, 1990), and presidential use of force (Ostrom and Job, 1986), as well as U.S. Cold War policies (Gaddis, 1982; Paterson, 1988; Dallek, 1983). Political influences are at the core of theoretical efforts among researchers interested in the comparative analysis of foreign policy, where there has long been interest in the idea that states with different domestic political arrangements engage in different patterns of foreign policy behavior. Various political factors are cited as primary sources of foreign policy in the field's major theoretical frameworks (Rosenau, 1966; Brecher, Steinberg, and Stein, 1969; East, Salmore, and Hermann, 1978; Wilkenfeld et al., 1980). Not only have these frameworks spawned numerous cross-national analyses of general foreign policy behavior patterns, but the comparing of political systems has been extended to the more focused phenomena of the war proneness of democratic and authoritarian systems (Small and Singer, 1976; Doyle, 1986) and the political roots of foreign policy restructuring (Moon, 1985; Hagan, 1989a).

The concern of this volume is the quality of political explanations in the comparative analysis of foreign policy.[1] Much of the empirical research that is cross-national in scope remains underdeveloped, with most analyses focusing on the broad structural attributes of political systems and, in particular, the level of democratization and to a lesser extent political development. As such, this research largely fails to incorporate the various non-structural conceptualizations of political influences in the comparative foreign policy frameworks, and thus far much the same can be said about most cross-national studies on domestic politics and war proneness or

1

foreign policy change. Perhaps more compelling is that this emphasis on political structure is by now very much out of touch with important analytic developments in the area studies literature on foreign policy making in various non-U.S. settings. Indeed, in the 1990s it still holds that "large gaps appear in the existing literature on foreign policy and political phenomena" (Wilkenfeld et al., 1980: 53; also Hermann and Hermann, 1980; Kegley, 1980). Political perspectives for executing comparative, cross-national studies remain largely undeveloped.

This book seeks to begin to fill the gap in this research through a detailed, yet largely exploratory, cross-national examination of the theoretical and empirical linkage between domestic political opposition and foreign policy. Its starting point is that foreign policy making is an inherently political process and that such domestic influences on foreign policy are a cross-nationally pervasive phenomenon. However, these effects can not be inferred entirely, or mainly, from the structure of a nation's political system, because, first, opposition does not simply exist in certain political systems (democracies) and not in others (authoritarian and less developed polities) and, second, the level of opposition in any political system may vary considerably across time and from one leadership to another. The book develops a conceptual framework in which the relationship between domestic politics and foreign policy behavior is recast in a way that captures equivalent types of opposition across diverse political systems. This framework is built around the idea of the "political regime," the particular political *group,* or *coalition of groups,* that controls the highest authoritative policymaking bodies of the national government. Political opposition, in turn, refers to those groups in the political system who challenge the current regime's hold on power and/or program of policies. This kind of perspective shifts the focus away from political system structure toward the domestic situation of a particular set of leaders *and* how they respond to these pressures in making foreign policy. The regime focus also facilitates judgments about the presence or absence of opposition across the full variety of political systems.

The addition of yet another conceptual framework, though, does little to advance the literature if the foreign policy effects of its core political components cannot be examined empirically in a reasonably large-scale comparative analysis. This project confronts the main barrier to executing these kinds of analyses of domestic politics and foreign policy: the lack of a cross-national data set on the kinds of political phenomena that theoretical works suggest influence foreign policy decisionmaking. This book details workable procedures for the construction of such a large-scale data set on regimes and opposition actors. A data set is constructed for a sample of eighty-eight political regimes in thirty-eight national political systems, followed by an exploratory analysis of the empirical association between domestic opposition and several basic dimensions of foreign policy behavior. The results from this analysis contribute to the body of findings in the existing literature, but, more importantly, they also provide insights for the direction of subsequent research on domestic politics and foreign policy.

The purpose of this introductory chapter is to explicate the research problem that frames the theoretical and empirical analyses and to place this project into the general literature on domestic politics and foreign policy.[2] There are two concerns here. The first is to clarify the theoretical assumptions underlying this research project, an exercise that will also demonstrate that the causal linkage between domestic politics and foreign policy is inherently complex, a situation with which any general or comprehensive theoretical effort must grapple. The other concern is to summarize the relevant cross-national research on domestic politics and foreign policy, as a means of isolating the major research themes and gaps in empirical research, particularly the ones that this project seeks to fill. The chapter closes with an elaboration on some of the book's basic concerns and premises, followed by an overview of its organization.

Why Opposition Matters:
Explicating the Theoretical Linkage to Foreign Policy

This section outlines elements of the general theoretical relationship of domestic politics to foreign policy. It does so by asking: Why assume that domestic political opposition matters to the extent that it can account for broad, cross-national differences in foreign policy behavior? In addressing this question, I keep coming back to three basic reasons: (1) foreign policy decisionmaking is inherently political, (2) domestic politics has substantively important effects on foreign policy behavior, and (3) political opposition is a pervasive phenomenon across nations with diverse political systems. However, when one looks to the prominent theoretical literature on domestic politics and foreign policy for answers, it quickly becomes apparent that theorists are not of a single mind on either of the first two issues. The implication of this is that the politics of foreign policy is intrinsically complex, involving diverse kinds of political phenomena, alternative causal mechanisms, and sharply divergent effects on foreign policy. Examining these three reasons for the importance of domestic politics, as well as their respective complexities, serves to explicate the theoretical premises underlying this research project; the first two are explored here, while an entire chapter (the next one) is devoted to the third, the cross-national pervasiveness of domestic politics.

The first reason for the overall significance of domestic politics is that foreign policy decisionmaking is intrinsically political. This holds that government leaders and decisionmakers routinely monitor domestic political conditions and incorporate them into their foreign policy calculations. This does not represent aberrant decisionmaking or an exceptional occurrence; rather, leaders do this regularly and do so in a way that can be assumed to be largely rational. Foreign policy decisionmaking is normally what Tsebelis (1991) calls "nested games of multiple arenas" and Putnam (1988) refers to as "two-level games," in which decisionmakers balance their perceived national interest with their expectations about domestic political constraints. Yet this linkage between domestic politics and foreign policy is complicated because leaders must engage in two, not one, domestic political games involving diverse opposition actors with different goals and interests. Rooted in Steinbruner's (1974) characterization of foreign policy as a "complex decision problem," the interconnection between domestic politics and foreign policy stems from two political tasks: coalition policymaking and retaining political power. The political nature of foreign policy lies in these two simultaneous, ongoing political imperatives for national leaders.

• Coalition policymaking concerns the requirement that agreement be achieved among actors who share (formally or informally) the authority necessary for committing the resources of the nation to a particular course of action in foreign policy. It stems from the fact that the making of foreign policy, as a complex decision problem, typically involves multiple actors (Steinbruner, 1974), such as contending leadership factions and executive bureaucracies, separate institutions such as the legislature or a politicized military, and/or nongovernment actors (e.g., interest groups) essential to the sustained implementation of the decision. Where there are disagreements among these authoritative actors, decision outcomes then take the form of a "political resultant" (Allison, 1971) reflective of the agreements necessary to gain approval for the action. This process, by which leaders build the authority for major policy initiatives, has long dominated U.S. foreign policy literature with its emphasis on political constraints on presidential initiative due to bureaucratic politics (e.g., Hilsman, 1971; Allison, 1971; Halperin, 1974), the assertion of congressional authority (e.g., Spanier and Nogee, 1981; Frank and Weisband, 1979), and the weakness of the U.S. state (e.g., Katzenstein, 1976; Krasner, 1978). It is also at the core of foreign policy models of domestic structure (e.g., Risse-Kappen, 1991; Mastanduno, Lake, and Ikenberry, 1989), as well as in models of single-group and coalition decision units (Hagan, Hermann, and Hermann, forthcoming; also Snyder and Diesing, 1977).

• Retaining political power is the second imperative of domestic politics, being associated with the second dimension of the complex foreign policy problem: mixed, competing values or goals (Steinbruner, 1974). One goal for foreign policy makers, acting in their concurrent role as national political leaders, is maintaining and, if possible, enhancing the political support base necessary for holding on to political power. Thus, foreign policy makers (at least senior ones) must balance foreign policy concerns with their need to maximize domestic political support for their regime. When foreign policy considerations are inconsistent with the regime's political situation at home, political leaders must adjust foreign policy to make it more compatible with those domestic realities. In U.S. foreign policy decisionmaking literature, the logic of presidential survival underlies such varied treatments as Halperin's (1974) "presidential interest," Mueller's (1971) "presidential popularity," and Hampson's (1988) "divided decisionmaker." The political fears of the Truman and Johnson administrations, respectively, are a dominant theme in postrevisionist literature on the origins of the Cold War (Gaddis, 1972; Patterson, 1979; Leffler, 1993) and the Vietnam War (Gelb with Betts, 1978; Berman, 1982; Schandler, 1977). General models of crisis decisionmaking, particularly those that contributed to the outbreak of war (and especially World War I), incorporate political explanations that stress leaders' perceptions of the domestic consequences of their foreign policy actions (e.g., Levy, 1989; Lebow, 1981).

The separate political imperatives of coalition policymaking and retaining political power form the theoretical premise here that domestic politics is a widespread and nonaberrant influence on a nation's foreign policy.[3] Equally important, though, it points to the need to cast conceptualizations of domestic politics in a broad manner. Any general theoretical formulation must consider opposition groups in multiple arenas, or levels, of the political system. Coalition policymaking, in its pure form, involves individuals and groups who occupy the authoritative structures of the central political leadership, or the political regime. As such, to get at this dynamic, it is necessary to focus on the extent of conflict and division among the actors within that central political leadership, along with any external groups essential to the implementation of the policy. In contrast, the essence of retaining political power is that leaders respond mainly to external challenges to their control of the regime, although in extremely fragmented regimes this opposition may come from factions in the regime. In this way political actors outside the regime (e.g., opposing political parties, a politicized military, and various forms of domestic unrest) are important, because over the long term they influence the selection of future leaders and compete for office. In sum, these dual domestic political games involve diverse types of opposition at multiple arenas of the political system.

The second reason domestic political opposition is important is because it has an impact on substantively important aspects of foreign policy. Even without taking the extreme position that domestic politics is the dominant, driving force behind a nation's foreign policy, it can still be argued that leaders respond to opposition in ways that adjust national foreign polices in significant ways. This occurs in several ways. First, political opposition affects the extent to which a government is willing and able to *commit* to a course of action in foreign affairs, for example, joining an international organization such as the League of Nations or European Economic Community, deploying military forces to fight aggression in such places as Manchuria or Vietnam, or entering into compromises necessary to break a deadlock in international trade negotiations, be it the 1930s or the 1990s. Second, domestic politics influences the precise mix of *confrontation and accommodation* with acknowledged adversaries, conditioning the propensities of leaders to use military force or resort to protectionist trading strategies. Compare, for example, how domestic politics and national legitimacy crises "pushed" pre–World War I European leaders toward confrontation, while the situation in the divided and polarized Western democracies right up to World War II "pulled" leaders away from stopping aggression at all costs. Finally, domestic politics is often at the root of the level of *assertiveness and passivity* in diplomatic posturing, examples of which range from the minimal activities of Japan's largely reactive post–World War II foreign policy to the dramatic shifts toward independence in the foreign relations of Gaullist France and revolutionary Iran. As suggested by these brief illustrations, domestic politics ultimately helps determine how the games of the balance of power and complex interdependence are played.

But as before, the evidence of the importance of domestic politics is not simple or direct. Instead, the precise impact of political opposition on foreign policy behavior occurs in completely divergent ways across different situations and episodes. Among the familiar cases just mentioned, domestic opposition prevented leaders from taking meaningful action in certain cases, while in others the effect was to propel them toward sharply intensified actions. The significance of this observation is that it indicates that leaders may respond to domestic opposition (at any level) in fundamentally different ways. Therefore, central to this research effort is the idea that there is no single dynamic by which political opposition affects foreign policy. Drawing upon established theoretical research, it can be argued that the causal linkage between domestic politics and foreign policy can take one of three forms: bargaining and controversy avoidance, legitimization of the regime and its policies, or neither, when leaders act to insulate foreign policy from domestic political pressures.

• Bargaining and controversy avoidance: The main feature of this political dynamic is that political leaders and foreign policy makers respond to opposition by attempting to accommodate it with some form of restraint in foreign policy. It would seem especially important in coalition policymaking, because a compromise or some other bargaining strategy is necessary if the support of other authoritative actors is to be gained (this is the particular focus of Putnam's [1988] "two-level games"). In the broader political arena, where opposition groups challenge the regime itself, it centers around the leadership's avoidance of controversial actions that could discredit the overall leadership, for example, by making it look weak or by having it associated with a widely recognized adversary (see Salmore and Salmore, 1978). In either case, the resulting foreign policy actions are similar. Domestic politics acts as a constraint that prevents foreign policy initiatives that are strong in intensity and commitment; in other words, the government engages in low-risk behavior. Bargaining constraints, as well as controversy avoidance, underlies much of the conventional literature on the allegedly incoherent and reactive nature of U.S. foreign policy making (Kennan, 1951; Morgenthau, 1951; most recently, Destler, Gelb, and Lake, 1984). Leader preoccupation with Congress and divided public opinion are the dominant political themes in analyses of the orientations of U.S. foreign policy under Franklin Roosevelt (e.g., Dallek, 1979) and Nixon and Kissinger (e.g., Brown, 1983). Much of the international relations theory on the pacific character of democratic foreign policies rests, in large part, upon the idea that domestic politics inhibits foreign policy makers (e.g., Doyle, 1986), while Lamborn (1985, 1991) treats domestic politics as a constraint on the risk propensities of all potential belligerents.

• Political legitimization: This dynamic is one in which the leaders confront the opposition and attempt to mobilize support for the regime and its policies (or prevent the loss of that support), all in a manner resulting in amplified foreign policy activity. This strategy is most widely associated with the task of political survival in which a leadership manipulates foreign policy issues as a means of (1) enhancing the legitimacy of the regime by pursuing popular policies (e.g., nationalistic ones), (2) demonstrating strong leadership, and/or (3) deflecting attention away from divisive domestic problems by emphasizing foreign threats in a way that also discredits domestic opponents. It also occurs in coalition policymaking when advocates of a policy aggressively confront opponents' arguments and try to mobilize support among those actors still uncommitted on the issue. Theoretical discussions by George (1980) and Trout (1975) have suggested the importance of legitimizing strategies as an aspect of coalition policymaking. Political legitimization is treated by a number of Cold War historians as a primary dynamic behind the hardline U.S. policies toward the Communist world (Gaddis, 1982; Paterson, 1988; and Dallek, 1983), while political motivation in the use of force by U.S. presidents has been systematically demonstrated in analyses by Ostrom and Job (1986) and James and Oneal (1991). Legitimizing strategies such as "bashing the foreigners" (Russett, 1990) and "scapegoating" (Levy, 1988) are also found throughout the extensive international relations literature on the relationship between domestic conflict and foreign conflict (see overviews by Stohl, 1980; James, 1988; and Levy, 1989).

• The insulation of foreign policy from domestic politics: While the above two dynamics point to a strong political impact on foreign policy, the third dynamic suggests there is a diminished effect on foreign policy even when significant opposition exists. This is where political leaders and foreign policy makers act to deflect or reduce opposition constraints on their foreign policy choices. Such is the case where regime preferences on a politically controversial issue are strong, and the leadership is willing to take the political risks associated with implementing the policy. Containing political opposition may involve a number of actions: leaders may either ignore opposition challenges, suppress their opponents entirely, or co-opt them with political favors or concessions on other policy issues. The foreign policy literature on decisionmaking and domestic politics suggests that governments are often able to do so, depending on the nature of the situation (Brady, 1974; Paige, 1968), issue-areas (Art, 1973), presidential personality (Krasner, 1972; Perlmutter, 1974), and the suppression of opposition (James, 1988). Whatever the case, it is important to keep in mind that, even in the face of strong opposition, leaders may attempt to insulate foreign policy from domestic pressures.

The research implication of these alternative strategies is considerable, particularly because literature has emphasized one dynamic or the other. Taken together, they suggest that the linkage between domestic politics and foreign policy is an inherently contingent relationship. Ascertaining the foreign policy effects of opposition thus involves a sequence of two general questions: first, does opposition have an impact on foreign policy behavior, and, second, if so, how, and reflective of which strategy? In other words, an additional question must be added to the basic issue of whether or not foreign policy is linked to domestic opposition: if leaders can not insulate foreign policy from domestic politics, the direction of that relationship—as well as its strength—must also be considered.

In sum, a premise of this research is that foreign policy making is an inherently (and nonaberrant) political process, but the linkage of domestic politics to foreign policy is by no means simple. As diagramed in Figure 1.1, any conception of the necessarily complex relationship between domestic opposition and foreign policy must recognize three core elements: (1) that political leaders engage in the dual domestic political games of coalition policymaking and retaining political power (facing diverse opposition both within and outside the regime), (2) that they may choose alternative political strategies for dealing with opposition (bargaining/controversy avoidance, political legitimization, or insulation of foreign policy), and (3) that their choices have important, yet divergent, effects on several basic dimensions of foreign policy (commitment, confrontation/accommodation, and assertiveness/passivity).

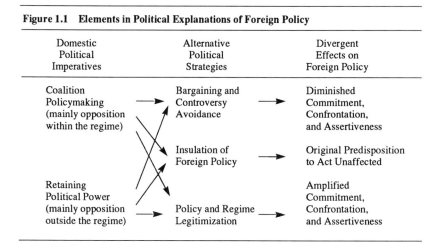

Figure 1.1   Elements in Political Explanations of Foreign Policy

Comparative Research on Domestic Politics and Foreign Policy: An Overview

This section overviews the major literature on domestic politics and foreign policy that has approached the relationship from a comparative perspective with an explicit concern for systematically ascertaining cross-national patterns between the two phenomena. The particular purpose of this brief review is to survey what political variables and explanations have been considered in the theoretical literature and then examine to what extent these frameworks and models have been examined in the empirical literature. Although this is not a comprehensive examination of all that this literature has to offer, it will serve to identify the research gaps that are the concern of this book.

Domestic political influences are, of course, a major component of Rosenau's (1966) long-influential "pre-theory" framework. Governmental factors, along with individual, societal, and systemic variables, constitute the four clusters of "source variables" that directly shape the nation's foreign policy. And two of his three "genotypic variables," which condition the effect of source variables, are essentially political variables; in other words, accountability concerning political structure and development is largely treated as indicative of political development. Although Rosenau does not specify the precise variables within the government variable cluster, he is clear about how accountability and development influence the relative potency of the three domestic source variable clusters. Quite simply, individual leader traits are the most important foreign policy influence in nations with either closed or less developed political systems. Only in modern democratic polities do societal and governmental influences out-weigh the leader's dominance on foreign policy, because of the constraints of competing political elites or parties, private interest groups, and estab-lished constitutional procedures guaranteeing open political activity. In closed regimes, competing elites and private interest groups are not allowed to exist, while in less modern states, leaders experience few of the pres-sures that "bureaucracies and large-scale organizations impose in more developed countries" (Rosenau, 1966: 47).

A number of early comparative foreign policy studies sought to assess the overall empirical validity of the Rosenau pre-theory. Some of these studies indicate that accountability has an important influence on foreign policy. Moore (1974a, 1974b, 1974c) reported significant differences in United Nations voting behavior of open and closed regimes when control-ling for size and development, while Rosenau and colleagues (Rosenau and Hoggard, 1974; Rosenau and Ramsey, 1975) found that the eight pre-theory genotypes rank in an expected order. However, most other compara-tive research uncovered a weak and more complex relationship (Butler and Taylor, 1975; East and Gregg, 1967; East and Hermann, 1974; C. Hermann, 1975; Salmore, 1972; Salmore and Hermann, 1969; Salmore and Salmore, 1970). Actually, the more consistent evidence comes from studies employing accountability as an intervening variable mediating the foreign policy effects of other source variables, for example, studies of leader per-sonality (M. Hermann, 1974, 1980), governmental and societal constraints (Moore, 1974b), and domestic conflict (Wilkenfeld, 1973).

Political factors, as well as the other sets of foreign policy influences, have been more fully specified in the frameworks of the Interstate Behavior Analysis (IBA) and the Comparative Research on the Events of Nations (CREON) projects.[4] The political component, one of five source compo-nents in the IBA framework (Wilkenfeld et al., 1980),[5] consists of three sets of influences: formal institutional factors, such as bureaucratic and leg-islative arrangements, linkage mechanisms, concerning the effects of the wider polity such as public opinion, and political system aggregate descrip-tor variables, referring to the overall features of the polity and the regime such as elite profiles. In the early CREON project, political phenomena and their effects on various dimensions of foreign policy behavior are outlined in the "regimes perspective" (East, Salmore, and Hermann, 1978).[6] As developed by Salmore and Salmore (1978), this perspective concerns the national leadership's ability to extract resources from the society (resource availability), political conditions that undercut its ability to act in foreign affairs (political constraints), and its orientation toward opponents and other domestic arrangements (disposition to use resources). Political con-straints most directly concern domestic opposition, focusing on "the degree of coherence or unity within the regime itself and between the regime and other governmental political institutions, the nature and extent of regime accountability, and the degree to which the regime represents the wider society" (p. 122).

The IBA and CREON projects have each produced substantial empirical findings, but in both projects the assessments of the political elements have, at best, been limited and incomplete. The IBA researchers did not collect data on their political phenomenon, and instead concluded that of the five source components "the political component is undoubtedly the most difficult to conceptualize" (Wilkenfeld et al., 1980: 53). Still, the IBA project has generated important findings about the role of political structure (as an aspect of nation-type) through an analysis of the relative importance of source components (which, again, exclude the political component) across five groups of nations.[7] Two sets of findings are particularly notable. First, the importance of societal influences was found not to be limited only to democratic states, but instead was correlated to the foreign policies of Western, closed, and unstable nations, although these effects are complex with different societal variables affecting foreign policy in varied ways across the three types of nations. Second, the influence of individual leaders was found to be particularly strong in certain types of nations, and Wilkenfeld et al. (1980: 22) conclude "that psychological source factors would exert maximal impact in closed states (because of the concentration of power) and developing systems (because roles are less clearly institutionalized)."

Much of the earlier CREON research on political regimes also turned out to be primarily on political structure and, in particular, the role of accountability (Butler and Taylor, 1975; East and Hermann, 1974; Salmore, 1972; Salmore and Hermann, 1969; Salmore and Salmore, 1970).[8] A couple of analyses, however, did conceptualize domestic political constraints directly and assess their impact on foreign policy behaviors. Salmore and Salmore (1972) examine the impact of two nonstructural properties of regimes: the genesis of a regime, essentially a measure of the regime's institutionalization, and its internal political coherence in terms of decisionmakers' "expectations that its actions will be accepted by internal support groups, and thus that the decision it takes will not be opposed" (p. 8). Although the Salmores find only regime genesis to be significantly linked to foreign policy, studies by Geller (1985) and Hagan (1987) elaborate upon their conceptualization in alternative ways and find regime constraints associated with conflict and independence in foreign policy.[9]

The final two bodies of research, neither of which is tied to mainstream comparative foreign policy research, concern political explanations of two specific foreign policy phenomena: the initiation of war and the restructuring of foreign relations. As evidenced by the citations in the previous section of this chapter, research into the political origins of war is an important tradition in international relations literature (see Levy 1989; Blainey, 1988). There are two seemingly separate areas of theory development here.

Political structure is the theme of the first, comparing the war proneness of democratic and authoritarian political systems and typically making the argument that democracies are less likely to initiate war than are authoritarian systems. Explanations of the pacific character of democratic polities hold that these polities produce leaders who are less bellicose in international affairs and/or that the pluralistic nature of democratic political constraints imposes greater institutional and opposition constraints on foreign policy decisionmakers (Wright, 1942; Doyle, 1986; Rummel, 1983; Russett, 1990). The other strand of theoretical work linking domestic politics and war focuses directly on leaders and their opposition and in ways that cut across democratic and authoritarian settings. Much of this literature associates domestic politics with aggressive and expansionist foreign policies, either because of leaders who try to manipulate opposition with various diversionary tactics (Levy 1989; also Levy, 1988; and Russett, 1990, as noted earlier) or because of hardline tendencies within the leadership group due to its political vulnerability (Lebow, 1981; Rosecrance, 1963) and coalition logrolling and imperial myths (Snyder, 1991; see also Lamborn, 1985, 1991).

Systematic research in this area has been impressive, with a cumulating body of historical evidence on the connection between domestic politics and war proneness using the Correlates of War data on international wars and disputes since 1815. Most of this research examines the question of the relative war proneness of democratic and authoritarian nations. The evidence consistently supports Wright's (1942) original finding that there has been little difference between the overall propensity of democracies and authoritarian regimes to go to war, while at the same time providing clear evidence of a complete absence of war among democratic political systems (Small and Singer, 1976; Chan, 1984; Doyle, 1986; Weede, 1984; Dixon, 1989; Maoz and Abdolali, 1989; Russett, 1990).[10] Systematic research into the other political sources of war proneness is, in contrast, far more limited. Two studies suggest, albeit with contradictory conclusions, the importance of a political system's level of development or, more precisely, institutionalization. Maoz (1989) finds that newly established polities (both democratic and authoritarian) created through revolutionary processes are more prone to international disputes, while Dixon (1989: 5) finds that older democracies are quite war prone as structural constraints "erode as the polity becomes entangled in alliances and accustomed to its role in the international system." Another body of research by Morgan and colleagues (Morgan and Campbell, 1991; Morgan and Schwebach, 1992) looks directly at political divisions in all types of political systems and provides preliminary evidence that decision constraints undercut the tendency of conflicts to escalate into war. These two studies of nonstructural phenomena suggest that politics in both democratic and authoritarian systems influence overall patterns of war proneness, not just interactions with similar types of political systems.

The growing research on foreign policy change and restructuring also provides important insights into the linkage between domestic politics and foreign policy, all cast in a way appropriate for comparative analysis. Political factors are central to the three major theoretical explanations of foreign policy change. The political element of Holsti's (1982: 14) multicausal framework is centered around political opposition in the form of factionalization, the foreign policy effects of which are conditioned by leadership attributes and dynamics, for example, their attitudes toward external actors, personality factors, policymaking processes, and decisionmakers' perceptions and calculations. The focus of the Goldmann (1988) framework is on the stabilization of new policies from domestic and international pressures. Political stabilizers—leader consensus, issue salience, and the institutionalization of policy—essentially affect the extent to which a policy can be insulated from domestic opponents seeking its termination (p. 248). Political influences on government decisions to change course in foreign affairs are interwoven throughout much of Hermann's (1990) framework in which he identifies several sets of agents for change and the sequence of decisionmaking phases by which leaders recognize and manage those pressures. The restructuring of opposition is one of four primary agents of change, and political dynamics underlay several of the processes through which decisionmakers identify and manage pressures for change. The specific decisionmaking phases involving political dynamics are leaders' initial policy expectations, the recognition of discrepant information, the development of alternatives, and the building of an authoritative consensus for new options.

Political sources of foreign policy restructuring have been examined in several cross-national analyses. These preliminary studies do not capture the subtle political dynamics in the above frameworks, but they do provide important, though indirect, evidence of the role of political phenomena in foreign policy change.[11] Two analyses find evidence that foreign policy changes do not result from the movement from democratic structures to authoritarian rule, or the reverse. Maoz and Abdolali (1989) find that the rise or fall of democratic institutions within countries has historically had little impact on their war proneness, while Andriole, Wilkenfeld, and Hopple (1985) report that changes in basic political structure have had little impact on trade patterns of Third World nations. Other studies move away from political structure and the democratic/authoritarian focus and, instead, focus on the foreign policy effects of other kinds of regime changes. Moon (1985; also Midlarsky, 1981) demonstrates that revolutionary changes in the Third World have had an important impact on those countries' voting alignments in the United Nations. But Hagan (1989a) shows that many of these realignments can be traced to less dramatic types of regime changes, involving nonstructural political phenomena such as shifts between mainstream parties or contending factions within a single party.

This brief survey is intended to provide some sense of the status of political explanations in the comparative study of foreign policy. The look at the major theoretical frameworks points to three distinct categories of political phenomenon in foreign policy. The first category concerns structural properties of the political system as a whole, often with the focus mainly on accountability and, to a lesser degree, political development. The focus on political system structure is apparent throughout the comparative foreign policy, international conflict, and regime change literatures. The second category concerns various domestic political pressures and is centered around conceptualizations of actual opposition. This includes nonstructural patterns of domestic politics, such as regime fragmentation/coherence and regime genesis in the CREON project, political linkage mechanisms in the IBA project, decision constraints in war proneness studies, as well as various political pressures in the Goldmann, Hermann, Holsti frameworks. Whereas the previous category concerns political divisions within the national political system, the third category of phenomenon, which is also nonstructural, focuses on the shared political orientation of the members of the regime or the national political elite. Falling into this category are the CREON project's notion of the "disposition to use resources" and the IBA project's "political system aggregate descriptor variables." The shared images and interests of the regime are also evident in the various regime change studies and are central to some explanations (e.g., Wright's logic) of the relatively bellicose nature of authoritarian regimes. Clearly, then, there is no shortage of attempts to conceptualize a broad range of internal political phenomenon.

However, a look at the empirical literature makes it equally evident that the range of research across the three categories of political phenomenon has been biased and incomplete. Quite simply, a large majority of empirical studies have focused on political structure in the form of formal accountability and, to a lesser degree, political development. In part this has been intentional. Some studies assumed that accountability was an important factor and sought to test it, both as a direct influence and a mediating factor. For example, assessments of the Rosenau pre-theory, as well as certain of the war proneness and foreign policy change studies, view structural phenomena as directly indicative of political constraints and/or indicators of the political orientations of leaders. However, in the cases of the CREON and IBA projects there has simply been a failure to measure effectively the other concepts presented in their elaborate theoretical frameworks. The IBA researchers cite the difficulty in accomplishing this task and then ignore the political source component in their analysis. Within the CREON project (in its earlier phase) there was an effort to measure political phenomena, but the regime's perspective was not as well developed as the project's other theoretical perspectives. In sum, empirical research has not matched the ambitions of the various theoretical frameworks.

There are two problems with this emphasis on political structure to the exclusion of other kinds of political phenomena. First, accountability and political development have not accounted for foreign policy behavior very well. One of the major findings of early comparative foreign policy studies has been that the conflict levels of democratic and authoritarian states are not markedly different. Accountability was useful when employed as a variable mediating the linkage between source variables and foreign policy. The democracy/war proneness studies have also consistently demonstrated that democratic states have been just as prone to initiate wars and militarize disputes as have their authoritarian counterparts; confirmation has been limited to showing that democracies rarely fight with one another. Foreign policy change studies also suggest in varying ways that there are limits to structural conceptions of political regime change.

The second problem with the emphasis on political structure is that it does not adequately capture domestic political phenomena of considerable theoretical importance. Rather, at least as a cross-national indicator of political constraints, its use rests upon the tenuous assumption that opposition exists in only certain types of political systems and not in others. Leaders in modern, democratic polities are viewed as being greatly constrained, while their counterparts in less developed or nondemocratic systems operate relatively free of domestic opposition. However, as will be shown in Chapter 2, neither condition is likely to hold entirely because the level of opposition can vary substantially in any type of political system; domestic opposition may be quite substantial in the regimes of closed and less developed political systems, while it may be rather mild in established democratic polities. Thus, although political structure may capture some other important aspects of domestic politics, used by itself it is an inadequate indicator of opposition, and dependence upon such conceptualizations oversimplifies cross-national assessments of how domestic politics influences foreign policy.

The Scope and Organization of the Book

The research reported in this book falls into the second category of political phenomenon above, that which attempts to account for cross-national differences in foreign policy patterns in terms of patterns of domestic politics, for example, regime and decision constraints, institutional and bureaucratic actors, linkage dynamics, opposition and support, and the like. Without making claims to being comprehensive, it focuses on what is arguably a primary, though largely unexamined, feature of domestic politics: the pattern of political opposition. As studied here, political opposition refers to those groups in the political system that are poised to compete for authority and control in national political structures and that aggregate interests across a broad range of policy issues. The chief conceptual task for this volume is to identify basic types of political actors and classify them in terms of their political position vis-à-vis the regime, with respect to both their relative resources and political orientations. Although this likely excludes certain relevant political actors and activities, it still captures the mainstream, ongoing domestic political activity that probably shapes leaders' perceptions of their immediate domestic political environment. Furthermore, it incorporates much of the political phenomena noted in the various comparative theoretical frameworks, but does so in a way that does not preclude broad, cross-national analyses of domestic politics and foreign policy.

The aspirations of this research effort are shaped by several additional overarching considerations. Chief among these is a concern, as noted above, that notions of political system structure (e.g., the democratic/ authoritarian distinction) do not adequately capture cross-national variations in the kinds of political opposition that influence foreign policy behavior. In other words, as will be demonstrated in Chapter 2, it cannot be assumed that leaders in some types of political systems (e.g., democracies) typically face major domestic opposition, while their counterparts in other types of systems (e.g., authoritarian systems) operate largely free of domestic political constraints. Therefore, a chief task throughout this effort is to conceptualize opposition in ways that capture important variations within political systems having fundamentally different structural arrangements, not only between democracies and authoritarian systems but also between established and less developed polities and between parliamentary and presidential systems. Ultimately, the hope is to be able to talk about equivalent levels of opposition across different types of political systems and to permit systematic comparisons in the role of domestic politics in their foreign policies. All this is not to say that political structure is irrelevant; as suggested in some of the comparative research (e.g., Wilkenfeld et al., 1980; Hermann, 1980), it mediates the impact of domestic sources of foreign policy in majors ways and will be considered as such in judging the impact of domestic opposition on foreign policy.

Another concern is to incorporate some of the theoretical complexity in the general linkage between domestic politics and foreign policy, as outlined earlier in this chapter. This applies to the range of opposition to be considered. The simultaneous importance of the political imperatives of coalition building and retaining political power points to the importance of opposition at multiple levels or arenas of the political system. At one level is opposition most immediate to foreign policy decisionmakers in the form of political divisions within the group, or among the coalition of groups, that controls the authoritative policymaking structures that constitute the regime. As best argued by Salmore and Salmore (1978), it is within the regime that policymaking authority is concentrated, and because of this it is mainly here that coalition policy processes are played out.[12] At the opposite level are political groups that are outside of the regime and challenge the ruling party's or coalition's control of the regime. From the perspective of the regime's leadership, the primary dynamic involved in its relationship with these opponents is political survival and the task of retaining control of the regime.[13] A third level of opposition, falling midway between these two extremes, is also important. This is opposition from within the support groups aligned with the regime. The regime's relationship with these groups likely involves a mix of coalition building and competition for control of the regime; namely, while these actors challenge the current leadership in the long term, they operate to keep the regime in power and thus are brought into the policymaking process. Any purportedly comprehensive research of political opposition patterns must necessarily attempt to examine opposition at multiple levels if it is to begin to tap the dual political games of coalition policymaking and retaining political power.

This research also attempts to incorporate some of the complexities in the causal mechanisms by which opposition becomes connected to foreign policy. Although beginning with the assumption that leaders are attentive to strong and intense opposition, the effects of those domestic pressures are dependent upon additional contingencies associated with the political strategies by which leaders cope with tensions between domestic politics and foreign policy imperatives. This contingent relationship suggests two interrelated tasks. The first is the juxtaposition of the alternative dynamics of bargaining/controversy avoidance and policy/regime legitimization with their respective diminishing and amplifying effects on foreign policy behavior. The question here is not only if leaders respond to opposition; of equal importance is how, and with what strategies, do they engage that opposition. The second task is to explore political conditions that might explain how leaders respond to opposition. Under what political conditions are foreign policy makers able to insulate foreign policy from domestic pressures; and, in those cases where they are not, what conditions predispose leaders toward accommodating opposition by bargaining or controversy avoidance as opposed to confronting it by legitimizing the regime and its policies?

Finally, let me acknowledge that all this is bounded (some might say limited) by a persisting interest in the idea that general domestic political patterns can account for some interesting broad features of foreign policy behavior. In this way, this book's analysis is rooted in the various literatures that have sought to uncover a broad association between political system structure, such as democracy, and patterns of foreign policy behavior, war proneness, and restructuring. However, the approach taken here involves a subtle, yet important, shift in the unit of observation. The approach taken here, following an imaginative analysis by Salmore and Salmore (1972), focuses on the political configurations of successive political regimes across time within national political systems.[14] Although the term "regime" is used in a variety of ways, I conceive of it as the group or set of groups that control the central authoritative political structures of a national political system.[15] The concept of regime is valuable for two reasons. It leads one to think in terms of opposition as it relates to the leaders who actually make policy; thus, throughout this analysis political opposition (including that within the regime) will be conceptualized and measured in terms of its position relative to the group or coalition occupying the regime. The regime notion also facilitates large-scale, cross-national analyses of opposition and foreign policy. As will be fully explained in Chapter 4, the political regime (defined as a single group or coalition in power) can serve as a unit of analysis that can capture changes in domestic political opposition across time, shifts that occur even though political structures remain entirely intact.

The organization of the remainder of the book is as follows. Theoretical and conceptual issues are the concern of the next two chapters. Chapter 2 examines the matter of the existence of political opposition in, and impact on foreign policies of, diverse types of political systems. The intent of that chapter is to develop, in an informed way (i.e., based on substantively rich area studies case study research), themes for conceptualizing opposition in diverse settings and linking it to foreign policy behavior in a way appropriate for cross-national analysis. These insights are the basis for Chapter 3: the development of nonstructural conceptualizations of political opposition and of the logic by which to link them to several dimensions of foreign policy behavior. Three sets of political influences are considered in this chapter: the fragmentation of political authority within the regime, opposition in the wider environment (e.g., ruling party factions, opposition parties in the legislature, the military, and regionally based leadership), and aspects of the political system and regime context. The explanatory logic is developed regarding the impact of these political influences on several dimensions of foreign policy and under what conditions.

An empirical analysis is executed in the next two chapters. Chapter 4 explains the operationalization of political variables and the procedures for constructing the political opposition data set used in the book. This discussion provides details on source materials, the use of the political regime as a unit of analysis, measurement procedures for the specific political variables, as well as the regime data set itself. An analysis linking opposition to foreign policy is reported in Chapter 5. This analysis explores the broader association between various types of opposition and dimensions of foreign policy behavior for a sample of eighty-eight regimes for the decade 1959–1968. These direct relationships are considered further by reexamining them across subsamples of regimes defined by aspects of political system structure and certain regime properties.

The findings in Chapter 5, while in some respects preliminary, raise clear insights into, as well as puzzles about, the dynamics of the basic linkage between domestic politics and foreign policy. Chapter 6 concludes the book with a summary of these wider implications for comparative research into domestic politics and foreign policy. Several puzzling findings are also identified, followed by a discussion of three avenues for further research that could possibly resolve some of the puzzling findings. What emerges from the book's effort is not a definitive set of findings, but rather several clear guideposts for further cross-national research.

Notes

1. Comparative foreign policy analysis, as defined here, refers to efforts to cast theoretical and empirical studies in a way that consciously permits systematic comparisons across different decision situations, episodes, and/or nations. The cross-national emphasis is especially important here, given my concern with contrasting different types of political systems and regimes.

2. This literature concerns major theoretical research in international relations and foreign policy decisionmaking with illustrations of the latter primarily from research on U.S. foreign policy. This analysis attempts to synthesize a large amount of literature normally treated separately, but does not attempt a comprehensive or thorough survey of the voluminous research on especially the politics of U.S. foreign policy. Good reviews of the literature on domestic political influences on U.S. foreign policy can be found in Kegley and Wittkopf (1991), Nathan and Oliver (1987), and Rosati (1993). Note that the primary literature review presented in this book, the subject of Chapter 2, analyzes the literature on the politics of foreign policy in non-U.S. settings.

3. "Uncertainty," Steinbruner's third dimension of the complex decision problems, is not included in the discussion here. However, it too is relevant in several less direct ways. First, national political leaders are generally more familiar with domestic politics than with foreign situations; as a result, they are probably more likely to act on what they perceive to be the more clear-cut threats of domestic opposition, even if such action could affect more ambiguous foreign relationships. Furthermore, the level of uncertainty is related to the scope and intensity of political debates over foreign policy. Political constraints on foreign policy action will be especially severe where there is fundamental disagreement over the nation's interests and/or the consequences of a particular course of action. Finally, these dynamics, as well as others, suggest that shifting levels of domestic and international uncertainty can account for the varying impact of domestic politics across different types of issues and situations; for example, domestic political constraints are likely to be diminished in situations of international crisis. This argument underlies the contextual role of conditioning influences, particularly institutionalization and vulnerability, in the framework developed in this book. It is developed further in Hagan (forthcoming-b).

4. The important Brecher, Steinberg, and Stein (1969) framework is not discussed in this brief survey because it did not spawn (nor did it seek to) large-scale,

cross-national analyses. Some of its findings on the Israeli case are, however, considered in Chapter 2.

5. The IBA's other four source components concern psychological, societal, interstate, and global influences. Note that phenomena such as domestic unrest and other forms of political instability are included in the societal component.

6. The CREON project's other theoretical perspectives concern leader personality, decisionmaking structures and processes, national attributes, international systems, and situational environment. Note that the identification of this as the early stage of the CREON is a reflection of certain difficulties in reviewing the efforts of what is now a two-decade-old project. As explained in East, Salmore, and Hermann (1978), "early" CREON involved the development of separate political perspectives and the execution of cross-national aggregate data studies. "Later" CREON has moved to a far more situationally and decision-specific posture (e.g., see Hudson, Hermann, and Singer, 1989; Hermann, Hermann, and Hagan, 1987; Hermann and Hermann, 1989; Hagan, Hermann, and Hermann, forthcoming). The research reported in this book actually spans both stages of the project. Its early roots are to be found in the early work of the Salmores (1970, 1972, 1978), although Geller's (1985) research is a much more direct extension of the Salmores' project. In addition, as will be discussed in this book's conclusion, the concepts and data presented here are intended to contribute to the more situationally oriented explanations of political opposition. Another initial effort in this direction is found in Hudson and Sims (1992).

7. Specifically, the IBA researchers empirically derive a typology of nations, similar to Rosenau's genotypes, based on four structural dimensions: capability, economic structure, government structure, and instability. The latter two dimensions are clearly political, and government structure is essentially a measure of democratization. Through a subsequent Q-factor analysis of these four structural dimensions, five nation groupings were then identified: Western, closed, large developing, unstable, and poor nations.

8. These studies are, though, significant in that they elaborate on the theoretical logic linking accountability to foreign policy and examine its impact (which again was found to be limited) on commitment, initiative, adaptability, and consistency in foreign policy behavior—not just conflict as has been the case in other accountability analyses.

9. The extensive empirical literature on the linkage of domestic and foreign conflict might also be considered to fit here. It is not included because the conceptualizations have mostly to do with broader domestic instability, much of which is nonpolitical in nature, and as discussed in Chapter 3, because much of it falls outside the scope of opposition as discussed here.

10. An important study by Schweller (1992) refines these analyses by contrasting the responses (preventive war versus nonwar options) of declining democratic and authoritarian powers to the challenge of rising new powers.

11. As best argued by Moon (1985), looking at differences in a nation's foreign policy across a sequence of regimes can provide insight (albeit indirect) into the deeper political roots of a nation's foreign policy. If it is found that a major shift in foreign policy occurs between successive regimes, then it can be argued that the different traits of the two regimes (e.g., changes in political structure, leader orientation, and/or political constraints) were at root in their respective foreign policies. For example, a finding that major foreign policy restructuring occurred only with regime changes involving a shift between democratic and authoritarian structures (in either direction) would indicate that accountability is the dominant domestic political influence on foreign policy.

12. As will be discussed, it is still important to recognize that power may become significantly dispersed such that actors outside the regime become directly involved in policymaking processes.

13. However, as will be argued, severe political competition for power occurs within politically fragmented regimes during periods of high uncertainty about the regime's internal distribution of power.

14. This logic is similar to Gurr's (1974) development of the concept of a "polity" as a unit of analysis in identifying changes in authority structures within national political systems. Gurr's focus is, of course, structural and as a result a single polity normally persists for several decades, if not longer. In contrast, the more fluid character of opposition patterns suggests that the time span of even a reasonably stable regime is likely to be less than a decade, while in a highly unstable system a regime does well to last a couple of years.

15. Although the term "regime" is used in different ways, its definition here is closer to that used in the comparative politics literature than in the international relations literature. A good overview of its various conceptualizations in comparative politics can be found in Lawson (1993).

2

The Politics of Foreign Policy in Non-U.S. Settings: A Reassessment of Themes for Comparative Analysis

This chapter extends the theoretical discussion in Chapter 1 to address in detail my third reason for assuming that domestic political opposition matters: namely, that opposition significant to foreign policy making is a pervasive phenomenon across widely different types of political systems. This is not a simple issue. As just noted, the conventional wisdom in most comparative research (and currently reigning in the research on democracy and war proneness) is that domestic political pressures are largely limited to some types of political systems (established democracies) and not others (closed and/or less developed ones). To assess the validity of this assertion, this chapter examines research on the politics of foreign policy in three basic non-U.S. settings: (1) established parliamentary democracies, (2) established authoritarian polities, and (3) various Third World nations with (presumably) less established political systems. These categories are admittedly simple (as will be even more clear at the end of the chapter) but are still a useful starting point, and the latter two correspond to the open/closed and developed/less developed dichotomies underlying the conventional comparative foreign policy schemes. Parliamentary democracies are also included to permit examination of the role of opposition in democracies other than the United States with its presidential system. Because of the diversity of parliamentary cases, this group is divided into those with multiparty coalition cabinets and those with factionalized single-party cabinets. The analysis of each setting demonstrates the third premise for this research project: that political influences are pervasive across all types of political systems.

Four questions are asked about the politics of foreign policy in each setting. First, does significant opposition exist in any of the three kinds of polities where conventional wisdom suggests that it would not? If so, what specific kinds of political actors operate in these settings, specifically, what are their organizational properties, and in what political arenas do they operate? Third, how does opposition influence foreign policy decisionmakers in these settings? Under what conditions are leaders most sensitive to opposition, and, if so, in what ways do leaders cope with these opposing groups, for example, by bargaining and controversy avoidance or through political legitimization? Finally, what impact does opposition have on decision outcomes, and what aspects of foreign policy are affected by these political processes? Not only will answers to these questions permit evaluation of conventional themes in comparative foreign policy analyses, this exercise will also provide the basis for identifying specific directions for further cross-national research.

Addressing these questions requires detailed information on specific decisions and some familiarity with these political systems. As a generalist, I do not claim any particular country or regional expertise. My strategy is, then, to base my discussion of each setting's politics on the analysis of case study research done by country/regional experts, and then to synthesize these insights in a cross-national fashion. The utility of case studies to the systematic development of foreign policy theory is now widely recognized (Eckstein, 1975; George and Smoke, 1974; Rosenau, 1987; Jervis, 1990).[1] Such collective work is especially important to the development of a more complex, yet cross-nationally applicable, framework linking domestic opposition to foreign policy. The premise of the chapter is that the simplicity of comparative research on domestic politics and foreign policy lies, in part, in the failure of generalists to recognize the accumulating theoretical insights in the now typically conceptually well-informed area study research on non-U.S. foreign policy decisionmaking. And, as such, the chapter serves a second purpose: it brings to light this extensive—yet quite scattered—case study literature for the benefit of generalists who work in this area. In no way is this meant to be a comprehensive literature review on each country or region, but a welcomed side-benefit would be to stimulate greater attention by generalists to case study research of foreign policy theorists with expertise on specific countries and regions.

If it is not already apparent, the reader should recognize the centrality of the chapter to all that follows. The literature synthesized in the chapter lays the groundwork for the theoretical framework in Chapter 3—indeed, the utility of that scheme should ultimately be judged by its success in capturing (in general form) the kinds of political actors and processes described in the case study literature. My bias is that this scattered case study research has much to offer about the precise nature of opposition in non-U.S. settings and how it influences foreign policy, and therefore this chapter's analysis of these case studies constitutes the major literature review for the volume. I will not expand further upon the brief treatment in Chapter 1 of the major works on the politics of U.S. foreign policy. Nor will I attempt to tackle in detail the extensive research on political opposition to be found throughout the comparative politics literature. At certain points, I draw upon core concepts in the literature on party systems, praetorian militaries, coalition politics, and the like for purposes of conceptualization (Chapter 3) and operationalization (Chapter 4). But, I do not go further in reviewing the comparative politics literature because it seems to be of less direct utility to understanding the precise kinds of opposition that influence foreign policy and mechanisms by which it does so.[2] At this preliminary stage of theoretical and empirical inquiry, the analytically well-informed case studies of actual foreign policy decisionmaking episodes appear to offer the most useful insights for developing empirical theories of domestic politics and foreign policy.

The Politics of Foreign Policy in Western Parliamentary Democracies

These countries are those that, like the United States, fall within the conventional categories of being politically open and developed. These are the established democratic systems found throughout Western Europe and in Canada, Australia, New Zealand, and Japan. They differ from the United States, though, in that they have parliamentary, not presidential, systems (Finland and France actually have quasi-presidential systems). The distinction between the two has not been emphasized in the comparative foreign policy literature, but there is a conventional wisdom that asserts that the institutional arrangements found in parliamentary systems, like the structures in authoritarian and less developed polities, result in general differences in political constraints as compared to those of presidential democracies. Specifically, it has been argued that cabinet leaders in parliamentary systems are less constrained than their presidential counterparts because of differences in the "separation of powers" in a presidential system and the "association of powers" in a parliamentary system. Whereas a parliamentary executive (if it has a majority in the legislature) effectively dominates the legislature, a president is confronted by an autonomous legislative branch; consequently, a parliamentary leadership is assumed to be less affected by domestic political constraints.

This conventional wisdom, however, assumes the cabinet in a parliamentary system is a cohesive body. Waltz (1967: 301), in his classic comparison of British and U.S. foreign policy, has shown the weakness of this assumption.

> The Prime Minister . . . , assured of formal backing especially in close divisions, must nevertheless worry lest between general elections his effective support dwindle and his position become politically insupportable. Prime Ministers must be, and must take pains to remain, acceptable to their Parliamentary parties. By the political system within which he operates, the Prime Minister is impelled to seek the support of his entire party, at the cost of considerably reducing his freedom of action.

Although able to dominate the legislature, the prime minister is at a disadvantage because he or she normally shares considerable political power with the collective party leadership in the cabinet, which in turn depends upon the support of the parliamentary party. Indeed, Waltz concludes that a prime minister is institutionally *weaker* than a president. Although he would probably now acknowledge the increased importance of Congress since the Vietnam War, his focus on party constraints suggests that opposition may be potentially important in even the stable British polity with its cohesive single-party government. The subsequent analysis seeks to build on Waltz's insight in two politically fragmented parliamentary situations: coalition governments and factionalized single-party cabinets.

Foreign Policy Decisionmaking in Coalition Cabinets

Among Western parliamentary democracies there is considerable diversity in opposition patterns and their impact on foreign policies, most basically between multiparty coalition governments and single-party governments. Coalition cabinets, which have actually been a prevalent form of government in Western Europe since World War II (Bogdanor, 1983), represent the most fragmented kind of political situation with ultimate government authority being formally divided among contending political parties. For a number of countries (France, Germany, Italy, the Netherlands, and Sweden) there is a sufficient number of analytic overviews and detailed case studies to explore the linkage between coalition politics and foreign policy.

Certain case studies, but not all, stress the inability of coalition governments to engage in effective and active foreign relations. A primary theme in studies of the foreign policy of the French Fourth Republic is the pervasive political constraints inherent in its succession of unstable, multiparty cabinets. Its foreign policy making was one of "governing without choosing" marked by a "growing crisis of inactivity, with energies of the representative regimes increasingly absorbed by its own procedural mechanisms" (Rioux, 1984: 195), and the result was that it was "extremely difficult for the various French governments to put together a coherent and effective foreign policy program" (Handreider and Auton, 1980: 154).[3] A parallel depiction is made about postwar Italian foreign policy under coalition cabinets led by the Christian Democratic Party. Spotts and Wieser (1986: 267) emphasize "the diffusion—and confusion—of authority" as amplifying tendencies toward "passivity" and "weak commitment(s)," while Willis (1971: chap. 13) documents how the "immobilismo" of Italian politics led to a succession of vague policies toward the EEC and ultimately a paralysis and passivity in what was originally an activist integration policy.[4] The late 1960s West German Grand Coalition between the Christian Democratic (CDU/CSU) and Social Democratic (SDP) parties, while not as unstable as French and Italian cabinets, also had a constrained and ambiguous foreign policy. Handreider (1970: 174; also Handreider and Auton, 1980) argues that "for essentially domestic political reasons, an authentic alternative to previous foreign policy orientations was thus precluded," even though declining Cold War tensions created new opportunities for German foreign policy. Finally, comparative Dutch case studies (Everts, ed., 1985) identify episodes of severe domestic political constraints on the country's traditionally insulated foreign policy elite.[5] On the controversial issues of the NATO deployment of the neutron bomb (Maessen, 1985) and cruise missiles (van Staden, 1985; Everts, forthcoming), "domestic groups have been relatively successful, for instance, in blocking—or at least delaying—decisions which the government wanted to make regarding nuclear weapons" (Everts, 1985: 5).

But, while the above cases of coalition foreign policy making point to highly constrained conditions, equally striking in this literature are coalition cabinets that *were* politically capable of taking substantively meaningful foreign policy action. The case studies of the Working Group on the Foreign Policy of the Netherlands show that the same coalitions deadlocked on NATO nuclear issues were politically able to act on other visible issues, such as arms shipments to Taiwan and Indonesia, the Arab-Israeli conflict, and human rights matters (Everts, ed., 1985: 326–327). While this illustrates issue-specific political constraints in some regimes, other more general country studies point to the overall workability of coalition decisionmaking in a way that achieves political agreements and, indeed, insulates foreign policy issues from broader political pressures. For example, the reemergence of multiparty rule in Fifth Republic France during the brief period of "cohabitation" between socialist President Francois Mitterrand and conservative Prime Minister Jacques Chirac did not produce the unstable deadlock of the Fourth Republic (LePrestre, 1984; Macridis, 1989). Similarly, in Finland, which also has a quasi-presidential executive, there eventually emerged a strong political basis for dealing with the Soviet Union (Arter, 1987: chap. 5; Joenniemi, 1978). Most striking, though, are characterizations of the general absence of constraints in Scandinavian political systems. Despite the fact that these nations are frequently ruled by coalition cabinets (and even minority governments), foreign policy making is concentrated in an executive that works closely with a professional bureaucracy in a largely depoliticized manner (Faurby, 1982; Goldmann, Berglund, and Sjostedt, 1986; Sundelius, 1982, 1989). Although there are exceptions (e.g., the 1946 Icelandic political turmoil over accepting U.S. military bases, as depicted by Nuechterlein, 1961), the example of the 1981 Swedish handling of a Soviet submarine in its waters taps the distinctly nonpolitical nature of its foreign policy decisionmaking. A cohesive subgroup of Defense and Foreign Ministry officials quietly handled the problem with periodic consultations with party leaders (inside and outside the cabinet) and with few political restraints (Sundelius, forthcoming).[6]

These two sets of case studies make an important theoretical point: there can be considerable difference in the level of internal constraint on the foreign policies of otherwise similarly fragmented regimes. In other words, not all coalition cabinets are automatically deadlocked or severely constrained. This, in turn, raises two key questions: what factors enable a coalition cabinet to overcome internal divisions and achieve agreement necessary to act in foreign policy, and what factors contribute to deadlock among contending parties? Although the case study authors cited above certainly do not operate from a common theoretical framework, the analytic rigor of these cases collectively points to several common political factors that condition the ability of coalition cabinets to act.

Probably the most basic factor influencing coalition decisionmaking is the precise distribution of power (i.e., cabinet ministries) among member parties. Although the simple number of parties in a coalition does not appear to be critical (e.g., Dutch and West German cases of deadlock involved only two parties), the presence of either a predominant or senior party within the coalition appears to be important. Compare, for example, the political situation of West Germany's Grand Coalition, in which the Christian Democrats and Social Democrats shared power equally, to that of succeeding governments. These later cabinets, in which either the Christian Democrats or the Social Democrats shared power with the smaller Free Democratic Party, were clearly more capable of achieving agreement on foreign policy matters (see Handreider and Auton, 1980). This also applies to the quasi-presidential systems of France and Finland. In both cases, the institutional distribution of power has allowed the president to dominate on foreign policy matters, particularly under strong leaders like Mitterrand (Macridis, 1989; LePrestre, 1984) and Kekkonon (Arter, 1987).[7] Yet Italian and Dutch cases show that a dominant coalition member is not by itself sufficient to create coherence in a coalition's foreign policy. In both countries, the supposedly dominant Christian Democratic Party has often been unable to break coalition stalemates. Factors other than political balances within the cabinet must also be important.

Broad policy disagreement, or polarization, over substantive foreign policy issues is a second factor affecting the ability of parties to achieve meaningful agreement. The deadlock in West Germany's Grand Coalition can be traced mainly to the contending foreign policy belief systems of the leadership of the two parties. As Handrieder (1970: 180–181) stresses, "the various viewpoints on the German question represented in the Grand Coalition were working at cross-purposes, with the more conservative CDU/CSU elements acting as a constant brake on the more innovative SPD elements" and "only rarely did [it] speak with one voice." At the other extreme, a strong leadership consensus on the nation's basic interests and role in world affairs provides for workable coalitions, for example, Sweden's "neutrality regime" (Sundelius, 1989), Fifth Republic France's "style and aspirations" in its independent foreign policies (Macridis, 1989), and Finland's acquiescent Cold War posture toward the Soviet Union (Arter, 1987; Joenniemi, 1978). But policy debates were more complex, or subtle, in the deadlocked coalitions of the French Fourth Republic, Italy, and the Netherlands. The dominant feature of these coalitions was that the coalition parties represented a relatively narrow range of the country's political spectrum; in other words, none spanned the left-right spectrum as in the Grand Coalition. In fact, the party leaders in the Dutch Christian Democratic–conservative cabinet fully agreed that the country should accept NATO cruise missile deployments (Everts, forthcoming). This is not to say that policy differences did not occur in these cases, but they were clearly not the defining characteristic in all of the deadlocked coalitions.

A third political condition is the overall nature of political relationships among the coalition parties. In Sweden, for example, the strong norm of consensus decisionmaking reinforced the agreement on neutrality. Not only does this norm provide for regularized consultations among party ministers, bureaucratic officials, and even opposition leaders, it also facilitates active cooperation and trust across the political spectrum. Political relationships in other coalitions were far more competitive and distrustful as parties plotted for position in the next cabinet government. In Italy and Fourth Republic France, policy differences on any issue were exacerbated by the ever present ministerial merry-go-round and uncertainty of any cabinet's tenure in office because of the repeated use of no-confidence votes by parliament.[8] Handreider and Auton (1980: 155–156) depict an extremely unstable situation in the French Fourth Republic:

> It [was] relatively easy for the "ins" and "outs" to shift positions and to support some government measures and not others. The center, shifting in its own composition, was a highly unstable coalition of interests preoccupied with holding off the Gaullists and other groups on the Right and Communists and Socialists on the Left. It was easier to mobilize the electorate against a particular government or policy than for an alternative.

Even among mainstream (prosystem) parties, the distrust and uncertainty in coalition relationships appear to have been as important a constraint as differences on substantive policy issues.

A final influence on coalition decisionmaking is the extent of opposition to the cabinet by elements within one or more of its parties. In the Dutch, Italian, and French Fourth Republic cases, cabinet leaders were severely pressured by organized opposition from members of their own parliamentary parties. The authority of each cabinet was, in effect,

incomplete because ministers had to negotiate with party leaders and factions outside the cabinet to avoid antigovernment votes that would bring
down the entire cabinet. In the Dutch situation this was critical. The
Christian Democratic and conservative-liberal ministers were prevented
from implementing their shared desire to accept NATO cruise missiles by
an antimissile faction of Christian Democratic parliamentarians whose support of the government was explicitly conditioned upon the refusal of the
missiles (Everts, forthcoming). Rampant party factionalism was at the root
of ongoing cabinet instability in Italy and Fourth Republic France, and foreign policy deadlock occurred on issues that became intertwined with
ongoing internal party competition for control of resources and policy. In
Italy, not only has factionalism within the Christian Democratic Party
undercut its control over junior coalition members, but according to Willis
(1971: 270) "the outcome of struggles within the party" have determined
that country's "conception" of European union. At the other extreme, cases
suggest that party cohesion and discipline are important to overcoming
coalition constraints. The comparative Dutch cases (Everts, ed., 1985)
show that coalition governments have been able to operate effectively
when not challenged by parliamentary factions, while Scandinavian
episodes illustrate how party cohesion contributes to the workability of
coalition arrangements (Faurby, 1982; Arter, 1987).

As a group, these case studies point to varying levels of political constraint in different coalitions, reflecting the mix of at least four political
conditions: the distribution of power within the cabinet, polarization over
policy issues, distrust and competition in political relationships, and opposition within the parliamentary parties of one or more of the coalition members. Where these combined pressures are strong, the result can be severe
constraint on the nation's foreign policy, which the cases here depict as
involving minimal commitment of resources, ambiguity in government
positions, and a passivity that is often broken only by altered international
conditions or increased foreign pressure on the government. Where these
pressures are absent, coalition cabinets do not appear to be prevented from
achieving the kind of agreements necessary for mounting major foreign
policy initiatives.

But this is not to say that even highly constrained coalitions do nothing
or avoid controversial foreign policy matters entirely. Along with handling
nonpoliticized issues, the literature suggests that even the most unstable
coalition may try to act on major foreign policy issues in order to demonstrate its ability to cope with policy crises and thereby achieve some legitimacy at home. Handreider and Auton (1980: 156), in their overview of
French foreign policy, make this point most clearly: "Yet internal weakness
pushed the Fourth Republic even more toward foreign matters. Unable to
fashion an internal sense of community, the Fourth Republic sought to
define itself through foreign policy." In effect, because of their political

fragmentation and vulnerability, these weakened actors were often compelled to deal with the most difficult issues in order to legitimize themselves, albeit again with only minimal initiative and coherence and often in a way that placed them at the mercy of foreign pressures.

Foreign Policy Decisionmaking
in a Factionalized Single-Party Cabinet

If, at first glance, foreign policy makers in coalition cabinets appear severely constrained, then their counterparts in single-party governments should have wide political latitude in international affairs. Such seems to be the case for countries like Great Britain, where "the linkage between domestic politics and the external environment, while profound, was less obviously problematic than in the West German and French cases" (Handreider and Auton, 1980: 264). Other overviews of British foreign policy making (e.g., Clarke, 1988; Vital, 1968; Wallace, 1976) usually downplay constraints from opposition parties and factions or cabinet politics.[9] Instead, the country's decision process is depicted as highly elitist, limited mostly to bureaucratic politics, and involving mainly problems of management and coordination.[10] Rarely is it suggested that there is a "breakdown both of partisanship in British foreign policy and of complete party solidarity in Parliamentary voting," as in the political disarray of the 1956 Suez crisis (Christoph, 1965: 91; also Epstein, 1964; Thomas, 1966). Rather, with the exception of Farrands (1988), the dominant theme in the literature on British foreign policy is that political opposition does not place severe constraints on foreign policy officials.[11]

But the case of another parliamentary system ruled by a single party— Japan under the Liberal Democratic Party (LDP)—suggests that not all cabinets in such seemingly cohesive governments operate free from major internal political constraints. Research on Japanese foreign policy making is exceptionally extensive and conceptually explicit, providing insights into the role of various actors and the dynamics of political effects on decision outcomes. There are a number of analytic overviews of how postwar Japanese foreign policy decisions have been made (Destler et al., 1976: chap. 3; Destler, Fukui, and Sato, 1979: chap. 2; Hellmann, 1969: chap. 1; Hosoya, 1976; Kosaka, 1974; Ori, 1976; Scalapino, 1977). There is also a large and diverse set of case studies examining internal political processes and carefully linking them to foreign policy decision outcomes. Some are major episodes defining Japan's basic international relationships, such as security ties with the United States (Destler et al., 1976; Scalapino and Masumi, 1962), treaties normalizing postwar relations with the Soviet Union (Hellmann, 1969) and Korea (Baerwald, 1970), and the sequence of decisions leading to diplomatic recognition of the People's Republic of China (Fukui, 1970 and 1977a; Kim, 1979; Langdon, 1968; Ogata, 1988;

Park, 1975; Welfield, 1976). Balancing these cases are studies of less dramatic, though not necessarily less critical, foreign policy issues. These include negotiations in the General Agreement on Trade and Tariffs (GATT) Tokyo round (Fukui, 1978a), the signing of the Nuclear Non-Proliferation Treaty (Frankel, 1977), matters of weapons procurement (Han, 1978), and economic crises with the United States over textile trade (Destler et al., 1979) and currency exchange rates (Fukui, forthcoming).

At first glance, Japanese foreign policy would seem to be largely free of any domestic political constraints. As a result of post–World War II constitutional reforms, power is concentrated in the hands of the prime minister and his cabinet, replacing the more institutionally fragmented and ill-defined pattern of prewar authority (see Hosoya, 1974; Fukui, 1977b). The government also has policy instruments that enable it to regulate strongly its own economy and society (Pempel, 1977; Katzenstein, 1978). The pattern of postwar politics has further contributed to this concentration of power. For the past thirty years the ruling Liberal Democratic Party has retained power with a persistent parliamentary (Diet) majority and the close support of big business and the major government ministries.[12] The political leadership of the LDP has been generally dominant in this setting. Ori (1976: 4) comes to the widely held conclusion that of the four major components in the foreign policy process (the ruling LDP, the foreign policy bureaucracies, big business, and the opposition in the Diet), "the ruling conservative party and its top leaders have dominated much of the postwar foreign policy process."[13]

This concentration of power might lead to the conclusion that domestic politics has little influence on Japan's foreign policy (other than the bureaucratic politics typical of any complex government). However, this would ignore the fact that the ruling LDP is actually a loose configuration of powerful political factions and has "operated frequently just like a fragmented multiparty system" (Richardson and Flanagan, 1984: 450).[14] Like separate political parties, LDP factions are well organized, each having "its own headquarters and a fairly fixed and stable membership drawn exclusively from among LDP Diet members" (Fukui, 1970: 128). These organizations are also well established and have since the mid-1950s shown "remarkable continuity, in the sense that the groupings around particular leaders have generally been very stable and at least parts of the factions remained an integrated whole even after that politician's death or retirement from politics" (Richardson and Flanagan, 1984: 101).[15] Finally, LDP factions are intensely political groupings and yet are distinctly nonideological. They are organized mainly to compete for party and government leadership positions; they do not represent distinctive ideological or policy orientations across the aggregate of foreign policy issues.

The above analogy to multiparty politics extends to LDP politics within the cabinet. Since the rise of the LDP in the mid-1950s, no single LDP faction has been able to achieve control of a majority of Diet seats. As a result, postwar Japanese cabinets have actually been a coalition of mainstream LDP factions, consisting of the most powerful factions and their allies and excluding opposing factions in the LDP.[16] This situation creates two levels of constraints for any prime minister: he must retain the support of the potential rival factions in his cabinet coalition, and he must not provoke defections by the antimainstream factions that are excluded from the cabinet yet hold seats essential to the LDP's control of the Diet. Rarely have LDP factional coalitions been stable for extended periods of time. As president of the LDP, the prime minister faces the uncertainty of reelection every two years, and historically there has never been much of a guarantee against factional defections threatening the cabinet's premature collapse. As depicted by Fukui (1970: 136), political constraints in this setting are severe: "a president (party president/prime minister) who dares to deal with any controversial policy issues runs the risk of arousing all the destructive passions of his opponents in the dissident factions and even some of his fair-weather allies and may well be found to be digging his own grave." These pressures are intensified by strong consensus norms of decisionmaking in Japanese culture, and these normally apply to processes of foreign policy making.[17]

The linkage of LDP factional politics to foreign policy decision outcomes is not, though, entirely simple. What emerges from the case study literature is that Japanese foreign policy decisionmaking varies with respect to the primacy of three kinds of political concerns: (1) the competition for power among leadership factions, (2) the contending perspectives on substantive policy issues, and (3) the interests of different bureaucratic actors.

The first situation occurs when dissident factions provoke a cabinet crisis by linking the survival of a highly vulnerable prime minister (and his cabinet coalition) to his handling of a highly controversial foreign policy issue. Government handling of the issue then becomes driven by leaders' expectations concerning its impact on increasingly tenuous internal factional balances. In the matter of the peace agreement with the Soviet Union, "the shift toward normalization was first introduced in the form of a slogan, primarily for domestic political effect, and the government moves in the weeks immediately following were guided largely by considerations of internal politics" (Hellmann, 1969: 58). Similarly, factional opposition to the 1960 revision of the security treaty with the United States was "more a reflection of anti-Kishi feeling and factional rivalry than of deep conviction" over the pact itself (Destler et al., 1976: 19). Finally, after the Nixon opening to the People's Republic of China (P.R.C.), "normalization was turning into a succession issue as prospective successors began to rally around it," involving opposition from not only the LDP's pro-P.R.C. elements (see below) but also its anti-Sato members who otherwise did not have strong preferences on the issue (Ogata, 1988: 45). The pattern is clear: despite the absence of strong policy convictions, political conflict over foreign policy issues can be intense if factions strive to use these controversies to evict the current prime minister and his factional coalition.

This is not to say, however, that LDP members never have strong policy preferences on specific policy issues or that they are always driven by purely factional interests. In the second pattern of LDP decisionmaking, as illustrated by the prolonged issue of establishing ties with the P.R.C., "the influence of the factions appears to have been far less direct and conspicuous" and "the major divisions were more explicitly ideological and related to policy" (Fukui, 1977a: 101).[18] By the mid-1960s, leadership disagreement on the "two Chinas" issue had become formalized with the creation of competing LDP study groups in parliament: the pro-Beijing Afro-Asian Problems Study Group and the pro-Taipei Asian Affairs Problems Group. These operated independently of the formal factions in at least two ways: first, "both groups [were] cross-factional in the sense that their members [were] drawn from all but two factional units identified in the party" (Fukui, 1970: 256), and, second, the pressures from the pro-Beijing and pro-Taipei wings of the party persisted largely independent of periodic leadership succession crises.[19] Even though the issue was not sharply politicized like the first set of episodes, the political crosspressures constrained successive prime ministers in balancing (often ambiguously) relations with the P.R.C. and Taiwan. Prior to the normalization of relations in 1972, the pro-Beijing wing kept the issue alive by agitating for an opening to the P.R.C. (Fukui, 1970; Ogata, 1988; Welfield, 1976). After normalization, it was the pro-Taipei group that constrained Japanese leaders (particularly Prime Minister Fukuda, whose own faction was sharply divided on the China issue) in the signing of a peace treaty with the P.R.C. and formally breaking relations with Taiwan in 1978 (Kim, 1979; Ogata, 1988).

The third pattern of politics in Japanese foreign policy occurs when the decision process is dominated by bureaucratic interests, with the political leadership being unwilling to intervene to resolve interministerial disputes. That this occurs is especially evident from case studies of foreign economic policy making. In the case of the GATT Tokyo round, decisionmaking was confined entirely to "equal ministries" and, indeed, "the most obvious characteristic of Japanese decision making . . . was that the top political leadership was seldom engaged" (Fukui, 1978a: 139). The same seems to be true in the government's response to the 1971 exchange rate crisis (Fukui, forthcoming).[20] The LDP leadership was closely involved in the 1969–1971 textile dispute with the United States, but the LDP politicians heading the major ministries (Foreign, Finance and Ministry of International Trade and Industry [MITI]) adhered closely to the views of their senior bureaucrats.[21] The absence of LDP political pressures does not, however, reduce the range of policy disputes. One pervasive bureaucratic cleavage (found in the textile dispute and the GATT negotiations) centers on the contending perspectives of the Foreign Ministry and MITI. MITI sees its role as promoting Japan's industrial development and international trading position, while the Foreign Ministry views trade relations in terms of Japan's overall foreign relations and, in particular, the overriding interest of maintaining good relations with the United States. MITI "was not as committed to free trade as the Foreign Ministry" in the GATT Tokyo round negotiations (Fukui, 1978a: 100), while throughout the textile dispute it prevented Prime Minister Sato and the Foreign Ministry from making major concessions to the United States on textile trade issues.

Whatever the pattern of political conflict within the Japanese government (factional competition, clashing policy positions, or contending bureaucratic interests), the constraining effect on the country's foreign policy behavior is evident across almost the entire set of case studies. For example, throughout the peace treaty negotiations with the Soviet Union, the prime minister's preoccupation with leadership politics forced Japan to "play a passive role, for [he] was effectively denied the opportunity for maneuver toward any form of agreement other than that desired by the Soviets" (Hellmann, 1969: 154). Similarly, the fragmented Japanese government was "unable to make its own decisions or put forward policy proposals" in the process leading up to the normalization of relations with China (Fukui, 1970: 260), while subsequently it was very slow in moving toward specific treaties and final diplomatic recognition (Ogata, 1988: 80). The inability to act was equally apparent in the negotiations with the United States on textile trade. MITI (and its industrial supporters) wielded veto power over any negotiated settlement so that it was "difficult for Japanese political leaders to be even minimally responsive to pressures for compromise" (Destler et al., 1979: 321). A clear pattern emerges here. Japanese foreign policy seems largely reactive with minimal, often ambiguous commitments, and is often only able to act in the face of strong external pressures (such as Soviet negotiating demands or the "Nixon shocks"). Not surprisingly, the terms "immobilisme" and "paralysis" are frequently used to describe the country's foreign policy process (e.g., Destler et al., 1978; Fukui, 1970; Hosoya, 1976; Hellmann, 1969; Kosaka, 1974; Tsuruntani, 1974), and these factors are very much at the core of Calder's (1988) recent characterization of Japan as a "reactive state."[22]

Despite the overall inhibiting effect of domestic politics on Japan's foreign policy, there is some evidence that "in some cases, [factional politics] can bring new policy initiatives and commitments to the surface" (Destler et al., 1976: 24). One frequent factor is the tendency of prime ministers to emphasize major foreign policy issues to legitimize their position in office. Sometimes issues are raised by prime ministers seeking to enhance their domestic stature; for example, Kishi initially pushed the idea of the revised security pact with the United States as part of a public visit by President Eisenhower (Scalapino and Masumi, 1962: 135), while candidate Sato initially pushed the idea of the Okinawa reversion as a way of distinguishing himself from the current prime minister (Destler et al., 1976: 26). Another dynamic is that cabinet crises can provoke factional realignments that ultimately break prior internal constraints on action. Accounts of Japan's negotiations with China (Welfield, 1969) and the Soviet Union (Hellmann, 1969) both link rare Japanese bargaining initiatives to new factional balances after LDP cabinet shakeups. In still other cases, cabinets came to power with the expressed purpose of tackling a controversial issue, realizing that the failure to do so would undercut its credibility. Fukuda's replacement of Sato as prime minister was intended to open the way for ties with the P.R.C., and the new leadership "believed that it was a matter of survival in domestic politics to achieve normalization before the United States did" (Ogata, 1988: 50). Domestic political pressure then becomes an important motivation to grapple with an issue, although often various persisting constraints ultimately permit only a rather feeble effort in that direction.

In sum, even in a one-party regime such as Japan's, domestic politics can have a pervasive impact on foreign policy. Indeed, the position of the Japanese prime minister appears to be institutionally weaker than that of a U.S. president, largely because the former "must necessarily rely upon political support from the leaders of the various factions of his own political party, as well as on the financial support of the business community, in order to attain and hold his position" (Hosoya, 1976: 119). These constraints are further intensified by the vulnerability of prime ministers during succession crises and by the well-established consensus decisionmaking norms that govern interfactional bargaining. In addition, the factionalization of the country's political leadership increases the access of bureaucratic and interest group actors because these entrenched actors serve as potential allies—or opponents—in factional rivalries. Not only does this impose external constraints on decisionmakers, but alliances with these powerful groups restrict the flexibility of political leaders in interfactional bargaining. Even one-party cabinets in parliamentary systems— when they have well-defined internal divisions—do not have any particular immunity from domestic opposition.

The Politics of Foreign Policy
in an Established Authoritarian System

If, as the conventional wisdom suggests, the structure of parliamentary regimes limits the impact of domestic politics on foreign policy, then these influences would be assumed to have much less effect on the foreign policy of a closed polity such as that of the former Soviet Union. The conventional view of closed political systems is based on the totalitarian model of Communist rule in the Soviet Union (Freidrich and Brzezinski, 1965). It posits that foreign policy reflects the highly centralized and unrestrained power of the Politburo leadership and that the sources of foreign policy are fundamentally different from those of a democracy. Domestic political influences are unimportant because there is no viable opposition to the regime's single party, which is itself assumed to be politically cohesive. Thus, it is concluded that authoritarian regimes have greater flexibility in foreign affairs. In addition, "because power in the Soviet foreign policy formulation is concentrated in relatively few hands, the influence of personalities is important" (Stern, 1974: 89; also Tucker, 1965). Foreign policy decisions are thus interpreted in terms of the personal style of the leader or the shared perspectives of the senior leadership (Adomeit, 1982).

A modification of this conventional view acknowledges the possibility of important domestic political influences on Soviet foreign policy—but only during periodic leadership succession crises such as those following Stalin's death (Rush, 1965; Armstrong, 1965; Pendill, 1971). Rush (1965: xi), the preeminent proponent of this view, notes "there is a qualitative difference between Soviet politics in a period of personal rule and Soviet politics in a period of succession." This interpretation "typically assumes that one view or another prevails; opposition is either overcome or power changes hands" (Horelick, Johnson, and Steinbruner, 1975: 46). The impact of internal politics is only temporary, and "in the long run . . . any Soviet leader victorious in the power struggle will return to the basic interests of Soviet policy" (Armstrong, 1965: 47).

These conventional perspectives have been under growing criticism for at least two decades, and well before the collapse of the Soviet system when that system seemed to be very well institutionalized. Political influences are emphasized in several general theoretical frameworks concerning the sources of Soviet foreign policy (e.g., Bialer, 1987; Schwartz, 1975; Dallin, 1981). There are also a number of theoretical formulations of the dynamics of leadership politics and bureaucratic constraints as they relate to foreign policy (Aspaturian, 1966, 1976; Hodnett, 1981; Juviler and Zawadzka, 1978; Morton, 1967; Simes, 1986; and Ross, 1984). In addition, and despite the difficulties of getting into the Soviet "black box," a number of valuable studies consider in some detail the foreign policy effects of political influences. These empirical studies fall into two general categories. Some are general Kremlinological assessments of leadership politics underlying the foreign policies of the Khrushchev and Brezhnev regimes (e.g., Linden, 1966; Gelman, 1984; Marantz, 1975; Slusser, 1967). The others are case studies of specific foreign policy decisions or episodes, and encompass at least three kinds of foreign policy initiatives: (1) foreign interventions in Czechoslovakia (Valenta, 1979, 1984a), Hungary (Valenta, 1984c; Fry and Rice, 1983), the Middle East (Golan, 1984; Spechler, 1987;

Ra'anan, 1973), Angola (Valenta, 1980a), Afghanistan (Valenta, 1980b, 1984b), and Poland (Anderson, 1982); (2) major international crises such as the 1961 Berlin Crisis (Slusser, 1973) and the Cuban Missile Crisis (Dinerstein, 1976); and (3) cooperative initiatives such as the Austrian State Treaty (Mastny, 1982) and the Nuclear Test Ban Treaty (Jonsson, 1977).

Before proceeding further, some mention should be made about the continued relevance of the Soviet foreign policy literature, now that the Communist system has collapsed and the country has fragmented into a weak confederation of independent states centered around the Russian Federation. I believe the insights of this literature remain quite useful for two reasons. First, from a theoretical perspective, the decisionmaking research on the Soviet Union is uniquely well developed as compared to any other established authoritarian states, Communist or otherwise. Even assuming that Russia has moved into the category of democratic systems, this literature still provides insights into other current (and future) regimes in bureaucratized and established authoritarian systems.[23] Second, from a more substantive perspective, it can be argued that there is significant continuity in the foreign policy processes from the Soviet Union to those of the still evolving democracy of the Russian Federation. Rigorous, detailed case study evidence has yet to emerge on the highly fluid foreign policy decisionmaking in the Gorbachev and Yeltsin regimes, and I will not pretend to be able to fill the void in that literature. However, using more impressionistic accounts and initial political analyses, it is possible to point out general aspects of current foreign policy processes that appear quite similar to those under the old Soviet apparatus.[24]

At the core of critiques of the conventional perspectives is the view that internal politics has been a persistent influence on Soviet foreign policy in the post-Stalinist era. In other words, "once we transcend Soviet constitutional and ideological myths, we find informal political behavior that comes closer to a 'conflict model' than to the stereotype of consensual authoritarianism" (Dallin, 1981: 362). Two general factors have contributed to the growing role of domestic politics in Soviet foreign policy and apparently continue to operate in the Russian Federation.

First, foreign policy issues became increasingly complex and the party ideology was recognized as offering fewer and fewer concrete answers, such that there was room for legitimate policy differences. Among contending actors there has long been a "predisposition to make different assessments of the 'correlation of forces' in world politics" (Dallin, 1981: 46). In Soviet bloc crises, such as that posed by the reformist Dubcek regime in Czechoslovakia, there was "under the cover of 'shared images' . . . plenty of room for disagreement among senior decision makers on when the Soviet Union should intervene in a socialist country if there is only a potential threat" (Valenta 1979: 87). Political debates also grew as Soviet leaders came to view foreign policy problems as being closely intertwined with domestic problems. Well before the Gorbachev reforms, there had been an "indisputable decline in the compartmentalization of foreign and domestic policy issues . . . [which] seems to have resulted in a situation in which no one institutional group, for example the defense complex, achieves or carries a preponderant influence" (Bialer, 1981: 414). These pressures have no doubt been intensified with the end of the primacy of Communist ideology and the openness of the system under Gorbachev and Yeltsin (Bialer, 1987; Bishop, 1990).

The second factor, and the one to be considered in detail here, is the growing dispersion of political authority in the post-Stalin era at two interconnected levels: among established bureaucratic actors and within the senior political leadership of the Politburo. The first level reflects the organizational fragmentation of government and party structures. Contrary to the totalitarian model, post-Stalinist bureaucracies displayed growing autonomy from and influence on the top leadership, and thus were not simply instruments (or "transmission belts") of the central authorities (see Skilling, 1966; Godwin, 1973; Eckstein, 1970; Huntington, 1970; Barghoorn, 1973; Johnson, 1970). This bureaucratic power system stemmed from several conditions of the post-Stalinist era. Effective management of the problems of a modern, complex society necessitates less reliance on terror and political ideology and greater dependence on bureaucratic expertise. Also, in their competition for power senior political leaders were likely to form alliances with actors outside of the Politburo, especially during periods of succession and instability. Khrushchev regularly appealed to bureaucratic allies in the Central Committee to circumvent Politburo factions (Linden, 1966), while Brezhnev's carefully crafted leadership coalition extended to major institutional interests (Gelman, 1984). Within this context bureaucracies took on the character of interest groups (Skilling, 1966) in some respects, working "within relatively circumscribed limits, to maximize the values and promote the interests of their particular professional or institutional groups" (Barghoorn, 1973: 39).

As a result of this growing bureaucratic involvement, the Soviet, and now Russian, policymaking process has taken the form of bargaining among various institutional interests along the lines of a pluralist or bureaucratic politics model. A dominant theme has been that there existed in post-Stalinist governments a broad, underlying cleavage, centered around the interests of competing bureaucracies and institutions. Almost three decades ago, Aspaturian (1966; 1976) argued that the supposedly monolithic Soviet regime had become broadly polarized between a "security-producer-ideological" grouping and a "consumer-agriculture-public service" grouping. Even under Brezhnev, the Soviet establishment was not an entirely homogeneous body after almost two decades of placid, if not stagnant, rule.[25] As Simes (1986: 158) then noted:

> Although the establishment puts a premium on developing consensus and avoiding conflicts between elite factions, inherent tensions exist—between the party apparatus and the economic managers, between consumer industries and agriculture on the one hand and the military-industrial complex on the other, between those with authority for maintaining rigid controls and indoctrination and those responsible for promoting scientific and technical progress.

The interplay of institutional interests, even in the absence of the framework of the Communist party, continues to the present. Contemporary reactions to Gorbachev's politics placed him in a pivotal position between radical reformers on the left and orthodox conservatives on the right (Hough, 1989; Winter et al., 1991), and after the August 1991 coup, it is clear that Yeltsin contends with entrenched bureaucratic and political opposition from the conservative sectors (*New York Times,* June 7, 1992: 1).

If this suggests that bureaucracies define the broader political context, other evidence indicates that bureaucratic and institutional actors directly participate in making decisions in a somewhat politically dispersed setting. Indeed, Simes (1986: 160), while not suggesting that the Politburo was somehow unimportant, argued that "under ordinary circumstances, real business [was] conducted behind the scenes, through a sort of informal inter-agency process," including agencies specifically assigned foreign policy tasks such as the Defense Council and the Military-Industrial Commission under the Council of Ministers. Bureaucratic actors dominated policymaking on several of what Art (1973) calls "institutionally grounded" issues concerning military force posture and arms development (Warner, 1974; Herold and Mahoney, 1974), the strategic arms race (Spielmann, 1978; Gallaher and Spielmann, 1972; Odom, 1975; Kolkowicz, 1970), and the evolution of military doctrine (Hudson, 1976). There is little reason to believe that these decisionmaking patterns on these kinds of issues changed dramatically under Gorbachev (e.g., Bialer, 1987).

The direct influence of bureaucratic actors on Politburo decisionmakers is documented in detail in the case studies of foreign intervention. These studies consistently make two points: first, the positions of certain senior decision participants were organizationally rooted, and second, bureaucratic actors pressured Politburo leaders directly and were essential elements in the eventual coalition favoring the use of force. As illustrated by the most detailed of these case studies, Valenta's (1979) analysis of the Czechoslovak intervention, bureaucratic actors were a major force behind the Brezhnev Politburo's decision to shift from political pressure to military force in order to suppress the Dubcek reforms. In fact, military force was originally advocated by the bureaucracies charged with party organization, ideological watchdog functions, and the rule of certain Union Republics, all of whom feared that the "cancer" of the Prague Spring would spread to the Soviet Union. Ultimately these domestic bureaucracies pressured a hesitant Politburo and foreign affairs bureaucrats, who feared an invasion would damage détente with the West and harm Soviet prestige in the international Communist community. Although not without its methodological problems (Dawisha, 1980; Simes, 1975), Valenta's (1979: 54) conclusion seems warranted that the "application of the bureaucratic politics paradigm—modified and tailored to Soviet circumstances—substantially illuminates certain aspects of the decision making process leading to the intervention which have not previously received sufficient attention." This conclusion is not fundamentally at variance with evidence about bureaucratic influence in the decisions leading to Soviet military intervention in Hungary (Valenta, 1984c; Fry and Rice, 1983), Afghanistan (Valenta, 1980b, 1984b), and Poland (Anderson, 1982).[26]

The bureaucratic politics or pluralist/interest group conception of Soviet foreign policy decisionmaking is, however, simplistic or at least incomplete. Although bureaucracies shape issues, provide information, and even wield some political power, they alone did not make final decisions on major foreign policy issues. These decisions were ultimately made at a second level: the senior political leadership in the Politburo, the central Soviet decisionmaking body. The membership of this body was not dominated by bureaucratic actors with narrow or organizational interests and perceptions as described above. Rather, as Valenta (1979: 7–8) noted, "several senior decision making 'generalists' within the Politburo have especially diversified responsibilities and enjoy power and position that do not depend on the interests of organizational parochialism. Because they are relatively little influenced by organizations, their decisions are characterized by *uncommitted thinking*." Yet, although bureaucratic and institutional concerns have been less dominant in this setting, this is not to say that Politburo policymaking was not political—only that it centered around "another aspect of group conflict, namely the struggle among top leaders and their closest associates and followers" (Skilling, 1966: 38).

At the root of Politburo politics was the shared nature of authority within that body, where there was a collective leadership actually similar to that found in parliamentary regimes. After Stalin, no secretary general of the Communist Party (the actual head of the Soviet government) was completely dominant, but rather each had to secure a voting majority if any major action was to be taken. He was, at most, a first among equals, and "compared within such chief executives in Western political systems as the American president, the Soviet secretary general probably [had] somewhat limited decision making power and enjoy[ed] fewer prerogatives" (Valenta, 1979: 27). Support for this assertion is that Gorbachev, in one of his major acts of political restructuring, shifted the system to a presidential system outside the Communist Party rule. However, this has not resolved the problems of dispersed authority and well-entrenched opposition; both Gorbachev and Yeltsin, as with their U.S. counterparts, have found themselves facing powerful opposition lodged in a politically autonomous legislature.

The intensity of Politburo politics was reinforced by the uncertainty surrounding leadership positions, because authority in the Soviet system was never entirely secure, even during the relatively well-institutionalized Brezhnev regime. In the absence of explicit procedures for leadership succession, "it was fully conceivable that [the leader] would suddenly find himself removed from office by a political conspiracy of his former political associates" (Schwartz, 1975; 177). As documented by the Kremlinological studies of foreign policy making under Khrushchev (e.g., Linden, 1966), Brezhnev (e.g., Gelman, 1984), and Gorbachev (e.g., Bialer, 1987; Hough, 1989; Simes, 1991), a continuous cloud of uncertainty over the Politburo's precise political balance preoccupied its members. The policy positions of the senior political leaders, who again were typically generalists on most foreign policy issues and not committed to any bureaucratic interest, reflected their own political calculations of the costs of supporting or not supporting a policy initiative. Political self-interest is a primary motive in this setting, and Valenta (1979: 8) went so far as to generalize that "in Soviet decision making, the challenges of internal politics are much more real and forceful than the alleged threats of 'U.S. imperialism,' 'German revanchism,' 'Czechoslovak reformism,' or 'Chinese adventurism.'" Anderson (1982: 24) suggests that in the 1980 and 1981 decisions not to invade Poland "the political leaders of the USSR were guided more by personal calculations about their own particular best interests—that is, by power relationships within the Politburo—than by considerations of international repercussions arising from their actions."

Although the above discussion suggests that Politburo conflict was an ongoing phenomenon, that is not to say that the specific pattern of leadership conflicts did not vary significantly across time and between different regimes. The intensity of the political conflicts was conditioned by varying levels of the above two factors—the dispersion of authority and leadership uncertainty (a point central to Kremlinological mapping of the evolution of the Khrushchev and Brezhnev Politburos).[27] The early Khrushchev and late Brezhnev years were marked by a considerable concentration of power in the hands of their respective party secretaries, while in his final years in power Khrushchev was far less dominant in a way comparable to Brezhnev's collective rule prior to his consolidation of power in the early 1970s. As to the level of political uncertainty, it is here that the focus on succession crises (Rush, 1965; Bialer, 1987) becomes relevant—not as a unique period of leadership conflict, but as representing the most extremely intense competition for power. The case studies of military intervention also indicate varying constraints within the Politburo. The Politburo seems to have been least capable of achieving a timely and consistent decision in the 1968 Czechoslovak (Valenta, 1979, 1984a) and 1956 Hungarian cases

(Valenta, 1984c; Fry and Rice, 1983), both periods of shared authority with no predominant leader. This is in clear contrast to the intervention in Afghanistan (Valenta, 1980b, 1984b) and Angola (Valenta, 1980a) where the Brezhnev-dominated Politburo was much less constrained.[28] The fragmentation of authority and political uncertainty in Soviet leadership politics probably reached its height in the latter years of the Gorbachev regime, when constitutional reforms dispersed authority across the structures of the new presidency, an autonomous legislature, the remaining Communist Party apparatus, and the increasingly powerful regional governments.[29]

Another important factor conditioning the pattern of leadership politics and bureaucratic constraints is the leader's political decisionmaking style. Although not focused directly on foreign and policy decisionmaking, Breslauer's (1982) comparative work on the authority-building strategies of Khrushchev and Brezhnev as leaders is relevant here.[30] He (1982:10) conceptualizes two approaches to leadership style: the consensual style of Brezhnev and the confrontational style of Khrushchev:

> The consensual approach is the province of the "political broker or artful synthesizer," whose authority derives in large part from his skill in building consensus for policies that will appease the masses without threatening the prerogatives of established, organized interests. The confrontational approach, in contrast, is adapted by the "populist hero," who tries to "stand above politics and particular interest." The populist is by definition anti-establishment, in that he confronts established interests by making common cause with masses.

Brezhnev's more cautious consensus style is evident throughout Valenta's (1978) depiction of the prolonged decision to invade Czechoslovakia, in which he was hesitant to commit to either the pro- or anti-intervention coalition and only approved the use of military force after he believed he would end up on the losing side politically.[31] This style contrasts sharply with "the classic Khrushchevian tactic—the sudden and bold initiative aimed at setting opponents off balance and producing a quick and decisive advantage in political struggle" (Linden, 1966: 152).[32] The ability of the leader to shape debates (and get around constraints) is further illustrated by the roles played by Gorbachev and Yeltsin, although it is now becoming evident that the former was more willing than the latter to moderate changes in the face of political opposition (Winter et al., 1991). Still, compared to Brezhnev, Gorbachev and Yeltsin have, even on politicized issues, been willing to act to get around establishment interests.[33]

Taken as a whole, this overview of Soviet foreign policy making suggests that it was inherently political, involving complex maneuvering among loose coalitions of bureaucratic actors and political leaders, each acting according to their own political interests and perceptions of complex issues. In a way that corresponds with Roeder's (1988) two-tier model of oligarchic decisionmaking, there were complex interactions across political arenas in which the clash of well-defined bureaucratic and institutional interests often became intertwined with the competition for ultimate authority among Politburo generalists.[34] The process was extremely fluid, involving not permanent factions or ideological groupings but rather "loose, issue-oriented, heterogeneous alliances of convenience among different subgroups for a temporary common purpose" (Valenta, 1979: 12). Not unlike the democratic settings examined in the previous section, it reflected the mix of interests and perceptions of varied actors in an environment where political power was significantly dispersed. Although the alignments in recent Soviet and Russian politics are arguably more fluid, there seems to be much continuity in the pattern of foreign policy processes from previous post-Stalinist regimes (*New York Times,* August 16, 1992: 12).

The impact of these ongoing political processes is complex and could "propel Soviet foreign policy in diverse directions" (Bialer, 1981: 415; Juviler and Zawadzka, 1978; Marantz, 1975). One direction is toward highly constrained foreign policy behavior marked by "ambivalence, inconsistency, and compromise" (Aspaturian, 1976: 95). Much of the literature argues that post-Stalinist "policies tend to be watered down in order to take the interests of all into account" (Schwartz, 1975: 189), and analyses of policies such as détente, for example, explain Soviet motivations in terms of political balances within senior government leadership (Leonard, 1973; Simes, 1977; Yanov, 1977).[35] Political factors also inhibited the Soviet use of force and other high-risk behaviors (Ross, 1984; Roeder, 1984; Simes, 1986). As Ross (1984: 239) argued, "the risk associated with a disruption or breakup of the leadership coalition is high and Soviet leaders will seek to avert or minimize it." The political factors isolated in especially the case studies of the Hungarian, Polish, and Czechoslovak interventions are argued to have inhibited the quick use of force or contributed to it not being used at all; for example, the latter intervention was decided upon "only after a long period of hesitation and vacillation" (Valenta, 1979: 155– 156).[36] Most analyses of the Gorbachev era—given his ongoing political balancing act—emphasize the "pull" of domestic politics on the restructuring of Soviet foreign policy, resulting in a substantively new orientation that still reflected the "ambivalence, inconsistency, and compromise" of earlier regimes.

Receiving almost equal emphasis in the literature is a second direction in Soviet foreign policy, one in which domestic politics *pushes* leaders toward greater international initiatives and confrontation. These dynamics center around the use of foreign policy to legitimize the positions of the ruling Politburo leadership and the Communist system as a whole (Bialer, 1981, 1987; Dallin, 1981). This legitimizing function has been especially important for any regime pursuing restraint or détente with the West, including even the generally cautious Brezhnev leadership to which it contributed a "growing internal predisposition to act" (Gelman 1984: 156).[37] In the Soviet-Cuban intervention in Angola, for example, bureaucratic factors were much less important than Brezhnev's political vulnerability over the détente issue (Valenta, 1978: 21).

> A weak stand on Angola by Brezhnev and his supporters could have provided ammunition to elements in the Soviet leadership who fear détente, arguing that it inhibits the USSR in its pursuit of activist globalism and assistance to clients in the Third World. A tough stand, on the other hand, could have been perceived by Brezhnev and his supporters as a convenient demonstration to critics at home and abroad that détente is not a "one-way street," that the USSR does not "betray" the revolutionary forces in the Third World.

Khrushchev found himself in a similar situation that contributed to the Cuban Missile Crisis (Linden, 1966: 154): "Being a leader who sought to justify reform internally and limited détente externally, he was constantly vulnerable to the charges that he had forsaken the struggle with the 'imperialist' adversary. He also needed to show his mettle for battle."[38] Not surprisingly, this opposition to cooperation with the West and domestic reform is becoming apparent in the post-Communist system. By mid-1992, anti-Yeltsin opposition had demanded that Russian forces be used to intervene to protect ethnic Russian minorities in the newly independent republics of Moldova and Georgia, and they have blocked the return of four northern islands to Japan. The lack of action on Yeltsin's part, as well as his cooperation (if not dependence) on the West, have become linked to the general opposition to the regime by old-style Communists and right-wing nationalists (*New York Times,* July 1992; Scott, 1992).

Although it is difficult to generalize about Soviet, and now Russian, foreign policy decisionmaking, this brief survey suggests that the conventional wisdom is quite limited, even in periods of relative stability. Since the death of Stalin, senior political leaders rarely operated in complete isolation from domestic political pressures, albeit within the bounds of Communist norms and structures. Even in this restrictive, one-party political setting, significant political divisions did occur, and policymaking was inherently political along the familiar lines of bargaining/controversy avoidance and political legitimization. Furthermore, the essential elements of these political patterns are evident in the emerging foreign policy processes in post-Communist Russian foreign policy: a well-entrenched conservative bureaucracy, fragmented political authority with an uncertain tenure, and the simultaneous push and pull of the imperatives of coalition policymaking and retaining political power. That such continues in an increasingly democratic Russia should not be entirely surprising; the foreign policy processes of the Soviet Union were never fundamentally different than those in democratic states, especially fragmented single-party regimes such as Japan's.

The Politics of Foreign Policy
in Various Third World Polities

If there has been some similarity in foreign policy processes in the advanced industrial nations, the process would still appear to be quite different in the Third World. The most salient contrast is the overall absence of established powerful political actors in most Third World polities. In particular, large complex bureaucratic and political structures are absent in many developing countries (East, 1973; Hill, 1977), and even to the extent they exist in the larger Third World countries, they are considered to be largely subordinant to political leaders (Ismael and Ismael, 1986; van Klaverin, 1984). Not surprisingly, it is widely argued that such approaches as bureaucratic politics have limited applicability to most Third World countries (Dessouki and Korany, 1984; Hill, 1977; Korany, 1983; van Klaverin, 1984; Weinstein, 1972, 1976). Both the conventional wisdom and many of the recent treatments of Third World foreign policy decisionmaking start from this observation to one degree or another.

For the conventional wisdom the key implication is that the national leader is likely to dominate the foreign policy decisionmaking process. Furthermore, from this it is inferred that decisions reflect the leader's personal characteristics, indeed "his anger and his ardor, his whims and his convictions, may become the mood of his country's policy" (Zartman, 1966: 130; Kissinger, 1966; Levi, 1968). Weinstein (1976: 21–22) has best captured the implications of this conventional view of Third World foreign policy making: "The leaders of new states are frequently said to engage in 'reckless' conduct and to make decisions on the basis of 'almost random' pressures. . . . Unfettered by the restraints of entrenched bureaucracy and large scale organizations, these leaders can set policies which primarily express their personal ambitions, ideologies, and frustrations." Third World foreign policies are pictured as being divorced from domestic and international pressures confronting the government, and in this context decisionmaking and domestic political constraints are considered largely irrelevant. Foreign policy is, for the most part, thought to reflect the personal traits of the leader.

More recent Third World studies have, to varying degrees, rejected the conventional view as simplistic. While not denying the prevalence of predominant leaders throughout the Third World, there appears to be agreement with Korany (1986) that there has been an "unhealthy monopoly" of the "great man" explanation of foreign policy. These critiques argue, instead, that foreign policy making in Third World states—as in modern states—is rooted in domestic and international pressures.[39] The implication of this insight is twofold. First, even where foreign policy making is dominated by a single dominant leader, that leader should be seen as coping with pressing international and domestic problems. Just like a politically predominant leader in a modern state, a strong leader in a Third World nation must deal with threats to his or her nation's security, economic well-being, and international status. Second, there are often decisionmaking and political constraints, and these are as pervasive as those found in the more established political systems of the advanced industrial states. Not only must the single predominant leader pay close attention to domestic political opposition outside the regime, but in many regimes there may be a considerable diffusion of power across intensely competitive actors in a highly fragmented setting. Indeed, the theme that comes out of this literature is that domestic political constraints occur as frequently (along the lines of several scenarios discussed below) as they do in modern polities. And if there is anything distinctive about Third World politics, it is the intensity and fluidity of those pressures compared to those of more established political systems.

The literature on the politics of Third World foreign policy is, though, by no means single-minded and, instead, points to varied political dynamics and foreign policy outcomes. In this section, I want to address three interwoven themes. The first two, found in the more general theoretical literature, concern the roots of the exceptionally pervasive and intense political pressures on Third World foreign policy makers, in other words, the political instability of most of the region's regimes and the highly divisive character of their foreign policy issues. The situation is, however, further complicated by a third factor: significant variation in the configurations of political authority and decisionmaking across Third World polities. These are illustrated by a number of case studies of specific foreign policy decisionmaking episodes, and this in turn enables the first two general conditions to manifest themselves in often—but not always—extreme ways.

Political instability, as it relates to the politics of foreign policy in Third World countries, involves a mix of several elements (Clapham, 1977; Heeger, 1974; Huntington, 1966; Rothstein, 1977). There is the absence of any trust between competing political groups, such that among contending players the "line between opposition and sedition is . . . tenuous" (Good, 1962: 4). Even in newly independent states, there have been long-existing hostilities between civilian parties, civilian and military elites, and members of different ethnic groups. Little agreement exists over the rules of the game, and basic elements of the political order itself are not well institutionalized. Not only are political system procedures governing leader succession weakly established, but even the means by which a leadership makes decisions is often equally ill defined. Political debates often raise fundamental questions over the legitimacy of basic political arrangements and the existence of the national political order itself. Ultimately, authority—even in a regime where there is a single predominant leader—is diffuse and complex, "for none of the groups that competes for control of the state really has the power to establish a stable equilibrium" (Rothstein, 1977: 111).

The condition of extreme political instability is linked to foreign policy decisionmaking in two ways. One implication is that these extreme political pressures act as an overriding factor in the foreign policy making process. Although acknowledging broader domestic and international constraints on the range of any leadership's foreign policy options, it is widely argued that the leadership's domestic political needs are a powerful factor behind foreign policy. Good (1963: 3) argues that the task of state-building in fragile and newly independent states is a primary determinant of the foreign policy of new states. "The demands of state-building in former colonies overwhelm all others. Inevitably, they impinge on foreign policy. The foreign policy of a new state cannot be understood exclusively in light of domestic necessities; but unless the omnipresent task of state-building is allowed to illumine the objectives and motives of foreign policy, it cannot be understood at all." More recently, David (1991: 236) broadens realist explanations of Third World alignments by incorporating domestic needs, claiming not only that "the dominant goal of Third World leaders is to stay in power," but that "they will sometimes protect themselves at the expense of the interests of the state."

A second implication of political instability is that the management of volatile and polarized opposition does not usually take the form of bargaining and compromise as emphasized in such approaches as bureaucratic politics. Rather, the tasks of political survival and state-building suggest that foreign policy issues are to be manipulated to legitimize the current regime's hold on power. Although just one of several strategies for political survival (Wriggins, 1969), the political use of foreign policy can serve a number of political purposes for keeping the current leadership in power. Weinstein (1972: 371) considers the political uses of foreign policy to be varied, including to "isolate one's domestic enemies," to focus "attention on certain kinds of issues than on others," to "create symbols of nationalism and patriotism, adherence to which may be seen as validating one's own nationalist credentials," and to "embarrass adversaries who fail to accept them." Among Middle East scholars, the focus on foreign policy as a means of coping with the "legitimacy problem in Arab politics" (Hudson, 1977) is a prominent theme in the analysis of the sources of the region's numerous conflicts (Dawisha, 1990, 1977; Taylor, 1982; Ismael and Ismael, 1986; Ajami, 1981; and most studies in Korany and Dessouki, 1984). Dawisha (1990: 284), for example, concludes that "it is no exaggeration to argue that . . . the efforts by regimes at domestic legitimization constituted a primary, if not the only, motivating factor" in most Middle East conflicts.

Furthermore, the political use of foreign policy results in external behavior that is hardly restrained or in any way watered-down, and not in line with the passive behavior often expected from the weak states of the Third World. It necessarily involves a strong element of nationalism, quite often in the form of picturing the international system as a hostile environment. The resulting hostility is a familiar theme in Third World foreign policy analyses, and as will be discussed below, extreme levels of hostility are very well documented, especially for relatively radical regimes in China, Iran, Cuba, Indonesia, and Syria. However, two cautions are in order here. The political use of foreign policy can also apply to relatively conservative, status quo regimes, as illustrated by the invasion of the Falklands/Malvinas Islands by Argentina and by the revival of "assertive nationalism" in Chinese foreign policy in the early 1980s. Nor does the political use of foreign policy always result in conflictual behavior. Rather, the key feature is that it be sufficiently dramatic to appeal to the public's nationalism and "demonstrate that the leader is being dealt with as an equal by the world's leading statesmen" (Wriggins, 1969: 228), frequently in the context of cooperation within the nonaligned movement and other forms of high-level diplomacy. Whatever the case, political instability and the resultant political use of foreign policy to legitimize the regime contributes to greater activity and assertiveness in foreign policy.

It would be a mistake, however, to suggest that this is the only dynamic of domestic political effects on Third World foreign policy behavior. The politics of foreign policy, in other words, is not limited to a situation where the leader merely manipulates foreign policy to contain domestic opposition. Such an image suggests that foreign policy issues themselves are not important and that foreign policy is affected only when the leader decides to employ it as a strategy for containing domestic opposition on unrelated issues. The view taken in the more recent Third World research suggests that these governments are often divided over pressing foreign policy issues. It is the highly divisive character of these issues that is the second source of conflict in Third World foreign policies.

For most Third World governments, the single most important policy issue is development.[40] It is a complex problem in all respects, and there is no single strategy of development. As conceptualized by Weinstein (1972), there are two competing uses of foreign policy as a means to achieving development. One is the "mobilization of resources of the outside world for the country's economic development" (p. 336). Because of severe domestic poverty, it is essential that foreign policy be used to acquire aid and investment from abroad. This requires restraint and cooperation with potential aid donors, as well as the projecting of an image of stability so as to minimize the perceived risk to multinational corporations. The other use of foreign policy is the "defense of the nation's independence against perceived threats" (p. 366), not simply from foreign military powers but also from excessive penetration by foreign economic actors and dependence on international markets. Foreign policy must be active and often hostile as the nation defends itself from foreign domination and asserts its status in an unequal world.

These two uses of foreign policy are mutually inconsistent, and few Third World countries have been able to pursue one strategy completely at the expense of the other. Instead, to one degree or another, all these nations face a "dilemma of dependence" (Weinstein, 1976): they seek to avoid domination by foreign powers but must attract aid and investment from them in order to modernize economically. Domestic politics is one of several factors (others include levels of dependence and superpower competition) that influence the relative emphasis a government gives to acquiring aid and investment and to protecting the nation's independence. Intense debates are likely over "how much dependence on outside assistance should be accepted and how much foreign control tolerated" (Weinstein, 1976: 28). Kautsky (1969) suggests that there are typically two groups in any Third World regime: revolutionary and managerial elites. Revolutionary modernizers adhere to the more radical strategies of development and take hardline positions stressing hostility and independence vis-à-vis the major powers. Managerial elites adopt relatively pragmatic positions that call for greater accommodation with the major powers and a toning down of revolutionary fervor.[41]

Debates over development questions and the competing uses of foreign policy are sharply intensified when they become linked to the political survival of competing factions and/or leadership succession crises. As Brown (1976: 10) noted with regard to factional conflict in post-Maoist China, "at a critical point in any policy debate between leaders at the pinnacle of power, differences over issues become so intense that it is not the policy itself which is paramount, but rather the authority, power, and influence of the leader advocating policy. And at this juncture, the debate over policy is transformed into a struggle for who will hold the ultimate power to decide the issue." And, once again, the usual outcome is not foreign policy restraint or inactivity. Rather, much of the Third World literature presents another scenario: a strong push toward asserting independence in foreign policy. As Weinstein (1972: 356) states:

> Given the prevailing perception of a hostile world, a competitive situation creates strong incentives for carrying out the nation's independence, while liabilities accompanying a policy designed to serve the needs of economic development are formidable; in a non-competitive political situation, however, the liabilities of a development-oriented foreign policy can easi-

ly be overcome, while the political incentives to carry out an independence policy are reduced.

In sum, there are sharp foreign policy debates in Third World governments, but the general view is that they are a further pressure for more—not less—assertiveness in foreign policy.

All this is not to say that political processes in the making of Third World foreign policy are uniform. In fact, emerging from the growing body of case study research is a third theme: there are different political configurations in Third World decisionmaking processes. There are arguably four types of situations: (1) noninstitutionalized and highly unstable coalitions of contending groups, (2) unstable regimes operating under some political constraints, (3) highly centralized regimes dominated by a single predominant leader who is sensitive to domestic politics, and (4) relatively well-established, though possibly fragmented, regimes in significantly bureaucratized polities. The first group is the most striking from a political perspective because it has extreme domestic political pressures resulting in equally extreme patterns of foreign policy. Examining these extreme situations in some detail here permits isolation of specific conditions that sharply politicize foreign policy in Third World settings. Subsequent consideration of the three other types of situations illustrates different configurations of political conditions and precludes excessive generalization about the politics of Third World foreign policies.

The first group consists of situations in noninstitutionalized political systems with highly fragmented and unstable regimes engaging in intensely conflictual and assertive foreign policy behaviors. Well-researched case studies are available for five episodes: the People's Republic of China at the height of the Cultural Revolution (Ahn, 1976; Brown, 1976; Fairbank, 1986; Hinton, 1972a, 1972b; Pye, 1984; Robinson, 1982; Thorton, 1982; Zagoria, 1968), the Indonesian confrontation over the creation of Malaysia (Weinstein, 1969, 1976), Iran's hostage crisis with the United States (Stempel, 1981, forthcoming), Syria's escalation of tensions with Israel prior to the 1967 war (Bar-Siman-Tov, 1983; Rabinovich, 1972; Kerr, 1971), and the Argentine invasion of the Falkland/Malvinas Islands (Levy and Vakili, 1990; Moneta, 1984).

What is striking about these cases is that they explain intense foreign policy behaviors in terms of a common set of four extreme political conditions. First, in each episode there was an extensive fragmentation of authority among groups with bases of power in different government institutions, all of which occurred despite authoritarian and one-party structures (and sometimes also a predominant leader). By the mid-1960s, Indonesian politics was dominated by a sharp three-way power struggle between the army leadership and the leftist Indonesian Communist Party (PKI), with the supposedly predominant Sukarno struggling to survive between these two contending centers of power. In China at the height of the Cultural Revolution, leadership factions had deteriorated into possibly five autonomous political groups: the party apparatus (Liu Shaoqi and Deng Xiaoping), government administrators (Zhou Enlai), the military (Lin Biao), various radical groups (e.g., the Red Guards and the Cultural Revolution Group), and Mao Zedong himself. There was a similar pattern in the postrevolutionary Iranian regime: relatively moderate elements in the Provisional Revolutionary Government and later the presidency (e.g., Barzargan and Bani Sadr), more hardline clerics of the Islamic Republican Party (Beheshti et al.), and the politically central Khomeini, who was surprisingly inactive and uncommitted in political decisionmaking. The Syrian and Argentine cases did not have predominant leaders, but still had considerable fragmentation. The Syrian regime under General Jadid continued to be plagued by tensions between the party and army wings of the Ba'athist regime, as well as sharp factionalism within each institution. The formal power-sharing arrangements within the Argentine military regime had begun to deteriorate with tensions between (and factionalism within) the army, air force, and navy.

Second, in each regime the political situation among the coalition of actors was extremely unstable, reflecting a complete lack of institutionalized processes within the regime and in relationship to the broader political system. Not only did no single group have control over policy, but procedures for reaching agreement (e.g., voting) were entirely absent, and there was ongoing uncertainty about the allocation of power within the regime. Weinstein (1972) and Stempel (forthcoming) both assert that there was rarely an identifiable decision group (did these actors ever meet together) or precise "occasion for decision" for major actions. The situation was further exacerbated by the essentially zero-sum conflict within most of these regimes. With the possible exception of the Argentine military regime, the groups within each regime were embroiled in an open fight for control of the regime, in which it was likely that the losers would be terminated politically. Not surprisingly, domestic political considerations dominated the motivations of the political players in their positions on foreign policy issues.

Third, leadership conflicts over foreign policy were further intensified by political instability in the wider political environment. The Syrian and Argentine regimes were the most vulnerable to pressures from external groups, facing attempted coups from opposing military factions and widespread public unrest, respectively. While this forced some cooperation among Syrian elites (Bar-Siman-Tov, 1983), mounting political and economic crises created divisions within the Argentine military regime over its basic political mission and policy strategies (Levy and Vakili, 1990). Either way, pressure on the foreign policy process was sharply intensified by the tendency of factions to appeal to outside political groups as a means of enhancing their power within the regime. The Chinese, Iranian, and

Indonesian cases were somewhat different: none faced a real threat of being overthrown by a contending group outside the regime, and each had a single predominant leader who held undisputed ideological legitimacy within the political system. However, this did not preclude contending actors in the regime from making appeals to the wider public, except that in these settings those appeals could be made most aggressively by a predominant leader, while the regime's rival factions had to cast their public appeals for support in an escalating rhetoric centered around the leader's ideology. Either way, the spilling of conflicts in the regime into the wider political arena sharply intensified the connection between political legitimacy and foreign policy in these highly unstable settings.

Finally, in each case there was general consensus supporting confrontation in foreign policy. None of the key regime actors doubted the legitimacy of China's confrontation with the West, Indonesia's opposition to Malaysian independence, the Iranian students' holding of U.S. hostages, Syria's demands for Arab unity and war with Israel, and Argentina's invasion of the Falklands. In other words, critical to each of these episodes was the existence of foreign policy issues that the regime (and its opposition) could readily manipulate to enhance their position or the regime's legitimacy. Even when there were policy splits within the regime over the appropriate level of foreign confrontation, the more moderate or pragmatic elements (e.g., the Indonesian military, Chinese pragmatists led by Liu Shaoqi, and Iranian moderates in the PRG) could at most quietly and cautiously call for restraint. If anything, the intense and open nature of regime conflicts required them to work even harder (at least in public) to match the ideological credentials of their more radical opponents. In sum, not only was there a broad consensus on these confrontations, but they were strongly amplified by the manipulation of the issue by hardline players (especially predominant leaders) as a means of embarrassing and destroying less hardline elements.

The impact of these domestic conflicts was considerable, and it is not an exaggeration to say that these confrontational episodes were driven in large part by the leadership crises and legitimacy problems of these regimes. At one level, the extreme internal conflicts were matched by intensely hostile foreign policy initiatives. Not only did the Argentine, Chinese, Indonesian, Iranian, and Syrian regimes involve themselves in major confrontations (the Falklands, the Vietnam War, the creation of Malaysia, the hostage crisis with the United States, and the 1967 Arab-Israeli war), but also each regime (with the exception of the less radical Galtieri regime) had overall foreign policies that were generally highly active and assertive. As Bar-Siman-Tov (1983) documents for Syria, these regimes engaged in a constant flow of bellicose behavior toward adversaries and were not just active in the affairs of their own immediate region. Weinstein (1976) shows that the Sukarno regime was active not only on the

Malaysia issue, but that it extended its anti-Western activity to concerns in the Middle East, Vietnam, and the international economic order. By any Third World standard (and by the standards of preceding and successor regimes in these countries), the intensity and scope of the conflict behavior of these regimes were quite distinctive.

Yet if the push of domestic politics seems to be uniquely strong in these cases, there is one aspect of foreign policy where the difference was not all that great: the inability to commit the nation (and its resources) to a particular course of foreign policy action. These regimes strongly expressed symbolic threats and promises to act in various ways, but (with the exception of the Argentine regime) these intentions were simply not implemented in concrete ways. This too can be traced to internal political constraints. According to Stempel (forthcoming), the Iranian regime was actually deadlocked over whether to release the hostages (as preferred by the moderates) or put them on trial (as demanded by the hardline clergy and students). Despite its public support for the confrontation with Malaysia, the Indonesian military actually dragged its feet in carrying out military actions and in other ways covertly cooperated with its Malaysian counterpart (Weinstein, 1976: 324–325). Chinese leaders could not agree on concrete actions to support the Vietnamese against the United States, reflecting their overall "very poor position to influence" important international developments (Hinton, 1972c: 149; Zagoria, 1967; Brown, 1976). The intense conflict in the Syrian regime led that regime "blindly to the brink" (Seale, 1988, chap. 8) of a conflict with Israel in ways over which it had little control. Again with the exception of the Argentine regime, in each regime there was an ongoing political inability to commit to policies in meaningful and coordinated ways, although at the time it seemed hidden by the intensely threatening verbal policy behaviors of these regimes.

In sum, these extreme cases collectively point to the most dramatic kind of linkage between domestic politics and foreign policy, in which internal political survival (not external pressures) seems to be the dominant force behind the government's escalation of foreign confrontations. The primacy of domestic politics is reflected in the combined weight of several extreme political conditions: significant divisions within the regime, low institutionalization, fluid and threatening political opposition, and the political nature of foreign policy issues. But although these cases expose a linkage between domestic politics and foreign policy in stark detail, it would be a mistake to assume that these extreme cases represent the typical linkage between domestic politics and foreign policy in Third World nations. As noted at the opening of this section, there are three exceptions to consider.

The first of these configurations also has extreme domestic instability but differs from the above cases in one very important respect: there were some constraints such that political pressures did not result in the extremely intense pattern of confrontation with adversaries. An illustration of this is

South Korea's decisionmaking throughout its treaty crisis with Japan in 1964–1965 (Kim, 1971).[42] The negotiation of a treaty with the former colonial power was a very explosive issue in the volatile political system of South Korea's Third Republic, and even the regime's politically predominant leader, President Chung-Hee Park, was hardly in a political position to act. Not only was his ruling Democratic Republican Party merely a "federation of factions" (Kim, 1971: 183), but the regime faced an extremely hostile domestic environment involving parliamentary opposition, the military, and student protests. The treaty presented "a great political opportunity for the opposition to exploit against the government" (p. i), and the crisis was intensified by the fundamental lack of legitimacy of the Korean political system and the fact that "Koreans' distrust of Japan was matched by their distrust and suspicion of their own government" (p. 104). Yet despite this extremely politicized setting, the resultant foreign policy was not an explosion of hostility toward Japan nor even a termination of the negotiations. Rather, despite extreme domestic pressures, the Park regime moved slowly, yet erratically, toward an agreement with the Japanese after a year and a half of domestic turmoil.

This foreign policy outcome is different from the aggressive hostility found in the previous set of cases of political instability. Although the South Korean regime faced a clear legitimacy crisis, was itself sharply fragmented, and had strong challenges from the outside, its political situation was different from the previous five cases in significant ways. First, the leaders in this otherwise weakly institutionalized and more open regime adhered to certain political rules and norms, and thus could not suppress or ignore opposition challenges to the controversial treaty. Equally important was that the regime's initiative of repairing relations with a former colonial ruler ran counter to domestically politically satisfying options. In Weinstein's formulation, the regime was pursuing an issue that was widely perceived to undercut the nation's independence (although contrary to his hypothesis the regime was willing and ultimately successful in carrying out the initiative). The value of the Korean case is that it shows that even partially different configurations of variables (as identified in the more extreme cases above) may produce widely different decision outcomes. Although it is only a single case, this episode suggests the need to avoid the premature conclusion that extreme domestic instability always leads to extreme foreign policy confrontation.

The second exception is the situation, widely emphasized in the literature, in which foreign policy decisionmaking is dominated by a predominant leader who faces no significant opposition groups in the regime or in the wider environment.[43] Despite this, it is striking that research into these situations still emphasizes the domestic political roots of foreign policies. In part, the argument stems from the emphasis on the role of leader personality, asserting that certain leaders are highly sensitive to pressures from their environment in making decisions. As argued by M. Hermann, these "pragmatic" leaders do not have a rigid attitudinal framework to guide their policy judgements (as do their more "principled" counterparts), but instead closely monitor both the domestic and international environment and act in a largely situationally conditioned manner in making decisions (Hermann, Hermann, and Hagan, 1991, 1987). The other part of this argument is that predominant leaders, despite their personal political dominance, remain preoccupied with the basic weakness of their regimes—namely, the lack of strong support groups and the regime's lack of widespread legitimacy. As noted earlier, this is a prominent explanation of Arab foreign policies (Dekmejian, 1971; Dawisha, 1990; Ismael and Ismael, 1986; Taylor, 1982; Korany and Dessouki, 1984), and is said to account for such actions as Syria's intervention in Lebanon, Morocco's claims to the Western Sahara, Iraq's invasions of Iran, and Libya's various African interventions (Dawisha, 1990).

One episode of decisionmaking by a predominant leader that has been examined in particular detail is the politics of Syria's 1976 intervention in the Lebanese civil war. Decisionmaking analyses by Lawson (1984) and Hermann (1988) focus on Hafez al-Assad as a predominant leader and show the subtle interaction between leader personality and domestic political pressures. Assad's decisionmaking style fits the definition of the pragmatic leader, and his sensitivity to the environment certainly extended to domestic politics (Hermann, 1988; Seale, 1988; Hinnebusch, 1984). Lawson (1984) argues that the invasion itself was driven by the regime's alarm over growing opposition, as well as by declining support by mid-1976 in the region of the country that traditionally supported the regime. The significance of the Lebanese intervention was that control of Beirut gave the Syrian regime regular access to resources and markets in a way that favored socioeconomic interests of groups normally favorable to Assad, while also preventing the further growth of opposition in these depressed areas. Thus the political logic of Syrian intervention went far beyond the widely cited task of legitimacy, representing instead a predominant leader's close reading of specific groups and use of a subtle political strategy enabling "the country's ruling coalition to reinforce its collective position in relation to its domestic opponents" (Lawson, 1984: 476).

The final decisionmaking situation here challenges the basic premise, as raised at the beginning of this section, that Third World foreign policy decisionmaking is fundamentally different from that in the advanced industrial nations. Namely, as Vertzberger (1984b: 70; Hill, 1977; Clapham, 1977) has cautioned, "there is a distinct class of states in the Third World which *do* have coherent bureaucracies acting in regularized patterns and routines." In other words, foreign policy decisionmaking clearly takes place in politically and organizationally complex settings, and these processes are sufficiently established to be insulated from extreme instability. That all along there have been certain exceptions is clear from structural analyses of foreign policy settings in Israel (Brecher, 1974, 1972; McLaurin, Peretz, and Snider, 1982), India (Bandyopadhyaya, 1970; Brecher, 1977; Brenner, 1985; Tharoor, 1982), Nigeria (Aluko, 1976), and the larger Latin American countries (Muñoz and Tulchin, 1984; Lincoln and Ferris, 1984; Fox, 1977; Schneider, 1976). The central role of bureaucratic and institutional actors is now cited in the relatively well-established regimes of such formerly unstable polities as Algeria (Korany, 1984b), China (Barnett, 1985; Bachman, 1989; Shirk, 1990–91), Egypt (Dessouki, 1984), South Korea (Koo, 1985), Thailand (Buszynski, 1989), and Saudi Arabia (Korany, 1984a).

Nor are the decision processes fundamentally different from the constraints widely cited in the advanced industrial states. Muñoz and Tulchin (1984: 15; also Lincoln and Ferris, 1984) conclude that "even though the [North American] bureaucratic politics perspective may not provide a complete explanation of Latin American foreign policies, it still can offer useful theoretical insights at more restricted levels." The play of well-institutionalized norms of consultation and consensus within the Saudi royal family (along with the involvement of senior technocrats) is, according to Quandt (1981: 108–111), at the root of indecision, lack of initiative, and very broad policy compromises in that nation's foreign policy. Even where decision dynamics diverge from the constraints of bureaucratic and institutional politics, the underlying processes do not seem to be much different from those in the governments of the advanced industrial states. For example, Vertzberger's (1984a, 1984b) case study of the 1959–1962 Sino-Indian confrontation shows that factional politics, groupthink, leader personality, and bureaucratic politics (not unfamiliar to Western cases) were all at the base of the Nehru government's risky behavior (and misperceptions) in that crisis.[44] Even in polities marked by instability and numerous leadership changes, there has not been a sharp departure from the effects of earlier patterns of domestic political constraints, but only an intensification of those pressures on foreign policy makers. The fragmentation and polarization of recent Israeli politics among Labour, Likud, and various smaller parties have caused that country's foreign relations to be deadlocked in major ways (Yaniv and Yishai, 1981: 1005–1128; Dowty, 1984; Aronson, 1982–83). Similarly, the factionalism behind post-Maoist Chinese foreign policy (Bachman, 1989; Harding, 1980; Lieberthal, 1984; Shirk, 1984) has not been fundamentally altered by the political crisis culminating in the Tiananmen Square repression (Quansheng, 1992). In these cases and others, processes in even severely politicized settings in otherwise established Third World polities do not appear to be all that different from those cases examined in the two previous sections of this chapter.

In closing, more recent literature on Third World foreign policy suggests that decisionmaking is complex. As in modern states, leaders are subject to a variety of domestic and international constraints, including political conditions that are often very fluid with a mix of political instability and intense policy disputes. However, beyond that, the precise configuration of specific political factors can vary significantly and lead to sharply divergent foreign policy patterns. At one extreme, highly conflictual and assertive foreign policies result from the otherwise opposite political configurations of an unstable, fragmented coalition and of a cohesive regime dominated by a predominant leader. Other scenarios lead to relatively restrained foreign policy behavior, and in one of these the sources of these constraints are well-established bureaucracies and government institutions. Compared to the instability of, for example, Italian democratic coalitions and the collapsing Soviet Union, the processes of all but the most unstable Third World polities do not seem to be all that different from those of advanced industrial states.

Revised Themes for Comparative Foreign Policy Research

This chapter has drawn upon area studies literature on foreign policy decisionmaking in several basic political settings as a means of evaluating comparative foreign policy research on domestic politics and opposition. Two general conclusions emerge from this exercise. Most basically, it has shown that domestic political influences on foreign policy are a widespread phenomenon across the full variety of political systems, which supports my third contention for the importance of political explanations in cross-national analyses of foreign policy. Equally important, it has illustrated that the causal linkage between opposition and foreign policy is not simple or direct. Not only is the occurrence of strong opposition by no means automatic in any type of political system (including democracies), but there is considerable variance in the configuration of opposition and the effects on foreign policy decision outcomes. Taken together, this literature demonstrates that comparative foreign policy theories (or pre-theories) have treated domestic politics simplistically by considering it solely in terms of political system accountability and level of development.

Although comparative foreign policy research has treated political influences simplistically, this is not to suggest that efforts at developing cross-national generalizations about domestic politics and foreign policy should be abandoned. Rather, comparative perspectives need to be adapted so as to incorporate the complexity and variety of political influences on foreign policy in all types of polities. It is here that this chapter offers a further benefit: it provides insights to guide further comparative research in the linkage between domestic politics and foreign policy behavior. These points provide the basis for the conceptual framework presented in Chapter 3, and in summary form they are as follows:

1. *Comparative research should have as a working assumption that significant political influences on foreign policy may—or may not—occur in any type of political system.* This is the primary implication of the above summary of this chapter's analysis of the politics of foreign policy making in non-U.S. settings. It runs directly counter to the conventional notion that foreign policy opposition exists in some types of political systems and not others. Instead, it has been shown that political constraints are equally important in authoritarian systems such as the former Soviet Union as well as a variety of Third World settings. In addition, though, it also shows that domestic opposition is by no means automatic. Not only does the level of opposition vary within and across various authoritarian states, but also the survey of democratic systems suggests that not all of them are sharply constrained by domestic opposition. While certain democratic regimes have opposition (including single-party systems such as Japan under the LDP), other democracies are relatively cohesive and do not face major domestic political constraints. In fact, cases such as the German Grand Coalition and the Israel Labour-Likud coalition stand out because they were far more politically fragmented than their relatively cohesive predecessors.

2. *Comparative research should focus on the conceptualization and measurement of patterns of political opposition that are likely to influence foreign policy behavior.* The open/closed dichotomy is hardly a satisfactory measure, and instead an immediate task is the development of conceptualizations and measurements of various types of opposition as they actually occur in diverse political systems, both democratic and authoritarian. Particularly striking is that the case studies consistently emphasize constraints from political divisions within the central leadership of the regime (e.g., factions, parties, and other autonomous groups), an arena of political activity common to all political systems. This is not to say that intraregime processes were insulated from outside pressures, and herein lies the importance of opposition outside the regime from, say, factions of the ruling party, opposition parties in the legislature, the military (and other paramilitary actors), and/or regional/ethnic groups. It is also essential that these conceptualizations and measurements be flexible enough to capture roughly equivalent patterns of opposition across systems with different structural arrangements. Not only should it be possible to compare fragmentation levels in democratic and authoritarian regimes, but also comparisons of the levels of constraints of differ types of opposition (e.g., military actors versus political parties) should not be precluded.

3. *Comparative research should focus on the political dynamics by which domestic politics is linked to foreign policy behavior.* With the assumption that opposition can exist, a primary research task becomes one of understanding the causal mechanisms by which it influences foreign policy behaviors. The alternative political dynamics of bargaining/controversy avoidance and political legitimization (and their respective divergent

outcomes) are evident in all three political systems examined here. Bargaining and controversy avoidance processes, of course, underlie the frequent deadlocks in multiparty and factional coalitions in parliamentary democracies, but the same sets of analyses note occasions in which political legitimacy concerns push the regime out of its constraints. Both dynamics are equally evident in analyses of the foreign policies of the former Soviet Union, and comparative case studies of military intervention even show that bargaining and controversy avoidance may constrain some decisions (e.g., Czechoslovakia) while legitimacy concerns may motivate others (e.g., Angola). Political legitimization themes are found in much of the Third World foreign policy literature, particularly in the cases of highly unstable coalitions or regimes with predominant (and sensitive) leaders. However, bargaining and controversy avoidance dynamics are apparent with the emergence of more complex, though not necessarily more stable, policymaking environments in some countries. As with the occurrence of political opposition, the alternative dynamics of bargaining/controversy avoidance and political legitimization can not be assumed to occur exclusively in one type of political system and not others.

4. *Comparative research needs to consider the impact of factors that account for the strength and direction of domestic political effects on foreign policy.* Although opposition and alternative political dynamics occur across widely different political systems, it would be a mistake to go to the other extreme and infer from the literature that domestic politics, even where strong opposition exists, is always the dominant influence in all situations and with a particular kind of impact. There were, for example, major differences in overall internal constraints between the otherwise similarly fragmented Italian and Swedish coalition cabinets, and the comparative case studies of Dutch coalition cabinets, the factionalized Japanese LDP, and the Brezhnev Politburo show that the foreign policy makers in each were strongly constrained on some occasions but not on others. The implication is that the linkage between political opposition and foreign policy is an inherently contingent relationship, one that poses two basic questions. First, under what conditions does domestic opposition most affect foreign policy—in other words, when are leaders able to insulate foreign policy from domestic political pressures, and, at the other extreme, when does domestic politics become a dominant consideration in foreign policy calculations? Second, under what conditions does domestic politics take the form of bargaining and controversy avoidance as opposed to political legitimization—in other words, when does a leadership accommodate opposition by working out some kind of settlement with them, and when do they confront their opponents by asserting the virtue of their policies and hold on power?

Implicit in the literature are two general approaches to accounting for the strength and direction of opposition effects on foreign policy. One explains foreign policy effects in terms of the characteristics of opposition actors, with the assumption that decisionmakers are more attentive to certain types of opposition and not others, depending on, for example, the strength of these actors, the intensity of their challenges, and their proximity to the leadership (e.g., opposition inside or outside the regime). Another equally important approach focuses on the conditioning effects of other political variables that define the context in which leaders and opposition interact in the making of foreign policy. Some have to do with the political situation of the regime itself, for example, when foreign relations becomes closely linked to periodic leadership succession crises. Other factors have more to do with the properties of the political system, particularly the extent to which political procedures and norms are well established. Although this approach seems to be the less obvious of the two, it is found throughout the case study literature and in ways that explain both the strength and direction of opposition effects.

Notes

1. In this context it should be emphasized that the conventional wisdom of the comparative foreign policy literature (as, for example, represented in the logic of the Rosenau pre-theory) reflects an accurate reading of the area studies literature *of the early 1960s*. In a sense, this chapter represents an effort to develop themes from more recent case study literature, much of which is far more theoretically explicit than that available to Rosenau at the time.

2. Also, many of the more impressive developments in the field (e.g., Skocpol's [1979] work on states and revolutions) have more to do with structural phenomena and are secondary to the concerns of this research at its current stage.

3. On foreign policy making in Fourth Republic France, particularly with respect to the Algerian crisis, see also Andrews (1962), Brown (1965), and Macridis and Brown (1960).

4. Other sources on the politics of Italian foreign policy include Kogan (1963), Posner (1977), and Vannicelli (1974). Posner (1977: 824) is the most blunt. After noting the vigorous efforts of other smaller European nations with similar internal and external constraints (Belgium, Denmark, and the Netherlands) "to make the Atlantic and European organs more responsive to their needs," he concludes that "the general pattern of Italian external policy, in both the military and economic sectors, has been one of passivity. The most important explanation of this pattern is the nature of the broad DC coalition, which diffuses responsibility and, while inhibiting decisive policy making, encourages competition among its various components."

5. Fitzmaurice (1983) raises a similar concern in his brief overview of the increasingly politicized character of Belgian foreign policy making, although he does not suggest that this country's foreign policy has faced the kind of deadlock found in the Netherlands.

6. This is not to say that the political nature of decisionmaking in Scandinavian countries is ignored. However, the focus is more on the impact of "bureaucratic politics" (Faurby, 1982) and the attendant problems of management and coordination (East, 1981; Karvonen and Sundelius, 1990; Sundelius, 1982).

7. The same applies to the early coalition cabinets of Fifth Republic France, in which no party was willing to challenge De Gaulle's predominance within the regime, particularly on foreign policy matters (see Kaminsky, 1975; Morse, 1973).

8. Even the relatively stable West German political system was not immune from these pressures: "in the election year of 1969, the programmatic differences that had all along strained the Grand Coalition intensified and contributed to the increased stagnation of Bonn's foreign policy line" (Handrieder, 1970: 190).

9. This is further illustrated by the fact that Neustadt's (1970) examination of the British-U.S. crisis over the Skybolt Affair focuses mainly on the dynamics of bureaucratic politics in the two polities.

10. Research on Canadian foreign policy decisionmaking also emphasizes bureaucratic politics (e.g., Nossal, 1989, 1979). An exception is a case study of nuclear weapons policymaking in which a leadership crisis politicized decisionmaking and brought bureaucratic processes into the broader political arena (Lentner, 1976).

11. Farrands (1988: 51), who "argues that a focus on administrative and elite processes is inadequate," emphasizes nationalism in British politics in that "it is an important guide to and constraint on policy, and the ability to manipulate national sentiment is important to policy-makers of all political persuasions" (p. 61). He argues that this created strong pressures for action in the British government's response to the Argentine invasion of the Falklands/Malvinas Islands.

12. Articles on specific bureaucratic and business actors in Japanese foreign policy making can be found in Scalapino (1977).

13. As will be noted below, there are exceptions where other actors are able to prevail, depending, as noted by Fukui (1977a) and Minor (1985), on the character of the issue and the willingness of political leaders to delegate or respond to pressures from the bureaucracy and business groups.

14. Detailed examinations of the LDP's factional organizations and internal politics include Fukui (1970, 1978b, 1985), Scalapino and Masumi (1962), Stockwin (1975), Thayer (1969), and Richardson and Flanagan (1984).

15. On the genealogy of postwar factions, see also Thayer (1969) and Fukui (1970).

16. Like multiple parliamentary parties, Japanese factions seek to attain a minimum winning coalition by having a stable majority of LDP votes to win the party presidency and thereby form a factional coalition cabinet.

17. Hellmann (1969: 19), in particular, emphasizes this dynamic, concluding that "each major postwar foreign decision has been accompanied by protracted consultation among various faction leaders, reflecting an effort to reach consensual agreement."

18. Other episodes fitting this pattern are brief studies by Frankel (1977) of Japan's ratification of the nuclear nonproliferation treaty and by Han (1978) of the procurement of the PXL antisubmarine aircraft. Both authors stress the role of right wing opposition within the LDP without reference to the party's factionalism, and in a way that suggests the opposition cuts across factions and crystallizes within various study groups.

19. That this was the general pattern of LDP politics on the China issue is evident from case studies that span multiple episodes of the China issue, for example, Fukui (1970 and 1977a), Welfield (1976), and Ogata (1988). Occasionally, though, the issue did become connected to leadership succession crises and thus was sharply politicized, as occurred with the fall of the Sato government after the Nixon administration's surprise recognition of the People's Republic of China.

20. According to Fukui (1978a) Japanese decisionmaking concerning the

GATT Tokyo round was dominated entirely by professional bureaucrats in the Ministries of Foreign Affairs, International Trade and Industry, Finance, and Agriculture and Forestry, as well as the Economic Planning Agency. With few exceptions, the LDP leadership had little involvement: "once the substantive negotiations were underway . . . neither the Cabinet nor individual ministers sought a leadership role in guiding and directing the bureaucracy" (p. 81). Similarly, the decisions to revalue the yen in the face of the floating of the U.S. dollar (the second of the 1971 "Nixon shocks") was left entirely to senior bureaucrats in the Ministry of Finance and its autonomous agency, the Bank of Japan. Throughout the crisis, the minister of finance refused to intervene to resolve disputes among the two equal bureaucratic players.

21. At one point, Prime Minister Sato appointed a senior member of his own faction to head the recalcitrant MITI, but this effort did not resolve MITI opposition because "the new minister, finding he could not persuade the industry and the MITI bureaucracy to seek accommodation with American demands, rather quickly. began to espouse the MITI view" (Destler et al., 1979: 43).

22. It is, however, important to keep these effects of domestic politics in proper perspective. Although sharp debates occur within the LDP leadership, a broad consensus does exist about Japan's international interests and goals: a pro-West, nonmilitary, and trade-oriented foreign policy. As Hosoya (1976: 121) notes, "the general direction is not in doubt, but the speed and manner of progressing is the resultant of thrusts from one side and counter-thrusts and restraints from the other."

23. Relatively little conceptual research was done on the politics of foreign policy in the Eastern European Communist systems, with major exceptions being a useful theoretical framework by Clark (1980) and research on Yugoslavia by Zimmerman (1987). Also, the People's Republic of China could be considered now to have taken on some of the character of an established authoritarian system, as represented by Barnett's (1985) institutional analysis of Chinese foreign policy making.

24. Along with media reporting, the points that follow on the Gorbachev and Yeltsin foreign policies are drawn from the following sources, which represent mainstream thinking about the still-changing political settings of Soviet and Russian foreign policy making. Analyses of the original foreign policy decision-making system of the Gorbachev regime (during the mid- to late 1980s) include Bishop (1990), Bialer (1987), Holloway (1989–90), Larrabee (1988), Larrabee and Lynch (1986–87), and Stewart and Hermann (1990). By the end of the decade, it was clear that the political situation was becoming far more fluid; along with ongoing media reporting, useful analyses of these changes include Bialer (1987), Winter et al. (1991), Hough (1989), and Simes (1991).

25. Literature on the orderly Brezhnev regime (e.g., Simes, 1986; Bialer, 1987; Dallin, 1981) stresses the expanding array of expert organizations routinely involved in the foreign policy process, including the Foreign Ministry and military as well as various policy institutes, such as the Institute for the U.S.A. and Canada (which continues to exist under Georgi Arbotov).

26. There is also evidence that pressure for Soviet political intervention in support of allies and liberation movements in Africa (Valenta, 1978) and the Middle East (Golan, 1984; Spechler, 1987; Ra'anan, 1973) was at least partially domestic, coming from the military and party ideologues with parochial predispositions favoring Cold War confrontation, regional strategic interests, and sympathy for "anti-imperialistic" activity.

27. These kinds of shifts in the intensity of leadership conflict have been effectively modeled by Roeder (1984), who identified several periods of post-

Stalinist rule depending on the interaction of the "level of completion" and "power dispersion" variables.

28. Similarly diminished constraints can be inferred from the case studies of the Soviet political intervention in the Middle East after Brezhnev had consolidated power in the 1970s and 1980s (Golan, 1984; Spechler, 1987). However, Anderson (1982) reports that constraints were a factor in the Brezhnev Politburo's decision not to intervene in Poland.

29. Constitutional reforms creating several independent centers of power are discussed in the regular reporting of the *New York Times,* throughout 1990.

30. Authority building is not simply the process by which a leader consolidates power after becoming head of state; it is a more or less permanent feature of a leader's tenure in office, "first to rise within the collective leadership, then to consolidate their authority and push their comprehensive programs, and finally to defend their policy effectiveness after those programs faltered" (Breslauer, 1982: 10).

31. The evidence from cases of Soviet intervention decisions concerning the Middle East (Ra'anan, 1973), Angola (Valenta, 1978), and Afghanistan (Valenta, 1980b) indicate that Brezhnev, long after consolidating power in the early 1970s, still had a cautious decisionmaking style, even on issues for which he had strong preferences (and political incentives) for advocating intervention.

32. Kremlinological overviews (e.g., Linden, 1966; Slusser, 1967) of the Khrushchev regime illustrate the ongoing erratic and confrontational style of this leader's foreign policy decisionmaking. Compared to the Brezhnev regime, there exist fewer relevant case studies of specific decisionmaking episodes by the Khrushchev regime after he had consolidated power, with the notable exception of Slusser's (1973) case study of the 1961 Berlin Crisis.

33. These two leadership styles are also relevant to the alternative political directions of foreign policy, as discussed below. Relatively speaking, the "pull" of coalition politics would dominate politicized issues in regimes with consensus-oriented leaders, while the "push" of the leader's own political interest would be reflected in the confrontation type of leader.

34. As in the Japanese one-party setting, competition among senior leaders creates a symbiotic relationship between bureaucratic and political leaders, and in this situation the influence of bureaucratic actors is enhanced—not diminished. As Roeder (1988: 285) summarizes: "the leaders need supporters among the interest elites to promote their careers or maintain their positions; and the interest elites need patrons at the top to support their specific program requests."

35. For example, one interpretation views Brezhnev's policy of détente with the West as providing him with a politically acceptable approach to the problem of a stagnant, overbureaucratized economy. The argument, best made by Leonhard (1973: 69), is that détente was a broad compromise between reformers and hardliners. The relaxation of Cold War tensions, favored by the moderates, enabled the government to attract foreign investment in the Soviet economy and to import technology and needed goods (e.g., foodstuffs) that could not be produced entirely at home. Yet, to the satisfaction of the conservatives, these policies were designed to enable the regime to avoid major domestic economic and political reforms, and to retain a growing commitment to military spending.

36. In the case of Middle East policy, Spechler (1987; see also Ra'anan, 1973; Golan, 1984) shows that during the 1982 Lebanese crisis political pressures resulted in restraint as well as less support for the PLO as compared to that given to Syria, in part because the latter had strong institutional interests in Moscow.

37. Even the otherwise risk-adverse Brezhnev Politburo, if not divided over

the issue at hand, found high-risk behavior attractive in order to impress domestic audiences in order to preserve the coalition from external pressures (Ross, 1980).

38. This is a consistent theme in the case studies of Soviet decisions to intervene in Afghanistan (Valenta, 1980b, 1984b), the Middle East (Golan, 1984; Spechler, 1987), and Angola (Valenta, 1978). Anderson (1982) illustrates that there were limits to this legitimizing function in the case of a possible invasion of Poland, because it would have directly undercut Brezhnev's overall policy of détente. Mastny's (1982; also Marantz, 1975) study of the Austrian State Treaty suggests how legitimacy dynamics in leadership politics resulted in a cooperative initiative with the West.

39. The major critiques of conventional themes, particularly the focus on the role of the single leader, in Third World studies include those by Clapham (1977), David (1991), Hill (1977), Korany (1986, 1983), Weinstein (1972, 1976), and Vertzberger (1984b). Other parallel assessments can be found for specific regions, including ones concerning Latin America by van Klaverin (1984) and Lincoln and Ferris (1984), the Arab States by Dessouki and Korany (1984a), sub-Saharan Africa by Shaw and Aluko (1984), and the People's Republic of China by Bobrow, Chan, and Kringen (1979) and Chan (1979).

40. Useful theoretical statements linking development to foreign policy include Anglin (1964), Biddle and Stephens (1989), Gitelson (1977), Ismael and Ismael (1986), Joffe (1976–77), MacMaster (1974), Moon (1985), Rothstein (1976), Shaw (1976), and Weinstein (1972).

41. It is important to keep in mind that these are differences of emphasis. "Managerial modernizers, too, can regard themselves as being part of the revolutionary tradition" and "revolutionary and managerial modernizers still can express their different attitudes by using these symbols with different degrees of emphasis and interest" (Kautsky, 1969: 454). Therefore, in any type of regime, these relatively different policy tendencies may coexist.

42. Unfortunately, these more restrained manifestations of instability are not widely considered in the Third World literature, perhaps because of an academic bias in the West toward only the most dramatic kinds of foreign policy episodes. Another interesting example of this situation is that of Jordanian foreign policy making during the Persian Gulf crisis (see Brinkley, 1990).

43. M. Hermann identifies a predominant leader when "a single individual has the authority to commit the resources of a nation in response to a particular problem and others cannot reverse his or her decision" (Hermann, Hermann, and Hagan, 1991: 2). This is not an unusual occurrence; it is the dominant theme in the literature on personal rule in sub-Saharan Africa (Jackson and Rosberg, 1982) and the "primacy of the executive and especially the personalized character of the decision making process" in most Arab nations (Korany and Dessouki, 1984: 414; also Friedman, 1990; Khadra, 1985), particularly Iraq under Sadaam (Ahmad, 1984; Dawisha, 1986), Libya under Khaddafi (Zartman and Kluge, 1984), and Syria under Assad as discussed below. See also Dominguez (1989) for a discussion of Castro's role in Cuban foreign policy.

44. Complex political and bureaucratic processes are also evident in Brecher's (1977) case study of India's devaluation crisis in 1966. Here, though, the "decision was made by a small group of politicians guided by a few technocrats" (Brecher, 1977: 3).

3

Conceptualizing Political Opposition and Its Cross-National Linkage to Foreign Policy Behavior

This chapter presents a conceptual framework linking domestic opposition and foreign policy in a way that is appropriate for executing broad cross-national analyses. The task is to conceptualize existing opposition across different types of political systems and to capture the diverse kinds of political actors and processes identified in the collective case study literature in Chapter 2. This should permit comparison of roughly equivalent levels of political constraints found in the different institutional arrangements not only of democratic and authoritarian polities but also those of presidential and parliamentary systems and the fluid configurations in less institutionalized polities. The framework is also structured to incorporate some of the theoretical complexity outlined in Chapter 1, as reinforced and extended by the theoretical insights gleaned from the case studies in Chapter 2.

The framework consists of a sequence of four components, the first two of which consider the presence or absence of political opposition actors. One of these concerns political divisions within the central political leadership, or regime fragmentation, which is the primary arena where policy is formulated. The other component here consists of several types of political opposition outside of a regime that challenge the regime's overall policies and its hold on power. These include opposition from within the ruling party, other political parties, the military and paramilitary actors, and regionally based groups. The framework's two other components incorporate some of the contingencies governing leader responses to opposition within and outside the regime. Thus, the third component emcompasses conditioning influences that mediate the strength and direction (i.e., bargaining/controversy avoidance or political legitimization) of opposition effects on foreign policy. These are the structure of the political system and the vulnerability of the regime. The final component of the framework has several dimensions of foreign policy behavior to which political opposition is hypothesized to be linked, and they are conceptualized in a way that can reflect the amplifying and constraining effects of domestic politics.

Before proceeding, however, let me emphasize that this framework, although cast in a general manner, is not intended to be comprehensive in scope. First, as noted earlier, my concern in this project is with capturing mainly the organized opposition actors that are regularly involved in the broad political process at the national level. I have not attempted to capture directly less organized, mass-based opposition (e.g., riots, demonstrations, and the like) that is emphasized in the literature on political instability and domestic conflict. Although related to certain notions developed in this chapter (e.g., institutionalization, vulnerability, and the intensity of opposition), a full consideration of these kinds of phenomena is beyond the scope of the current effort. Second, the treatment of opposition is constrained by the need to have concepts that can realistically be operationalized in a cross-national analysis, and this chapter's framework includes only those phenomena that can be incorporated into the empirical analyses to follow. Although this does not exclude any major types of political actors or essential theoretical dynamics, it does result in the exclusion of more fluid kinds of domestic politics (particularly interest group activity and public opinion), because they can not be adequately measured for aggregate data analysis (given that their political involvement and positions literally vary from one decision to another).[1] Like others before it, this project is limited by the reality that some types of opposition are so situationally based and issue-specific that it is very difficult to develop aggregate measures of them for broad cross-national analyses. In sum, the focus here is on relatively permanent, general types of opposition actors, that is, the various groups that are active across the full array of issues (aggregating interests themselves) and in more or less constant competition with the current leadership in power. These are the actors that are widely emphasized in the comparative politics literature and that the comparative cases in Chapter 2 point to as the primary, ongoing political environment in which decisionmakers operate.

Regime Fragmentation

This pattern of opposition concerns the extent to which the central political leadership of a national government is fragmented by persisting internal political divisions in the form of competing personalities, institutions/ bureaucracies, factions, and/or competing parties or other autonomous groups. (Alternatively, it can be thought of as a measure of the ability of a single leader or group to dominate its immediate political environment.) A basic premise of this research is that political constraints most immediate to the central political leadership (and thus senior foreign policy makers) are of special importance. The area studies literature reviewed in Chapter 2 consistently pointed to political pressures within the top leadership, be it the Soviet Politburo and Central Committee, the Japanese cabinet controlled by the Liberal Democratic Party, or the ruling coalitions of the unstable regimes of Indonesia under Sukarno, China during the Cultural Revolution, or initially Iran under Khomeini.

The importance given to regime fragmentation is also grounded in three theoretical assumptions about why foreign policy decisionmakers would be most sensitive to debates and challenges from within the regime. First, because the political power necessary to allocate the nation's resources lies in the authoritative positions constituting the regime, divisions within this leadership can actually prevent decisionmakers from committing the government to a substantively meaningful course of action in foreign policy. In contrast to other types of opposition, dissenting groups within a regime are directly able to block any initiative. Second, even if not all elements of a regime's coalition actually participate in the making of decisions, policymakers must still be concerned that their decisions do not alienate powerful groups within the regime. These groups are essential to the power base of the regime, and their defection from the regime could bring its immediate collapse, taking with it all its members. It is assumed that leaders strongly value retaining power, and will seek out policy options that do not seriously threaten to destroy their hold on power. Finally, permanent divisions within the central leadership significantly enhance the influence of groups outside the regime. As illustrated in a number of the cases in Chapter 2, actors within a divided regime may try to strengthen their position by aligning with (or certainly not alienating) important actors in the bureaucracy, party, or legislature, with the result that the latter gain increased influence over policy.

For purposes of broad cross-national analyses, information on three dimensions of regime fragmentation appear useful: (1) the extent to which power is dispersed among separate political groups within the regime, (2) the presence or absence of a politically predominant leader, and (3) whether or not members of a regime are divided over broad foreign policy issues. This conceptualization is broader than those found in earlier efforts (Salmore and Salmore, 1978; Hagan, 1987), where the focus was mainly on the range of groups (e.g., factions, parties) within the leadership, as in the first dimension here. The other two dimensions are added separately in order to tap pressures that enhance their ability to achieve agreement despite that dispersion of power. These are factors that various theories have suggested are important to understanding political decision processes and, in particular, the ability of contending groups to work together and achieve agreement. Also, as will be seen in its operationalization, this kind of separate conceptualization allows greater flexibility in subsequently combining the three dimensions into a composite measure.

The Internal Group Structure of the Regime

This is the primary aspect of regime fragmentation, and it concerns the extent to which power is divided among separate groups in the regime. Is the regime controlled by a single, cohesive political group, or is power dispersed across multiple groups sharing control of the regime? For purposes here (and for subsequent cross-national data collection) there are three basic configurations of group structure: (1) a single cohesive group, (2) a single factionalized group, and (3) a coalition of autonomous groups. Associated with the three are progressively stronger internal political constraints. They are conceptualized here in a manner that captures equivalent configurations across various institutional arrangements.

Regimes controlled by a single, politically cohesive party or group. This is the least constrained type of regime, being controlled by a single political group that is internally cohesive. These bodies are, politically speaking, unitary actors in that they have no persisting, reinforcing divisions in the form of organized cliques or factions. Although there are likely bureaucratic and personal conflicts among elements of the ruling party, these divisions and debates vary from issue to issue and from situation to situation. Nor do these conflicts involve sustained competition for political control of the regime itself or its basic political makeup. All this means that foreign policy making in these regimes is facilitated because there exists a broad consensus on foreign policy issues and on the distribution of authority inside (and outside) the regime.

There are, of course, numerous cases of single-party governments, although not as frequently as is widely assumed (Bogdanor, 1983). In the United States with its presidential executive, it occurs when a single party controls the executive, has a majority in the Congress, and is itself reasonably cohesive in both institutions. Parliamentary systems in Britain and Canada have an especially long history of single-party rule by cohesive and disciplined ruling parties. But certainly not all such cases are Anglo–North American. Note the stable patterns of cohesive authority in the ruling parties of Mexico, Taiwan, and Kuwait, countries that have had remarkable order in their leadership politics across successive leaders. Still, even in more fluid systems, this pattern replaces more fragmented situations with the rise of a strong leader who is able to bring to office colleagues of a similar mentality, for example, the Soviet Union under Brezhnev in the 1970s as well as various single-party regimes in the less institutionalized systems in Africa, Asia, and the Middle East.

Regimes controlled by a single party or group that is internally divided by factions. As in the first case, central authority is controlled by a single political group, but here that group has persisting, organized subunits, or factions. The regime is best considered to be a composite of actors competing for control over policy and, in many cases, overall dominance within the regime. These divisions are structured in the sense that they exist through the life of the regime and potentially pervade decisionmaking across the full range of issues. Decisionmakers likely align with members of their factions again and again across most, if not all, issues confronting the regime. This might simply reflect the policy beliefs common to members of the factions, but where infighting for control of the regime is paramount, the purely political interests of these factions probably define the policy positions of each of their members. Together, or separately, the two factors suggest that factionalism broadly constrains the regime's foreign policy. The only factor mitigating these constraints (which are absent in coalition governments) is the fact that the party's members have a shared interest in seeing their party retain control of the regime. In this last sense, political debates in the foreign policy process in these regimes remain relatively contained.

Factionalism is defined broadly here so as to capture diverse phenomena that can take at least three forms. *Structural factionalism* is found in a political party that is nothing more that what Sartori (1976: chap. 4) refers to as a federation of subparties. Such factions are subparties in that they have the primary organizational attributes of a political party, including formal membership rosters, financial resources, and media facilities such as newspapers. They also compete openly for control of party leadership posts; indeed, candidates for office in public elections are often identified by factional, as well as party, labels. With such factions, government formation becomes an exercise of putting together a workable coalition of a majority of these actors within the ruling party. It is not surprising, therefore, that a factionalized party in a single-party regime exhibits much of the behavior of a coalition cabinet, all within the bounds of a shared interest in the continuing dominance of the ruling party. As seen in Chapter 2, these kinds of factional organizations have had a strong imprint on the politics of foreign policy in Japan under the Liberal Democrats and Italy under the Christian Democrats.

However, factionalism is not limited to these well-established subparty organizations. In more fluid political systems such as those in Third World polities (recall, for example, Indian and Chinese foreign policy making), leadership competition is not nearly as structured but instead is organized around highly contentious leadership cliques, resulting in a pattern of *clientelist factionalism* (see Belloni and Beller, 1978). In contrast to structural factions, patron-client networks are more individually based, being centered around the personal following of the individual leader who is able to deliver government and party resources to "clients" in exchange for their support. These cliques, given their largely personal basis, also tend to be more fluid in structure and smaller (but more numerous) than structural factions. Political competition is likely to be pervasive and intense as these fluid cliques compete for power. Although these factions lack the organizational strength of structural factions, leaders are considerably constrained by the overall atmosphere of political uncertainty resulting from shifting relations among factions and the lack of norms and structures regulating their behavior. To ignore them in comparative research would be to bias the phenomenon of factionalism toward leadership divisions in more established political systems.

The third kind of factionalism concerns largely policy-based divisions, which may be less directly associated with competition for control of the regime. In the case of *policy factionalism,* the leadership in the regime is organized into two or more groups, or wings, that are defined primarily by contending policy orientations (not necessarily linked to foreign policy). The groups are defined largely by their members' adherence to a set of shared policy (domestic or foreign) beliefs that transcend any single policy issue. Such divisions may permeate organized factions (e.g., leftist, centrist, and rightist factions of Italy's Christian Democrats) or the clientelist networks (e.g., "reds" versus "experts" in the Chinese Communist Party since the late 1950s). Most notably, though, policy-based factions are, by themselves, interesting because they can occur in parties that are otherwise well disciplined and without any kind of structural or clientelist factionalism. However, even in these situations, leaders may become sharply divided over a broad set of political issues, and as a result find themselves organized into reinforcing cleavages across multiple issues. Such has been the case of occasional Communist regimes where moderates and hardliners coexist, the United States in the Carter administration with the split between Brzezinski and Vance, and the divisions within the Dutch Christian Democratic Party on arms control issues. As with other forms of factionalism, these kinds of broad policy divisions are significant in that they constrain the ability of the regime to agree on policy, although in this case it is mainly substantive policy differences that preclude the ability to reach policy consensus.

Regimes composed of a coalition of two or more autonomous political groups. This third configuration includes cases in which no single party or group has control over the regime. Authority in these regimes is shared by politically autonomous actors, either within the collective leadership of a single executive body (e.g., a coalition cabinet or military junta) or by some interinstitutional arrangement such as separation of powers. Regimes of this type are theorized to be most strongly constrained because (a) no single group has the authority to commit the nation's resources on its own and (b) there is little long-term shared interest in sustaining the unsatisfactory compromise arrangement of a multiparty coalition (i.e., member parties would prefer to gain sole dominance over the regime in the future). The threat of bringing down the regime is assumed to be a powerful constraint on foreign policy makers who propose controversial policy initiatives. Another factor is that where substantive foreign policy disputes do occur, it is quite possible that their resolution will be difficult because of the lack of fixed procedures for resolving disputes between separate actors and institutions. While there are some polities with very well established norms for coalition policymaking (e.g., the Scandinavian countries), there are probably far more cases where ongoing political distrust and different ideological orientations make it quite difficult for separate parties and institutions to work together to achieve agreement.

As before, cross-national analysis requires recognition of varied (yet roughly equivalent) types of coalitions, across the different institutional arrangements of parliamentary, presidential, and authoritarian government structures. The classic case is a parliamentary system in which no party has enough seats in the legislature to take full control of the cabinet, and thus control of the regime necessarily passes to two or more parties. Postwar Italy and Fourth Republic France had a long succession of weak cabinets composed of several parties with little willingness to cooperate in dealing with certain major foreign policy issues. Israel with its Likud-Labour cabinets entered the ranks of parliamentary regimes internally deadlocked on major foreign policy questions, and subsequent Likud-dominated (and now Labour) coalitions have done little better. Such coalitions are not unique. Coalition government has been the postwar norm throughout much of Western Europe (Bogdanor, 1983), and since 1989 it has replaced Communism as the primary form of cabinet structure in the new democracies of Eastern Europe. The Anglo–North American image of single-party government is hardly the norm for most democracies.

Coalition regimes are not, however, limited to parliamentary democracies. The equivalent level of fragmentation occurs in presidential democracies when the party controlling the presidency does not control the congress. Because neither institution has full authority to commit the nation's resources, a de facto coalition exists in which policymaking authority is shared by different parties. And even though no group can by itself bring down the regime (because of their separate bases of power), the various forms of veto power held by the presidency and the congress create an equivalent ability to prevent the regime from acting. This situation regularly occurs in the United States with its Republican presidents and Democratic-controlled Congress, and the same is true for presidential systems in Latin America, which often have multiparty situations reflective of their fragmented party systems. Quasi-presidential systems in postwar Finland and Fifth Republic France also fit this pattern, in that the president is independently elected but must work with a cabinet (with its own premier) whose composition is determined by the partisan distribution of seats in parliament. One of the reforms in the Soviet system instituted by Gorbachev was the creation of an autonomous presidential executive, and this separation-of-powers system has been maintained thus far in the Russian Federation under Yeltsin, who must now deal with a very contentious, autonomous parliament that includes holdovers from the Communist order.

Coalition arrangements can also be found in authoritarian polities if no single group has been able to achieve or maintain dominance over the system's multiple centers of power. Following Perlmutter (1981), authoritarian systems can be said to consist of at least three types of structures: the state or governmental apparatus; the official party; and a variety of parallel or auxiliary structures that support the regime (e.g., militant gangs, the secret police, or the military). A stable authoritarian regime is characterized by the dominance of one structure, usually a strong official party. During certain periods (e.g., ones of political consolidation or decay), however, relations among these structures may become very unstable with no single group having dominance, as was the case in China during the Cultural Revolution and in Syria during the succession of military-Ba'athist coalitions throughout the 1960s. Where such separate structures are not well established, the situation can be even more complex. In Iran during the hostage crisis, the new revolutionary regime found authority ill defined and dispersed across various legislative, paramilitary, and even multiple executive institutions such as the Provisional Revolutionary Government, the Revolutionary Council, and Khomeini as the revolution's overseer. Coalition arrangements were also at the core of the dramatic changes in the Soviet Union under Gorbachev. His political reforms (or maneuvers) not only created autonomous presidential and legislative institutions, but also withdrew the primacy of the Communist Party, strengthened representation of Republican governments at the national level, and yet continued to face powerful institutions such as the military and the KGB.

Presence of a Predominant Political Actor

This dimension of fragmentation concerns whether or not there is a single individual or group with relatively preponderant political power within the regime. The notion of the "predominant leader" (M. Hermann, 1976, 1980) underlies several critiques of the bureaucratic politics model (Allison, 1971), which assert that the "ability of bureaucracies to independently establish policies is a function of presidential attention" (Krasner, 1972: 169; Destler, 1974; Perlmutter, 1974). Achen (1989) has argued that the presence of a "focal actor" enables bureaucratic decisionmaking to be modeled as a unitary actor, while C. Hermann (1992) asserts that a strong leader can define foreign policy decision outcomes in ways far different from the highly constrained image portrayed in the bureaucratic politics literature. However, predominant actors are not limited to individual leaders; predominant groups, such as factions or parties, are of equal significance in more fragmented regimes. The coalition theory literature has established that the presence of one party with a disproportionate share of parliamentary seats (and with it the ability to enter into alternative coalitions), what de Swaan (1973; see also Pridham, 1986) calls a "pivotal actor," facilitates agreement among contending parties to form a coalition cabinet. This same logic can be extended to explaining the likelihood of a coalition decision unit achieving agreement and the precise shape of that agreement (Hermann, Hermann, and Hagan, 1991). The cross-national frequency and importance of predominant actors—individual leaders, powerful groups, or both—in the foreign policy process is quite evident throughout the case studies discussed in Chapter 2.

The notion of a predominant actor is relevant in assessing political constraints in each of the three types of group structures, but "predominance" must be defined differently across the three configurations. In a regime with a single cohesive group, a predominant actor is the individual leader who is personally so dominant that he or she controls all power within the regime. That leader is, in effect, the regime. No power within the regime exists independently of the leader, and other senior officials serve merely as advisors and can not directly challenge the leader. It is also possible to have predominant individual leaders in more fragmented regimes (which adds a fourth kind of actor to Perlmutter's authoritarian scheme above). While leaders in this setting can be expected to have their preferences indirectly challenged, there is no question of their predominance within the regime. Although subordinates may debate policy because the predominant leader does not impose his or her preferences, in no way will they openly challenge the professed policy position of the leader.

Some individual leaders attain this kind of political power because they are exclusively identified with the creation of a new political order, either as a leader of national independence (e.g., Ghana's Nkrumah or India's Nehru) or a revolutionary leader (e.g., Egypt's Nasser or Cuba's Castro). Predominant leaders may also occur in more complex and established political systems, as when an individual achieves dominance (though usually temporarily) within the regime because he or she alone is credited for the political victory that brought the party/group to power (e.g., Adenauer in West Germany, Thatcher in Britain, and Gasperi in Italy). Another case is where a leader has established (sometimes coercively) his or her political power base over the ruling party to such an extent that others in the party will pose no challenge (e.g., Syria's Assad, Iraq's Sadaam, and Taiwan's Chiang Kai-shek). De Gaulle's dominance of the 1960s French Fifth Republic scene probably reflects all these sources of political predominance.

Theoretically, in a more fragmented regime, the political power of a predominant actor (with or without any kind of individual charisma) stems from one of two factors, or both. One is when a single group controls an institution that has formal veto power over groups in other institutions because of constitutional arrangements, for example, the role of the president in presidential and quasi-presidential systems. The other situation is more subtle but probably more pervasive, being central to parliamentary cabinets and fluid authoritarian coalitions. This occurs when one group can lay claim to a preponderant amount of the resources critical to the base of the regime's authority, for example, votes in the parliament, military force, legitimizing ideology, and financial resources. In either case, the implication is that the range of policy options considered in the decision process will be narrowed because those of the predominant actor can not be overruled. Also, on many issues a predominant actor with clear preferences may impose his or her wishes on others in the regime, particularly when weaker actors have a narrower range of strong policy preferences and/or fear that the predominant actor will evict them from the regime and enter into an alternative coalition.

Predominant groups in fragmented regimes appear in a variety of settings, although here their common feature is that they have more resources than other factions. In parliamentary coalitions, pivotal actors occur when there is a senior party with a large majority of the ministries by virtue of its dominance of the parliament; for example, recall cases involving the dominant Christian Democratic parties in Italy, the Netherlands, and West Germany. Presidential and quasi-presidential systems are, by virtue of their institutional arrangements, naturally prone to have predominant actors. The party that controls the executive usually has predominance over the legislature on foreign policy issues (with or without the formal veto), as evidenced by the relative dominance of post–World War II U.S. presidents, as well as powerful executives in the fragmented quasi-presidential regimes of France under Mitterrand (versus Chirac) during the "cohabitation era" and Finland under Kekkonen. Finally, this situation occurs in authoritarian regimes when power is dispersed across multiple institutions, one of which is controlled by a group with control of relevant political resources. Examples of these are fragmented regimes with either a charismatic leader with strong ideological credentials (e.g., the case of Indonesia under Sukarno or Iran under Khomeini) or a strong military that is coercively able to dominate the civilian leadership (e.g., Syria by the end of the 1960s).

Polarization over Foreign Policy Issues

This dimension of fragmentation occurs when actors in a regime are divided over substantive aspects of foreign policy issues. Is there agreement among the regime's contending actors on the identification of core threats and problems facing the nation? Are there differences on the basic strategies for coping with those threats, between, say, moderates favoring diplomatic accommodation and hardliners arguing for increased confrontation?

In other words, is there an overall consensus on the national interest? Where policy splits occur it is likely that group constraints will be intensified as foreign policy debates (which themselves must be resolved) become tied up with the political competition for office. This kind of concern is found in research on crisis decisionmaking (Snyder and Deising, 1977) and the outbreak of war (Vazquez, 1987), while Art's (1973) critique of the bureaucratic politics model emphasizes the importance of "shared images" in facilitating agreement on certain issues. The emergence of polarized belief systems is the central theme in Holsti and Rosenau's (1984) research on post-Vietnam foreign policy leadership and is a key feature underlying domestic constraints on U.S. foreign policy over the past two decades (Destler, Gelb, and Lake, 1984; Vazquez, 1985). Parallel concerns about "ideological distance" and "policy space" are found in the coalition theory literature, where it is argued that parties with relatively proximate ideological orientations are more likely to agree to enter into a coalition than are parties with sharp differences (Axelrod, 1970; de Swann, 1973).

Like the concept of the predominant actor, the theoretical significance of policy polarization is as a condition affecting the likelihood of agreement among contending groups in a fragmented regime. Where such actors differ in basic ways over general aspects of the nation's foreign relations, it can be expected that their contending orientations will be related to debates on specific foreign policy issues. Not only will these policy differences intensify political disputes throughout the life of the regime, but they will cause such political divisions to be more directly linked to foreign policy debates. Indeed, in relatively cohesive regimes such policy disputes may be the primary factor driving foreign policy debates. Equally interesting, though, is that actors in even highly fragmented regimes will find that they can often work together if there is a general consensus on foreign policy issues. Agreement on at least certain kinds of issues is regularly possible, largely because of an overarching consensus on the nation's foreign policy interests and, in time of crisis, foreign threats. Furthermore, if some actors in the regime do not have strong preferences on an issue, then their support could likely be "bought" by advocates of a policy through political "sidepayments." Either way, the absence of polarization over foreign policy within the regime likely reduces the constraints characteristic of factionalized and coalition arrangements.

Not surprisingly, actors in fragmented regimes often have basic differences about the nation's foreign policy. As seen in Chapter 2, numerous fragmented regimes are composed of parties, factions, or party wings representing distinct leftist versus rightist tendencies, for example, the Grand Coalition in West Germany, the factions of the Italian Christian Democratic Party, or the United States with the collapse of the Cold War consensus after Vietnam. And in certain cases (e.g., Fourth Republic France on the Algerian question, Iran during the hostage crisis, and the Labour and Likud

Coalition in Israel) the intense political constraints on foreign policy decisionmakers stemmed in part from the fact that competition for political office was intrinsically tied to immediate foreign policy dilemmas. Substantive foreign policy splits are important, even in fairly cohesive, single-party regimes. Recall the prolonged debates within Brezhnev's Politburo over what means to use to overthrow the Dubcek regime. Even within the president-dominated U.S. executive, fundamental splits can occur, such as those over détente and Third World issues between Vance and Brzezinki in the Carter administration.

However, what is especially striking is that some very fragmented regimes are clearly not polarized over foreign policy issues. Their factions and parties are essentially nonideological, being instead organized primarily for purposes of gaining control of the party leadership and ministerial resources. The clearest example is Japan's Liberal Democratic Party, whose factions are not formed around contending policy positions and who adhere to an overall consensus on Japan's national interests. Multiparty regimes, and even minority governments, are capable of functioning effectively if there is a well-established foreign policy orientation, as illustrated by Sundelius's (1989) research on Sweden's entrenched "neutrality regime" during the Cold War. In fact, what was most notable about the Dutch crisis over arms control issues was that normally the country's foreign policy process is elitist and consensual (Everts, 1985).

Summarizing thus far, constraints on foreign policy makers resulting from the fragmentation of power within the regime are theorized to reflect the interaction of three basic conditions. At the core is the group composition of the regime across cohesive single parties, factionalized single parties, and coalitions of multiple groups. These constraints are, in turn, conditioned by two factors: the presence or absence of a politically predominant actor and the extent of polarization over foreign policy issues. The absence of a predominant leader and sharp polarization over foreign policy issues intensifies the constraints inherent in the division of authority among contending factions and groups. Equally important is that the reverse is true: political constraints are diminished if there is a predominant actor or if there is no polarization on basic questions of foreign policy. The significance of regime fragmentation is twofold: it encompasses the opposition most immediate to foreign policy makers, and these internal divisions likely force the leadership to be more responsive to opposition outside the regime.

Political Opposition to the Regime

The nation's central political leadership in the regime does not, of course, function in a political vacuum. The regime itself operates in a complex political environment, and a primary goal of any leadership is to retain power. Even though political divisions within the regime are assumed to be the most important form of opposition, it is critical to consider organized opposition in the wider polity if a complete assessment of domestic political constraints is to be attempted. This is important in two respects. First, there are numerous internally cohesive regimes that are still affected by opposition in the wider environment, and ignoring such opposition would greatly diminish any estimates of domestic constraints. Second, as some of the case studies show, the impact of regime fragmentation does not become fully apparent unless the responses of factional and/or party members to their wider constituencies are considered. The effects of regime fragmentation are greatly compounded by opposition from a volatile political environment.

This section presents cross-national conceptualizations of several basic types of opposition: (1) opposition from within the ruling party or group, (2) opposition from other political parties, (3) opposition from the military and/or paramilitary actors, and (4) opposition from regionally based groups. Although not a comprehensive coverage of every possible type of opposition (interest and corporatist groups, in particular, are excluded), this is a logically complete list of the types of organized actors who regularly challenge the regime. Basic dimensions of national political conflict are captured here: the ideological, coercive, and regional elements of political competition within the wider political system, as well as challenges to authority from within a regime's own party. The activities of these political actors are also usually well covered in the political accounts of area experts, such that the realistic collection of data on a cross-national basis is not precluded.

The foreign policy effects of opposition from outside the regime—or actually foreign policy decisionmakers' sensitivity to it—is theorized to be a function of two attributes of opposition actors: their organizational strength and the intensity of their challenges. The strength of the opposition refers to its organizational capabilities relative to those of the regime, with the assumption that foreign policy makers are more attentive to opposition groups who appear strong enough to threaten the regime's long-term hold on power. It is most basically a function of the relevant resources it commands in the political system (e.g., legislative seats, coercive force). But as with regimes themselves, the strength of any opposition group is determined also by its internal cohesion. If an opposition group has internal factional divisions, or if it is divided into separate groups, then it is assumed that its members will be less willing or able to work together in challenging the regime. An internally unified opposition is far more likely to be effective in challenging the regime than one in which political resources are dispersed across infighting factions and/or separate actors.

The intensity dimension of opposition concerns the severity to which a group opposes the regime. Regardless of type of opposition, the intensity of challenges to the regime can be viewed across three basic levels: opposition (1) to the regime's overall policy program, (2) to the continuation of the regime in power, and (3) to the basic norms and structures of the established political system. The least intense kind of challenge is one in which opposition is limited to basic aspects of the regime's policy program, but does not extend to demanding the leadership's removal from office. More intense is an effort by an opposition group to evict the current leadership and, presumably, take control of the regime itself. The most intense form of opposition calls into question basic arrangements in the political system. Such antisystemic opposition challenges not only the regime, but also the legitimacy of the regime's hold on power and the political system norms and procedures upon which it entered office. Extremist opposition groups will be highly assertive in challenging the regime, often to the point of violating basic political norms in the system. It is assumed that more intense challenges, particularly if the opposition has substantial resources, are likely to capture the attention of the regime's leadership. Common to the conceptualization of the four types of opposition discussed below is the theoretical assumption that their impact on foreign policy makers is a function of the interaction of the strength of the opposition and the intensity of its challenges.

Opposition from Within the Ruling Party or Group

This is opposition to the regime and its policies from within its own national organization and leadership. The question is to what degree can the party leadership that controls the regime depend on the political support of its own senior membership? Intraparty opposition is still fairly proximate to the central leadership, but it is different from that of regime fragmentation because it refers to the party/group leaders who are outside the regime's authoritative structures, for example, political leaders who hold positions in the legislature, the military, or the ruling party's machinery or policymaking bodies. Thus, in parties and groups organized around structural factions or polarized wings and tendencies, a key issue is whether or not certain of these actors are excluded from the regime and therefore seek to change it or its policies. Important to keep in mind is that, although parties are often formally represented in the regime, there are important cases in which some factions or leaders are clearly excluded from the leadership body and subsequently oppose it.[2]

The wider membership of any political group, even if some of it is actually outside of government leadership positions, is critical to the survival of the regime because it represents the resource base of the leadership. The loss of support in any ruling political group—democratic or authoritarian—can ultimately mean that the leadership is forced to give up control of the regime. In a parliamentary regime, the dependence of the cabinet on the party or parties in parliament is clear: it cannot retain power if it loses its legislative majority because of the defection of its junior, or backbench, party members. In the Dutch cabinet, it was precisely this fear of defection by the anti–cruise missile faction that precluded any flexibility by the promissile party leadership in the cabinet. Similarly, leaders and factions in one-party regimes fear the loss of support from broader party bodies, such as the roughly three-hundred-member Central Committee of the former Communist Party of the Soviet Union. The sensitivity of Politboro leaders to this constituency is illustrated by the Brezhnev Politburo's eventual adoption of the military option against the Dubcek reforms in Czechoslovakia, a position originally advocated by Central Committee hardliners. In military regimes, a junta must also exert discipline on subordinate units of the military that also wield coercive power, as illustrated by the fluid politics in army-party regimes in Syria before Assad with their successive coups d'état. Intraparty opposition is a key arena of political constraints in both democratic and authoritarian polities.

The strength dimension of intraparty opposition essentially asks to what extent is the national party/group leadership organized into contending political groups, and if any of these actors are excluded from the regime or operate outside of its control. The most cohesive ruling party is one that is well disciplined with no organized factions or wings. In cases such as the usually cohesive and centralized British Conservative Party, the cabinet is able to depend fully on the support of their party in the legislature and faces no organized challenges to its control of the party. At the other extreme are parties such as the Japanese Liberal Democratic Party or the Italian Christian Democratic Party where there are major constraints on their leadership. Here the regime depends on the support of a party that is itself organized around autonomous factions—in other words, as noted above, ones that are organizationally autonomous and operate as subparties outside of the regime. The defection of these factions may bring about the collapse of the entire cabinet, as well as intensify competition among factions included in the regime (by offering alternative factional alignments).

As with regime fragmentation, there are other forms of intraparty/ intragroup divisions falling between the extremes of highly cohesive parties and those with structural factions. These are parties with more fluid internal organization that undercuts the discipline of the ruling group. One situation is where there are broad divisions between opposing wings or tendencies (e.g., reformist versus orthodox wings with some likely centrists), as was manifested in the cases of Soviet and Israeli foreign policy decisions. Minimally, such opposition will mean that the regime, whatever its makeup, will have to work hard to balance the policy preferences of the opposing wings. Another situation occurs when the party leadership contends with a membership that is largely undisciplined in an otherwise cohesive party (i.e., with no formal factions). Instead of broadly defined wings, the main feature here is that the wider party has numerous centers of autonomous power resisting the directives of the leadership. This might take the form of parties that are loosely structured around numerous patron-client networks, whose members are not ideologically polarized but rather act mainly in the interest of gaining resources from the party. This limited opposition was at the root of Indian political infighting throughout the 1962 border conflict with China. U.S. presidents face a similar lack of discipline because of their lack of control over their own party in the institutionally autonomous Congress.

The intensity of intraparty opposition may vary at each of these levels. The mildest form of dissent is where the membership of the ruling party generally supports the leadership and its overall policy program, although the leadership must remain attentive to inevitable political infighting that might weaken or distort its support base. This characterizes personalist regimes in ethnically fragmented African ruling parties. A bit more intense are opposition challenges to the overall policy program of the regime, but which do not directly call for a change of leadership itself. Except during open succession crises, this was the norm in Soviet foreign policy decisions. The most intense level of opposition occurs when the opposing element is excluded from the regime and openly seeks to have the leadership removed from power. Periodic leadership succession crises revolve around this level of conflict (regardless of the strength of that opposition), while in systems such as Japan's LDP and Italy's DC, excluded factions pose an ongoing threat to the life of the regime. At each level, the interaction of strength and intensity captures the extent to which leaders are challenged by their own supporters and thus are constrained by them.

Opposition from Other Political Parties

This type of opposition concerns challenges to the regime from other political parties in the legislature. This is a largely ideological dimension of politics, getting at challenges from other civilian groups organized to aggregate interests and to compete publicly for control of the national regime. In competitive democratic party systems where no one party has been historically dominant, political parties in the legislature are a very important type of opposition. Indeed, in the cases with disciplined, cohesive ruling parties (e.g., Great Britain), opposition political parties in parliament are the primary challengers to the regime. There is an especially extensive and directly relevant theoretical literature on political party systems (Lijphart, 1977; Sartori, 1966, 1976; McDonald, 1971; Almond and Powell, 1978; Dahl, 1966; Luebbert, 1986). Although focused on the overall pattern of party competition within a political system, various party system typologies can be usefully adapted to conceptualizing the strength and intensity of party opposition as it relates to the regime.

The strength of an opposition party is based on the single resource critical to party politics: seats in the national legislature.[3] In the party systems literature, the power balance between competing political parties is determined by the number of legislative seats controlled by each. For purposes here, this kind of scheme can be adapted by comparing the number of seats controlled by the regime's party (or coalition) to the combined total controlled by all opposition parties. Party opposition becomes significant when it controls enough seats to threaten the government's control over the policy process and maintain high public visibility as an alternative voice in national politics. Furthermore, control of a sizable number of seats by opposition parties can be taken as an indicator of the possibility that the regime might lose its majority in a future election.

The most extreme situation for a regime is when the cabinet does not command a majority of seats in the legislature. In both presidential and parliamentary systems, this gives the legislature a constant veto over regime policy initiatives, and in the latter system it also means that the legislature can bring about the collapse of the cabinet at any time.[4] The cases of Italian decisionmaking illustrate how such extreme legislative constraints compounded the deadlock of its postwar minority governments. More typical of this level of party opposition is where a regime retains a legislative majority, but it is not very large and an opposition party controls almost as many seats. Although in better shape than minority governments, these regimes must in the short term worry about defections from their own parties and other parliamentary maneuvers to block legislation, and over the long term be concerned about losing that majority in the next election. In political systems with two major parties, as in Israel, Germany, and Great Britain, legislative parties are an important and persistent influence on an otherwise dominant ruling party or coalition.

Other levels of party opposition are not nearly as severe but are still significant. First, like the regime's itself, the strength of party opposition depends upon its own internal cohesiveness. If a sizable number of opposition seats are controlled by different parties, then it is less likely that they will be able (or even willing) to work together to mount an effective assault on the regime and its policies (e.g., the fragmentation of opponents of earlier Mapai-Labour coalitions in Israel and the usual dominance of India's Congress Party). Even when opposition resources are controlled by a single party, the same applies if that party is internally factionalized, because its leadership will be absorbed in the intrigues of its own party. As illustrated by Japanese foreign policy making, structural factions in the otherwise substantial Japanese Socialist Party have undercut its challenges to the LDP. Second, legislative opposition is naturally undercut if the ruling party has a large majority so that it can feel relatively immune from opposition threats. Control of, say, two-thirds of legislative seats provides the regime with pretty much of a veto-proof situation (even with some voting defections from within its own parliamentary party) and at least an expectation that the majority will remain intact after the next election. But this is not to say that such opposition is insignificant. Even parties with few seats can have some imprint on policymaking, because their control of mainstream, national political resources gives them a visible and legitimate voice in national politics.

The intensity of political party opposition is also emphasized in the party systems literature, and in fact the above examples take on only partial significance unless the extent to which they are polarized from the regime is considered. The most extreme situation (reflective of Sartori's notion of "polarized pluralism") is where a party, even as it participates in the established electoral system, challenges the very legitimacy of the political system, for example, the Nazi Party in Weimar Germany, the Communist Party of Italy in the 1950s and 1960s, and the German Social Democrats until the late 1950s. This level of opposition is more severe because it likely challenges the basic assumptions of foreign policy alignments, as well as the very rules of political competition and government rule. The demands and strategies inherent in such challenges would seem particularly difficult to ignore, even if they come from relatively small parties. Even as charismatic a leader as Kenya's Kenyatta could not tolerate the existence of an independent party (Odinga's Kenyan People's Union) with fewer than 10 percent of the legislative seats. This is not a unique situation in one-party dominant systems with authoritarian tendencies.

Less severe, and more typical, is where a party opposes the regime, but its challenge is tempered by its acceptance of the democratic norms of the political system. In these situations, the primary question is the extent to which the contending parties disagree over policy issues. In some cases regimes and their opposition are ideologically similar and fall onto the same area of the political spectrum (e.g., those of the restrictive Central American democracies, as well as the centrist Democratic and Republican parties in the United States in the 1950s and 1960s), while in other cases there is sharp polarization over basic domestic and foreign policy issues (e.g., Israel's Labour and Likud parties and the British Labour and Conservative parties). Finally, even milder opposition is possible: auxiliary parties that do not question the dominance of the ruling party in otherwise authoritarian systems.

Opposition from the Military and Paramilitary Actors

This type of opposition concerns the coercive dimension of domestic politics and focuses on the position of the military vis-à-vis civilian elements of the political system.[5] In most cases this simply concerns the nation's military establishment, but in others it may also include other actors who command substantial coercive resources in the society (often having been created as counterweight to the military establishment), for example, police forces or paramilitary groups such as China's Red Guards, Iran's revolutionary guards, and the Nazi's brownshirts. In many nations it is critical to consider the military's influence because it is regularly active in national politics, either as a key support group for a civilian regime or as a contender for control of the regime itself. Either way, the military's role in domestic politics goes well beyond professional or corporatist military concerns and, instead, extends to the full aggregate of domestic and foreign policy issues. The political role of the military is a prominent theme in the comparative politics literature (e.g., Huntington, 1966; Janowitz, 1964; Perlmutter, 1977, 1981; Decalo, 1976).[6] The typologies of military orientations and civil-military relations in this literature provide a good basis for conceptualizing both the strength and intensity of military opposition toward a political regime.

The literature points to three factors that together determine the strength of military opposition: (1) the size of the military establishment (simply, does one exist?), (2) institutional arrangements and norms defining the military's actual role in domestic politics, and (3) the internal cohesion of the military and the possible presence of paramilitary actors. The militaries of some countries have so few resources that they are almost politically irrelevant, for example, Costa Rica and the Ivory Coast. In most countries, though, there is a relatively sizable military establishment, but in well-established civilian polities (democratic and authoritarian) its influence is limited because of its subordination to, or exclusion from power by, civilian elites. In other words, its influence is largely bureaucratic and centered mainly around defense policy issues, and it generally has little effect on the broader competition for control of the regime.

Stronger levels of military opposition occur when it is regularly and directly involved in the broader processes by which policies are developed and the leadership is selected. A relatively moderate form of such involvement occurs in many established, civilian-dominated systems. Here, military leaders occupy major political positions at the highest levels of the regime and, as a result, wield significant authority that inevitably goes beyond the military's institutional interests. For example, as depicted by Valenta and others, the role of the Soviet military in foreign intervention decisions involved more than simply providing military advice and then carrying out the intervention. A much stronger level of military involvement occurs when it operates as an autonomous actor outside normal regime and party structures. For example, usually following the return to power of civilian authorities, the former military rulers retain a formal veto over certain government actions, as found in various Latin American democracies. Another case is when the military becomes, in effect, an independent actor in the context of a decaying one-party regime (e.g., the role of the military in the Chinese Cultural Revolution or in Sukarno's decaying regime in Indonesia) or a praetorian democracy (e.g., the Japanese military's defiance of civilian control in the early 1930s). However, note that the military's ability to influence the regime in these settings depends on its own internal cohesion. Military opposition is far weaker if the organization is factionalized or if it shares coercive resources with paramilitary groups such as party militias and national police forces.

Huntington's (1966) concept of the "praetorian army," as well as Perlmutter's (1977) elaboration on it, provides a good basis for judging the intensity of military opposition and thus its likelihood of challenging civilian leaders in a regime. The mildest level of military opposition is where this politicized actor basically supports the current regime and is in agreement with its overall policy program. Somewhat more intense is military opposition to the current leadership (or overall distaste for its policies), but it still accepts the rules of the game that give the civilian leaders dominance. Characteristic of this "professional revolutionary" orientation (Perlmutter, 1977) is that the military does not seek power unilaterally and instead works with others civilian actors to undercut the current leadership. Military opposition to Gorbachev's reforms occurred at this level: the military opposed his leadership but only acted with other civilian party hardliners in the attempted August coup. Most extreme are militaries with "praetorian" political orientations (Huntington, 1966). These armies are clearly antisystemic and thus are far more likely to assert their influence against civilian leaders in unilateral and extraconstitutional ways. They are also likely to be in sharp disagreement with regime leaders over basic policy matters and even the proper shape of the domestic political order. The severity of these kinds of challenges is illustrated by Sukarno's sensitivity to the Indonesian military. This is probably not an unusual situation, even though it has not been widely considered in the comparative foreign policy literature.

Opposition from Regionally Based Groups

This dimension of opposition is concerned with the decentralization of political authority within the country. It considers political constraints that often emerge from federal political structures and that reflect regional (often ethnic) subdivisions. It is a dimension of opposition that is not usually considered in the comparative foreign policy literature and only a bit more in the theoretical comparative politics literature (e.g., Deutsch and Foltz, 1966; Duchacek, 1970; Enloe, 1972; Lijphart, 1977). However, after decades of "political development," many countries—both developed and less developed ones—have not achieved national integration. A large number of current political crises can be traced not to ideological clashes, but to ones involving extremely hostile regional groups and/or to demands for autonomy or even full independence. Not only does this now include the collapse of the Soviet Union, Yugoslavia, and Czechoslovakia, but also persisting tensions in Canada over Quebec, China and several regions (especially Tibet), Britain's Northern Ireland, Israel's Arab Palestinians, India's Sikhs, and any one of a number of civil wars in Sub-Saharan Africa. For many regimes, it seems the primary leadership task is to prevent national disintegration by maintaining tenuous regional balances among sharply antagonistic ethnic groups. The importance of these constraints on foreign policy is demonstrated by a number of the earlier case studies, ranging from the Ukrainian and Byelorussian pressure for the Soviet military intervention in Czechoslovakia to the underlying rationale of state-building in the nonaligned foreign policies of Third World states.

The strength of regionally based opposition, at least for purposes of the institutional focus considered in this project, stems largely from the structures governing relations between the national and regional governments and ruling parties. The question is to what degree are regional groups represented in party and government politics at the national and regional level? The representation of regional actors at the former level provides these groups with access to the policy process and possibly the selection of leaders. Regionally oriented groups may also exert influence by virtue of their control over the nation's territorial subunits, and this influence may be substantial if these regional governments have considerable autonomy. National parties will be constrained if they perceive opposition control of regional governments to be a threat to their ability to rule the nation as a whole. Taken together, the representation of these subnational interests adds a territorial dimension to national politics.

Regional actors, if they exist, are weakest in unitary political systems. As in Great Britain, Japan, and France, there are no autonomous regional governments, and the representation of regional interests is downplayed by the national government and the ruling party. Regional opposition is a bit stronger in quasi-federal systems, because these systems allow open representation of regional and ethnic interests within the structures of the national regime, although regional bodies do not have effective autonomy from central authorities. This was/is the norm in orthodox Communist regimes in the Soviet Union, Yugoslavia, Czechoslovakia, and China. Considerably stronger representation of regional interests combines this kind of representation at the national level with powerful regional governments whose leaders are locally elected and have significant control over the region's internal policies. Such federal systems, in other words, are based on a significant division of powers between the regional and national governments, as for example in the United States, Canada, Mexico, and India. The situation where regional opposition is the strongest is a confederal system, the primary feature of which is that regional actors have dominance over national politics and policy processes. Not only do these actors have regional autonomy, but they also have either constitutional or de facto veto power over the actions of any other groups in the national regime. Lijphart (1977) treats this as a central feature of the consociational polities of Lebanon, Malaysia, and Lebanon. These kinds of structures were also a central feature of post-Tito Yugoslavia before its collapse, and they are now at the core of the new Commonwealth of Independent States.

The intensity of regional opposition depends on the orientation of the leaders controlling regional positions within the national political system as well as regional governments. Regional opposition becomes significant to national decisionmakers when its demands go beyond local matters and extend to the overall policies of the regime (including foreign policy), the composition of national leadership, and relations between national-regional structures. The mildest level of regional opposition is when its actors (at the national and/or regional level) support the regime and its major policies. More intense regional opposition challenges the current regime and/or its overall policies, but does not call into question basic arrangements between the national and regional authorities. Regional opposition is far more intense when it demands reforms in the relationship between the national government and regional authorities, even if it does not call into question the basic structures of the political system or the nation's territorial integrity. U.S. politics during the civil rights crises of the 1950s and 1960s represents this kind of reformist movement. More dramatic are cases in which a regional leadership is essentially antisystemic. These leaders oppose the basic norms of the political system and/or they seek full independence for their region or province. To the surprise of many, probably the most intense opponents to emerge under Gorbachev's political reforms were radical nationalist leaders ultimately demanding a dismantling of the Soviet Union. Recent crises in Canada and Czechoslovakia also reflect the increasingly antisystemic nature of demands for changes between national and regional authorities.

Summarizing this section, the second component of this model of domestic political constraints on foreign policy makers focuses on four types of opposition outside the regime: (1) opposition within the ruling party/group, (2) opposition from other political parties, (3) opposition from the military and paramilitary actors, and (4) regionally based opposition. The strength and intensity of each opposition interact to determine the level of political pressure on foreign policy decisionmakers, with the assumption that leaders are more sensitive to opposition that has relatively substantial resources and poses strong challenges to the regime and the political order. Keep in mind, these influences are partially channeled through the first, and primary, component of the framework: the political regime. Furthermore, these effects are also mediated by the broader political context, the framework's third component, which is the subject of the next section.

Political Factors that Condition
Opposition Effects on Foreign Policy

Thus far, the conceptual framework presented in this chapter has focused on the existence of opposition groups and the strength and intensity of their threat to the regime and its policies. However, a further theoretical task is to consider how this direct opposition–foreign policy linkage is conditioned by the broader political context. As shown in Chapter 2, the properties of the political system and the more immediate political situation of the regime can provide further insight into the sensitivity of a leadership to opposition and the way it responds to it. In other words, these contextual factors can influence the strength of opposition effects on foreign policy, as well as the direction of those effects in terms of the alternative dynamics of bargaining/controversy avoidance and political legitimization. Thus, even with knowledge of the strength and intensity of opposition, leader responses to that opposition are by no mean obvious and are, instead, further shaped by broader political system structures and the regime's immediate political situation.

Comprehensive research on this question is far beyond the scope of the book. Ultimately, a wide variety of conditioning variables must be considered, ranging from political structures and state-society relations to transitory properties of the decision setting, issue-area, and international situation. The book, though, takes a first step by exploring the conditioning dynamics of two key political properties: political system structure and institutionalization and the vulnerability of the regime currently in power.

Political System Structure

The book has been concerned with moving beyond broad political system variables, such as accountability and political development, in comparative research on domestic politics and foreign policy. But this is not to argue that the structural attributes of political systems are not important. Although they do not directly account for the presence or absence of opposition groups, these structures seem to influence if, and how, leaders respond to those opposition actors. Actually, this role is more consistent with Rosenau's (1966) open/closed and developed/less developed genotypic variables, and the one consistent finding out of the comparative foreign policy research has been that political structure (i.e., accountability) mediates statistical relationships between various domestic factors and foreign policy; for example, recall findings reported by Hermann (1974a), Moore (1974), Wilkenfeld (1972), and the Interstate Behavior Analysis project (Wilkenfeld et al., 1980). In addition, while case studies showed the pervasiveness of opposition across different political systems, at no point did any suggest that these political procedures are identical, a point noted in research on such diverse settings as Japan (Destler et al., 1976), the Soviet Union (Valenta, 1978), and India (Vertzberger, 1984b).

The primary dimensions of political system structure are accountability and institutionalization (as a more precise conception of political development).[7] Accountability refers to the extent of democratization, with respect to the ability of the public to participate in the political process and their ability to contest officials and their policies in meaningful ways (Dahl, 1973). Even though it does not directly account for levels of opposition, there is good reason to suspect that leaders in open systems are generally more responsive to equivalent levels of opposition than are their counterparts in authoritarian systems. Democratic leaders must tolerate the legitimacy of challenges of a wider array of institutional and noninstitutional actors outside of the regime, and they are less able to insulate controversial foreign policies by restricting public discussion and coercively suppressing it. This same logic might also account for alternative leader responses to opposition, in other words, bargaining/controversy avoidance versus political legitimacy. Democratic norms and open political processes predispose leaders to emphasize various forms of accommodation as a means of coping with opposition at all levels. In contrast, authoritarian leaders are in a better position to manipulate opposition and policies via political legitimization. All this is not to say that leaders in closed systems are immune from opposition, but only that they are probably better able to insulate it from domestic politics and have greater options for dealing with domestic opponents.

Institutionalization (Huntington, 1966) concerns the extent to which political system processes (especially those within the regime) have become widely accepted (at least by major political players) and are thus an established feature of the political order. Well-institutionalized political systems have structures and norms that arc widely accepted, so that decisionmakers cannot easily violate the "rules of the game" and must recognize the legitimacy of opposition challenges to policy, and ultimately to their hold on political office. Outcomes of elections (however restrictive) are respected, opposition groups are tolerated and trusted, and the rules for policymaking and allocating political power are well established. At the other extreme, in less institutionalized political systems, regime leaders can readily suppress opposition groups and/or violate constitutional norms in order to achieve policy goals and retain power. These behaviors reflect the lack of established political procedures and extreme distrust among competing political groups.

The contextual role of institutionalization, as portrayed by the case studies in Chapter 2, is more complex than that of accountability. In fact, case studies of highly institutionalized systems (e.g., Scandinavian polities) and noninstitutionalized polities (e.g., various unstable Third World settings) have a common point: the political context enables leaders to insulate foreign policy from severe domestic political constraints. In the former, highly developed political networks enable leaders and opposition to work together in a consensual fashion and thereby insulate foreign policies from severe political distortions. Leaders in noninstitutionalized polities are also able to insulate foreign policy from domestic politics, but for an entirely different reason: they can manipulate and violate political norms to get around opposition constraints. As a result, it makes sense to argue that political pressures are most severe on leaders of regimes in moderately institutionalized political systems. These leaders must adhere to political system norms and procedures, even though they are not well defined and are likely open to continuous challenge by opposition groups. It is in this political atmosphere that leaders will be most affected by opposition, for they have fewer options for dealing with opponents with whom there is much less trust.

The concept of institutionalization also points to divergent political processes at its different levels. A dominant theme in the Third World literature is that leaders in these often noninstitutionalized political systems are particularly prone to use foreign policy to enhance the legitimacy of their regime and its policies. Not only is their hold on power open to question, but these are settings in which the give and take of bargaining and controversy avoidance are often irrelevant, either because opposition is absent or entirely distrusted and thus to be controlled. Accommodative processes of this kind are more prevalent in situations in which formal political procedures and the role of opposition are acknowledged, and are particularly evident in moderately institutionalized systems because of the severity of political constraints in these fluid settings.

Regime Vulnerability

How leaders respond to opposition also likely reflects more transitory, nonstructural aspects of the regime's own, more immediate political situation. The vulnerability of a regime concerns conditions that suggest its leaders would expect that opposition efforts might well be successful in removing them from power. Although it is difficult to tap leaders' perceptions of the shifting domestic fortunes of their regime, two properties generally indicate the possible collapse of the regime in the face of strong and intense opposition. They are the historical competitiveness of the political system and its regime, and the degree of political uncertainty within the current regime. Both properties, particularly if viewed interactively, provide some insight into the stability of the regime and its vulnerability to outside opposition pressures.

The first of these properties concerns whether or not control of the regime has alternated between different political groups in recent history.

In other words, has a single party (and single faction within it) historically controlled the regime and thus dominated the political system; has it achieved such a predominant position that it has been able to retain power for extended periods of time and does not appear to face any major challenge? Although many democracies have competitive party systems and certain authoritarian polities have long retained the same ruling group, vulnerability is not simply a function of democratization. There are some democracies with one-party-dominant party systems in which a single party or coalition has long dominated, for example, the PRI in Mexico, the LDP in Japan, and the Federal Council in Switzerland. Nor do authoritarian structures guarantee the dominance of any one group. Some authoritarian regimes (e.g., China and Syria) have had highly competitive internal politics with major exchanges of power between party factions and/or competition between party, state, and military institutions. Also, recall Brezhnev's fears throughout the Czechoslovakia intervention decision episode that he, like Khrushchev, might be voted out of power by his political colleagues in even the relatively cohesive Politburo. And of course, there are political systems with continuous exchanges between military and civilian leaders (e.g., Turkey, Nigeria, and various Latin American polities). Thus, whatever the structure of the system, regimes may or may not have had histories of political competition, and the leaders of ones that have are unlikely to forget the past and remain sensitive to the prospect that they too may be turned out of office.

Leaders' concern for holding on to power is intensified by a second property of regime vulnerability: the current level of political uncertainty within the regime itself. Regimes are destabilized if their own component factions or groups are not firmly supportive of their own regime. Often this occurs when a previously stable regime becomes plagued by growing divisions, and elements within it seek to overthrow its leader. Other regimes are largely transitory (even if they hold on to power for years) in that their members are actually acting out a prolonged succession crisis after the passing of a predominant leader. Revolutionary regimes, having just come to power after transforming the entire political order, are themselves typically racked by internal conflicts as former allies reject each other's legitimacy (i.e., revolutionary credentials) and fight to the death to see who will dominate still-evolving structures of the new political order. All of these cases represent very fluid situations within the regime itself, and it is likely that these leaders will be quite sensitive to the need to respond to external opposition (as well as internal opposition). After all, not only do opposition groups threaten the very tenuous internal balance, but they also are potential allies in a new regime if the current arrangement collapses.

Regime vulnerability is, then, a combination of both the historical competitiveness of the political system and the internal stability of arrangements within the regime itself. Where both conditions are present in extreme forms, leaders will be preoccupied with the task of retaining power, and foreign policy making will largely be a function of domestic political needs. Equally important are regimes whose leaders seem almost invulnerable in that they face few internal threats and have long retained power. Even substantial opposition is perceived to have little chance of actually evicting the current leadership from power, and thus the latter is more willing to take domestically controversial foreign policy actions. The logic of regime vulnerability also provides insight into how leaders respond to opposition, either through bargaining/controversy avoidance or political legitimization. Assuming the regime's manipulation of foreign policy for political survival is the more extreme and desperate response (e.g., as in Argentina's invasion of the Falkland Islands), then it would make sense that the most highly vulnerable regimes would be relatively prone toward political legitimization. More moderately vulnerable regimes, in contrast, would have the ability and willingness to accommodate opposition through bargaining and controversy avoidance. Like political system properties, regime vulnerability can be linked to both the strength and direction of opposition effects on foreign policy makers.

Linking Political Opposition to Foreign Policy

The final component of the framework concerns the dependent variable: foreign policy behavior. This component makes the final link from opposition to foreign policy behavior, and in a way compatible with the theoretical logic outlined in Chapter 1. Political effects on four basic dimensions of foreign policy behavior are considered: commitment, independence of action, affect direction, and affect intensity. Each, it will be argued, is deeply rooted in the rational two-level game in which leaders balance foreign policy concerns with domestic political imperatives. All four are also reflective of the processes of both bargaining/controversy avoidance and political legitimization.

Before turning to the specific foreign policy dimensions, it should be made clear from the onset that we are not talking about the basic goals, strategies, and interest in a nation's (or regime's) foreign policy. Rather, the political processes outlined in this chapter affect not so much the substance of policy, but rather the degree to which it is implemented in the face of domestic political constraints. In this way, this framework diverges from others (e.g., Salmore and Salmore, 1978; Hudson and Sims, 1992) in that it does not claim that domestic politics influences all dimensions of foreign policy. Foreign policy dimensions such as amount of activity, types of instruments, and alliance and targeting behavior are primarily reflective of the substantive basis of the nation's orientation to foreign affairs. In contrast, the foreign policy dimensions of commitment, independence, and affect are more indicative of the give and take of domestic politics as constraints on the regime's pursuit of the national interest.

Commitment

This dimension of foreign policy concerns the ability of political leaders to commit their nation to a particular course of action in international affairs. As conceptualized by Callahan (1982), commitment in foreign policy has two interwoven elements. The first is the allocation of resources for the implementation of foreign policy goals and strategies. The second, though less obvious, is the creation of expectations in the minds of other political actors as a result of statements by national leaders. Commitment is built around the distinction among "deed behaviors," involving the actual use of resources, "pledging behaviors," with expression of threats or promises to act, and "verbal commentary," in which leaders express judgments about foreign situations. At each level, commitments are further differentiated by considering whether these actions are irreversible, whether pledges to act are made by senior or junior government officials, and what kinds of qualifying conditions are placed on their use (Callahan, 1982).

Committing the nation's resources, or even stating the intention to do so, is a major political act domestically. The former, especially, brings to a head processes of bargaining and consensus building by requiring formal votes within the regime and imposing trade-offs in the allocation of material resources. The latter does the same for controversy avoidance and political legitimization by making clear, in often irreversible ways, the orientation and preferences of the regime. The most severe manifestation of the political inability to commit to a course of action—deadlock—is, of course, the most striking feature of weak and fragmented cabinets in parliamentary democracies dealing with politicized issues. Constraints on action are most striking when leaders agree to carry out policy changes only to have them blocked by opposition at home. Recall, for example, that the Dutch cabinet, despite its pro-NATO policies and willingness to take responsibility for accepting cruise missiles, was blocked in exercising its preferences because of the threat of defection by the antimissile faction in the parliament. Not all political divisions lead to deadlock, of course, and in less divided regimes the outcome is more of a broad compromise and a watered-down decision emerges—as for example in the Brezhnev Politburo's use of political and economic sanctions instead of military intervention in dealing with reformist Czechoslovakia.

Although the logic of bargaining/controversy avoidance and political legitimization are similar with respect to the use of resources in foreign policy, they differ with respect to the expression of threats or promises to act. The logic of political legitimization suggests that although leaders generally avoid the actual use of resources (that might prove costly in the long term at home and abroad), they often have strong incentive to express threats or promises to act in order to generate support inside and outside the regime. In the theater of domestic politics, repeated threats and promises to act probably serve to legitimize the regime and its policies as well as actually committing fully to a course of action. Documentation of this kind of threatening verbal crisis behavior (while being unable to carry out those threats) is common to the case studies of Syria's road to the 1967 war, Indonesia during the Malaysia confrontation, and Iran during the hostage crisis.

Independence of Action

This dimension of foreign policy is concerned with "the amount of autonomy a government tries to maintain in its foreign policy actions" (M. Hermann, 1982: 243). Independence of action (IOA) has two elements: an initiative-reactive dimension and a unilateral-multilateral dimension. The first concerns whether the government initiated the action itself or reacted directly to an action by another government, while the second dimension concerns whether the government acted on its own or if its actions were taken jointly with other nations. Actions taken in concert with other nations, as well as ones responding directly to foreign actors, are indicative of low independence of action in foreign policy.

The matter of independence in foreign policy is deeply rooted in domestic political processes, but in completely divergent ways reflective of the alternative political dynamics of bargaining/controversy avoidance and political legitimization. The former dynamics point to diminished initiative and unilateralism, particularly where there is an inability to reach agreement except when forced by external pressures (thus leading to a largely reactive foreign policy), as well as an unwillingness to initiate controversial actions on one's own for fear of generating public disenchantment. Japanese negotiating episodes (e.g., the peace treaty with the Soviet Union, the textile wrangle with the United States, and the recognition of the People's Republic of China) best fit this pattern, all involving factional politics that precluded any negotiating initiatives and ultimately left the government at the mercy of their negotiating adversaries.

The logic of political legitimization suggests precisely the opposite pattern of foreign policy behavior. Here, *domestic* politics is the chief stimulus for action when a leadership will necessarily take highly visible, often dramatic actions to impress domestic audiences and give the regime prestige. Unilateral initiatives are precisely the kinds of action that can allow a regime to demonstrate its leadership qualifications (and on a global stage) and emphasize widely popular (i.e., nationalist) aspects of its orientation. The theme of independence in foreign policy is a chief means for mobilizing support and isolating adversaries, and, as discussed in Chapter 2, is widely cited as a driving factor in the more assertive foreign policies of a variety of Third World regimes. The commitment of a regime to military force, such as the Argentine invasion of the Falklands and Syria's intervention in Lebanon, are typically considered as having been driven by mainly domestic considerations in a way that enhanced the image of the regime. But this is not limited to Third World polities; recall that certain cases of Soviet intervention (e.g., Angola and the Middle East) were argued to have been influenced by Politburo politics, as were occasional initiatives of the constrained factionalized or coalition cabinets in Europe and Japan.

Affect: Direction and Intensity

This dimension is related to conflict in foreign policy, referring to the expressed feelings, ranging from strong friendliness to extreme hostility, that policymakers express toward the policies, actions, or government of another nation. Its focus is on the overt "emotions regarding another actor in the international arena as shown in the verbal and nonverbal behaviors of policymakers of the acting government . . . , as reflected in what they are saying and doing at the moment" (Hermann, Hermann, and Hutchins, 1982: 211). It has two distinct elements. Direction of affect distinguishes among positive, negative, and neutral feelings toward the recipient of the action, and as such approximates the more familiar notion of cooperation and conflict.[8] The other element is affect intensity, which concerns the strength with which feelings are expressed, regardless of whether they are positive or negative. Intensity of affect ranges from strong to weak or neutral. The separate focus on affect direction and intensity is warranted because the separate (and statistically independent) dimensions offer contending perspectives on the political manifestations of foreign policy. It may well be that the domestic political essence of affect in foreign policy is not its direction, but rather how strongly it is expressed to domestic audiences. The dynamics of bargaining/controversy avoidance and political legitimization can be tied to both positive and negative behavior as long as the tone of that behavior is consistent with the political needs of the regime.

As noted above, the affect direction measure is a variant of the cooperation/conflict measure in foreign policy, and the logic of bargaining/controversy avoidance and political legitimization suggests a strong political connection with affect direction. The accommodation inherent in the bargaining/controversy avoidance predisposes leaders toward less hostility (and greater neutrality) in foreign policy affect, if it is assumed that any conflictual foreign policy action is politically risky, in that it is more divisive within the regime and likely to generate opposition from the wider public. Various cases of Japanese and Dutch foreign policy suggest that leaders, for whatever reason, were politically adverse to engaging in Cold War confrontations. And, of course, the divided Politburo under the cautious Brezhnev sought to deal with Czechoslovak reforms through nonmilitary sanctions.

The logic of political legitimization suggests just the opposite kind of outcome. Hostility in foreign policy is considered to be an effective means by which a regime can legitimize its hold on power. Conflict enables the leadership to demonstrate its ideological and political credentials and/or take advantage of the internal unifying effects of foreign threats, as was most clearly the case in the invasion of the Falklands by the domestically threatened Galtieri regime. The opposite applies to cooperative behavior, in that foreign cooperation might undercut the regime's legitimacy by suggesting excessive conciliation or dependence on foreign powers or other recognized adversaries. There were, for example, political limits on the Brezhnev Politburo's international cooperation with the West. Even the advocates of détente in the Soviet Politburo (including Brezhnev) had strong political incentive for supporting action in the Angolan episode.

But it might be that intensity—not direction—is the dimension of affect more reflective of domestic opposition, if we assume that drama of any kind, and not just conflict, is the essence of government posturing for domestic audiences. Bargaining/controversy avoidance indicates that leaders avoid any kind of strong expression of affect in foreign policy; any strongly expressed position, positive or negative, is likely to attract opposition within or outside the regime. Also, if the watering down of preferences of contending actors is central to coalition building, then this would seem to preclude the full expression of any one actor's positions. Very mild behavior would also minimize the domestic political risks of a controversial action that is actually carried out, particularly if we assume that cooperation as well as conflict can irritate domestic audiences and undercut the legitimacy of the regime and its policies. This is clearly a problem for regimes seeking to align with more powerful partners. Thus, for example, the South Korean government acted very cautiously in negotiating a peace treaty with Japan; similarly, and at roughly the same time, domestic controversy forced the Japanese government to temper its enthusiasm for renewing the security pact with the United States. Political legitimization, in contrast, suggests that domestic politics will lead to far more intense patterns of foreign policy behavior. Although the central feature of the literature on political legitimization is that foreign conflict behavior is the chief means for generating support for the regime, affect intensity suggests that cooperative actions can also capture the imagination of political audiences. Cooperative diplomatic activity, if it is highly visible and with widely recognized friendly nations, can also enhance the stature of the regime and its policies. According to Good (1963) and others, nonalignment served an equally important function in the politics of new state foreign policy during the Cold War.

Summary: The Overall Conceptual Framework

This chapter has developed the elements of a conceptual framework for linking domestic opposition to foreign policy behavior, all in a way that is cross-nationally applicable and can be effectively tested with available data. Four components of the model have been presented, and their causal ordering is diagramed in Figure 3.1. The first is regime fragmentation. This arena of politics is important for two reasons: (1) these leadership divisions are assumed to be the most immediate political constraints on decisionmakers, and (2) they operate as a conduit by which opposition groups outside the regime influence foreign policy. The second component is political opposition operating outside the regime and competing for control of the regime and dominance of the political system. Four types of opposition are: (1) dissenting actors in the regime's ruling group or party, (2) other political parties in the legislature, (3) military and paramilitary groups, and (4) regionally based actors. The level of opposition is conceptualized in terms of two dimensions: strength and intensity. The framework's third component concerns aspects of the political context that mediate the opposition's effects on foreign policy behavior. These conditioning factors are the accountability and institutionalization of political system structures and the regime's political vulnerability. Finally, these three sets of political phenomena are linked to several dimensions of foreign policy behavior: commitment, independence of action, and affect direction and intensity. The remainder of this book is devoted to testing, and expanding upon, this basic framework for these dimensions of foreign policy behavior. First, however, it is necessary to explain the operationalization of these concepts and present the cross-national data on each.

Figure 3.1   Conceptual Framework Linking Domestic Political Opposition to Foreign Policy

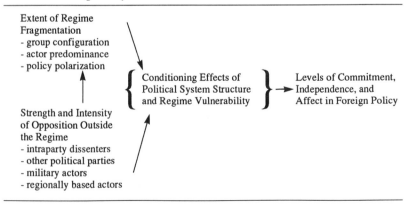

Extent of Regime
Fragmentation
- group configuration
- actor predominance
- policy polarization

Conditioning Effects of
Political System Structure
and Regime Vulnerability

Levels of Commitment,
Independence, and
Affect in Foreign Policy

Strength and Intensity
of Opposition Outside
the Regime
- intraparty dissenters
- other political parties
- military actors
- regionally based actors

Notes

1. Getting at the situationally and decision-specific effects of interest group and public opinion pressures (as well as the subtle effects of other opposition) is now best left to case study research and more focused comparative methodology. One such effort, with which the author is involved, might bridge the gap between quantitative and case study assessments. This is the CREON project dealing with decision units, in which general models of decisionmaking by specific types of decision units are developed and subjected to tests across a variety of decisions (Hermann and Hermann, 1989; Hagan, Hermann, and Hermann, forthcoming). This approach will be considered in the conclusion of the book.

2. The factionalism literature discussed in the previous section is also relevant to intraparty literature. The themes discussed here are most explicitly considered in discussions of Japanese and Italian politics.

3. If a party is illegal or refuses to participate in the political system, then it is not included as a party opposition but instead is considered to be a form of noninstitutionalized opposition. Keep in mind, though, there are often antisystemic parties who still participate in the electoral system, and these would be counted here.

4. Minority governments exist with the external support of at least some parties in the parliament, but such agreements should not be equated here as support for policy. These outside parties are, de facto, part of the ruling coalition, even though they act as part of the legislative opposition by challenging the regime's policies while still sustaining the cabinet's control.

5. In some cases military opposition occurs vis-à-vis a military-dominated regime. In these cases, though, this opposition would be measured with the intraparty opposition measure, with a subleadership element of the military opposing the senior elements of the military.

6. The role of military actors have received relatively little systematic treatment in the comparative foreign policy literature. In U.S. foreign policy literature, the most impressive empirical study is Bett's (1977) comparative case studies of the civilian and military positions on the use of force in various Cold War crises.

7. Accountability and institutionalization are usually considered as separate phenomena, and for reasons to be explained later will be treated as such in the analyses to follow. However, it should be recognized that the mediating effects of accountability and institutionalization are probably closely intertwined, and a complete conceptualization of political structure would classify polities in terms of their interactive effects. At one extreme would be democratic systems with well-institutionalized democratic norms with inviolate norms of representation and pluralist political competition. At the other extreme are political systems that are neither democratic nor well institutionalized, and in which leaders have few restraints on suppressing opposition. Cases falling between the two extremes are democratic regimes in noninstitutionalized settings and authoritarian systems that have well-established political and decisionmaking norms that place major constraints (albeit from within the ruling party) on the leadership. The concept of institutionalization softens the sharp distinction between open and closed systems, in which the former are often presumed to be well established and the latter are not. The two should be used interactively in future studies employing larger samples of regimes.

8. There is a clear connection between affect and conventional measures of cooperation and conflict, "but these concern the actual intent to harm or benefit the recipients, whereas affect indicates the actor's feeling of pleasure or displeasure with the recipient" (Hermann, 1978).

4

Classifying Regimes by Political Opposition: Procedures and Data

The categorization of regimes in terms of opposition for cross-national empirical analysis is a central, and original, feature of this research project and thus requires detailed attention. The purpose of this chapter is to explain the specific procedures necessary to construct cross-national data on political opposition. The chapter seeks to show how the concepts developed in the previous chapter can be operationalized in a valid and efficient manner in the construction of cross-national data. Several specific features are important: First, procedures are presented for the identification of political regimes, an important preliminary task because the "regime," as opposed to the "nation-state," constitutes the unit of analysis in the statistical analyses in the next chapter. Second, the classification of regimes by opposition is based on a set of questions developed to guide the interpretation of largely descriptive country accounts by area experts. This chapter outlines the basic coding rules used to make judgements about the strength and intensity of oppositions across diverse political settings and using varied kinds of information sources. Third, the data on each nation's regimes and their opposition are explained, in part to illustrate coding procedures but also to facilitate the interpretation of findings reported in the next chapter. This regime data set is for the sample of thirty-eight nations in the Comparative Research on the Events of Nations (CREON) data set (the foreign policy data set used in the analyses below) for the decade 1959–1968. I hope the discussion of these mechanical issues will make it possible for an interested researcher to collect opposition data.

Constructing the Data Set: A Note on Source Materials

Before presenting the data itself, an explanation of source materials on the regimes and their political opposition is in order. Much of the effort in this research project has been devoted to building a conceptually rich data set that could capture opposition characteristics and other political conditions in a way that is cross-nationally valid and yet not simply tied to political system structure. This kind of information cannot be acquired simply from major existing data sets, even those as impressive as the *World Handbook III* (Taylor and Jodice, 1983), the *Cross-Policy Data* (Banks, 1971), and the *Polity Data* (Gurr, 1974). Although the structural data (largely connected to democratization) in these data sets provide clues about some—but not all—opposition actors and political conditions, little can be gleaned from them regarding the precise strength and intensity of any of that opposition. The other kinds of variables in these data sets are political events such as coups, strikes, and demonstrations. This data concerns noninstitutionalized opposition and extreme forms of political behavior, and there are few event indicators of the strength and intensity of institutional opposition such as party factions, specific opposition parties, and the military. While extreme acts such as no-confidence votes and coups are relevant to party and military opposition, a comprehensive and balanced image of political opposition across diverse political systems cannot possibly be acquired from the political event data sets.

The strategy employed here involved researching the general pattern of political activity for the thirty-eight countries during the ten-year period in the CREON sample. The process involved three steps. The first was to identify systematically books, book chapters, and journal articles on each national political system.[1] The objective was to compile a reasonably comprehensive sampling of the major comparative politics/area study literature and regular accounts of major political episodes on each country. Multiple sources were sought for each country (indeed, each of its regimes) so as to tap the collective expertise of recognized (i.e., frequently cited) major country specialists, and not simply the views of a single scholar. The second step was to write up extensive descriptive country files in order to document key commentary by each area specialist, all in a format that could be consulted repeatedly throughout the process of coding the data. This was a very extended stage of the project and resulted in about 750 pages of typewritten documentation, or on average about twenty pages for each country in the sample. The third step was to interpret these country files in terms of the opposition concepts presented in Chapter 3. As explained below, a standard set of questions was asked about each regime's political situation and its opposition actors. Repeated passes through the descriptive files were necessary to insure that coding judgements were made in a consistent manner for the varied political systems of all thirty-eight countries.

Four types of bibliographical materials were considered in compiling sources for each country. Preliminary general background on each country's political arrangements and history was provided by several major political handbooks: the annual editions of Arthur Bank's *Political Handbook of the World* and the more detailed Europa volumes entitled *The Far*

East and Australasia, The Middle East and North Africa, and *Sub-Saharan Africa.* The Europa handbooks were especially valuable because they were written with considerable historical detail and authored directly by regional and country specialists. And even though they were available for only certain regions (the most notable exception is Latin America), it happened that they were available for precisely those countries that had relatively few other sources.[2]

Although a good introduction to successive leaders (but not necessarily separate regimes) and relevant political actors, these handbooks rarely provided adequate detail on the political makeup of specific regimes and the strength and intensity of their opposition. Additional kinds of sources were therefore always required, and the second kind was overviews of specific national political systems (e.g., actors and institutional arrangements), especially ones written in the 1960s or early 1970s. Although it was usually possible to identify at least one important book on each national political system, it was not possible to compile an adequate set of multiple sources using book-length country studies alone (nor were these necessarily the most useful sources). Chapter-length overviews were especially important for the smaller, less intensively studied countries that made up most of the sample used here. The best of these were found in edited volumes on the politics of certain regions, for example, sub-Saharan Africa (Duignan and Jackson, 1986; Mazrui and Tidy, 1984), Eastern Europe (Ionescu, 1967; Benes, Gyorgy, and Stambuk, 1966; Griffith, 1964; Rakowska-Harmstone, 1984), Southeast Asia (Rose, 1963), the Middle East and North Africa (Abboushi, 1970; Entelis, 1980; Hudson, 1977; Peretz, 1986; Zartman, 1963), and Latin America (Burnett and Johnson, 1968; Kantor, 1969; Martz, 1959; Skidmore and Smith, 1984; Wiarda and Kline, 1985).

A third type of source was edited volumes on a particular kind of political phenomenon with chapters on specific countries. Not only did these chapters usually examine a particular type of opposition in considerable detail, they often had precise information on the makeup of specific regimes and opposition activities for designated time periods. The most useful of these volumes included studies of cabinets and coalitions in parliamentary democracies (e.g., Baylis, 1989; Blondel and Muller-Rommel, 1988; Bogdanor, 1983; Brown and Dreijmanis, 1982; Luebbert, 1986; Pridham, 1986), personalist regimes in sub-Saharan Africa (Jackson and Rosberg, 1982), factional politics in single-party regimes (Belloni and Beller, 1978; Pempel, 1990), opposition within one-party systems (Dahl, 1973; Huntington and Moore, 1970; Carter, 1962), parties and party systems in various democracies (Dahl, 1966; Daalder, 1987; Sartori, 1976; Henig and Pinder, 1969; McDonald, 1971; Bernard et al., 1969; LaPolombara and Weiner, 1966), military opposition (Perlmutter, 1977; Johnson, 1962), and federal arrangements and regional opposition (Lijphart, 1977; Duchacek, 1970). Several cross-national handbooks on political parties in democratic and authoritarian states (again, especially the smaller ones) were also essential: *Political Parties: A Cross-National Survey* (Janda, 1980), *Political Parties of Asia* (Fukui, 1985), and *Political Parties of the Americas: Canada, Latin America, and the West Indies* (Alexander, 1982a).

The final kind of source was general political histories and reports on specific political episodes and crises. Although not conceptually focused, these narrative sources provided detailed information on fluid aspects of regime composition and shifting opposition for precise time periods. Some excellent books covered the postwar political histories of certain countries such as Italy (Kogan, 1983) and China (Thorton, 1982) as well as selected regimes in Turkey during the 1960s (Dodd, 1969) and the Soviet Union under Khrushchev (Linden, 1966). However, most of the available reports were articles, and the best of these came from journals that reported regularly (at least once a year) on political events and conditions in specific countries. Two journals—*World Today* and *Current History*—were the best for regular reports on all geographical regions, while *Asian Survey* reports every January and February on all nations throughout Asia. With the benefit of hindsight, these accounts were more thorough than the short-term, situationally conditioned reporting by newspaper journalists, who were themselves usually not academic area specialists.[3] The well-informed, descriptive detail of these reports was essential in filling in gaps in the other sources for even the most extensively covered countries (e.g., Japan and India) as well as for smaller countries with few other sources.

The mix of these four kinds of sources enabled me to put together the multiple sources on each country's relevant opposition. Chart 4.1 lists the primary sources used in collecting opposition data on the nations in the sample used here.[4] The information in the chart is presented so that the reader can judge the validity of the opposition data in at least two ways. First, the list of sources can be examined to see if any major works on any country are missing and, if so, whether their absence distorts the subsequent development of data on that country. Second, the list permits some generalizations about the number and types of sources for the countries in the sample. The number and types of sources varied across countries in the sample, and the chart allows for judgments about biases in the sources used for the different types of countries and political systems. With respect to the second issue, the number of sources for each country in Chart 4.1 varied in interesting ways, although most countries clustered near the sample mean of about twelve and one-third sources per nation. Eighteen nations, about one half of the sample, had between ten and fifteen sources. Only three countries had a sharply larger number of sources: China (thirty-two), the Soviet Union (twenty-seven), and India (twenty-five). At the other extreme were countries with relatively few sources: Iceland (six), Ivory Coast (five), Spain (five), and New Zealand (five).

Chart 4.1   Major Sources for Each Country in the CREON Sample

Belgium: Dewachter (1987); Dewachter and Clijsters (1982); Fitzmaurice (1983); Henig and Pinder (1969); Lorwin (1966); de Meyer (1983); Rudd (1986); Weil (1970).

Canada: Campbell (1977); Drummond (1972); Janda (1980); Kornberg and Clarke (1982); Lentner (1976); Lijphart (1977); Meisel (1967); Milburn (1965); Thordarson (1972); Thornburn (1979, 1967).

Chile: Alexander (1982b); Bernard et al. (1973); Burnett (1970, 1968); Fleet (1984); Janda (1980); Kantor (1969); Nef (1978); McDonald (1971); Sigmund (1977); Skidmore and Smith (1984); Valenzuela and Valenzuela (1985).

China: Ahn (1976); Baum (1969, 1964); Bennett (1970); Brugger (1969); Chang (1975, 1972); Cheng, C. (1966); Goodman (1984); Fairbank (1986); Gottlieb (1977); Halpern (1962); Hinton (1972a, 1972b, 1972c); Hsieh (1985); Hsiao (1967); Joffe (1976–77); Nathan (1978); Oksenberg (1971); Perlmutter (1977); Pye (1984, 1981); Ra'anan (1970, 1968); Sutter (1978); Teiwes (1984); Thorton (1982); Yu (1964); Zagoria (1968, 1967).

Costa Rica: Ameringer (1982); Denton (1985); Gardiner (1966); Kantor (1969); Mijeski (1977); Martz (1959); McDonald (1971); Skidmore and Smith (1984); Tomasek (1968).

Cuba: Angell (1967); Dominguez (1987, 1981, 1978); Janda (1980); Kantor (1969); Kline (1985); McDonald (1971); Roca (1982); Skidmore and Smith (1984); Suarez (1967); Valdes (1984); Wiarda (1968).

Czechoslovakia: Beck et al. (1976); Benes et al. (1966); Brzezinski (1967); Ionescu (1967); Korbonski (1976); Leff (1988); Szulc (1971); Skilling (1974, 1973a, 1973b, 1972, 1965); Taborsky (1965); Toma (1979); Ulc (1984).

Egypt: Baker (1978); Binder (1966); Dekmejian (1971); Dessouki (1984); Harik (1973); Hudson (1977); Kerr (1968); Lenczowski (1965); McLaurin et al. (1982); Perlmutter (1977); Safran (1975); Zartman (1963).

France: Andrews (1966); Campbell and Charlton (1978); Ehrmann (1968); Grosser (1966); Janda (1980); Macridis and Brown (1960); Noonan (1980, 1970); Henig and Pinder (1969); Wahl (1959); Williams (1970); Williams and Harrison (1972).

East Germany: Benes et al. (1966); Brzezinski (1967); Croan (1972); Grote (1979); Harnhardt (1984); Heidenheimer (1971); Janda (1980); Korbonski (1976); Ludz (1974, 1970); Krich (1985); McCauley (1983, 1979); Scharf (1984); Schulz (1982); Skilling (1973a); Sontheimer and Bleek (1975); Starrels and Mallinckrodt (1975).

West Germany: Alleman (1967); Baylis (1989); von Beyme (1983); Derbyshire (1987); Edinger (1968); Hanrieder (1970, 1967); Heidenheimer (1971); Henig and Pinder (1969); Janda (1980); Keller (1960); Kirchheimer (1966); Merkl (1980, 1978, 1974); Norpoth (1982); Rosmoser (1966); Schmidt (1983).

(continues)

Chart 4.1   (*continued*)

Ghana: Austin (1967); Bebler (1973); Bretton (1966); Europa (1985c); Ibingira (1980); Jackson and Rosberg (1982); Janda (1980); Kilson (1970); Kraus (1981); LeFever (1970); Mazrui and Tidy (1984); Pellow and Chazan (1986); Pikney (1972); Smock and Smock (1975); Thompson (1969).

Guinea: Cowan (1962); Europa (1985c); Hapgood (1963); Jackson and Rosberg (1982); Janda (1980); Kaba (1977); Mazrui and Tidy (1984); Riviere (1977).

Iceland: Banks (1985); Faurby (1982); Grimsson (1987); Henig and Pinder (1969); Janda (1980); Nuechterlein (1961).

India: Brecher (1959, 1967); Cohen (1988); Hanson (1968, 1967); Hardgrave (1970); Kochanek (1968, 1966); Kothari (1973, 1970, 1967, 1964); Morris-Jones (1967, 1964); Narain (1985); Nicholson (1978); Palmer (1967, 1965, 1961); Park (1967); Tharoor (1982); Vertzberger (1984a); Wallace (1969, 1968); Weiner (1962, 1957).

Israel: Aronoff (1978); Brecher (1972); Fein (1967); Luebbert (1986); Medding (1972); Paltiel (1975); Peretz (1979); Perlmutter (1977); Rouleau (1968); Safran (1978); Seliktar (1982); Yishai (1981).

Italy: Barnes (1966); Belloni (1978); Bognetti (1971); Di Palma (1977); Franeti (1985); Germino and Passigli (1968); Henig and Pinder (1969); Kogan (1983, 1963); Marradi (1987); Pridham (1983, 1986b); Sartori (1966); Spotts and Wieser (1986); Zariski (1980).

Ivory Coast: Europa (1985c); Jackson and Rosberg (1982); Thompson (1962); Zolberg (1971, 1969).

Japan: Destler et al. (1976); Destler et al. (1979); Fukui (1985, 1970, 1978b); Hellmann (1969); Koichi (1982); Leiserson (1973); Muramatsu and Kraus (1990); Ori (1976); Richardson and Flanagan (1984); Scalapino and Masumi (1962); Stockwin (1975); Thayer (1969).

Kenya: Bennett (1966, 1963); Bienen (1974); Europa (1985c); Gertzel (1970); Jackson and Rosberg (1982); Janda (1980); Lamb (1969); Mueller (1984); Sanger and Nottingham (1964).

Lebanon: Abboushi (1970); Gilmore (1983); Gordon (1980); Hudson (1977); Hudson (1968); Janda (1980); Kerr (1966); Lijphart (1977); Peretz (1986); Rabinovich (1984); Rondot (1966); Smock and Smock (1975); Weinberger (1986); Yamak (1966).

Mexico: Alisky (1982); Gellner (1964); Hellman (1983); Johnson (1968, 1985); Kantor (1969); McDonald (1971); Needler (1984, 1982); Ross (1963, 1960); Scott (1965); Skidmore and Smith (1984); Stevens (1985).

Norway: Baylis (1989); Christophersen (1968); Eckstein (1966); Faurby (1982); Fitzmaurice (1986); Henig and Pinder (1969); Nilson (1980); Pesonen and Thomas (1983); Rokkan (1966); Sarlvik (1983); Storing (1963).

(*continues*)

Chart 4.1 (*continued*)

New Zealand: Aimer (1985); Banks (1985); Europa (1985a); Janda (1980); Milburn (1965).

Philippines: Fischer (1963); Guzman and Reforma (1988); Lande (1968); Machado (1978); Noble (1986); Starner (1963); Wurfel (1988, 1964).

Poland: Beck et al. (1976); Benes et al. (1966); Brzezinski (1967); Chrypinski (1972); Dziewanowski (1979); Groth (1972); Ionescu (1967); Korbonski (1976); Linden (1978); Skilling (1973a); Stehle (1964).

Soviet Union: Aspaturian (1976); Azrael (1981, 1970); Barghoorn (1973); Bialer (1980); Breslauer (1982); Brzezinski and Huntington (1964); Dallin (1981); Dallin and Larson (1968); Daniels (1971); Gelman (1984); Griffiths (1971); Hammer (1974); Hodnett (1981); Hough (1980); Kolkowicz (1971); Linden (1978, 1966); Morton (1967); Roeder (1988, 1984); Ross (1980); Rush (1965); Skilling and Griffiths (1971); Slusser (1967); Tatu (1967).

Spain: Arango (1985); Linz (1973, 1970); Medhurst (1977); Wiarda (1980).

Switzerland: Baylis (1989); Gruner and Petterle (1983); Henig and Pinder (1969); Kerr (1987); Lijphart (1977); Steiner (1982, 1983).

Thailand: Badgley (1969); Darling (1969, 1968, 1962); Girling (1981); Nuechterlein (1967, 1966, 1964); Riggs (1966); Simmonds (1963); Wilson (1965, 1964a, 1964b, 1963, 1962a, 1962b); Wit (1968); Wyatt (1984).

Tunisia: Ashford (1965); Entelis (1980); Europa (1985b); Hudson (1977); Janda (1980); Moore (1965, 1962); Robert (1965); Zartman (1963).

Turkey: Abboushi (1970); Dodd (1969); Erogul (1987); Ellis (1962); Janda (1980); Peretz (1986); Tachau (1984); Sayari (1978).

Uganda: Chick (1970); Decalo (1976); Europa (1985c); Hopkins (1964); Jackson and Rosberg (1986, 1982); Legum (1971, 1970); Mazrui and Tidy (1984); Mittelman (1975); Twaddle (1973); Uzoigwe (1983).

Uruguay: Bernard et al. (1973); Bray (1968); Janda (1980); Kantor (1969); McDonald (1982, 1971); Porzecanski (1974); Shapiro (1972, 1969); Socolow (1966); Taylor (1985); Weinstein (1975).

Venezuela: Alexander (1982c); Bernard et al. (1973); Blank (1984); Janda (1980); Martz (1968); McDonald (1971); Kantor (1969); Wiarda (1985).

Yugoslavia: Beck et al. (1976); Benes et al. (1966); Burg (1983); Campbell (1972); Ionescu (1967); Korbonski (1976); Linden (1978); Meier (1964); Ramet (1984); Remington (1984); Rusinow (1977); Shoup (1979); Skilling (1973a).

Zambia: Europa (1985c); Gann (1986); Gertzel (1984); Gertzel et al. (1984); Jackson and Rosberg (1982); Legum (1970, 1971); Pettman (1974a, 1974b); Rasmussen (1969).

Does the sampling distribution undercut the quality of data in major ways? Is there biased source coverage for different types of countries and, in particular, different types of political systems? One might, for example, suspect that smaller and less developed countries would have fewer sources, which might result in sketchier and probably biased coding judgments. This does not appear to be the case. Although several small Third World countries (e.g., Ivory Coast and Guinea) had relatively few sources, some of the nations with the most sources were also small Third World states (e.g., Thailand, Ghana, Lebanon, Cuba, and Uganda). Meanwhile, even certain large countries such as Venezuela and Turkey also had relatively few sources. Nor did there appear to be a maldistribution across types of political systems; the number of sources for democratic and authoritarian polities were roughly equal throughout the sample.

Two other factors, instead, accounted for differences in the source coverage of nations. One was the political visibility of the country in international affairs, especially during the 1960s. Thus a country such as Thailand (then "the next Vietnam") received extensive coverage, while countries less directly involved in Cold War crises, such as Iceland, the Ivory Coast, and New Zealand, received much less coverage. The other factor was the complexity of the nation's political system and extent of political turbulence during the 1960s. China, India, and most countries with an above average number of sources all had major political crises, a wider variety of political opposition, and multiple regime changes. In contrast, the countries at the bottom range of the scale were ones with fairly simple and stable (at least then) political systems. While Turkey and Venezuela were two exceptions to this rule, the countries with fewest sources had no regime changes (e.g., Guinea, Ivory Coast, Switzerland, Spain, Tunisia, and Zambia) or had orderly regime changes and a limited range of opposition (e.g., Iceland, New Zealand, and the Philippines). Given the less complex nature of their political systems, even a few good sources provided adequate information to answer coding questions. The distribution of sources did not, then, appear to be significantly biased, and in many ways was compatible with the complexity of coding tasks for the country. Thus sufficient sources were available to make critical coding judgments for all countries, and almost always with multiple sources on each regime and type of opposition.[5]

Identifying Political Regimes

In the empirical analyses, the task will be to compare the foreign policy behavior of regimes classified in terms of fragmentation and by measures of intraparty, political party, military, and regional opposition. Thus the political regime, as opposed to the nation-state, serves as the unit of analysis. Even though it is widely used in cross-national research, the nation-state is not an appropriate unit of analysis for research on political opposition. The attributes of nations are not subject to change except over very extended periods of time. It is too gross a unit of measurement for the kinds of comparisons to be made, because within any nation there can be, over time, major changes in the level of domestic opposition and other political conditions. (Nor is the alternative of aggregating data by one-year intervals attractive: this results in very small aggregations of the foreign policy events data, which disrupts findings due to very few annual events for some nations.)

Yet the use of the regime as a unit of analysis raises the question of what exactly constitutes a regime change—defined as the exchange of power between separate political groups or a basic change in the political environment? What kinds of political events should be treated as indicators of the termination of one regime and the beginning of another? The most basic procedure is to focus simply on the head-of-state position, with a regime change occurring in the event of a change in the individual occupant of this position. This criterion is relatively easy to employ, and it results in the identification of regimes that have a degree of "face validity," as it deals with the coming and going of more or less well known political leaders.

But the use of the head-of-state criterion in this research was problematic for two reasons. First, in many cases a change in the incumbent head of state did not represent a major political change because the same basic group (or coalition) remained in power. Most notable here were cabinet shuffles in a parliamentary system in which the prime minister changed without any effect on the regime's internal party structure, as for example in Italy when the same coalition of Christian Democratic factions and smaller parties continued in office. The same occurred in presidential democracies, as for instance the succession of power from Kennedy to Johnson or Nixon to Ford, in which the political makeup of the administration changed little except for the head of state. Therefore, the head-of-state criterion could not be used alone if the head of state changed, but the same faction, group, or coalition continued in office.

Another problem with the head-of-state criterion was that it was not sufficiently precise to capture some changes in opposition. Used by itself, it can blur major changes in the level of opposition that might occur during the tenure of a particular head of state. Accordingly, another supplementary rule for identifying regimes was needed. For purposes of this cross-national research project, the best strategy was to focus directly on the occurrence of significant changes in the primary arena of opposition: the level of regime fragmentation. Where there was a clear change in one of the three dimensions of regime fragmentation, that marked the termination of one regime and the beginning of another, even though the same head of state might have remained in power. Several situations indicated a basic change in the level of regime fragmentation during the ongoing tenure of the head of state. A change in the regime's group structure could occur with the rise or demise of major factions or coalition partners; it could also occur in democratic systems when the cabinet gained or lost a legislative majority due to elections or defections. Shifting levels of polarization could also account for regime changes, for example in cases where the leadership became divided as a result of an approaching succession crisis or an escalating policy dispute. Finally, a leader's tenure in office could be marked by his or her rise to or fall from predominance, the latter occurring when the leader suffers a major political defeat undercutting his or her political position permanently. The occurrence of any one of these three conditions (which could occur together) was by itself adequate for identifying a new regime.[6]

The national political regimes identified for the thirty-eight nations in the CREON sample for the decade 1959–1968 are listed with accompanying information in Chart 4.2. Included under each country is the name of the regime's ruling party or group, along with additional information to be used in interpreting regime labels in the charts later in the chapter. Specifically, abbreviations of member groups are indicated, as is supplemental information about the extent of fragmentation if it was relevant for identifying the regime and distinguishing it from a subsequent one. The names of the incumbent heads of state are also indicated for purposes of convenience, but again keep in mind that these regimes represent groups in power rather than just individuals (except where there is a predominant leader). If a country has two regimes with the identical group makeup (e.g., Belgium), then they are differentiated by simple numbering. Finally, the dates the regime was in power are listed; note that some regimes began before the CREON decade or lasted beyond it, or both in the case of a few countries.

For the ten-year period under consideration, a total of ninety-four regimes were identified for the thirty-eight nations in the sample. However, four regimes (one each for Cuba, West Germany, Norway, and Turkey) were of such short duration that they did not overlap with the months included in the quarterly based CREON data set, thus leaving a sample of ninety regimes. Twenty-nine countries, about three-fourths of the sample, had more than one regime, and on average each country had about two and one-third regimes for the decade. There was, though, much variation in the number of regimes across the sample. Six nations had four or more regimes: Turkey had the most with six regimes,[7] while Belgium, Canada, Italy, Norway, and Venezuela each had four. At the other extreme were nine nations with only one regime—Egypt, East Germany, Guinea, Ivory Coast, Poland, Spain, Switzerland, Tunisia, and Zambia—most having a one-party system with a predominant leader but also one with a stable, ongoing coalition cabinet. Twenty-one nations, more than half the

Chart 4.2   Regimes in the CREON Sample of Nations for the Years 1959–1968

Belgium
Christian Socialists (CVP/PSC) and Liberal Party (PVV/PLP) coalition-1
(Eyskens-1), November 1958 to April 1961.
Christian Socialists (CVP/PSC) and Socialist Party (PS/SP) coalition-1 (Lefevre,
Harmel), April 1961 to March 1966.
Christian Socialists (CVP/PSC) and Liberal Party (PVV/PLP) coalition-2
(Vanden Boeynants), March 1966 to June 1968.
Christian Socialists (CVP/PSC) and Socialist Party (PVV/PLP) coalition-2
(Eyskens-2), June 1968 to January 1972.

Canada
Progressive Conservative Party (PC; Diefenbaker-1), April 1958 to June 1962.
Progressive Conservative Party (PC-minority cabinet; Diefenbaker-2), June 1962
to April 1963.
Liberal Party (LP-minority cabinet; Pearson), April 1963 to April 1968.
Liberal Party (LP; Trudeau), April 1968 to October 1972.

Chile
Conservative Party (PC), Liberal Party (PL), and Radical Party (PR) coalition
(Alessandri), November 1958 to November 1964.
Christian Democratic Party (PDC; Frei), November 1964 to November 1970.

China
Chinese Communist Party (CCP-factionalized; Mao and Liu), April 1959 to July
1966.
Cultural Revolution coalition (CCP-military–Mao Zedong–Red Guards), July
1966 to April 1969.

Costa Rica
National Union Party (PUN-minority executive; Echandi), May 1958 to May
1962.
National Liberation Party (PLN; Orlich), May 1962 to May 1966.
National Union (UN-minority executive; Trejos), May 1966 to May 1970.

Cuba
Revolutionary coalition (Castro-1), January 1959 to June 1959.[a]
Cuban Communist Party (PCC; Castro-2), June 1959 through 1988.

Czechoslovakia
Communist Party of Czechoslovakia-1 (CPCS-cohesive; Novotny-1), March
1953 to September 1963.
Communist Party of Czechoslovakia-2 (CPCS-factionalized; Novtony-2),
September 1963 to January 1968.
Communist Party of Czechoslovakia-3 (CPCS-factionalized; Dubcek), January
1968 to April 1969.

Egypt
Revolutionary Command Council (RCC; Nasser), November 1954 to September
1970.

(continues)

Chart 4.2   *(continued)*

France
Gaullist-led grand coalition (de Gaulle-1), November 1958 to November 1962.
Gaullist parties (de Gaulle-2), November 1962 to July 1968.
Gaullist Party cabinet (de Gaulle-3), July 1968 to July 1969.

German Democratic Republic
Socialist Unity Party (SED; Ulbricht), October 1945 to May 1971.

Federal Republic of Germany
Christian Democratic Union/Christian Socialist Union (CDU/CSU; Adenauer-1),
    September 1957 to September 1961.
Christian Democratic Union/Christian Socialist Union (CDU/CSU) and Free
    Democratic Party (FDP) coalition (Adenauer-2, Erhard), September 1961 to
    October 1966.
Interregnum, October 1966 to December 1966.[a]
Christian Democratic Union/Christian Socialist Union (CDU/CSU) and Social
    Democratic Party (SDP) Grand Coalition (Kiesinger), December 1966 to
    October 1969.

Ghana
Conventional People's Party (CPP; Nkrumah), March 1957 to February 1966.
National Liberation Council (NLC; Ankrah), February 1966 to April 1969.

Guinea
Democratic Party of Guinea (PDG; Toure), October 1958 to March 1984.

Iceland
Social Democratic Party (SDP–caretaker cabinet), December 1958 to November
    1959.
Independence Party (IP) and Social Democratic Party (SDP) coalition (Thors,
    Benediktsson), November 1959 to October 1970.

India
Indian National Congress (INC; Nehru predominant), December 1950 to May
    1964.
Indian National Congress (INC; Shastri, I. Gandhi-1), May 1964 to February
    1967.
Indian National Congress (INC; I. Gandhi-2 predominant), February 1967 to
    November 1969.

Israel
Mapai, Achdut Ha'avodah, and varying junior parties (Mapam, National
    Religious Party, and/or Progressives) coalition (Ben Gurion predominant),
    November 1955 to June 1963.
Mapai, Achdut Ha'avodah, and varying junior parties (Mapam, National
    Religious Party, and/or Poalei Agudah) coalition (Eshkol-1), June 1963 to
    June 1967.
National Unity Coalition (Eshkol-2), June 1967 to August 1970.

(continues)

Chart 4.2   (*continued*)

Italy
> Christian Democratic (DC) center-right minority cabinet (factionalized; Segni, Tambroni, Fanfani-1), February 1959 to July 1960.
> Christian Democratic Party (DC) centrist minority cabinet (factionalized; Fanfani-2), July 1960 to February 1962.
> Christian Democratic Party (DC), Social Democratic Party (PDSI), and Republican Party (PRI) center-left minority coalition cabinet (Leone), February 1962 to December 1963.
> Christian Democratic Party (DC), Socialist Party (PSI), Social Democratic Party (PDSI), and Republican Party (PRI) center-left coalition (Moro), December 1963 to June 1969.

Ivory Coast
> Democratic Party of the Ivory Coast (PDCI; Houphouet-Boigny), August 1960 through 1988.

Japan
> Liberal Democratic Party (LDP; Kishi faction), February 1957 to July 1960.
> Liberal Democratic Party (LDP; Ikeda faction), July 1960 to November 1964.
> Liberal Democratic Party (LDP; Sato faction), November 1964 to July 1972.

Kenya
> Kenyan African National Union (KANU; Kenyatta-1 factionalized), December 1963 to March 1966.
> Kenyan African National Union (KANU; Kenyatta-2 cohesive), March 1966 to August 1978.

Lebanon
> Chehab/Consociational coalition cabinets, September 1958 to August 1964.
> Helou/Consociational coalition cabinets, April 1964 to September 1970.

Mexico
> Institutional Revolutionary Party (PRI; Lopez Mateos), December 1958 to December 1964.
> Institutional Revolutionary Party (PRI; Diaz Ordaz), December 1964 to December 1970.

New Zealand
> Labour Party (Nash), December 1957 to December 1960.
> National Party (Holyoake), December 1960 to February 1972.

Norway
> Labour Party (DNA; Gerhardsen-1), January 1955 to September 1961.
> Labour Party (DNA–minority cabinet; Gerhardsen-2), October 1961 to September 1963.
> Liberal Party (V), Christian People's Party (KRF), Center Party (SP), and Conservative Party (H) center-right coalition (Lyng), September 1963 to September 1963.[a]

(*continues*)

Chart 4.2   *(continued)*

Norway (continued)
    Labour Party (DNA–minority cabinet; Gerhardsen-3), September 1963 to
        September 1965.
    Liberal Party (V), Christian People's Party (KRF), Center Party (SP), and
        Conservative Party (H) center-right coalition (Borten), October 1965 to
        March 1971.

Philippines
    Nationalista Party (NP; Garcia), March 1957 to November 1961.
    Liberal Party (LP; Macapagal), November 1961 to November 1965.
    Nationalista Party (NP-minority executive; Marcos), November 1965 to February
        1986.

Poland
    Polish United Workers Party (PZPR; Gomulka), October 1956 to December
        1970.

Soviet Union
    Communist Party of the Soviet Union (CPSU-cohesive; Khrushchev-1), June
        1957 to April 1960.
    Communist Party of the Soviet Union (CPSU-factionalized; Khrushchev-2),
        April 1960 to October 1964.
    Communist Party of the Soviet Union (CPSU-cohesive; Brezhnev and Kosygin),
        October 1964 to April 1973.

Spain
    Falange (Franco), October 1936 to November 1975.

Switzerland
    Federal Council coalition, 1946 through 1988.

Thailand
    Military Junta (Sarit predominant), September 1957 to December 1963.
    Military Junta (Thanom and Praphat), December 1963 to October 1973.

Tunisia
    Neo-Destour Party (Bourguiba), April 1956 to November 1985.

Turkey
    Democratic Party (DP; Mendares), April 1950 to May 1960.
    Committee of National Unity (CNU-1; Gursel-factionalized), May 1960 to
        November 1960.
    Committee of National Unity (CNU-2; Gursel-cohesive), November 1960 to
        October 1961.
    Justice Party (JP) and Republican People's Party coalition (RPP) coalition
        (Inonu-1), November 1961 to May 1962.[a]
    Republican People's Party (RPP), New Turkey Party (NTP), and Republican
        Peasant's National Party (RPNP) coalition (Inonu-2), June 1962 to February
        1965.

(continues)

Chart 4.2 *(continued)*

Turkey (continued)
Justice Party (JP), Nation Party (NP), New Turkey Party (NTP), and Republican Peasant's National Party (RPNP) coalition (Urguplu), February 1965 to October 1965.
Justice Party (JP; Demirel), October 1965 to March 1971.

Uganda
United People's Congress (UPC) and Kabaka Yekka (KY) coalition (Obote and Mutesa II), October 1962 to February 1966.
United People's Congress (UPC; Obote), February 1966 to January 1971.

United States
Republican Party (minority executive; Eisenhower), January 1953 to January 1961.
Democratic Party (cohesive; Kennedy, Johnson-1), January 1961 to June 1966.
Democratic Party (factionalized; Johnson-2), June 1966 to January 1969.

Uruguay
Blanco Party and Colorado Party coalition (collegial executive) December 1958 to March 1967.
Colorado Party (Gestido, Pacheco), March 1967 to December 1971.

Venezuela
Democratic Action Party (AD), Social Christian Party (COPEI), and Democratic Republican Union (URD) coalition (Bentancourt-1 predominant), February 1959 to November 1960.
Democratic Action Party (AD), Social Christian Party (COPEI), and independents coalition (Bentancourt-2), November 1960 to March 1964.
Democratic Action Party (AD) and independents coalition (minority executive; Leoni-1), March 1964 to November 1964.
Democratic Action Party (AD), Democratic Republican Union (URD), and National Democratic Front (FND) coalition (Leoni-2), November 1964 to March 1969.

Yugoslavia
League of Yugoslav Communists (LCY-cohesive; Tito-1), December 1945 to November 1961.
League of Yugoslav Communists (LCY-factionalized; Tito-2), November 1961 to March 1969.

Zambia
United National Independence Party (UNIP; Kaunda), October 1964 through 1988.

Note: a. Regime deleted from sample because its short duration does not correspond with the CREON "quarterly" foreign policy data.

sample, fell midway between these two extremes, having either two (twelve) or three regimes (nine) during the decade. And while the greatest number of regimes was found only in the democratic countries, half of the countries with nondemocratic political systems during the decade did have more than one regime: China, Czechoslovakia, Ghana, the Soviet Union, Thailand, Turkey, Uganda, and Yugoslavia.

A significant proportion (about 19 percent) of the regimes resulted from changes in which the same incumbent head of state remained in power. Some of these were regimes in democratic systems whose cabinets were altered by the shift from a single-party cabinet to a coalition (or the reverse) due to the loss or gain of a legislative majority, as in Canada, France (twice), West Germany, Norway, and Venezuela. Other sub–head-of-state changes were the result of a change in level or pattern of factional or coalition constraints, as in China, Israel, Italy, and Venezuela. In some cases a predominant leader continued in office, but only with rising opposition to his rule and a loss of political infallibility (e.g., Novotny in Czechoslovakia, Adenauer in West Germany, and Khrushchev in the Soviet Union). In still other situations a predominant leader retained predominance, but there was rising or diminishing factionalism, either within the cabinet or junta or in the congressional party (e.g., regime changes in Kenya under Kenyatta, Turkey under Gursel, the United States under Johnson, and Yugoslavia under Tito). Finally, there were some occurrences in which the head of state changed, but this did not change the basic group structure of the regime and thus did not warrant identification of a new regime. This not only included two cases of a collegial executive with a rotating head of state (Uruguay until 1967 and Switzerland), but also West Germany from Adenauer to Erhard, India from Shastri to Ghandi, Iceland from Thors to Benediktsson, the United States from Kennedy to Johnson, and several occurrences of the ministerial merry-go-round in Italy.

Before moving on to the analysis, one further issue should be addressed. How substantively meaningful is a data set on regimes that were in power in the 1960s, many of whose leaders have since retired or died or, even worse, whose national political systems have disappeared, (i.e., East Germany, the Soviet Union, and Yugoslavia)? While the value of (as well as problems with) using the CREON foreign policy events data set, which defines this sample, is explained in Chapter 5, let me briefly point out the continuing viability and relevance of this sample of nations and their regimes. My basic response is that the theoretical dynamic by which domestic opposition affects foreign policy is not time bound. The domestic process remains essentially the same for any period in time, a point demonstrated by the historical analyses of democracy and war proneness. Beyond that claim, two other points can be made. First, many of the specific opposition patterns in this data set continue to this day, while others are similar to some of the newer patterns of the 1990s in other countries. In particular, the new parliamentary democracies of Eastern Europe appear similar to the fragmented, polarized, and less institutionalized politics in Japan and Italy in the 1960s. Second, if the Cold War time frame of this data set seems to be less relevant, it also results in a more conservative test of the link between domestic politics and foreign policy. The tight bipolar structure of the international system at that time provided relatively little autonomy for the foreign policies of many nations. In a tense and threatening world, conforming well to Realist images of international affairs, one would expect domestic politics to have relatively little impact. Any aggregate relationship between domestic politics and foreign policy found in this analysis is likely even more prevalent in the looser bipolar system of the 1970s and 1980s and especially in the post–Cold War environment of the 1990s. Substantively and theoretically, the admittedly dated sample of regimes used here does not undercut the relevance or credibility of the findings reported in Chapter 5.

Classifying Regimes by Domestic Political Phenomena

Having identified the sample of regimes, the next step is to classify them by the three kinds of political phenomenon conceptualized in Chapter 3: regime fragmentation, political opposition outside the regime, and aspects of political system structure and regime vulnerability. There are two tasks in the presentation of the data on each variable. The first is to explain the operationalization of each variable. In line with the interpretive, or "soft," character of the data developed here, there are no quick or simple rules for measuring opposition, but this should not preclude documentation of basic coding rules. The other task is to report the distribution of the sample of regimes just identified as classified by each political measure. This will provide a further understanding of the data and, in turn, will enhance the interpretation of the statistical results in Chapter 5. This also provides an opportunity for judging the validity of the data, including the critical issue of whether or not the CREON sample of nations leads to a maldistribution of types of regimes defined by opposition traits.

Grouping Regimes by Political Fragmentation

It has been argued here that regime fragmentation is the primary arena of political opposition, because it concerns political divisions within the central political leadership that has the power to make major authoritative decisions. At the core of this concept is group structure in three possible variables, and the magnitude of those constraints as conditioned by two other factors: the presence/absence of a predominant actor and the extent of polarization over foreign policy issues. The procedures for coding these three variables are explained in this section, followed by an examination of the actual distribution of the sample of regimes in terms of a composite measure of regime fragmentation.

Ascertaining group structure. This variable classifies each regime by one of three group configurations: a single cohesive group, a single group with factional divisions, or a coalition of autonomous groups. The identification of a regime as a coalition, the most highly fragmented configuration, requires that two or more politically autonomous groups share control of the authoritative structures that constitute the regime. Operationally, the criteria of political autonomy is critical, and for coding purposes it can take two forms. One is autonomy in the form of a group having its own established organizational bases (e.g., its own headquarters, financial resources, and members), as with political parties. The other is institutional autonomy in which groups are identified with different structures of the government (e.g., legislature, military) and are in a competitive relationship. In both situations there cannot be any superior overarching party or institutional body.

The specific coding rules are dependent upon the institutional peculiarities of parliamentary, presidential, and authoritarian systems. In parliamentary systems, a coalition was identified by the presence in the cabinet of ministers from two or more separate political parties, as dictated by the lack of any party having a parliamentary majority. Also included were parliamentary coalitions in which a minority cabinet ruled for an extended period with the tacit support of opposition parties in the legislature. Coalitions in presidential systems were identified when the institutionally autonomous congress and executive were controlled by different political parties, while coalitions in quasi-presidential systems occurred when the president shared power with a legislatively based cabinet that was controlled by one (or more) opposing parties. For authoritarian regimes, the key question was whether or not different institutional centers of power were controlled by separate political groups, and in such a way that sources stated that the dominance of any one institution (usually the official party) was directly challenged by other institutions. For coding purposes, these institutional bases of power were the government apparatus (e.g., cabinet), the party apparatus, the military establishment, a charismatic leader and his/her personal "court," and possibly separate paramilitary groups.

If multiple political groups were not found, then the question was if the single ruling group had structural factions, political cliques, or opposing party wings. Any of these divisions were identified when sources argued consistently that the regime was composed of such competing groups and if it could be documented that these groups were represented by leaders in the ruling body of the regime. Structural factions were identified when party leaders in the regime were the heads or representatives of recognized factions that had their own organization (e.g., headquarters, media, labels) and that had formally competed for control of party offices. Political cliques are a far more fluid form of political organization, and while it was not always possible to trace the exact representation of cliques to specific individuals in the regime, general sources (and occasionally specific country reports) on patron-client networks clearly pointed to the prevalence of leadership clientelism within the regime's senior leadership. The remaining factionalized regimes were ones with actors who were organized around opposing general political orientations (and not specifically to foreign policy, as done below). This involved divisions over the party's general policy, as indicated by consistent reference (occasionally in connection to a leader succession crisis) to left, center, and right wings, to orthodox and reformist tendencies in especially authoritarian parties, or to divisions within a military junta over return of civilian rule.

The final group of regimes was the most cohesive in that these did not have permanent political divisions. In one sense, the coding procedures for these cases were simple: if sources on the regime's leadership consistently did not make any reference to political divisions within the cabinet, party politburo, or junta, then it was assumed that a regime was structurally cohesive. However, confirming evidence in most cases turned out to be quite helpful. Country accounts were often as striking in their discussion of the cohesion of a leadership as in that of the presence of sharp political splits. For example, literature on the politics of certain democracies emphasized the consensual or disciplined character of the party leadership and leader selection, for example, the sources on Norwegian, Canadian, and New Zealand politics. For especially authoritarian polities, accounts were often available that documented the fact that a leader had brought subordinates into the regime or had removed any major opponents, thereby creating a cohesive collective leadership. Finally, other treatments stressed the personal dominance of an individual leader and thus made clear the lack of any opposition, as in the case of regimes with strongly charismatic leaders who personally dominated all government institutions.

Identifying predominant actors. There are operationally two types of predominant actors: a politically predominant individual who personally dominates the regime or, in more fragmented situations, a political group that has preponderant political resources within the ruling coalition. In relatively cohesive regimes, a predominant leader was identified if, according to country sources, the individual head of state had such power that his or her hold on office could not be directly questioned by anyone in the regime and was able to prevail in any policy decision in which he or she participated and had clear preferences. The unchallenged authority of a single individual was determined by several, sometimes intertwined criteria. One was a source's depiction of a leader having widely acknowledged prestige because of his or her leading role in creating the political system. Specific indication of such political charisma was acknowledged leadership of the nation's successful independence movement from a colonial or occupation power or of the revolution (civilian or military) that brought the regime to power. While this indicated that other actors in the regime owed their position to the charismatic leader, sources were carefully checked for evidence that the leader might have subsequently lost complete control over the postindependence or postrevolutionary movement.

If only the above criteria were used, the sample of predominant leaders would be limited to mainly postindependence and postrevolution/coup leaders. To avoid this bias, the achievement of individual predominance was operationalized in terms of additional, regime-specific criteria. In established democracies individual predominance occurred when the leader was personally credited for having led the party to victory in the previous election, while in authoritarian systems it was indicated by a leader having consolidated power through the appointment of personal supporters and the eviction of personal opponents. In a political system penetrated by a foreign power, a leader could achieve predominance if strongly supported by the key external foreign power, as was the case with certain pro-Soviet regimes in Eastern Europe during the 1960s. Also useful were careful discussions that demonstrated the near impossibility of the emergence of a predominant leader, because of the existence of either strong norms of collective rule and consensus politics (e.g., Scandinavian systems as well as Mexico's PRI) or strong factional constraints such that no prime minister could ever dominate (e.g., Japan's LDP).[8]

The other kind of predominant actor occurred when a single group had preponderant power in more fragmented settings. For parliamentary coalitions, the main criteria for this was a single party's control of at least three-fourths of those legislative seats controlled by the coalition—for example the Christian Democratic coalitions with the Free Democrats in West Germany. Additional criteria were necessary, however, to catch exceptions to this rule. One was the situation in which the senior coalition party had structural factions (as in Italy's Christian Democratic–led majority coalitions), with the assumption that the presence of contending subparties negated the party's ability to dominate the coalition. The other exception was a minority government in competitive systems. Here it was assumed that the cabinet was so vulnerable to parliamentary overthrow that they were coded as not having predominant actors, except where there were strong norms of consensus policymaking governing relations between the cabinet and the legislature (e.g., as in Norway).

As for coalitions in presidential and quasi-presidential systems, the institutional dominance of the executive was considered indicative of the presence of a predominant actor when the presidency and the legislature were controlled by opposing parties. (The reverse could also apply here: a predominant leader was identified if sources showed that a prime minister and his cabinet were able to dominate the presidency, as happened during Uganda's ill-defined power-sharing arrangement between Obote's United People's Congress and Mutesa II's Kabaka Yekka.) But, as above, this dominance was assumed to be negated if the executive branch was itself internally factionalized or consisted of multiple political parties, which occurred in Venezuela throughout the 1960s. In authoritarian systems with coalitions, predominant actors were identified if sources indicated that one actor was recognized by others as having exclusive control over relevant political resources, for example, military power, ideological or nationalist legitimacy, or financial resources.[9] Thus, for example, the strained coalition in China during the Cultural Revolution clearly had a predominant actor: Mao Zedong and his "court" by virtue of his continued standing as the revolution's leader and chief articulator of its legitimizing ideology.

Judging polarization on foreign policy issues. This dimension asks if the political leadership in the regime is clearly divided over foreign policy issues. Although it was quite difficult to ascertain the specific policy position of every regime member on each issue, country accounts and political reports typically provided more general information on the contending orientations of different political groups (party wings, factions, or parties) on the nation's overall foreign relations.

As a general rule, a regime was considered polarized if actors within it had basic foreign policy differences that were directly tied (in a manner that could be documented) to general political orientations in national or party politics, in other words, left versus right, orthodox versus reformist, hardline versus moderate. Alternatively, the lack of disputes was inferred if parties and factions were relatively adjacent along the ideologically spectrum, or if sources stressed the nonideological character of the regime's factions. However, two supplementary rules were employed to identify frequent exceptions to these initial inferences; in other words, sources were examined for further information regarding foreign policy differences extending from general political orientations. The first rule identified regimes in which contending actors did not have broad ideological differences, but they were still considered polarized because sources clearly pointed out clear divisions over the major, overarching foreign policy issue(s) facing the regime (e.g., Johnson's Vietnam policies or de Gaulle's early Algerian policies). The second rule accounted for situations in which there were clear ideological differences, but the sources emphasized a strong consensus over foreign policy issues (e.g., Israel's National Unity Coalition under threat of Arab attack or the United States during the Cold War consensus). In these ways, it was possible to check the validity of the linkage between general political orientations and foreign policy positions.

A composite measure of regime fragmentation. To simplify the explanation of coding rules, the fragmentation dimensions of group structure, actor predominance, and policy polarization have been thus far treated separately. I now want to turn to the full, composite measure of regime fragmentation. This is the measure used in the analyses in Chapter 5, with the theoretical premise being that factional and coalition constraints become fully apparent only when the effects of leader predominance and policy polarization are taken into account. The computation of this variable is based on the following values, with higher values indicating greater fragmentation. The scale for the group structure dimension is:

3 = regime is a coalition of autonomous parties or groups
2 = regime is a single party or group with internal factions
1 = regime is a single party or cohesive group

The two other dimensions are based on dichotomous variables. The measure for predominant actors is:

2 = political predominant actor is absent
1 = politically predominant actor is present

The measure for polarization on foreign policy issues is:

2 = actors have broad differences on foreign policy issues
1 = actors are not divided over foreign policy matters

As used in this project, the three variables are combined (via multiplicative weighting) to create a seven-point scale with values ranging from 1 to 12.[10] The distribution of the sample of eighty-eight regimes across this scale is reported in Chart 4.3.

At the high end of the scale (points 12 and 8) are highly fragmented regimes. These regimes had either coalition or factional divisions that were intensified by both the absence of a predominant actor and the polarization of leaders on foreign policy issues. At the highest point of the scale are broad-based (i.e., no predominant actor) coalitions or minority governments whose members were polarized on foreign policy issues. All four of Italy's Christian Democratic–led cabinets fell into this group, as did certain of the Belgian, Canadian, West German, Norwegian, and Venezuelan coalitions. Ranked just below this group are factionalized single-party regimes (two of them are in authoritarian systems) that do not have predominant leaders and are internally polarized on foreign policy. Actually, in each there was a succession crisis that was linked to foreign policy, but as of then no predominant actor had emerged to break out of power-sharing

Chart 4.3   Classification and Ranking of Regimes by Regime Fragmentation

12 = Coalition/no predominant actor/polarized [3*2*2]
BEL/ChrSoc+Socialist-1; BEL/ChrSoc+Socialist-2; CAN/PC-minority;
FRG/Grand Coalition; ITA/DC-minority(ctr-right); ITA/DC-minority(centrist); ITA/DC+PDSI+PRI-minority(ctr-left); ITA/DC+PSI+PDSI+PRI;
NOR/Lib+ChrPP+SP+Cons; VEN/AD+inds(Leoni-1).

 8 = Divided single group regime/no predominant actor/polarized [2*2*2]
PRC/CCP(Mao+Liu); COS/PLN(Orlich); CZE/CPCS(Dubcek);
IND/INC(Shastri,Gandhi-1); IND/INC(Gandhi-2).

 6 = A. Coalition/no predominant actor/not polarized [3*2*1]
BEL/ChrSoc+Liberal-1; BEL/ChrSoc+Liberal-2; CAN/Liberal-minority;
CHL/PC+PL+PR(Alessandri); ICE/IP+SDP; ISR/Mapai coalition(Eshkol-1); ISR/National Unity Coalition; SWI/Federal Council;
TUR/RPP+NTP+RPNP; TUR/JP+NP+NTP+RPNP;
URG/Blanco+Colorado; VEN/AD+COPEI+inds(Bentancourt-2);
VEN/AD+URD+FND(Leoni-2).

B. Coalition/predominant actor present/polarized [3*1*2]
CHL/PDC(Frei); PRC/Cultural Rev coalition; COS/PUN(Echandi);
COS/UN(Trejos); FRN/de Gaulle+coalition cabs; FRG/CDU-CSU+FDP;
LEB/Chehab+coalition cabs; LEB/Helou+coalition cabs; NOR/Labour-2(minority); NOR/Labour-3(minority); UGA/UPC+Kabaka Yekka;
VEN/AD+COPEI+URD(Bentancourt-2).

 4 = A. Divided single group/no predominant actor/not polarized [2*2*1]
GHA/NLC Junta; JAP/LDP(Kishi faction); JAP/LDP(Ikeda faction);
JAP/LDP(Sato faction); PHI/Nationalist(Garcia); SOV/CPSU(Khrushchev-2); THI/Military Junta(Thanom+Praphat).

B. Divided single group/predominant actor present/polarized [2*1*2]
CZE/CPCS(Novotny-2); IND/INC(Nehru); KEN/KANU(Kenyatta-1);
POL/PZPR(Gomulka); USA/Dem Pty(Johnson-2); YUG/LCY(Tito-2).

 3 = Coalition/predominant actor present/not polarized [3*1*1]
ISR/Mapai coalition(Ben Gurion); PHI/Nationalist(Marcos);
USA/Republican(Eisenhower).

 **2 = A. Divided single group/predominant actor present/not polarized
       [2*1*1]**
FRN/de Gaulle+Gaullist ptys cabs; KEN/KANU(Kenyatta-2);
PHI/Liberal(Macapagal); THI/Military Junta(Sarit);
USA/Democratic(Kennedy,Johnson-1); URG/Colorado(Gestido,Pacheco);
ZAM/ZANU(Kaunda).

(continues)

Chart 4.3   *(continued)*

    B. Cohesive single group/no predominant actor [1*2*1]
    CAN/Liberal; MEX/PRI(Lopez Mateos); MEX/PRI(Diaz Ordaz);
    NZE/Labour; NZE/National; NOR/Labour-1; SOV/CPSU(Khrushchev-1);
    SOV/CPSU(Brezhnev+Kosygin); TUR/Democratic; TUR/Justice;
    UGA/UPC(Obote).

1 = **Cohesive single group/predominant actor present [1*1*1]**
    CAN/PC(Diefenbaker); CUB/PCC(Castro); CZE/CPCS(Novotny-1);
    EGY/RCC(Nasser); FRN/de Gaulle+Gaullist cab; GDR/SED(Ulbricht)
    FRG/CDU-CSU(Adenauer-1); GHA/CPP(Nkrumah); GUI/PDG(Toure);
    IVR/PDCI(Houphouet-Boigny); SPN/Falange(Franco); TUN/Neo-
    Destour(Bourguiba); TUR/CNU Junta(Gursel-2);YUG/LCY(Tito-1).

---

arrangements (e.g., Mao and Liu's tenuous power-sharing arrangement after China's disastrous Great Leap Forward, India's post-Nehru leadership, and the Dubcek leadership of Czechoslovakia's ill-fated Prague Spring).

    Highly cohesive regimes are at the opposite end of the scale in Chart 4.3 (points 1, 2A/B, 3), and each of these regimes was ruled by a single group with minimal internal divisions. The most cohesive type of regime here (point 1) had a cohesive single party dominated by a single predominant leader in a diverse set of political systems. Included here were several democratic regimes with exceptionally (but usually only temporarily) strong party leaders (e.g., West Germany's Adenauer and France's de Gaulle), several Communist polities (e.g., Cuba's Castro and East Germany's Ulbricht), two conservative authoritarian polities (Spain's Franco and Turkey's Gursel), and several cases of personal rule in Africa (e.g., Egypt's Nasser and Ghana's Nkrumah) in which the leader was, in effect, the regime. The regimes at point 2B, in contrast, had more collective (yet still cohesive) leadership bodies, reflective of either strong power-sharing norms in well-established institutions (e.g., Mexican, Norwegian, and New Zealand regimes) or the inability of any one individual to gain dominance yet (e.g., Khrushchev and Brezhnev in the Soviet Union or Uganda's Obote). The other regimes (points 2A and 3) had group divisions (either coalition or factions), and yet are appropriately ranked toward the cohesive end of the chart. The political intensity of factional and coalition conflict was diminished by either the distinctly nonideological nature of regime politics (e.g., Philippine and Thai cases) or because of the presence of a predominant leader containing these political rivalries (e.g., Israel under Ben Gurion and France under de Gaulle).

    The remaining four regime groupings, falling in the middle range of

Chart 4.3 (points 6A/B and 4A/B), are relatively complex with a hybrid of values on the fragmentation dimensions. Each regime had significant internal structural divisions, but these coalitional (point 6) or factional (point 4) configurations were only partially intensified because of either the lack of a predominant actor or polarization over foreign policy, but not both. Group 6A includes essentially broad-based coalitions composed of members who were ideologically similar (e.g., center-right coalitions in Belgium, Chile, and Iceland) or grand coalitions with no differences on foreign policy (e.g., Turkey's Justice Party and Republican People's Party). The coalitions listed in 6B were internally divided on foreign policy matters, but the presence of a predominant actor moderated these pressures. Some of these were coalition cabinets with a senior party (e.g., West Germany's CDU-CSU coalitions with the Free Democrats), while others were quasi-presidential systems with institutionally subordinate cabinet or legislative partners (e.g., the Lebanese coalitions or the presidencies in Costa Rica and Chile confronted by hostile legislatures). The factionalized regimes at points 4A and 4B had similarly mixed values on leader predominance and policy polarization. Japan under the LDP typified the kind of regime grouped under point 4A. Factional competition, particularly given the lack of a predominant leader or faction, was severe but pressures were moderated by the consensus on the nation's foreign relations. In contrast, the factionalized regimes at point 4B had fundamental policy splits, but these conflicts were contained by a predominant leader. This leader, who often appeared not to have strong preferences, allowed debates between factions and the leadership (e.g., India's Nehru and Tito's Yugoslavia).[11] In sum, points 4A and 4B tap diverse patterns of factionalism, even though they fall within a relatively moderate range of fragmentation.

The regimes derived from the interaction of the three fragmentation dimensions have some face validity. The groups of regimes are conceptually interesting and compatible with discussions found in the comparative politics literature. Authoritarian regimes appear at all but the highest level of regime fragmentation. Also, even though there are more democratic regimes at the higher fragmentation levels, this does not preclude other democracies from clustering at the lower, more cohesive levels. Another interesting feature is that the scale places coalitional and factional regimes at a wide range of points on the scale. The multiplicative measure does not preclude certain factionalized parties or coalitions from being ranked as moderately fragmented or even as relatively cohesive.

Grouping Regimes by Their Political Opposition

Conceptualizations of four basic types of opposition, each operating in a distinct institutional arena outside of the regime, were presented in Chapter

3. They are opposition from (1) elements within the ruling party or group, (2) other political parties in the legislature, (3) the military and other paramilitary actors, and (4) regionally based actors. Measures of each are based on the combination of two dimensions: strength and intensity. In this section, the basic procedures for the operationalization of these two dimensions are explained for each opposition, followed in each case by a presentation of the distribution of the sample regimes across a composite measure combining the two.

Measuring opposition within the ruling party or group. This refers to opposition to the regime and its policies by key actors in the regime's own ruling party or group who do not hold major positions in the regime itself. Operationally, intraparty opposition should not be confused with leadership divisions within factionalized single-party regimes. Whereas the unit of observation for regime fragmentation is something like a cabinet or politburo, the focus of subleadership opposition data is on the entire ruling party's/group's leadership in structures outside the regime—and, in particular, the possible exclusion of some party/group leaders from the regime itself. In democratic regimes this is both the leadership of the party apparatus (machine) and the party members in the parliament or congress. Important opposition in one-party authoritarian systems is often lodged in bodies such as a party's central committee, while in military regimes this opposition centers around senior commanders of military units.

The strength of intraparty opposition concerns the extent to which opposition groups within the ruling party are organized in ways ranging from powerful structural factions to more fluid cliques and party wings. As with regime fragmentation, structural factions were identified when sources provided evidence of organizational autonomy within the party (e.g., own financial resources, media facilities, and membership rosters) and open competition in party elections. An equivalent form of factionalism occurred when an electoral coalition of several parties began to deteriorate, after having successfully brought the regime to power. Any party with ties to the coalition, but that subsequently challenged the regime, was treated as the equivalent of a structural faction.[12] In military regimes, major units or branches commanded by senior officers were treated as the organizational equivalent of structural factions. A less severe form of intraparty opposition is the organization of the entire party/group into two opposing party wings. This situation was indicated by sources in either of two ways, or both: the depiction of the overall party as divided into, say, conservative/orthodox versus moderate/reformist wings (one being excluded), or reference to major tensions between the regime and another branch of the party, such as the party machine or the parliamentary party.[13]

In the case of relatively cohesive parties, the empirical task was to ascertain just how disciplined the parties were: was the party organized around political cliques or other kinds of small leadership groups, or was it a centrally disciplined body? Answers to these kinds of questions could be derived from general country or party overviews. Even if these sources did not identify specific groups or individuals by name, splits were identified simply by description of the internal workings of the political party in terms of clientelist politics or the occurrence of parliamentary rebellion. However, even in cases where sources emphasized party discipline, it was necessary to recognize that most cohesive parties can dissolve into contending cliques and party wings because of new policy debates or a leadership crisis. Thus annual political reports were carely examined to identify periodic internal party crises and the polarization of a party into opposing elements. Whatever the case, it was assumed that the lack of control by the regime over its own party membership was significant, even if it was relatively unorganized and without well-established leadership.

The intensity of intraparty opposition concerns the extent to which the above actors challenge major policies or even the regime itself. Critical to tap here is the extreme situation in which an element of a party acts to overthrow the regime throughout much of its time in office. Documentation of the purposeful exclusion of the leadership of specific factions or wings from positions in the regime was taken as evidence of their subsequent opposition to that regime. Anti-regime opposition was also inferred from reports of party-wide revolts against the effective head of state and resulting (and often prolonged) succession crises in even otherwise fairly cohesive parties. Reports of attempted coups in military regimes were considered evidence of anti-regime opposition by disaffected military units outside the ruling junta.

Less intense forms of intraparty opposition were indicated by broad controversies over the regime's general policies, but which did not directly challenge the tenure of the regime's leadership. The most direct evidence of this was reports of ongoing debates throughout the life of the regime over (and limited to) broad policy questions. In the case of coalition cabinets in which all of the major factions of each party were represented, it was assumed that the wider membership of each party still challenged the original compromises that enabled the coalition to be created (the only possible exception to this could occur if each coalition party was controlled by a predominant leader). The same applied to collective leaderships that incorporated all wings of polarized parties. Finally, the lack of any intraparty opposition (even from organized wings or cliques) was inferred from statements that party members were coerced into subordination by the regime or that the party was highly disciplined and not currently facing any major policy or leadership crises.

The measure of intraparty opposition is based upon the interaction of its strength and intensity dimensions. The scale for the strength dimension is:

4 = ruling party or group is organized around structural factions
3 = ruling party or group is organized around contending wings
2 = ruling party or group is organized around competing leader cliques
    or groups
1 = party or group is a cohesive organization

The intensity dimension is based on a three-point scale:

3 = opposition seeks to overthrow the regime
2 = opposition is limited to regime's policies
1 = no challenges to either policies or leadership

The combination via multiplicative weighting of these two measures results in an eight-point scale with values ranging from 1 to 12. The distribution of the sample of regimes is reported in Chart 4.4. Along with the label for each category, separate strength and intensity scores are reported in brackets. There are two groups at point 6 of the scale, because of the alternative combinations of scores of 2/3 or 3/2. The distribution of regimes is good (i.e., no empty cells), and authoritarian regimes can be found at most levels.

The top third of the scale (points 12 and 9) represents situations of the most severe intraparty opposition. At the highest point are regimes with the strongest and most intense levels of intraparty opposition: structural factions, some of which were excluded from the regime and thus opposed it throughout its duration. The regimes of Japan, Italy, and Uruguay fit this pattern throughout the decade, as did Costa Rica's when ruled by a loose alliance of conservative groups whose unity lasted only through the election.[14] The other group of regimes here (point 9) had parties with opposing wings whose normally policy-based opposition had escalated into demands for either major changes in the regime's leadership or, more typically, an end to the party's participation in a controversial coalition. The regimes of a diverse set of polities are at this level, but the common feature is that each party/group was in at least temporary internal disarray. In some regimes the crisis reflected severe debates over major policy issues (e.g., ideological splits in Chilean regimes and anti–Vietnam War opposition in Congress toward the end of Johnson's tenure as U.S. president). However, most cases were due to crises involving the overall future of the party that were raised by (1) the passing of a predominant leader (Israel and India), (2) participation in transitional coalitions in newly emerging political systems (postmilitary coalitions in Venezuela and Turkey and Uganda's tense postindependence coalition), or (3) attempts to reform an authoritarian order (e.g., Communist parties in Czechoslovakia and China during the late 1960s).

Relatively moderate levels of intraparty opposition are found in the middle range of Chart 4.4, which consists of four groups of regimes (points

---

Chart 4.4   Classification and Ranking of Regimes by Opposition Within the Ruling Party or Group

---

12 = **Party has structural factions and some oppose the regime [4*3]**
COS/PUN(Echandi); COS/UN(Trejos); ITA/DC-minority(ctr-right); ITA/DC-minority(centrist); ITA/DC+PDSI+PRI-minority(ctr-left); ITA/DC+PSI+PDSI+PRI; JAP/LDP(Kishi faction); JAP/LDP(Ikeda faction); JAP/LDP(Sato faction); URG/Blanco+Colorado; URG/Colorado(Gestido, Pacheco).

9 = **Party has opposing wings and some oppose the regime [3*3]**
CHL/PC+PL+PR(Alessandri); CHL/PDC(Frei); PRC/Cultural Rev coalition; CZE/CPCS(Dubcek); IND/INC(Gandhi-2); ISR/Mapai coalition(Ben Gurion); ISR/Mapai coalition(Eskhol-1); TUR/RPP+NTP+RPNP; TUR/JP+NP+NTP+RPNP; TUR/Justice; UGA/UPC+Kabaka Yekka; USA/Democratic(Johnson-2); VEN/AD+COPEI+URD(Bentancourt-1); VEN/AD+COPEI+inds(Bentancourt-2); VEN/AD+inds(Leoni-1); VEN/AD+URD+FND(Leoni-2).

8 = **Party has structural factions; opposition limited to regime policies [4*2]**
BEL/ChrSoc+Liberal-1; BEL/ChrSoc+Socialist-1; BEL/ChrSoc+Liberal-2; BEL/ChrSoc+Socialist-2; FRN/de Gaulle+coalition cabs; ISR/National Unity Coalition.

6 = **A. Party has opposing wings; opposition limited to regime policies [3*2]**
COS/PLN(Orlich); CZE/CPCS(Novotny-2); KEN/KANU(Kenyatta-1); POL/PZPR(Gomulka); USA/Democratic(Kennedy,Johnson-1); YUG/LCY(Tito-2).

B. Party cliques and autonomous elements and they oppose the regime [2*3]
CAN/PC-minority; FRG/CDU-CSU+FDP; GHA/NLC Junta; TUR/CNU Junta(Gursel-2).

4 = **Party cliques and autonomous elements; opposition limited to regime policies [2*2]**
PRC/CCP(Mao+Liu); FRN/de Gaulle+Gaullist Ptys; FRN/de Gaulle+Gaullist cab; FRG/CDU-CSU(Adenauer); FRG/Grand Coalition; IND/INC(Nehru); IND/INC(Shastri,Gandhi-1); LEB/Chehab+coalition cabs; LEB/Helou+coalition cabs; MEX/PRI(Lopez Mateos); MEX/PRI(Diaz Ordaz); SOV/CPSU(Khrushchev-1); SOV/CPSU(Khrushchev-2); SOV/CPSU(Brezhnev+Kosygin); SWI/Federal Council; USA/Republican(Eisenhower).

(continues)

Chart 4.4 *(continued)*

3 = **Party has opposing wings; no opposition to policy program [3*1]**
CUB/PCC(Castro); CZE/CPCS(Novotny-1).

2 = **Personal cliques and autonomous elements; no opposition to regime policies or government program [2*1]**
GHA/CPP(Nkrumah); KEN/KANU(Kenyatta-2); PHI/Nationalist(Garcia); PHI/Liberal(Macapagal); PHI/Nationalist(Marcos); SPN/Falange(Franco); THI/Military Junta(Sarit); THI/Military Junta(Thanom+Praphat); TUR/Democratic; UGA/UPC(Obote); YUG/LCY(Tito-1); ZAM/ZANU(Kaunda).

1 = **No divisions or opposition within the ruling party [1*1]**
CAN/PC(Diefenbaker); CAN/Liberal-minority; CAN/Liberal; EGY/RCC(Nasser); GDR/SED(Ulbricht); GUI/PDG(Toure); ICE/IP+SDP; IVR/PDCI(Houphouet-Boigny); NZE/Labour; NZE/National; NOR/Labour-1; NOR/Labour-2(minority); NOR/Labour-3(minority); NOR/Lib+ChrPP+SP+Cons; TUN/Neo-Destour(Bourguiba).

8, 6A/B, and 4) in which there was a hybrid of high strength and low intensity scores, or vice versa. The regimes at point 8 had parties with structural factions whose leaders supported the regime (in other words, all factions were included in the regime), but members of each party questioned the ongoing policy compromises forced upon their party in order to participate in the coalition. Along with the normally well-represented factions of the Belgian coalitions, these regimes included emergency coalitions in the newly created French Fifth Republic (to deal with the Algerian question) and in Israel under threat of Arab attack in 1967. Point 6 includes two groups of regimes. The first (6A) is a seemingly normal situation: regimes with parties organized into opposition wings who oppose the regime's policies without directly challenging the leadership. Along with a few internally polarized democratic regimes, these cases consisted of parties with predominant leaders who permitted open policy debates; these included regimes for Kenyatta's Kenya, Tito's Yugoslavia, Gomulka's Poland, and Novotny's Czechoslovakia. The regimes at point 6B were ones with leadership cliques that sought to remove the top leadership from power. These otherwise cohesive parties had temporarily decayed with key party leaders vying for control of the party (e.g., personality struggles surrounding the otherwise disciplined parties in Canada and West Germany, as well as conflicts [including abortive coups] in the military regimes in Ghana and Turkey). Finally, at point 4, are regimes with major policy disputes that intensified normally limited internal divisions. Some of these regimes, such as those listed for Lebanon, China, India, and Turkey, had political cliques that became broadly politicized over policy issues. Other cases were organizationally complex parties with various crosscutting policy conflicts (but which would not be the basis for separate party wings) and included ruling parties in Mexico, France, the Soviet Union, and West Germany.

The final set of regimes (at points 3, 2, and 1) had largely cohesive parties. Each had only the mildest opposition, involving at most relatively narrow political conflicts over the allocation of party/government resources that were not directed at the regime itself or its overall policy program. At point 3, there are two parties with distinct organizational wings (Cuba's Castro regime and the early Novotny regime in Czechoslovakia), but which in neither case offered much opposition because the dominant leader had suppressed all open dissent. Point 2 consists of what might be expected from parties organized around political cliques: powerful political bosses who had little concern for broader issues and were instead largely co-opted by the resources offered by the regime. Cases included here were regimes in the Philippines, Thailand, and several African one-party states. The last group, at point 1, represents the most cohesive type of situation in that these parties had no clear divisions. Several of these regimes were in authoritarian systems (Egypt, East Germany, Guinea, Ivory Coast, Tunisia), where any dissent had been contained by a mix of coercion and co-optation. Otherwise, the parties listed here had traditionally disciplined memberships and strong consensus norms, as usually found in Canadian, New Zealand, and Norwegian politics in the 1960s.

Measuring political party opposition. This concerns opposition to the regime and its policies from other civilian political groups that also aggregate broad sets of interests and that compete via elections for control of the government. The measurement of the strength of party opposition was based on two criteria. The primary one was the proportion of seats in the national legislature controlled by political parties that were not controlled by the regime. Specifically, party opposition was measured in terms of the proportion of opposition seats relative to those held by the regime's ruling party or coalition. There are several levels of party opposition: "very strong" opposition in which the regime lacks a legislative majority, "strong" opposition in which the opposition holds one-third to one-half of the seats, "weak" opposition in which the opposition holds one-tenth to one-third of the seats, and "minor" opposition in which the opposition holds fewer than one-tenth of the seats. The other criterion concerns the cohesiveness of the opposition, distinguishing between fragmented and cohesive opposition when there is strong opposition as just defined. Party opposition was considered to be cohesive when a single party had control of 75 percent of total opposition seats and, if so, did not have structural factions. If party opposition seats were dispersed among multiple parties or factions, then this opposition was downgraded to "moderately strong."[15]

Like intraparty opposition, the operationalization of the intensity of party opposition required judgements from country sources about the extent to which the regime and its policies were challenged.[16] Beginning with the mildest level of opposition, the initial question was simply whether or not the party openly opposed the regime. A party was coded as not challenging the regime if it was a creation of the ruling party within an authoritarian framework or if it was allowed to exist only so long as it did not question ruling party policies. Most political parties, of course, competed for power, and for these the question was the ideological distance between the main opposition parties and the regime's party. A sequence of two judgments was important here: the extent of polarization in terms of mainstream policy issues (e.g., left-right continuum) and, if parties were polarized, then in terms of mainstream (prosystem) versus antidemocratic (antisystem) parties. If the ruling party and the main party opposition were ideologically similar, then that opposition was considered to be relatively mild, whereas more intense opposition was ranked higher if the regime's party and the opposition party were from opposite ends of the spectrum. Finally, the most intense level of party opposition was if an opposition party rejected the basic legitimacy of the democratic political norms and institutions and professed an intention to introduce major structural changes in the domestic political order upon taking power.

The political party opposition measure is based upon the combination of the following strength and intensity scales, as before, with multiplicative weighting. The strength measure is a six-point scale (note: labels are used here to simplify category headings in Chart 4.5):

5 = opposition parties control the legislature
4 = strong party opposition: has 33–49 percent of seats and is dominated by a single cohesive party
3 = moderately strong party opposition: has 33–49 percent of seats and is fragmented by multiple parties and/or structural factions
2 = weak party opposition: has 10–32 percent of seats
1 = minor party opposition: has 1–9 percent of seats
0 = no opposition parties

The intensity dimension is a four-point scale:

4 = major opposition party has antisystem orientation
3 = major opposition party is from the opposite end of mainstream political spectrum

2 = major opposition party is from the same end of mainstream politi-
      cal spectrum

1 = no major opposition party opposes the current regime

Chart 4.5 reports the distribution of the eighty-eight regimes for the composite party opposition measure. The combination of the strength and intensity measures results in a scale with thirteen points ranging from 20 (minority governments with antisystem parties) to 0 (no opposition parties). As
with previous measures, the separate strength and intensity scores are indicated in the adjacent brackets, and several points on the scale include two
groups of regimes. The distribution of regimes across categories is generally good, although regimes from one country dominate the highest point
(20), and there are no cases of strong opposition with an antisystem orientation (note: procedures are used in the analyses below to control for this
problem).[17]

The highest range of political party opposition encompasses points 12
through 20 on the scale. At the most extreme level are three Italian regimes
in which minority governments faced a parliament dominated by the then
antisystemic Italian Communist Party (as well as small, but important,
rightwing antisystemic parties). The regimes at point 15 are also minority
governments and with opposition parties at the opposite end of the political
spectrum, but which are not antisystemic. These included Norway's Labour
minority governments (facing a variety of nonsocialist parties), a short-
lived Democratic Action cabinet in Venezuela, and two conservative presidencies in Costa Rica that had a congress controlled by the leftist National
Liberation Party. At point 12, there are two groups of regimes, and in both
the regimes had a legislative majority. The regimes at point 12A were
opposed by a single strong political party (a cohesive one with one-third to
one-half of the legislative seats) that was ideologically polarized from the
regime's ruling party (West Germany's Christian Democratic regimes
[with or without the Free Democrats] against the cohesive Social Democratic Party, as well as Norway's nonsocialist coalitions confronting the
disciplined Labour Party). The group at point 12B includes regimes with
moderately strong (i.e., factionalized) opposition parties in which there was
at least one major antisystemic party. The legislative opposition at this
level controlled a large number of seats, but they were internally divided
into several parties (e.g., the cases of Chile under Frei, France under de
Gaulle, and India under Gandhi) or were large single parties with structural
factions (e.g., Italy's majority DC regime and the factionalized Communist
Party opposition).

The scale's middle range (points 10 through 6) consists of more moderate levels of party opposition. The common feature here is that opposition
parties were either organizationally strong or intense in their orientation
vis-à-vis the regime, but not both. Another set of minority governments is

Chart 4.5   Classification and Ranking of Regimes by Political Party Opposition

20 = **Opposition parties control legislature; has antisystemic elements [5*4]**
ITA/DC-minority(ctr-right); ITA/DC-minority(centrist);
ITA/DC+PDSI+PRI-minority(ctr-left).

16 = **Strong opposition party with anti-systemic orientation [4*4]**
no cases

15 = **Opposition parties control legislature; has polarized mainstream elements [5*3]**
COS/PUN(Echandi); COS/UN(Trejos); NOR/Labour-2(minority);
NOR/Labour-3(minority); VEN/AD+inds(Leoni-1).

12 = **A. Strong opposition party with polarized mainstream orientation [4*3]**
FRG/CDU-CSU(Adenauer-1); FRG/CDU-CSU+FDP;
NOR/Lib+ChrPP+SP+Cons.

B. Moderately strong party opposition; has antisystemic elements [3*4]
CHL/PDC(Frei); FRN/de Gaulle+Gaullist ptys cabs; IND/INC(Gandhi-2);
ITA/DC+PSI+PDSI+PRI.

10 = **Opposition parties control legislature; nonpolarized mainstream elements [5*2]**
CAN/PC-minority; CAN/Liberal-minority; PHI/Nationalist(Marcos);
USA/Republican(Eisenhower).

9 = **Moderately strong party opposition with polarized mainstream orientation [3*3]**
BEL/ChrSoc+Liberal-1; BEL/ChrSoc+Socialist-2;
BEL/ChrSoc+Liberal-2; CHL/PC+PL+PR(Alessandri); COS/PLN(Orlich);
ICE/IP+SDP; ISR/Mapai coalition(Ben Gurion); ISR/Mapai
coalition(Eskhol-1); JAP/LDP(Kishi faction); JAP/LDP(Ikeda faction);
JAP/LDP(Sato faction); NOR/Labour-1;
VEN/AD+COPEI+inds(Bentancourt-2); VEN/AD+URD+FND(Leoni-2).

8 = **A. Strong opposition party with nonpolarized orientation [4*2]**
NZE/Labour; NZE/National; PHI/Liberal(Macapagal);
TUR/JP+NP+NTP+RPNP; USA/Democratic(Kennedy,Johnson-1);
USA/Democratic(Johnson-2).

B. Weak party opposition; has antisystemic elements [2*4]
FRN/de Gaulle+Gaullist cabs; GHA/CPP(Nkrumah); IND/INC(Nehru);
IND/INC(Shastri,Gandhi-1); SWI/Federal Council.

(continues)

Chart 4.5 (*continued*)

6 = **A. Moderately strong party opposition; nonpolarized opposition [3*2]**
CAN/Liberal; LEB/Chehab+coalition cabs; LEB/Helou+coalition cabs;
TUR/RPP+NTP+RPNP; TUR/Justice; URG/Colorado(Gestido,Pacheco).

B. Weak party opposition; has polarized mainstream elements [2*3]
FRN/de Gaulle+coalition cabs; UGA/UPC+Kabaka Yekka.

4 = **A. Weak party opposition; has polarized mainstream elements [2*2]**
BEL/ChrSoc+Socialist-1; CAN/PC(Diefenbaker); PHI/Nationalist(Garcia);
TUR/Democratic; ZAM/ZANU(Kaunda).

B. Minor party opposition; has antisystemic elements [1*4]
ISR/National Unity Coalition; KEN/KANU(Kenyatta-2);
MEX/PRI(Lopez Mateos); UGA/UPC(Obote); URG/Blanco+Colorado;
VEN/AD+COPEI+URD(Bentancourt-1).

3 = **Minor party opposition; has polarized mainstream elements [1*3]**
MEX/PRI(Diaz Ordaz).

2 = **Minor party opposition; nonpolarized orientation [1*2]**
FRG/Grand Coalition; KEN/KANU(Kenyatta-1).

1 = **Minor party opposition; does not challenge the regime [1*1]**
CZE/CPCS(Novotny-1); CZE/CPCS(Novotny-2); CZE/CPCS(Dubcek);
GDR/SED(Ulbricht); GHA/NLC Junta; POL/PZPR(Gomulka);
THI/Military Junta(Sarit); THI/Military Junta(Thanom+Praphat).

0 = **No opposition parties**
PRC/CCP(Mao+Liu); PRC/Cultural Rev coalition; CUB/PCC(Castro);
EGY/RCC(Nasser); GUI/PDG(Toure); IVR/PDCI(Houphouet-Boigny);
SOV/CPSU(Khrushchev-1); SOV/CPSU(Khrushchev-2);
SOV/CPSU(Brezhnev+Kosygin); SPN/Falange(Franco); TUN/Neo-
Destour(Bourguiba); TUR/CNU Junta(Gursel-2); YUG/LCY(Tito-1);
YUG/LCY(Tito-2).

---

at point 10, but they were from the same end of the political spectrum as their opponents. These include two Canadian Liberal Party minority cabinets (opposed by the similarly moderate conservative Progressive Party), as well as presidential regimes without congressional majorities in the United States under Eisenhower and in the Philippines under Marcos. Point 9 has opposition parties that were polarized vis-à-vis the regime, but the strength of these parties was undercut by their own fragmentation. Most were regimes opposed by multiple parties in the legislature (e.g., regimes in Chile, Costa Rica, Iceland, Israel, Norway, and Venezuela), while the Belgian and Japanese regimes faced single parties with structural factions. There are two groups of regimes at point 8. One of these (8A) has regimes opposed by a single strong opposition party, but it and the regime were ideologically similar; these cases included certain regimes in New Zealand, the Philippines, and the United States. The other group (8B) consists of weak party opposition with at least one major antisystemic party. These were regimes in which the Communist Party was a significant player in an albeit small opposition (e.g., Switzerland's broad consociational coalition, the initial Indian regimes, and France's last Gaullist cabinet after sweeping the 1968 election).[18] Finally, at point 6 there are another two sets of regimes. One (6A) had large, though fragmented, opposition, and they were not polarized vis-à-vis the ruling party or its coalition (e.g., certain cases for Canada, Lebanon, Turkey, and Uruguay). The other group (6B) consists of regimes with weak but polarized parties, and in it are two regimes with very broad coalitions in newly created political systems: the first Gaullist regime of the new French Fifth Republic and the Obote and Mutesa II regime immediately after Uganda's independence.

The lowest range of regimes, constituting the bottom third of Chart 4.5 (points 0 through 4), is mainly parties with low levels of strength (mostly minor parties), and it was mainly the intensity of their orientation vis-à-vis the regime that varied. The sole exception is group 4A, in which weak opposition (10 to 33 percent of seats) was polarized against the ruling coalition, for example, very broad coalitions in Belgium and Turkey or single-party cabinets with massive legislative majorities after dramatic election victories (Canada under Diefenbaker-1, Philippines under Garcia, Turkey under Mendares, and Zambia under Kaunda). At point 4B are regimes with minor opposition (fewer than 10 percent of seats) with antisystemic orientations. Most were in one-party systems (e.g., Mexico, Uganda, and Kenya) in which the ruling party had not fully consolidated power, and a small party actively resisted the regime's authoritarian tendencies. The other two regimes (in Israel and Venezuela) had small, antisystem parties challenging an emergency (domestic or foreign) grand coalition. Minor party opposition is also found at points 3 and 2, but the intensity of opposition was considerably diminished, as in Mexico, Kenya, and the Grand Coalition in Germany. The last two points on the scale are essentially one-party regimes. The regimes at point 1 consisted of auxiliary political groups that existed only at the benevolence of the regime and thus posed no major challenge to the regime. This occurred in several Eastern European Communist countries, as well as in military regimes that allowed some civilian input. The final group of regimes are in the strict one-party states of China, Cuba, Guinea, Ivory Coast, the Soviet Union, Spain, and Tunisia, as well as military regimes in Egypt and Turkey.

Measuring military and paramilitary opposition. This concerns the degree to which a regime encounters a politicized military and possibly paramilitary groups. Of course, not all regimes had politicized military establishments, and the initial coding task was to identify political systems with politically neutral military actors (and no paramilitary actors). Political neutrality was defined as not being involved in the politics surrounding the selection of leaders; in other words, the military's role did not extend beyond the pursuit of bureaucratic interests related to defense and foreign affairs. Along with broad country studies suggesting that the military was not politically active, political neutrality was confirmed by political histories documenting the absence of any recent military intervention and by reports that there were no political crises contributing to the military's politicization during the time. Similarly, there had to be equivalent evidence that there were no paramilitary actors, including armed elements of any political party. Note: military regimes were coded as having no military opposition (unless challenged by paramilitary actors); opposition from other military elements was, instead, captured by the intraparty opposition variable.

Where there was a politicized military, the primary indicator of the strength of this opposition was the extent of its de facto involvement in national political processes.[19] The basic distinction was between actors involved in the politics of an otherwise civilian regime and those who competed against civilian elites for dominance within the regime or political system. Two questions determined if the military limited its role to participating within a largely civilian framework: did the military occupy key positions within the civilian regime, giving it routine input into all major political issues, and/or was the military an active participant in the selection of the regime's civilian leadership (particularly the head of state) by virtue of its membership in elective bodies, by wielding veto power over the selection of certain leaders or parties, or by having engineered the violent coming to power of the regime?[20] The strongest form of military opposition (i.e., open competition with civilian actors) was indicated when one of three criteria was met: (1) during the regime's tenure there had been an attempted military coup, (2) either of the country's two preceding regimes had to have been a military regime, and/or (3) source accounts documented episodes of military threats to intervene against the civilian regime outside the bounds of established procedures.[21]

The other question about the strength of military opposition concerns the organizational coherence of the military, and it distinguishes between cohesive and factionalized patterns of military/paramilitary opposition. Fragmented opposition was indicated by the presence of factionalism within the military or its units and/or by the existence of separate paramilitary forces (often associated with a ruling party) independent of the military establishment. This factionalized/cohesive distinction was applied to the moderate level of military involvement in which it operated within civilian institutions.[22]

The intensity of military/paramilitary opposition at each of the above levels ranged from support for the regime and its policies, to opposition to those policies or even the regime itself, and even to a challenge of basic norms and structures of the civilian system.[23] The extreme, antisystemic orientation was inferred from source assertions that the military sought to dismantle civilian (democratic or authoritarian) political structures and establish a permanent military regime or a military veto power over civilian government leaders. Opposition to the current leadership and its policies (but without challenging the civilian political system itself) was inferred from accounts of (1) military leaders seeking greater influence within a ruling party, (2) military elements as part of a loose civilian coalition overthrowing a regime, and/or (3) broad policy differences between the regime and military/paramilitary elements.[24] The military was considered generally supportive of the regime if no evidence of this kind was found, although it was usually possible to find direct evidence for the overall commitment of the military to the regime's policy orientation.

The military opposition measure used in the analyses below is based on the combination of these strength and intensity dimensions. The measure for strength of military opposition is:

3 = military and/or paramilitary groups is/are active contender(s) for political dominance
2 = cohesive military is a major political actor in a civilian regime
1 = factionalized military or paramilitary groups is/are major political actor(s) in a civilian regime
0 = military is politically neutral

The scale for the intensity of military opposition is:

3 = the military and/or a paramilitary group have an antisystemic orientation
2 = the military and/or a paramilitary group opposes the current leadership and its policy program but does not challenge political system norms and structures
1 = the military and any paramilitary groups support the current regime and its overall policy program

The classification of the eighty-eight regimes by the military opposition measure is reported in Chart 4.6. Based on the multiplicative weighting of the four-point strength variable and three-point intensity variable, this composite military opposition scale has six points and values ranging from 0 to 9.

Chart 4.6 Classification and Ranking of Regimes by Military Opposition

---

9 = **Military establishment/paramilitary actors are contenders for power, have antisystem orientation [3*3]**
TUR/RPP+NTP+RPNP; VEN/AD+COPEI+URD(Bentancourt-1);
VEN/AD+COPEI+inds(Bentancourt-2).

6 = **Military establishment/paramilitary actors are contenders for power; oppose regime but do not have antisystemic orientation [3*2]**
PRC/Cultural Rev coalition; FRN/de Gaulle+coalition cabs;
UGA/UPC(Obote).

4 = **Politicized, cohesive military establishment in civilian dominant system; opposes regime's leadership [2*2]**
CZE/CPCS(Dubcek); SOV/CPSU(Khrushchev-2).

2 = **Politicized, factionalized military establishment and/or paramilitary actors in civilian dominant system; oppose regime's leadership [1*2]**
PRC/CCP(Mao and Liu); GHA/CPP(Nkrumah); LEB/Chehab+coalition
cabs; LEB/Helou+coalition cabs; TUR/JP+NP+NTP+RPNP; TUR/Justice;
UGA/UPC+Kabaka Yekka.

1 = **Politicized military establishment in civilian dominant system; supports regime's policy program [2*1 and 1*1]**
CUB/PCC(Castro); CZE/CPCS(Novotny-1); CZE/CPCS(Novotny-2);
EGY/RCC(Nasser); FRN/de Gaulle+Gaullist Ptys cabs; FRN/de
Gaulle+Gaullist cab; GDR/SED(Ulbricht); GUI/PDG(Toure);
POL/PZPR(Gomulka); SOV/CPSU(Khrushchev-1);
SOV/CPSU(Brezhnev+Kosygin); SPN/Falange(Franco); TUN/Neo-
Destour(Bourguiba); VEN/AD+inds(Leoni-1);
VEN/AD+URD+FND(Leoni-2); YUG/LCY(Tito-1); YUG/LCY(Tito-2).

0 = **Regimes with nonpoliticized military establishments and no paramilitary actors.**
BEL/ChrSoc+Liberal-1; BEL/ChrSoc+Socialist-1; BEL/ChrSoc+Liberal-2;
BEL/ChrSoc+Socialist-2; CAN/PC(Diefenbaker-1); CAN/PC-minority;
CAN/Liberal-minority; CAN/Liberal; CHL/PC+PL+PR(Alessandri);
CHL/PDC(Frei); COS/PUN(Echandi); COS/PLN(Orlich);
COS/UN(Trejos); FRG/CDU-CSU(Adenauer-1); FRG/CDU-CSU+FDP;
FRG/Grand Coalition; ICE/IP+SDP; IND/INC(Nehru);
IND/INC(Shastri,Gandhi-1); IND/INC(Gandhi-2); ISR/Mapai
coalition(Ben Gurion); ISR/Mapai coalition(Eskhol-1); ISR/National Unity
Coalition; ITA/DC-minority(ctr-right); ITA/DC-minority(centrist);
ITA/DC+PDSI+PRI(ctr-left);

(continues)

Chart 4.6 *(continued)*

ITA/DC+PSI+PDSI+PRI; IVR/PDCI(Houphouet-Boigny); JAP/LDP(Kishi faction); JAP/LDP(Ikeda faction); JAP/LDP(Sato faction); KEN/KANU(Kenyatta-1); KEN/KANU(Kenyatta-2); MEX/PRI(Lopez Mateos); MEX/(Diaz Ordaz); NZE/Labour; NZE/National; NOR/Labour-1; NOR/Labour-2(minority); NOR/Labour-3(minority); NOR/Lib+ChrPP+SP+Cons; PHI/Nationalist(Garcia); PHI/Liberal(Macapagal); PHI/Nationalist(Marcos); SWI/Federal Council; TUR/Democratic; USA/Republican(Eisenhower); USA/Democratic(Kennedy,Johnson-1); USA/Democratic(Johnson-2); URG/Blanco+Colorado; URG/Colorado(Gestido,Pacheco); ZAM/ZANU(Kaunda).

Military opposition variable is not applicable in the case of military regimes, which in this sample include:
GHA/NLC Junta; THI/Military Junta(Sarit); THI/Military Junta(Thanom+Praphat); TUR/CNU(Gursel-2).

Points 9 and 6 represent relatively high levels of opposition from the military or paramilitary actors. Three regimes in two countries (Turkey and Venezuela) had the maximum level of military opposition, in which the military was an active contender for power and had at least some elements with an antisystemic orientation. The military presence in Turkish and Venezuelan politics during the early 1960s was severe. The respective regimes under Inonu's Republican People's Party and Bentancourt's Democratic Action Party were successors to military regimes, and both lived with the constant threat of military intervention (including several abortive coups) on issues concerning the makeup of the civilian coalition as well as its relations with the military. At point 6 are also regimes in which the military was a contender for power, but here the evidence was that the military sought to change the leadership and its policies without questioning the civilian political order—for example, Lin Biao's wing of the Chinese military sought to dominate the Communist system (as did radical forces of the Red Guards), the French military sought to reverse the Algerian policy of de Gaulle's new Fifth Republic, and Uganda's Idi Amin confronted Obote on policy issues but as of late 1968 had not ended his overall support for the regime he helped put in power.

The remainder of the scale involves less severe levels of military opposition. At points 4 and 2 are regimes in which the military participated in processes of the civilian regime but did not compete with civilian elites and was not antisystemic in orientation. The difference between the regimes at these two points lies in the extent to which the military was factionalized. Cohesive militaries in Czechoslovakia and the Soviet Union were, respectively, part of the growing coalition of opponents to the reformist Dubcek and the later Khrushchev regimes (point 4). Factionalized militaries, in which some portions of the military were opposed to the regime and others supported it, include regimes in China under Mao and Lin, in Turkey after the antimilitary Justice Party was allowed to take power, and in Uganda under the tense coalition between Obote's United People's Congress and Mutesa II's Kabaka Yekka (point 2). At point 1 are regimes in which the politically active military supported the regime (indeed was probably a key support group); this included militaries in then stable and cohesive authoritarian regimes such as Castro's Cuba, Franco's Spain, and Tito's Yugoslavia, along with certain democratic regimes where a previously interventionist, but not yet entirely neutral, military had accepted civilian rule (the later Venezuelan and French regimes). At the bottom of the scale (point 0) are the regimes with nonpoliticized (or politically insignificant) military establishments; most regimes in the CREON sample of countries fell into this category.

Measuring regionally based opposition. This concerns opposition to the regime from political actors who represent the interests of, and have their primary base of political power in, the nation's geographic subregions (e.g., provinces, republics, and states). The strength of regional opposition was defined in terms of the general relationship (formal or de facto) between the national government and regional political actors. The coding of this variable was based on two general questions. First, did the regional leadership exert control over important (though not all) aspects of politics in the region without the interference of the national regime? This was indicated by autonomous regional institutions (executive and legislature) with substantial control of regional public policy, and by the election of regional leaders in local governmental and party elections that were held independent of the central government. Second, were regional actors represented in the regime or other national institutions? One indication of this was regime positions that had formal regional designations, as indicated by their official titles or party/factional labels. These positions could be (1) regional party secretaries in the central committee or politburo of a one-party regime, (2) regional party leaders (or their factions) as members of a cabinet or as key figures in the ruling party or the national legislature, and/or (3) a branch of the legislature (e.g., a senate) or some other national body whose membership was regionally based. The other way regional positions at the national level were evident was when country sources documented the informal allocation of government positions by region or ethnic group, even if official government policy disavowed such political necessity (e.g., as was done in certain Middle East and African regimes).

If country sources indicated negative answers to both questions, then the system was coded a unitary system, in which political power was fully centralized with no regionally organized actors. An affirmative answer to only the second question indicated a quasi-federal system with representation of regional interests at the national level in the parliament or the ruling party of an otherwise centralized political system. Affirmative answers to both questions pointed to either a federal or confederal system, with the difference concerning the extent of balance between the two arenas. Distinguishing between the two required judgments about just how much power was wielded by regional governments and their representatives at the national level. Whereas federal systems have a division, or sharing, of authority between national and regional governments, the case of confederal systems is more clear-cut. Not only do regional governments have near complete autonomy, but at the national level regional actors have a de facto veto power over other national actors within the regime.

Judging the intensity of regional opposition required a look at the political orientation of regional leaders within the national government and, where regions had political autonomy, the parties in control of provincial governments. Antisystemic opposition by regional leaders was operationalized in two ways: these leaders sought to have their region withdraw from the nation or to restructure its borders with other provinces and/or were from an ideologically antisystemic national party seeking to transform the overall political system. Less extreme regional opposition demanded the reform of certain relationships between central and regional authorities, such as calls for greater regional autonomy (e.g., language use or states rights), although in a way that did not question the nation's territorial integrity. Still milder opposition occurred when regional leaders opposed the regime on largely national, nonfederal matters. In federal systems this occurred when a regional government was controlled by another mainstream national party, while in quasi-federal systems this happened when regional leaders were from a different political party/group or an opposing wing or faction of the ruling party/group.

The measure for regionally based opposition is based on the combination of the strength and intensity dimensions. The strength measure ranges from highly decentralized to highly centralized systems, with the values as follows:

3 = confederal arrangements
2 = federal arrangements
1 = quasi-federal arrangements
0 = unitary system

The scale for the intensity measure consists of four points:

4 = regional actor(s) has antisystemic orientation
3 = regional actor(s) seeks reforms in national-regional arrangements without challenging basic political system norms and structures
2 = regional opposition group(s) opposes the current regime and its policy program, but does not question basic national-regional arrangements
1 = regional leaders are all supportive of the regime

Chart 4.7 reports the distribution of the sample of eighty-eight regimes across the composite regional opposition scale. The multiplicative weighting of the strength and intensity dimensions resulted in an eight-point scale ranging from unitary systems (point 0) to confederal regimes with elements that were antisystemic (point 12). In contrast to the other opposition measures, the distribution of regimes here is incomplete. There were no regimes with opposition operating in confederal arrangements that challenged basic federal arrangements, either from an antisystemic or a reformist orientation (points 12 and 9).

The highest level of regional opposition was found, instead, in three regimes in federal systems with antisystemic orientations (point 8). During the 1960s, federal systems in Uganda and India experienced major internal political crises due to the control of regional governments by antisystemic parties. The first years of Ugandan independence were dominated by the struggle between the Bugandan leadership (under Mutesa II) demanding confederal arrangements and Obote's United People's Congress insisting on unitary structures; in other words, both groups rejected the existing federal arrangements. The crises in India were due to the ruling Indian National Congress's alarm over the election of antisystemic parties to head certain state governments. During the Nehru regime, the Communist Party took power in the state of Karela, while during Indira Gandhi's regime a revived Communist Party dominated a new coalition government in Karela and a Tamil nationalist party came to power in Madras. Although not the highest level of regional opposition, these situations were portrayed by the Ugandan and Indian sources as major crises for all three regimes.

Points 3, 4, and 6 fall within the middle range of regional opposition and include five groups of regimes, and in contrast to the higher levels of regional oppositions, there is a substantial number of cases (twenty-one) at this level. There are two groups of regimes at point 6. The first (6A) consists of the sample's only polities with confederal arrangements (Switzerland and Lebanon), and the opposition in their regimes was relatively mild and limited to mainly national issues. The other group here (6B) consists of regimes in federal systems in which regional leaders demanded reform of federal arrangements, as in the United States (southern governors and senators demanding states' rights) and in Canada (demands for greater

Chart 4.7   Classification and Ranking of Regimes by Regionally Based Opposition

12 =   Confederal arrangements; has regional actors with antisystemic orientation [3*4]
no cases.

8 =   Federal arrangements; has regional actors with antisystemic orientation [2*4]
IND/INC(Nehru-1); IND/INC(Gandhi-2); UGA/UPC+Kabaka Yekka.

6 =   A. Confederal arrangements; regional actors oppose regime but not federal arrangemnts [3*2]
LEB/Chehab+coalition cabs; LEB/Helou+coalition cabs; SWI/Federal Council.

B. Federal arrangements; has regional actors seeking reform in federal arrangements [2*3]
CAN/PC(Diefenbaker); CAN/Liberal(minority); CAN/Liberal; PRC/Cultural Rev coalition; USA/Republican(Eisenhower); USA/Democratic(Kennedy,Johnson-1); USA/Democratic(Johnson-2).

4 =   A. Quasi-federal arrangements; regional actors have antisystemic orientation [1*4]
BEL/ChrSoc+Socialist-2; CZE/CPCS(Dubcek).

B. Federal arrangements; regional actors oppose regime but not federal arrangements [2*2]
CAN/PC(minority); FRG/CDU-CSU(Adenauer); FRG/CDU-CSU+FDP; FRG/Grand Coalition.

3 =   A. Quasi-federal arrangemnts; regional actors seek reform of federal arrangments [1*3]
BEL/ChrSoc+Liberal-1; BEL/ChrSoc+Socialist-1; BEL/ChrSoc+Liberal-2; CZE/CPCS(Novotny-2); YUG/LCY(Tito-2).

B. Confederal arrangements; regional actors do not challenge regime or its policies [3*1]
no cases.

2 =   A. Federal arrangements; regional actors do not challenge regime or its policies [2*1]
IND/INC(Shastri,Gandhi-1); MEX/PRI(Lopez Mateos); MEX/(Diaz Ordaz); VEN/AD+COPEI+URD(Bentancourt-1); VEN/AD+COPEI+inds(Bentancourt-2); VEN/AD+inds(Leoni-1); VEN/AD+URD+FND(Leoni-2).

(continues)

Chart 4.7 (*continued*)

B. Quasi-federal arrangements; regional actors oppose regime but not federal arrangements [1*2]
no cases.

1 = Quasi-federal arrangements; regional actors do not challenge regime or its policies [1*/1]
PRC/CCP(Mao+Liu); CZE/CPCS(Novotny-1); GHA/NLC Junta;
IVR/PDCI(Houphouet-Boigny); KEN/KANU(Kenyatta-1);
KEN/KANU(Kenyatta-2); SOV/CPSU(Khrushchev-1);
SOV/CPSU(Khrushchev-2); SOV/CPSU(Brezhnev+Kosygin);
YUG/LCY(Tito-1); ZAM/ZANU(Kaunda).

0 = Unitary arrangements
CHL/PC+PL+PR(Alessandri); CHL/PDC(Frei); COS/PUN(Echandi);
COS/PLN(Orlich); COS/UN(Trejos); CUB/PCC(Castro);
EGY:RCC(Nasser); FRN/de Gaulle+coalition cabs; FRN/de Gaulle+Gaulist
Ptys cabs; FRN/de Gaulle+Gaullist cabs; GDR/SED(Ulbricht);
GHA/CPP(Nkrumah); GUI/PDG(Toure); ICE/IP+SDP; ISR/Mapai coalition(Ben Gurion); ISR/Mapai coalition(Eskhol-1); ISR/National Unity
Coalition; ITA/DC-minority(ctr-right); ITA/DC-minority(centrist);
ITA/DC+PDSI+PRI-minority(ctr-left); ITA/DC+PSI+PDSI+PRI;
JAP/LDP(Kishi faction); JAP/LDP(Ikeda faction); JAP/LDP(Sato faction);
NZE/Labour; NZE/National; NOR/Labour-1; NOR/Labour-2(minority);
NOR/Labour-3(minority); NOR/Lib+ChrPP+SP+Cons;
PHI/Nationalist(Garcia); PHI/Liberal(Macapagal);
PHI/Nationalist(Marcos); POL/PZPR(Gomulka); SPN/Falange(Franco);
THI/Military Junta(Sarit); THI/Military Junta(Thanom+Praphat);
TUN/Neo-Destour(Bourguiba); TUR/Democratic; TUR/CNU(Gursel-2);
TUR/RPP+NTP+RPNP; TUR/JP+NP+NTP+RPNP; TUR/Justice;
UGA/UPC(Obote); URG/Blanco+Colorado;
URG/Colorado(Gestido,Pacheco).

French autonomy in Quebec by its Union Nationale government). The normally quasi-federal Chinese polity also fits here during the Cultural Revolution, when provincial leaders attained considerable autonomy to the point that the provinces had different governments (often coalitions) depending on the local fortunes of the party, military, and Red Guards. At point 4A are two quasi-federal systems that saw the rise of antisystemic challenges by the end of the decade: in Belgium it was the election of several regional parties to the national parliament, while in Czechoslovakia it was Slovak demands for the dismantling of the unitary system during part of the Prague Spring. Also at this level (4B) is routine regionally based opposition in federal systems, where national opposition parties were in control of state/provincial governments (e.g., West German regimes in which Christian Democratic regimes confronted some Laender governments led by the Social Democrats). The final group in the moderate range (point 3) are quasi-federal systems in which national elites were increasingly concerned with regional and federal issues (e.g., regimes in Belgium, Czechoslovakia, and Yugoslavia).

The regimes at the lowest three points of Chart 4.7 had weak regional opposition. At point 2A, India, Mexico, and Venezuela were all federal systems in which the regime's ruling party had control of all state governments, without any indication by sources of any opposition to the regime or its policy program. The situation at point 1 is similar. These are quasi-federal systems in a variety of mainly authoritarian regimes where sources did not identify regional leaders openly opposed to the regime. As with the single-party state governments at point 2, the representation of regional concerns remained issue specific and challenged neither the regime nor essential federal structures (e.g., cohesive regimes in Yugoslavia, the Soviet Union, and China). The final group consists of regimes in unitary systems and included regimes with no autonomous regional actors (e.g., Japan, New Zealand, and Norway) or in which such political phenomena were entirely repressed or ignored and/or had no institutional outlet (e.g., Turkey, Guinea, and France). A little more than half of the CREON regimes had unitary regimes.

Grouping Regimes by Contextual Political Conditions

The final component of the framework (besides foreign policy behavior, which is operationalized in Chapter 5) concerns aspects of the broader political environment that condition if, and how, leaders respond to political opposition. Two contextual conditions are developed here: political system structure and regime vulnerability. Each has two components: the former is based on political accountability and institutionalization and the latter on uncertainty within the regime's leadership and competitiveness in the wider political system. Measures of political system structure and regime vulnerability are presented in this section, along with the distribution of regimes in the sample used.

Measuring political system structure. This concerns the formal structures that link a regime to the wider political system (accountability) and the degree to which major political actors adhere to these norms, as well as to ones internal to the regime (institutionalization). Accountability is measured as a simple dichotomy grouping regimes as democratic and nondemocratic. A political system was classified as democratic if, according to country sources, its regime was publicly elected through reasonably open procedures ensuring the rights of the opposition to contest the ruling party's policies and ultimately its hold on office. This is, no doubt, a rather simple measure, but keep in mind two things. First, it gets at the essential concern of accountability: that the regime and other institutional actors are subject to pressures from the wider polity and that such opponents cannot be widely suppressed. Second, as will be clear in a moment, this dichotomy can be embellished further by incorporating some sense of how well these structural arrangements are institutionalized.

The classification of regimes by political institutionalization was based on two criteria as documented by country sources: first, the pattern of regime changes prior to its coming to power and, second, the presence of major antisystemic actors in the current political system. Regimes were classified at three levels. A well-institutionalized regime satisfied two conditions: its political system had not experienced a political revolution since before World War II, and yet had at least two "regular" regime changes involving separate political groups;[25] and there were no major antisystemic actors operating within the political system.[26] Moderate institutionalization was marked by the following exceptions to the above criteria: there had been a political revolution since World War II and the same basic group (or its immediate successor) that created the political system remained in power, or there were important antisystemic actors in the political system environment of the current regime. Noninstitutionalized regimes met neither criteria: they were ruled by a political group that came to power via a political revolution, thus meaning that a previously antisystemic group now dominated a transformed and restructured political system.[27] Note that both democratic and authoritarian systems could be considered highly institutionalized, even if the latter had not been subject to open elections. The assumption here is that we are looking at norms and structures regulating the behavior of organized actors operating in the institutions of the national political system, in other words, the regime and its immediate organized opposition within the party, the legislature, the military, and/or regional governments. The behavior of these actors may be well institutionalized, even if groups or the bulk of the mass public and other actors are excluded from the system and even though that system might collapse in the long term.[28]

The distribution of the sample of eighty-eight regimes for the composite political structure variables is reported in Chart 4.8. The combination of the accountability (democratic = 2; authoritarian = 1) and institutionalization (high = 3; moderate = 2; low = 1) measures resulted in six groups of regimes across a five-point scale with values ranging from 1 to 6. At the high end of the scale (point 6) are well-institutionalized democracies consisting mainly of those Western polities that predated (even in exile) World War II, for example, regimes in Belgium, Canada, Iceland, New Zealand,

Chart 4.8   Classification of Regimes According to Political System Structure

6 = **Regimes in well-institutionalized democratic political systems [2*3]**
BEL/ChrSoc+Liberal-1; BEL/ChrSoc+Socialist-2; BEL/ChrSoc+Liberal-2;
BEL/ChrSoc+Socialist-2; CAN/PC(Diefenbaker); CAN/PC(minority);
CAN/Liberal(minority); CAN/Liberal; FRG/Grand Coalition; ICE/IP+SDP;
IND/INC(Nehru); IND/INC(Shastri,Gandhi-1); IND/INC(Gandhi-2);
ISR/Mapai coalition(Ben Gurion); ISR/Mapai coalition(Eskhol-1);
ISR/National Unity Coalition; NZE/Labour; NZE/National; NOR/Labour-
1; NOR/Labour-2(minority); NOR/Labour-3(minority);
NOR/Lib+ChrPP+SP+Cons; PHI/Nationalist(Garcia);
PHI/Liberal(Macapagal); PHI/Nationalist(Marcos); SWI/Federal Council;
USA/Republican(Eisenhower); USA/Democratic(Kennedy,Johnson-1);
USA/Democratic(Johnson-2); URG/Blanco+Colorado;
URG/Colorado(Gestido,Pacheco).

4 = **Regimes in moderately institutionalized democratic political systems
[2*2]**
CHL/PC+PL+PR(Alessandri); CHL/PDC(Frei); COS/PUN(Echandi);
COS/PLN(Orlich); COS/UN(Trejos); FRN/de Gaulle+Gaullist Ptys cab;
FRN/de Gaulle+Gaullist Pty cabs; FRG/CDU-CSU(Adenauer); FRG/CDU-
CSU+FDP; ITA/DC-minority(ctr-right); ITA/DC-minority(centrist);
ITA/DC+PDSI+PRI-minority(ctr-left);   ITA/DC+PSI+PDSI+PRI;
JAP/LDP(Kishi faction); JAP/LDP(Ikeda faction); JAP/LDP(Sato faction);
LEB/Chehab+coalition cabs; LEB/Helou+coalition cabs; MEX/PRI(Lopez
Mateos); MEX/(Diaz Ordaz); TUR/Justice; VEN/AD+inds(Leoni-1);
VEN/AD+URD+FND(Leoni-2).

3 = **Regimes in well-institutionalized authoritarian political systems [1*3]**
SOV/CPSU(Brezhnev+Kosygin); THI/Military Junta(Sarit);
THI/Military Junta(Thanom+Praphat).

2 = **A. Regimes in moderately institutionalized authoritarian political sys-
tems [1*2]**
PRC/CCP(Mao+Liu); CZE/CPCS(Novotny-2); CZE/CPCS(Dubcek);
SOV/CPSU(Khrushchev-1); SOV/CPSU(Khrushchev-2);
SPN/Falange(Franco); TUN/Neo-Destour(Bourguiba); YUG/LCY(Tito-1);
YUG/LCY(Tito-2).

B. Regimes in noninstitutionalized democratic political systems [2*1]
FRN/de Gaulle+coalition cabs; GHA/CPP(Nkrumah);
KEN/KANU(Kenyatta-1); KEN/KANU(Kenyatta-2); TUR/Democratic;
TUR/JP+RPP; TUR/RPP+NTP+RPNP;

(continues)

Chart 4.8   *(continued)*

> TUR/JP+NP+NTP+RPNP; UGA/UPC+Kabaka Yekka;
> VEN/AD+COPEI+URD(Bentancourt-1);
>   VEN/AD+COPEI+ind(Bentancourt-2);
> ZAM/ZANU(Kaunda).

1 = **Regimes in noninstitutionalized authoritarian political systems [1*1]**
PRC/Cultural Rev coalition; CUB/PCC(Castro); CZE/CPCS(Novotny-1);
EGY/RCC(Nasser); GDR/SED(Ulbricht); GHA/NLC Junta;
GUI/PDG(Toure); IVR/PDCI(Houphouet-Boigny); POL/PZPR(Gomulka);
TUR/CNU(Gursel-2); UGA/UPC(Obote).

Norway, Switzerland, and the United States (West Germany qualified by the end of the 1960s). The Third World countries of India, Israel, the Philippines, and Uruguay were also considered to have had established democratic norms and structures, even though they (except for Uruguay) were not fully independent until the late 1940s. By the 1960s, their political systems could be considered institutionalized, because long before independence the regime's ruling group was well established, in terms of its own leadership and organization and its growing role in governing the country.[29]

Regimes in moderately well-established democracies are at point 4. Several are democracies that in the 1960s were still emerging from postwar transformations in which fascist regimes were dismantled: West Germany and Japan, still under essentially the original Christian Democratic and Liberal Democratic leadership (neither had yet had two significant changes), as well as Italy, with its significant antisystemic Communist Party and various extreme rightwing parties. France's Fifth Republic, despite orderly elections, had not experienced a major regime change given that its second and third regimes still operated under the personal tutelage of de Gaulle. Several Third World democracies were also included in this group. Chile, despite having had a long history of democratic rule, was considered only moderately institutionalized because of the presence of the antisystemic Communist Party on the left and emerging extremist elements on the right. Two other regimes (Leoni in Venezuela and Demirel in Turkey) were the elected successors to the original democratic regimes that evicted the military from office, while the Costa Rican and Lebanese regimes followed antisystemic disruptions. Mexico, with its continuously ruling PRI, was not counted as a fully institutionalized system because its democratic system had still not had a major exchange of power between separate political actors, a judgment reinforced by the regime's widespread manipulations of national elections and the presence of small dissenting parties.

At point 3 are regimes in well-institutionalized authoritarian systems, including regimes in political systems that predated World War II and had experienced at least two leadership changes involving different factions or wings of the ruling party. The emergence of the Brezhnev regime in the Soviet Union was the second orderly succession for its by then well-established Communist regime. Thailand's military polity dated back to a 1932 military revolution. While the first regime considered here, under General Sarit, came to power by a coup, sources consistently pointed out that this was a regular exchange of power between mainstream elite factions (or "khanas") of the post-1932 political establishment. The exchange of power from Sarit to his protégés, Thanom and Praphat, was quite routine by the standards of the restrictive bounds of Thai military politics.

Two groups of regimes are at point 2 of Chart 4.8. The first group (2A) is composed of moderately institutionalized regimes in authoritarian systems. Although some had ruling parties that were well established by the mid-1940s, they were still ruled by essentially the same political leadership. Some of the cases were situations of continued dominance by the same pre-1945 predominant leader: Tito in Yugoslavia, Bourguiba in Tunisia, and Franco in Spain. Regimes in China (Mao and Liu), the Soviet Union (Khrushchev), and Czechoslovakia (Novotny-2 and Dubcek), in contrast, had just experienced their first regular exchange of power between contending factions (including a predominant leader's demise) of the ruling party. In all cases, this represented an initial shift away from a single predominant leader and toward a more collective, routinized party leadership. The other group here (2B) is made up of regimes in noninstitutionalized democracies. The Turkish and Venezuelan regimes were the immediate successors to military regimes and continued to face threats of military intervention, widespread instability, and/or frequent use of repressive measures. The first de Gaulle regime came to power by what was, in effect, a political revolution, and it too continued to face antisystemic actors on the extreme left and right (including some military factions). The remaining regimes—those in Ghana, Kenya, and Zambia—were ruled by newly established parties in elections hastily arranged just prior to independence from Great Britain, and especially Ghana's Nkrumah increasingly placed restrictions on opposition groups.

The final group of regimes (point 1) are authoritarian regimes with a minimal level of institutionalization; in other words, all were nonelected ruling parties that came to power after World War II as a result of various kinds of revolutions. These included political revolutions (Cuba/Castro and Egypt/Nasser), antidemocratic military coups (Ghana/National Liberation Council, Turkey/the Gursel junta, and Uganda/Obote's United People's Congress), military intervention by the Soviet Union (Czechoslovakia/

Novotny-1 and Poland/Gomulka), and the seizure of power immediately after independence (Ivory Coast/Houphouet-Boigny and Guinea/Toure). Although these had minimal levels of the kinds of political opposition groups discussed above, these regimes had equally little to show in the way of institutionalized bases of support or political norms.

Measuring regime vulnerability. This concept tries to capture a general sense of the possibility that a regime will be removed from power, reflective of the interaction of two levels of political activity: uncertainty among leaders of the regime and overall political system competitiveness. The operationalization of political uncertainty was based on indications from source accounts of overt competition within the regime for control. The question was were there actors within the regime (e.g., factions, cliques, individuals) actively seeking to alter the basic political makeup of the current leadership? Two kinds of evidence were critical: documented episodes of key leaders maneuvering to overthrow other leaders, and/or more general discussions of extreme distrust among members and/or ongoing infighting such that it could be concluded that any power sharing was tenuous at best. Political uncertainty was measured at three levels, depending on the scope of conflict within the regime. High political uncertainty was marked by a direct and immediate threat to the regime's overall leadership. Specifically, at least one member of the regime actively worked for the removal of the head of state or, in the case of more fragmented regimes, the dominant faction or party. Moderate political uncertainty referred to situations of intense infighting "below" the regime's dominant actor, such that the head of state or dominant faction or party was not directly challenged. Indicators of these situations were ongoing competition for cabinet ministries and party posts by other leaders and factions; in minority governments this took the form of leaders having to maintain the confidence of parliamentary supporters. Regimes with low political uncertainty did not have conflicts of these kinds, and source materials were normally able to confirm explicitly that the allocation of power among their members was well defined and stable. Thus, although important debates occurred among these leaders, these conflicts in no way questioned the political makeup of the regime.

The operationalization of political system competitiveness was based on the documented record of regime changes preceding the current regime, specifically the frequency and types of regime changes prior to its coming to power and since 1945 or the country's independence. It, too, was measured at three levels. A highly competitive system was one with a prior history of exchanges of power between separate political parties or other groups such as the military—and these actors continued to be active players during the current regime.[30] In moderately competitive systems (both democratic and authoritarian) the range of competition had been contained to a single party or group; namely, the same party or coalition had been in power for an extended period of time, but there had been significant power shifts between different factions or wings of the party.[31] There also had to be clear indication that these opposing wings and factions continued to exist. Noncompetitive conditions were ones in which the current leadership (a predominant leader or faction) had been continuously in power since the end of World War II. These were usually postindependence or postrevolutionary situations in which the new regime had decimated the opposition so that it was politically irrelevant.

The distribution of regimes across the vulnerability measure is reported in Chart 4.9. The measure was derived from combining the measures of uncertainty (high =3; moderate = 2; low = 1) and competitiveness (high = 3; moderate = 2; low =1) by multiplicative weighting, which resulted in nine groups of regimes across a six-point scale with values ranging from 1 to 9. At point 9 are several regimes in the extreme situation of having immediate internal threats and ongoing strong competition from actors outside the regime. As a result of national elections, Canada's second Diefenbaker regime had lost a large parliamentary majority, which in turn provoked an open internal revolt against the party's previously predominant leader. In Turkey, the postmilitary coalition (following a brief coalition between the intensely antagonistic Justice Party and Republican People's Party) was on the verge of collapse and continuously threatened by military intervention. The extreme vulnerability of Uganda's first regime reflected, in contrast to most African postindependence regimes, the extended process by which Obote sought to centralize and consolidate national power, first by an electoral alliance with Mutesa II and then later by purging him from the subsequent coalition regime.

The two groups of regimes at point 6 were also highly vulnerable regimes in that they ranked high on one of its dimensions and moderate on the other. The group with high uncertainty and moderate competitiveness (point 6A) consists of regimes with system-dominant parties or coalitions that were themselves internally fragmented. Among the regimes listed, these divisions had resulted from a leadership crisis involving efforts to remove a politically discredited leader (e.g., the Gandhi, Khrushchev, and Adenauer regimes), zero-sum strife between contending elements of Communist parties in China (during the Cultural Revolution) and Czechoslovakia (under Dubcek), and the continuous jockeying within Italy's minority DC-led cabinets as they struggled to find a formula for a majority government. The other group (point 6B) consists of regimes with moderate internal uncertainty in highly competitive political systems. The leadership competition in these regimes did not directly challenge the dominant leader or faction, but past experience suggested the very real possibility of an alternative group coming to power. This frequently occurred in competitive Latin American presidential systems (e.g., those of Chile,

Chart 4.9   Classification and Ranking of Regimes by Vulnerability

9 = **Regimes with high internal uncertainty in highly competitive political systems [3*3]**
CAN/PC(minority); TUR/RPP+NTP+RPNP; UGA/UPC+Kabaka Yekka.

6 = **A. Regimes with high internal uncertainty in moderately competitive political systems [3*2]**
PRC/Cultural Rev cCoalition; CZE/CPCS(Dubcek); FRG/CDU-CSU+FDP; IND/INC(Gandhi-2); ITA/DC-minority(ctr-right); ITA/DC-minority(centrist); ITA/DC+PDSI+PRI(ctr-right); ITA/DC+PSI+PDSI+PRI; SOV/CPSU(Khrushchev-2).

B. Regimes with moderate internal uncertainty in highly competitive systems [2*3]
CAN/Liberal(minority); CHL/PC+PL+PR(Alessandri); CHL/PDC(Frei); COS/PUN(Echandi); FRN/de Gaulle+coalition cabs; NOR/Labour-2(minority); TUR/JP+NP+NTP+RPNP; VEN/AD+COPEI+URD(Bentancourt-1); VEN/AD+COPEI+inds(Bentancourt-2); VEN:AD+inds(Leoni-1); VEN:AD+URD+FND(Leoni-2).

4 = **Regimes with moderate internal uncertainty in moderately competitive systems [2*2]**
PRC/CCP(Mao+Liu); CZE/CPCS(Novotny-2); GHA/NLC Junta; ISR/Mapai coalition(Ben Gurion); JAP/LDP(Kishi faction); JAP/LDP(Ikeda faction); JAP/LDP(Sato faction); LEB/Chehab+coalition cabs; LEB/Helou+coalition cabs; NOR/Labour-2(minority); SOV/CPSU(Brezhnev+Kosygin).

3 = **A. Regimes with high internal uncertainty in noncompetitive systems [3*1]**
no cases.

B. Regimes with low internal uncertainty in highly competitive systems [1*3]
BEL/ChrSoc+Liberal-1; BEL/ChrSoc+Socialist-1; BEL/ChrSoc+Liberal-2; BEL/ChrSoc+Socialist-2; CAN/PC(Diefenbaker); CAN/Liberal; COS/PLN(Orlich); COS/UN(Trejos); FRN/de Gaulle+Gaullist Ptys cabs; FRN/de Gaulle+Gaullist cabs; FRG/Grand Coalition; ICE/IP+SDP; NZE/Labour; NZE/National; NOR/Lib+ChrPP+SP+Cons; PHI/Nationalist(Garcia); PHI/Liberal(Macapagal); PHI/Nationalist(Marcos); TUR/CNU(Gursel-2); TUR/Justice; UGA/UPC(Obote); USA/Republican(Eisenhower); USA/Democratic(Kennedy,Johnson-1); USA/Democratic(Johnson-2) URG:Colorado(Gestido,Pacheco).

(continues)

Chart 4.9   (*continued*)

2 = A. **Regimes with moderate internal uncertainty in noncompetitive systems [2*1]**
KEN/KANU(Kenyatta-1); YUG/LCY(Tito-2).

B. **Regimes with low internal uncertainty in moderately competitive systems [1*2]**
CZE/CPCS(Novotny-1); FRG/CDU-CSU(Adenauer);
GHA/CPP(Nkrumah); IND/INC(Nehru); IND/INC(Shastri,Gandhi-1);
ISR/Mapai coalition(Eskhol-1); ISR/National Unity Coalition;
MEX/PRI(Lopez Mateos); MEX/PRI(Diaz Ordaz); NOR/Labour-1;
POL/PZPR(Gomulka); SOV/CPSU(Khrushchev-1); SWI/Federal Council;
THI/Military Junta(Sarit); THI/Military Junta(Thanom+Praphat);
TUR/Democratic Pty; URG/Blanco+Colorado.

1 = **Regimes with low internal uncertainty in noncompetitive systems [1*1]**
CUB/PCC(Castro); EGY/RCC(Nasser); GDR/SED(Ulbricht);
GUI/PDG(Toure); IVR/PDCI(Houphouet-Boigny); KEN/KANU(Kenyatta-2); SPN/Falange(Franco); TUN/Neo-Destour(Bourguiba); YUG/LCY(Tito-1); ZAM/ZANU(Kaunda).

Costa Rica, and Venezuela), where an institutionally protected president survived an intense electoral contest only to see the collapse of his power with the defection of coalition partners and/or loss of supporters in the congress.

Points 4 and 3 represent the moderate range of regime vulnerability. The group at point 4 has moderate levels of both internal uncertainty and system competitiveness. Included here were some standard situations: single-party regimes with ongoing factional struggles for certain leadership positions that did not threaten the head of state or the coalition's overall political makeup. The authoritarian regimes in China under Mao and Liu and the Soviet Union under the new Brezhnev-Kosygin leadership were cases in which the previously predominant leader had not yet been replaced with a stable collective leadership. Among the democratic polities (Japan, Lebanon, and the majority cabinet in Italy), there was ongoing competition among factions and parties (e.g., cabinet shakeups), but it did not threaten the regime's basic composition. Turning to point 3, only one of the two possible configurations (point 3B) has any cases in the sample: regimes with low internal uncertainty in highly competitive systems. This group, which has the largest number of regimes of any in Chart 4.9, consisted of stable coalitions and cohesive single-party regimes in otherwise highly competitive political systems. Included here were regimes in Belgium, Costa Rica, France, West Germany, Iceland, New Zealand, Norway, the Philippines, the United States, and Uruguay, as well as the new democracies of Venezuela and Turkey that by the mid-1960s had survived for several years without a return to military rule. There was one authoritarian regime in this group: the second Turkish military junta resulting from General Gursel's suppression of a coup by hardline dissident officers, which stabilized the junta's internal situation, as it allowed civilian parties to resume political activity.

At the low end of the scale are three groups of regimes that were not very vulnerable, each having at most moderate levels of uncertainty within the regime or competitiveness outside of it, or no threats at all. At point 2A, there were two regimes in noncompetitive polities: the first Kenyatta regime and the second Tito regime. Each had growing policy splits within the regime, but in neither case was the authority of the predominant leader questioned. Far more regimes were found in the group at point 2B. These were cases with system-dominant parties that had, at least during the current regime, achieved some stability with the emergence of a strong leader or consensual power-sharing arrangement. Most were single-party regimes with leaders who had consolidated power (e.g., the initial regimes under Czechoslovakia's Novotny, the Soviet Union's Khrushchev, Ghana's Nkrumah, West Germany's Adenauer, Norway's Gerhardsen as well as those for India's Nehru, Shastri, and Gandhi [initially], Turkey's Mendares, and both Mexican presidents during the decade), although a few cases were stable coalitions in Uruguay, Switzerland, and Israel after Ben Gurion. Finally, at point 1, there are the relatively few regimes that appeared to be free of political pressure, although recall from Chart 4.8 that most were completely lacking in any kind of institutionalization. These were mainly cases with single predominant leaders who had maintained cohesion within the regime, and since independence or the revolution had been able to suppress or co-opt any organized opposition outside the regime (e.g., leaders in Cuba, Egypt, East Germany, Guinea, Ivory Coast, Kenya, Spain, Tunisia, Yugoslavia, and Zambia).

Summary: A Look at Combined Levels of Opposition

By way of a final look at the data explained in this chapter, Chart 4.10 summarizes the data in terms of the ranking of regimes by their "total" opposition as defined by the combination of the measures of regime fragmentation and intraparty, political party, military, and regional opposition. Combining these opposition scores was complicated by the fact that the scales for the

Chart 4.10 Summary of Opposition Data for Political Regimes

	Fragmentation	Intra-Party	Opposing Parties	Military Actors	Regional Actors
13 IND/INC(Gandhi-2)	***	***	***	*	***
12 UGA/UPC+Kebaka Yekka	**	***	**	**	***
11 PRC/Cultural Rev coalition	**	***	*	***	**
11 CZE/CPCS(Dubcek)	***	***	*	**	**
11 ITA/DC-minority(ctr-right)	***	***	***	*	*
11 ITA/DC-minority(centrist)	***	***	***	*	*
11 ITA/DC+PDSI+PRI	***	***	***	*	*
11 ITA/DC+PSI+PDSI+PRI	***	***	***	*	*
11 TUR/RPP+NTP+RPNP	**	***	**	***	*
11 VEN/AD+COPEI+URD (Bent)	**	***	**	***	*
11 VEN/AD+inds(Leoni-1)	***	***	***	*	*
10 BEL/ChrSoc+Socialist-1	***	**	*	*	**
10 BEL/ChrSoc+Socialist-2	***	**	**	*	**
10 CAN/PC(minority)	***	**	**	*	**
10 CHL/PDC(Frei)	**	***	***	*	*
10 COS/PUN(Echandi)	**	***	***	*	*
10 COS/UN(Trejos)	**	***	***	*	*
10 FRN/de Gaulle+coalition cabs	**	**	**	***	*
10 FRG/CDU-CSU+FDP	**	**	***	*	**
10 IND/INC(Shastri,Gandhi-1)	**	**	**	*	***
10 LEB/Chehab+Consoc Cabs	**	**	**	**	**
10 LEB/Helou+Consoc Cabs	**	**	**	**	**
10 TUR/JP+NP+NTP+RPNP	**	***	**	**	*
10 USA/Democratic(Johnson-2)	**	***	**	*	**
10 VEN/AD+COPEI+inds(Bent)	**	***	*	***	*
9 BEL/ChrSoc+Liberal-1	**	**	**	*	**
9 BEL/ChrSoc+Liberal-2	**	**	**	*	*
9 CHL/PC+PL+PR(Alessandri)	**	***	**	*	*
9 PRC/CCP(Mao and Liu)	***	**	*	**	*
9 COS/PLN(Orlich)	***	**	**	*	*
9 FRG/Grand Coalition	***	**	*	*	**
9 IND/INC(Nehru)	***	**	**	*	*
9 ISR/Mapai coalit(Eshkol-1)	**	***	**	*	*
9 JAP/LDP(Kishi faction)	**	***	**	*	*
9 JAP/LDP(Ikeda faction)	**	***	**	*	*
9 JAP/LDP(Sato faction)	**	***	**	*	*
9 NOR/Lib+ChrPP+SP+Cons	***	*	***	*	*
9 SWI/Federal Council	**	**	**	*	**
9 TUR/Justice Pty	*	***	**	**	*
9 VEN/AD+URD+FND(Leoni-2)	**	***	**	*	*
8 CAN/Liberal(minority)	**	*	**	*	**
8 CZE/CPCS(Novotny-2)	**	**	*	*	**
8 FRN/de Gaulle+Gaullist ptys	*	**	***	*	*

(continues)

Chart 4.10 (*continued*)

8 FRG/CDU-CSU(Adenauer)	*	*	***	*	**
8 ISR/Mapai Coalit(Ben-Gurion)	*	***	**	*	*
8 NOR/Labour Pty-2(minority)	**	*	***	*	*
8 NOR/Labour Pty-3(minority)	**	*	***	*	*
8 SOV/CPSU(Khrushchev-2)	**	**	*	**	*
8 USA/Republican(Eisenhower)	*	**	**	*	**
8 USA/Democ(Kennedy,Johnson-1)	*	**	**	*	**
8 URG/Blanco+Colorado	**	***	*	*	*
8 URG/Colorado(Gestido,Pacheco)	*	***	**	*	*
8 YUG/LCY(Tito-2)	**	**	*	*	**
7 CAN/Liberal	*	*	**	*	**
7 FRN/de Gaulle+Gaullist cab	*	**	**	*	*
7 GHA/CPP(Nkrumah)	*	*	**	**	*
7 GHA/NLC Junta	**	**	*	*	*
7 ICE/IP+SDP	**	*	**	*	*
7 ISR/National Unity Coalition	**	**	*	*	*
7 KEN/KANU(Kenyatta-1)	**	**	*	*	*
7 POL/PZPR(Gomulka)	**	**	*	*	*
7 UGA/UPC(Obote)	*	*	*	***	*
6 CAN/PC(Diefenbaker)	*	*	*	*	**
6 MEX/PRI-1(Lopez Mateos)	*	**	*	*	*
6 MEX/PRI-2(Diaz Ordaz)	*	**	*	*	*
6 NZE/Labour	*	*	**	*	*
6 NZE/National	*	*	**	*	*
6 NOR/Labour-1	*	*	**	*	*
6 PHI/Nationalist(Garcia)	**	*	*	*	*
6 PHI/Liberal(Macapagal)	*	*	**	*	*
6 PHI/Nationalist(Marcos)	*	*	**	*	*
6 SOV/CPSU(Khrushchev-1)	*	**	*	*	*
6 SOV/CPSU(Brezhnev+Kosygin)	*	**	*	*	*
6 THI/Milt Junta(Thanon+Praphat)	**	*	*	*	*
6 TUR/CNU(Gursel-2)	*	**	*	*	*
5 CUB/PCC(Castro)	*	*	*	*	*
5 CZE/CPCS(Novotny-1)	*	*	*	*	*
5 EGY/RCC(Nasser)	*	*	*	*	*
5 GDR/SED(Ulbricht)	*	*	*	*	*
5 GUI/PDG(Toure)	*	*	*	*	*
5 IVR/PDCI(Houphouet-Boigny)	*	*	*	*	*
5 KEN/KANU(Kenyatta-2)	*	*	*	*	*
5 SPN/Falange(Franco)	*	*	*	*	*
5 THI/Military Junta-1(Sarit)	*	*	*	*	*
5 TUN/Neo-Destour(Bourguiba)	*	*	*	*	*
5 TUR/Democratic	*	*	*	*	*
5 YUG/LCY(Tito-1)	*	*	*	*	*
5 ZAM/UNIP(Kaunda)	*	*	*	*	*

Note: *** indicates a high level of opposition; ** indicates a moderate level of opposition; and * indicates a low level of opposition. Totals are placed in front of regime labels.

various regime/opposition measures were not identical in their range of values. However, as was done in presenting the data on each variable, it is possible to talk in terms of low, moderate, and high levels of each type of opposition. This scheme permits some rough comparisons across significantly different measures of opposition scales, and does not require further data development itself. In Chart 4.10, the level of each type of opposition for each regime is indicated across the columns: a high level of opposition is indicated by three asterisks ("***"), a moderate level by two ("**"), and a low level by one ("*"). In addition, the "total score" is indicated in front of the label of each regime; it is simply the sum of the levels of the five opposition measures. The highest possible score is 15 (high on all five measures) and the lowest is 5 (low on all measures). Note that many regimes have the same scores, and where this occurs the regimes with the same scores are listed alphabetically within their group.

The first point apparent from the chart is that none of the regimes in the CREON sample had high levels of opposition on all five measures. In fact, in only three cases (Uganda's UPC/Kebaka Yekka coalition and the two Lebanese regimes) did a regime have high or moderate scores for the five opposition measures. Rarely, then, was a regime confronted from all directions by even moderate opposition. The two regimes with the highest total opposition were, first, India's third INC (Gandhi-2) regime with a score of 13 with considerable regime fragmentation and high levels of intraparty, opposition party, and regional opposition, and, second, Uganda under the UPC and Kebaka Yekka coalition (score of 12) with strong or moderate opposition from all five sectors of the political system. Otherwise, two groups of regimes cluster at the top third of Chart 4.10, each having strong opposition from three sectors or at least moderate opposition from four. The first group (scores of 11) included are highly fragmented authoritarian regimes (China during the Cultural Revolution and Czechoslovakia under Dubcek), praetorian democracies with strong opposition from the military, other political parties, as well as their own party (e.g., postmilitary regimes in Turkey and Venezuela), and weak coalition cabinets and parties of Italian politics. The other group (score of 10) had mostly unstable democratic coalitions (e.g., some of those in Belguim, Costa Rica, India, Lebanon, Turkey, Venezuela, and France at the outset of the Fifth Republic) or single-party cabinets undergoing open succession crises (e.g., Canada's second Progressive Conservative government under Diefenbaker and West Germany's CDU-CSU and Free Democratic Party coalition), as indicated by high fragmentation and strong opposition from within their party and from other political parties.

Regimes with a score of 9 include highly fragmented regimes with relatively cohesive parties and little legislative opposition (e.g., China under Mao and Liu, Costa Rica under Orlich, and India under Shastri/Gandhi-1), while others were moderately fragmented with stable factional coalitions and strong or moderate opposition from intraparty and legislative opponents (e.g., some of the Japanese, Israeli, Turkish, Soviet, and Yugoslav regimes). Regimes with a score of 8 had relatively cohesive regimes, but faced strong and moderate opposition from within the party or from the opposition (e.g., several West German, Norwegian, Uruguay, and U.S. cases). Only in a few cases did regional opposition play a key role in this moderate group, while the military was significant in even fewer ones.

The regimes with scores of 7, 6, or 5, which constitute the lowest third of Chart 4.10, had no more than two types of opposition reaching the moderate level. These included cohesive democratic regimes and/or disciplined ruling parties, either of which had at most moderate opposition from mainly the legislature. A substantial number of authoritarian regimes were also found at this range. These were ones with some moderate opposition, primarily in the form of splits within the regime (e.g., nonideological cliques in the military regimes in Thailand and Ghana) or opposing political wings that extended outside the regime (e.g., Poland, Soviet Union, and the Turkish military cabinets). The only other case was the Obote regime in Uganda, which faced growing challenges from Amin's military. The remaining regimes had low levels of all types of opposition. Three of these were elected cohesive democratic regimes with minimal external opposition (Kenya under KANU/Kenyatta-2, Turkey under the Democratic Party, Zambia under UNIP/Kaunda). All of the other regimes were authoritarian. This is not striking, except that they were all of a particular type. Not only were most less institutionalized, but all but one had a fairly cohesive regime ruled by a single group (party or military) with a single predominant leader.[32]

Several general observations can be made about the overall distribution of regimes in terms of total opposition. First, as should be evident from the summary above, the distribution of regimes was fairly good with a roughly even split of the sample across high, moderate, and low levels of total opposition. Second, the concept of the political regime as a unit of aggregation was validated by the fact that the regimes of most countries (with multiple regimes during the decade) differed in terms of their opposition levels (the only exceptions were Iceland, Lebanon, and Mexico). Finally, the measures used were at least partially successful in getting beyond political structure in that not all democracies had opposition and not all authoritarian systems did not. Several authoritarian regimes had high opposition rankings and many had moderate rankings, while a sizable number of democratic regimes had low opposition rankings. As to political development, both institutionalized and noninstitutionalized regimes were dispersed throughout the rankings of total opposition.

Notes

1. A thorough attempt was made to identify all available sources on each country's politics. All of the books available in the University of Wyoming libraries were examined for useful sections on opposition and political episodes. In addition, the tables of contents for issues of general and regionally focused academic journals were surveyed, and those with titles that appeared relevant were examined for useful information. For the case study material desired here, the following journals were most useful among general focus journals: *Current History, Government and Opposition, World Politics,* and *World Today.* Certain regionally focused journals provided numerous essential articles for countries within their geographical range of coverage: *African Affairs, Asian Survey, Cooperation and Conflict* (for Nordic nations), *Journal of Modern African Studies,* and *Studies in Comparative Communism.*

2. Another excellent source is the annual volumes edited by Colin Legum on regional and national politics for the Middle East and Africa: *Middle East Contemporary Survey* and *African Contemporary Record.* However, they were of limited utility for this project because the Middle East series goes back only to the mid-1970s while the African series was initiated in the late 1960s. Thus, use of these sources was limited to the final years of the African regimes in the sample.

3. It was rare that I had to consult data banks on news sources, and only then when very specific information, usually on election results or cabinet composition, was needed. The source used was *Keesing's Contemporary Archives,* which covers major political episodes in detail (while ignoring more routine situations).

4. Sources for all of the thirty-eight nations are listed, except for the United States, whose sources are too voluminous to include here. Furthermore, familiarity with the United States and the stable routine of its politic made most coding judgment rather clear-cut.

5. If there is any deficiency in the use of these sources, it is that I was not able to arrange for my coding judgments to be validated by external country specialists, but hopefully the use of multiple sources reduces challenges from country specialists.

6. It might be argued that changes in the other types of opposition should also be considered in identifying regime changes. This is not done for a number of reasons. First, shifts in most types of opposition (e.g., legislative and intraparty) are reflected by changes in the level of regime fragmentation, for example, the gain or loss of a parliamentary majority or the rise or demise of party factionalism. Second, incorporation of all fluctuations in opposition (particularly minor ones such as a gain or loss of a few legislative seats) would lead to regimes with very short periods in office and thus result in smaller units of aggregation in the analyses below. Finally, coding procedures are developed below in a way that averages out any variation in the level of opposition outside the regime—and this occurs in relatively few cases.

7. Another Turkish regime (as well as one for Iceland) will be deleted because it had too few foreign policy events in the CREON data set, a procedure that will be explained in Chapter 5.

8. Leaders were not judged to be predominant solely in terms of the institutional power of their leadership positions. Thus in such systems as in the United States and Mexico, presidents were not automatically assumed to be politically predominant simply because they controlled powerful executive institutions. Leaders in these cases had to have such prestige that they were unchallenged and often made policy on their own, otherwise it was assumed that they operated in more collective settings.

9. The relevance of various types of political resources within the fluid politics of an authoritarian coalition depends on the basic character of the regime and the means by which it holds on to power. One-party regimes are likely to be legitimized by their ideology, and thus the party's leader may manipulate ideology to retain power and the other figures in that regime must play that game. In contrast, in military regimes that depend on force to retain power, coercive resources are likely to be a primary currency of politics. Finally, in "kleptocracies" access to money (from external sources such as foreign aid or drug/arms trade) is likely to define the relevant balances among players.

10. I recognize there is a problem in how to incorporate the relative importance, or weights, of the three variables in any composite measure. Should the dimensions be combined additively or multiplicatively? Is group structure twice as important as leader predominance or policy polarization? Are the latter two variables to be weighted equally? The decisionmaking and coalition literature, as well as intuitive observations, only suggests that their effects are to be combined, but not how. Accordingly, the three variables are assumed to be equally important and can be combined in a simple multiplicative fashion.

11. The one exception here was the United States under the second Johnson regime, which was factionalized by the rebellion of some congressional Democrats over the administration's Vietnam policy. Clearly, Johnson was not above the fray, but retained dominance because of the institutional autonomy of the executive branch.

12. As identified below for our regime sample, this often occurred in volatile Latin American presidential party systems, in which one member of the electoral coalition took the presidency but lost the support of former allies in the congress.

13. Often more specific labels were used to indicate contending political tendencies, such as the "Natolinist" and "Pulawska" wings of the United Polish Workers Party or the "officialistas," "rebels," and "terceristas" in Frei's Christian Democratic Party in Chile. Care was taken to make sure that formal labels were not interpreted as evidence that these were structural factions.

14. Conservative elements in Costa Rica were not nearly as cohesive as the leftist National Liberation Party. Just prior to an election, conservative leaders dissolved their parties and unified into a new, broader-based party. This party was not simply an electoral alliance but instead remained, at least in name, in place over the next few years, at least during the duration of the subsequent regime. But it was by no means unified; the president faced intense opposition from autonomous elements (usually in congress) of the new party, elements that could be traced directly to previously independent parties.

15. I have resisted the temptation to distinguish between cohesive and fragmented party opposition at the other levels. In the case of minority governments, it is logically impossible to have a cohesive party opposition with a majority of seats because it would have control of the regime. In the case of weak opposition, the assumption is that the distinction adds little to what is already a rather weak level of opposition, and only further complicates the measurement scale.

16. Ascertaining the main opposition party (or parties) was a complicated task if the regime faced more than one sizable party (i.e., each having more than 10 percent of opposition seats). If that was the case, then the intensity measure was defined by the party with the most intense orientation.

17. The country exclusively represented here is Italy, and it could be suggested that this concentration of cases for one country would undercut the statistical analyses in Chapter 5. However, in those analyses care was taken to insure that correlations for party opposition did not reflect only the Italian regimes. The validity of correlations reported for this measure was also checked by replicating them without

the three Italian regimes and by collapsing these extreme cases at point 20 with those at point 15 of the scale. Also, as explained below, all correlations were checked closely for any outliers.

18. The one exception is the Nkrumah regime in Ghana, where the United Party was not Communist but instead was antisystemic by virtue of its challenge to the increasingly authoritarian character of Nkrumah and his Convention People's Party.

19. The strength of opposition from the military and paramilitary actors was not based on the size or resources of the military, because in any political system the military is relatively large compared to other actors in the polity, and no matter what its size it likely commands relatively significant coercive power. While number of troops and the like might relate to aspects of foreign policy, such a measure would be meaningless for cross-national comparisons of the domestic role of military actors.

20. At least one of these conditions usually applied to authoritarian regimes and some less institutionalized civilian ones too, but there were cases of other such regimes where they did not, and country accounts were often found to confirm that the military was politically passive (e.g., Mexico's well-established PRI regimes by the 1960s as well as charismatic leaderships in Kenya, Ivory Coast, and Zambia).

21. Critical to note here is that military competition for dominance does not necessarily mean an attempt to overthrow the established system and establish a Communist regime. It may simply be a desire to dominate the existing civilian system (e.g., a Communist regime) without actually dismantling it. Lin Biao's quest for dominance of the Chinese Communist system is a good example of this. The extent of political changes intended by the military is captured by the intensity measure.

22. There were no cases in this data set in which the military acted as a fully cohesive force in competing with civilian groups for political dominance. Somewhat surprisingly, after some research and data collection it was clear that in all challenges to civilian dominance the military was factionalized over this role in the political system. It remains, though, an open question if it is ever possible that the military is fully unified (or immune from paramilitary challenges) when it gets so involved in politics that it competes with civilian actors.

23. If there were multiple factions or paramilitary groups, this variable was coded for the group with the most intense or extreme orientation.

24. This could be based on open challenges on specific policy issues, but also could include likely differences between a presumably conservative military and a highly reformist regime. Also fitting here were militaries opposed to certain members in a coalition.

25. In democratic systems, regular regime changes were those involving the exchange of power between separate political parties (e.g., West Germany's Christian Democrats to the Social Democratic Party) or coalition members (e.g., varied Christian Democratic coalitions in Italy), and not just factions within a single party. A regular regime change in an authoritarian regime was considered to have occurred if the regime had experienced a major leadership succession in an orderly manner and that did not disrupt basic system norms, as evidenced by the passing of the dominant faction or predominant leader in power at the creation of the political system.

26. By "major" I mean a political group that was a significant player in the nation's political scene and not just a very small fringe party with few political resources.

27. A political (not necessarily societal) revolution is identified by the coming

to power of an antisystem group that fundamentally restructures political structures and norms. Revolutionary changes are not limited to changes between democratic and authoritarian systems. They can also include the exchange of power between conservative and leftist authoritarian leaders (e.g., Nasser's overthrow of the Egyptian monarchy in 1952), or the fundamental restructuring of democratic structures by an irregular seizure of power by a largely antisystemic group (e.g., the change in France from the Fourth Republic to the Fifth Republic was a political revolution).

28. The now defunct Communist system in the Soviet Union is an excellent example of this concern. As discussed in Chapter 2, its regimes were well institutionalized by the time Brezhnev held power in the 1960s and 1970s. However, it is clear now that its base of public support was deteriorating and probably was never fully accepted. The latter, though, is beyond the scope of the measure used here.

29. The recognition of Third World regimes, even in newly independent nations, as potentially well institutionalized is critical because it (as well as other rules below) prevents this variable from simply being a measure of development.

30. Thus, for example, the Egyptian political system under Nasser would not be considered a competitive system because all prerevolutionary political groups had been effectively dismantled.

31. Regimes with a continuously dominant coalition partner were also included here, if they had shared power with only very minor parties. The Italian Christian Democratic Party is a case in point.

32. The well-institutionalized Thai regime was the only exception to the first point, and the Turkish regime under the Democratic Party the sole exception to the second (its leader, Mendares, was not dominant, but his regime was very cohesive).

5

An Analysis of
the Linkage Between
Opposition and Foreign Policy

This chapter reports the main findings of a statistical analysis of the relationship between opposition and foreign policy behavior for the regimes identified in Chapter 4. The analysis compares regimes, as classified by opposition measures, in terms of their overall foreign policy behavior using aggregated foreign policy events data. The foreign policy data are drawn from the CREON (Comparative Research on the Events of Nations) data set. Four dimensions of foreign policy are examined: commitment, independence of action, affect direction, and affect intensity. The research design is grounded in a set of correlational tests employed to ascertain general statistical associations between aggregate measures of opposition and foreign policy behavior.

This analysis is in many respects largely exploratory and, as such, is designed to address three basic issues about the linkage between domestic politics and foreign policy. The first issue is whether basic patterns of domestic political opposition can account for broad cross-national differences in foreign policy behavior. Are the foreign policy patterns of regimes with relatively high levels of opposition distinctive from those with lesser amounts of domestic opposition? If such a relationship is identified, the second issue is what political dynamics underlie these effects and with what kind of impact on foreign policy; in other words, do these correlations reflect the constraining effects of bargaining and controversy avoidance or the amplifying effects of political legitimization? The third issue has to do with the mediating effects of political system structure (accountability and institutionalization) and regime properties (vulnerability and fragmentation). (Note that subsamples defined by regime fragmentation are considered in order to gauge its mediating impact on the effects of opposition outside the regime.)[1] Do these contextual conditions enhance the basic bivariate association between opposition and foreign policy measures and/or do they effect the direction of those relationships as indicative of alternative political dynamics? Furthermore, for those political system and regime properties found to have significant effects, is the pattern of these effects consistent across the different types of opposition and foreign policy behavior?

The chapter is organized around the four dimensions of foreign policy behavior. Two sets of statistical findings are presented in each subsection: correlations for the overall relationship (i.e., for the full sample of regimes) between the five types of opposition and four foreign policy dimensions; and the same correlations for subsamples of regimes defined by the two political system and two regime properties. The chapter concludes with an attempt to tie together these subsections by generalizing about domestic political effects (opposition and conditioning influences) across all four foreign policy dimensions. Before moving to the statistical analysis itself, it is important to consider the data used for this analysis's dependent variable—foreign policy behavior.

Using the CREON Foreign Policy Data Set

Thus far, much of the book has been devoted to conceptualizing and measuring political opposition in a way appropriate for cross-national analysis. Little has been said about the kind of foreign policy data used here and, in particular, the source of those data: the CREON data set. The CREON data set is a foreign policy events data set, which is described fully in Hermann et al. (1973) and Callahan, Brady, and Hermann (1982). The unit of measurement in this kind of data set is the "event," which is defined in the CREON project as "a minimally aggregated action resulting from a decision by the political authorities of a state who have the power to commit the resources of the nation's government" (Hermann et al., 1973: 19). As with other foreign policy events data sets, an event consists of an actor, an action, and one or more recipients of that behavior (CREON distinguishes between direct and indirect targets). The final version of the CREON data set (version 6.01) used here consists of 12,710 such events for a sample of thirty-eight nations between 1959–1968. These countries are listed in Chart 4.2.

While events data sets are by now familiar to most foreign policy researchers, they remain controversial because of their dependence on public news sources.[2] Why then use this kind of data set? I have done so because, most basically, events data get at those decision "process" outcomes that are most likely affected by domestic politics: initiative, commitment, and affect in foreign policy. Other kinds of data, although they might employ more reliable (or seemingly more concrete) public sources, do not tap the kinds of outcomes theoretically linked to decisionmaking processes. An act of casting a vote in, say, the United Nations does not capture gradations in a government's commitment or initiative; indeed, most votes are routinely handled by delegations without the direct involvement of national political leaders. Similarly, international transaction data, such as foreign trade and communication flows, do not reflect discrete decisions of national authorities, and thus would not reflect the give and take of domestic politics.

The CREON data set is particularly appropriate for this project in two ways. It captures major foreign policy actions in that the actions are taken by national political authorities or their representatives and multiple actions on a single issue across time are included only if they involve major new commitments and new actors. The foreign policy events in the CREON data set likely lean toward major decisions taken by senior political leaders (i.e., in the regime) rather than the more routine actions of lower-level bureaucratic officials. But the more important feature of the CREON data set, for this research project, is that it alone among the major events data sets has measures of multiple dimensions of foreign policy behavior. It includes not just conflict and cooperation (i.e., affect direction), which is the primary feature of other events data sets (e.g., the World Event Interaction Survey [WEIS] and the Cooperation and Peace Data Bank [COPDAB]), but also other dimensions that are critical to ascertaining the foreign policy effects of domestic politics. These theoretically relevant measures, each of which will be fully explained below, are commitment, independence of action, and affect (intensity and direction). The CREON data set, alone, provides a preliminary opportunity to examine a broader array of theoretically relevant foreign policy dimensions.[3]

The use of the CREON data set, though, involves special costs, because it consists of a rather restrictive, and potentially biased, sample of nations and years. It has two specific validity problems. The first is that the CREON sample is relatively small (thirty-eight nations for only a ten-year period), and this results in a sample of ninety regimes. A regime sample of this size is clearly adequate for overall correlational analyses, but analyses of subgroups of regimes necessitate far smaller samples. The typical sub-sample of regimes defined by political structure, vulnerability, or fragmentation is about thirty cases. In subsamples of this size, correlational findings could easily be disrupted by outlying regimes with extreme scores on political opposition and/or foreign policy behavior.

The other problem with the CREON sample of nations is that it was not randomly selected (Hermann et al., 1973: 23–24). Smaller and less developed states are underrepresented, while practically all the major powers are included—the United States, the Soviet Union, India, China, West Germany, Japan, France, and Italy, as well as such regional powers as Egypt and Israel. The sample is thus biased toward larger and more modern nations. Compounding the problem is that larger and more modern states have far greater levels of almost all types of foreign policy actions, some of which are precisely those that we will be hypothesizing are linked to political opposition. Nation-size is particularly correlated with CREON measures of foreign policy activity, independence, and conflict, while modernity is tied to commitment. The difficulty this poses is that spurious correlations are likely to appear if opposition measures are found to be tied to modernity and nation-size, especially when using the smaller samples of regimes just noted.

In this project specific strategies were taken to protect against the CREON data's two potential problems of statistical outliers and the spurious effects of nation-size and modernity. Along with the usual procedures for standardizing foreign policy scores across nations with different numbers of events,[4] two additional procedures were used to insure that Pearson correlation coefficients were credible given the constraints of the CREON data set. *Specifically, for a Pearson correlation coefficient to be treated as meaningful in this study, it not only had to be statistically significant but also had to achieve significance using two additional statistical tests that checked for outliers and spurious effects.* The first procedure was used to catch highly disruptive outliers. Not only was the scatterplot for each correlation examined, but Pearson correlation coefficients were further evaluated by a nonparametric statistic, Spearman's Rho, which simply computes the correlation with rank-ordered data. If the Spearman's coefficient was not statistically significant, then a statistically significant Pearson correlation coefficient was rejected. The second procedure checked Pearson correlation coefficients for the spurious effects of nation-size and modernity. Each statistically significant correlation between opposition and foreign policy was reexamined using nation-size and modernity as control variables. If the resulting partial correlation coefficient was not statistically significant, then it was assumed that the bivariate Pearson correlation was spurious, and it was therefore rejected. In sum, Pearson correlation coefficients in the following tables are ones that meet multiple statistical criteria: not only is each statistically significant on its own, but the validity of its significance is confirmed by reanalyses using nonparametric correlations and by partial correlations controlling for nation-size and modernity. Taken together, these tests should serve to correct for biases inherent in the relatively small CREON data set.[5] (Because multiple statistical procedures are used, only Pearson correlation coefficients that are statistically significant—at the $p < .10$ level using a one-tailed test—for all three procedures are reported in the tables.)[6]

Another quality-control procedure should also be mentioned here. Although not inherent in the use of the CREON data, the aggregation of events data by regime necessitates some judgment about how many foreign policy actions, or events, are enough to be representative of a pattern of activity. A regime in power for just a few months (or days) is likely to have very few events, and these are potentially subject to the highly disruptive effects of just one or two unusual actions. Therefore, a regime was excluded from the analyses if it did not have at least ten events in the CREON data set. This resulted in the dropping of two more regimes (one each for Iceland and Turkey) from the sample identified in Chart 4.2, leaving a sample of eighty-eight regimes.[7] Note that not only does this enhance the validity of the data, it is also a more conservative test of opposition effects on foreign policy. It rids the sample of not only those regimes with the least activity, but also some with the highest levels of fragmentation and opposition (e.g., coalitions and minority cabinets). Along with the coding rules for identifying regimes, this prevents any single country with numerous leadership changes (e.g., Turkey and Italy) from dominating the data set.[8]

Analyses and Basic Findings

In this section, the chapter's lengthiest, statistical findings are presented for the four foreign policy dimensions of commitment, independence of action, affect direction, and affect intensity. Statistically significant (according to the multiple criteria) Pearson correlation coefficients are reported between measures of each foreign policy dimension and the five types of opposition: regime fragmentation, as well as opposition from intraparty, political party, military/paramilitary, and regional groups. Both the strength and direction of these correlations are essential as evidence of the theoretical arguments developed in Chapter 3. The size of correlation coefficients is indicative of the strength of opposition effects. The overall absence of correlations (i.e., for the full regime sample and all of the subsamples) indicates that opposition effects are unimportant; this would support a null hypothesis.[9] However, the absence of a relationship under some conditions but not others (i.e., theoretically sensible correlations were found for only certain subsamples of regimes) would indicate that leaders were able to insulate foreign policy from opposition in certain situations but not others. The direction of correlation coefficients is also important because we are juxtaposing the alternative dynamics of bargaining/controversy avoidance and political legitimization for each foreign policy behavior. Depending on the construction of the particular foreign policy scale, whether a correlation is negative or positive will be taken as evidence of the presence of one political dynamic and not the other.

The presentation of findings for each foreign policy dimension is done in two stages. In the first, the strength and direction of the correlations between opposition and foreign policy for the overall sample of eighty-eight regimes are examined. In the second stage, these overall opposition/ foreign policy correlations are reexamined for subsamples of regimes defined by political system properties (accountability and institutionalization) and by the two regime properties of vulnerability and fragmentation.[10] How these groups are defined, as well as their sample sizes, is summarized in Chart 5.1. Comparing the correlations across the subsamples with those for the overall correlations serves two purposes: first, it enables a further consideration of the significance of opposition effects, and second, it provides the basis for generalizing (in the chapter's final section) about the effects of the conditioning effects of political system and regime properties.

Before proceeding further let me acknowledge that more powerful statistical procedures were also used, particularly multiple regression, in

---

Chart 5.1   Subsamples of Regimes Defined by Political System and Regime Contextual Variables

---

Political system accountability
        Closed polities [n = 23]
        Open polities [n = 65]

Political system institutionalization
        Noninstitutionalized polities [n = 22]
        Moderately institutionalized polities [n = 32]
        Highly institutionalized polities [n = 34]

Regime vulnerability[a]
        Minimally vulnerable regimes [n = 29]
        Moderately vulnerable regimes [n = 36]
        Highly vulnerable regimes [n = 23]

Regime fragmentation[b]
        Cohesive regimes [n = 38]
        Moderately fragmented regimes [n = 27]
        Highly fragmented regimes [n = 23]

Notes: a. These three groups are based on the regime vulnerability scale as presented in Chart 4.9. The minimally vulnerable group consists of the three types of regimes at the scale's lowest points (1 and 2); these are ones with low internal uncertainty in noncompetitive systems, low uncertainty in moderately competitive systems, and moderate uncertainty in noncompetitive systems. Moderately vulnerable regimes (points 3 and 4) include regimes with low uncertainty in highly competitive systems and those with moderate uncertainty in moderately competitive systems. Highly vulnerable regimes (points 6 and 9) are those with moderate uncertainty in highly competitive systems, high uncertainty in moderately competitive systems, and high uncertainty in highly competitive systems.

b. These levels of regime fragmentation are based on the interaction of the group and actor dominance dimensions of this regime property. See Chart 4.3 but note that the polarization dimension is excluded, because it resulted in a severe maldistribution of data across regime subsamples. The low fragmentation group includes regimes with cohesive single groups (with or without a predominant actor) and ones with divided single groups with predominant actors. The moderately fragmented group consists of regimes with divided single groups with no predominant actor and coalitions that have a predominant member. The highly fragmented group of regimes consists of coalitions in which there is no predominant actor.

assessing the combined foreign policy effects of five opposition measures as well as the contextual effects of political system and regime properties. However, for purposes of this exploratory analysis, I have chosen not to report extensively on the multiple regression results for two reasons. First, as summarized later in this chapter, multiple regression of the five opposition variables does not account for much more than the bivariate correlations. Namely, in the large majority of cases, only one opposition variable achieved statistical significance in a multiple regression equation, and therefore the bivariate correlations seemed to convey the most information about possible relationships. Second, multiple regression to assess the contextual effects of political system and regime properties would, at this exploratory stage, hide important effects and reduce the amount of information to be conveyed. In particular, standard multiple regression would complicate the examination of significant relationships at the middle range of the institutionalization, vulnerability, and fragmentation conditions. While perhaps a bit cumbersome, my emphasis of bivariate correlations and subsamples of regimes permits a richer look at the dynamics of the relationships between opposition and foreign policy behavior across various political conditions. This is consistent with the preliminary nature of this research at this stage.[11]

Commitment

The CREON commitment measure, as developed by Callahan (1982), is based on an eleven-point scale and is built around the distinction between "deed behaviors" involving the actual use of resources, "pledging behaviors" with the expression of threats or promises to act, and "verbal commentary" in which leaders comment on foreign situations. The scale further differentiates commitment at these three levels by considering whether these actions are irreversible, whether pledges to act are made by senior or junior government officials, and what kinds of qualifying conditions are put on their use. Four commitment variables are used in this analysis. The primary measure is "mean commitment," which is a regime's overall commitment level during its tenure. It is computed by averaging the regime's total commitment scores on the eleven-point scale by its total number of events. The three supplementary commitment variables concern the proportion of a regime's activity at the three basic commitment levels: percent comment behaviors, percent verbal intent behaviors, and percent deed behaviors.

As theorized in Chapter 3, domestic politics strongly influences the extent to which a regime is able to commit itself to a particular course of action in foreign policy. The dynamics of bargaining/controversy avoidance and political legitimization suggest partially similar effects on commitment in foreign policy, with the assumption that extensive resource use can be politically risky and provoke opposition within and outside the regime. With respect to bargaining and controversy avoidance, even the expression of intent to act in the future is assumed to be politically divisive and thus is to be avoided. The hypothesis for bargaining/controversy avoidance is:

> The foreign policies of politically constrained regimes involve the use of fewer resources and less pledging behaviors, and instead have mostly verbal comment behaviors.

Support for this hypothesis would be indicated by negative correlations between opposition measures and the mean commitment, percent deed behavior, and percent intent behavior measures. There should be a correspondingly large positive correlation between opposition and percent comment behavior. The logic of political legitimization diverges mainly with respect to verbal commitment, given that strong threats and promises to act can be useful ways of asserting the stature of the regime and/or its policies. The hypothesis for political legitimization is:

> The foreign policies of politically constrained regimes have low commitments in the form of deed behaviors, but a strong propensity toward increased verbal intent behaviors.

Support for this hypothesis is indicated by the disaggregated commitment measure; in other words, positive correlations are expected for its middle range (verbal intent behaviors) and negative ones for its high (deeds) and low (comment) behavior.[12] The general absence (for the full sample and all subsamples) of significant correlations indicates support for a null hypothesis.

The results for the full sample of regimes are reported in Table 5.1A, which lists statistically significant Pearson correlations between the five opposition measures and the four commitment variables.[13] Significant findings are not widespread and, as will be seen, are much more complex than those for the other foreign policy dimensions. Only intraparty opposition is significantly correlated with commitment in any kind of clear pattern. It is correlated with mean commitment as well as comment and deed behaviors, but not with intent behaviors. None of the other opposition measures is at all significantly associated with any commitment measure. Furthermore, although not reported in the table, commitment is not even correlated to any of the separate strength and intensity dimensions of political party, military, and regional opposition. The only exception is regime fragmentation: its group structure dimension is weakly correlated with the same commitment variables that were found for intraparty opposition.

The direction of these correlations is perplexing, fitting with neither

Table 5.1A Significant Correlations Between Political Opposition and Commitment in Foreign Policy for the Full Sample of Regimes

	Mean Commitment of Action	Percent Comment Behaviors	Percent Intent Behaviors	Mean Deed Behaviors
Regime Fragmentation	—	—	—	—
Intraparty Opposition	.268**	–.268**	—	.252**
Political Party Opposition	—	—	—	—
Military Opposition	—	—	—	—
Regional Opposition	—	—	—	—

Significance levels: ** p < .01; * p < .05; p < .10. Table reports only those Pearson correlation coefficients that also meet significance tests (at the .10 level) for correlations using a non-parametric test and controls for nation-size and modernity.

the logic of bargaining/controversy avoidance nor of political legitimization. Intraparty opposition is positively correlated with the full commitment scale, and this is largely due to decreased verbal comment behavior and increased deed behavior. But increased commitment of resources by politically constrained regimes is precisely the opposite of what is expected by the logic of both hypotheses. The regimes facing internal party opposition have a larger percentage of deeds and a conversely lower proportion of the seemingly politically neutral comment events. Clearly, political constraints inherent in bargaining and controversy avoidance are not present here—in fact, just the opposite occurs. These regimes, if anything, appear constrained only in the sense that they engage in less commentary. However, there is equally little evidence to support the competing logic of political legitimization, which hypothesizes that domestic politics would stimulate greater commitment in the form of more verbal intent behavior. The intent variable is unrelated to opposition, and the politically risky increased deed behavior alone cannot be regarded of as indicative of a general pattern of domestically driven political legitimization.

Table 5.1B presents the correlations for the subsamples of regimes

Table 5.1B　Contextual Effects of Political System and Regime Conditions on Correlations Between Domestic Opposition and Commitment in Foreign Policy

	Accountability (closed/open)	Institution-alization (low/mod/high)	Regime Vulnerability (low/mod/high)	Regime Fragmentation (low/mod/high)
Regime Fragmentation 1.	–/–	–/ – /–	–/ – /–	not applicable
Regime Fragmentation 2.	–/–	.327/ – /–	–/ – /–	not applicable
Intraparty Opposition 1.	–/.263*	–/ .352* / .364*	–/.534**/–	.404**/.307 /–
Intraparty Opposition 2.	–/.315*	–/ .326* /–	–/.281**/.309	–/.397*/–
Political Party Opposition 1.	n.a./–	–/ .349* /–	–/ – /–	–/ – /–
Political Party Opposition 2.	n.a./–	–/ – /–	–/ – /–	–/ – /–
Military Opposition 1.	–/–	–/ –.345* / n.a.	–/ – /–	–/ – /–
Military Opposition 2.	–/–	–/ –.427** / n.a.	–/ – /–	–/ – /–
Regional Opposition 1.	–/–	–.359*/ – /–	–/ .344* /–.297	–/ –.311 /–
Regional Opposition 2.	–/–	–/ – /–	–/ – /–.364*	–/ – /–

1.: correlations for mean commitment variable.
2.: correlations for percent deed behavior variable.

Significance levels: ** p < .01; *p < .05; p < .10. Table reports only those Pearson correlation coefficients that also meet significance tests (at the .10 level) using a nonparametric test and controls for nation-size and modernity.

defined by political structure and regime properties. To simplify the presentation of results in this table, as well as ones to follow, correlations are reported for only two of the foreign policy variables. In the case of foreign policy commitment, the mean commitment and percent deed behavior variables are used.[14] The evidence is that conditioning variables have an important mediating effect on the overall correlations between opposition and foreign policy commitment in several ways. Most of the significant correlations for the subsamples are larger (in the .300–.400 range) than those identified for the overall sample. Along with confirming the overall intraparty effects, significant correlations are also identified for the other types of political opposition, although in some cases these are rather scattered. Finally, the direction of these correlations varies in interesting ways that indicate some support for both alternative hypotheses.

The most obvious pattern in Table 5.1B is the correlation of intraparty opposition with commitment at certain levels of all four of the control variables. As hypothesized in Chapter 3, it is in the democracies that intraparty opposition effects are more significant, although the manifestation of these constraints is still a greater proportion of deed behaviors, and not the expected inability to commit resources. The contextual effect of political system institutionalization is a bit more complex, with intraparty opposition effects occurring at both moderate and high levels of political system institutionalization. The overall positive correlation with deed behavior holds only for the subsample of regimes in moderately institutionalized polities.

The impact of intraparty opposition on foreign policy commitment is also mediated by the two regime properties. The effects of this type of opposition on commitment are especially pronounced for moderately vulnerable regimes, but not for highly vulnerable regimes as hypothesized. The mediating role of regime fragmentation is even less clear, and just the opposite as hypothesized. The most highly fragmented regimes are the only ones that appear unconstrained, and the correlations are strongest for the most cohesive regime group, reflecting greater intent behavior but not deed behaviors. The association for the moderately fragmented regimes is a bit weaker and reflects mostly actual resources and not verbal intentions. As with institutionalization, the effects of vulnerability and fragmentation vary sharply with respect to the intent and deed levels of commitment.

The introduction of political system and regime conditioning variables also uncovers correlations for the other types of opposition. The contextual effects of institutionalization are the most impressive in that they uncover correlations for the other four types of opposition. In the case of military and political party opposition, these effects occur in moderately institutionalized polities, which is again consistent with the hypothesis outlined in Chapter 3. However, the directions of these relationships are just the opposite: party opposition, like intraparty opposition, is positively correlated with commitment, while military opposition is associated with especially diminished deed behavior. Unexpected are the correlations for noninstitutionalized systems, where fragmentation and regional opposition have significant effects. Finally, other than those of intraparty opposition, the contextual effects of regime vulnerability and fragmentation are very limited and scattered and involve mainly regional opposition.

What sense, then, can be made of these findings? Three items stand out. First, political opposition relatively proximate to foreign policy decisionmakers—opposition within the ruling party—is most closely associated with commitment in foreign policy. This makes sense given that the commitment of resources, at least, requires the agreement of the regime's key support groups (as well as actors within the regime itself) and offers some indication of the dynamics of coalition policymaking. Second, the examination of regime subsamples demonstrates that opposition effects are conditioned by the broader political system and regime context; the contextual effects of institutionalization are particularly pervasive across multiple types of opposition. Third, the correlations across subsamples of regimes simply reinforce the puzzling findings for the overall sample: that of the unexpected positive correlations between intraparty opposition and commitment. Intraparty opposition is positively associated with commitment across all of the political system and regime conditions. In only a couple of seemingly isolated cases is commitment negatively correlated (as hypothesized) with political opposition: military opposition in moderately institutionalized polities and regional opposition facing highly vulnerable regimes. While this offers some isolated support for the logic of bargaining/controversy avoidance, no clear pattern of theoretically sensible effects emerges as a result of political system and regime controls.

Independence of Action

This dimension concerns the extent to which a regime acts on its own in foreign affairs, as indicated by self-initiated and unilateral activity. Four measures of independence of action (IOA) are used in the analyses. The primary one is mean IOA and is computed on the basis of the interaction of IOA's two dimensions. This juxtaposition creates four categories, ranging from high to low independence: initiatory-unilateral, initiatory-multilateral, reactive-unilateral, and reactive-multilateral. The actual mean IOA scale used in this analysis has three points, with the middle, hybrid categories being collapsed into a single category. This results in an ordinal scale in which initiative-unilateral actions equal 1, the two mixed categories equal 2, and reactive-multilateral actions equal 3 (high independence is indicated by low values on this scale). Two of the other IOA variables are measures of its separate dimensions: the percentage of a regime's events that are self-initiated and the percentage of its events that are multilateral. The fourth variable combines independence of action with the commitment dimension of the previous section; it computes the mean IOA score for relatively high commitment actions.[15] This combined variable permits further examination of the puzzling commitment findings in the previous section.

Independence in foreign policy, as argued in Chapter 3, is well grounded in the domestic political processes of bargaining/controversy avoidance and political legitimization, although with sharply divergent effects. The accommodation in the former set of dynamics contributes to diminished initiative and unilateralism (particularly when substantial resources are involved), reflecting, first, the inability to reach agreement within the regime except when forced by strong foreign pressures and, second, an unwillingness to take the initiative on domestically controversial actions. Accordingly, the logic of bargaining/controversy avoidance suggests:

> The foreign policies of politically constrained regimes are characterized by less independence of action, particularly for actions involving high commitment.

Confirmation of this hypothesis would find negative correlations between opposition and the initiative and unilateral measures, and positive ones between the mean IOA measures and especially the high-commitment IOA measure.[16] The logic of political legitimization suggests opposite correlations. Here, domestic politics is a stimulus for action as the leadership seeks to impress domestic audiences with clear policy imperatives and dramatic leadership. However, because legitimization is a largely domestic exercise, increased independence would not extend to actions requiring substantial resources, in other words, deed behaviors. The hypothesis suggested by the logic of political legitimization is:

> The foreign policies of politically constrained regimes are marked by high levels of independence, although this does not generally extend to high commitment actions.

Positive correlations are expected between opposition and the initiative and unilateral measures. Negative correlations are hypothesized in the case of mean IOA scale and ones for the high commitment–IOA variable.

The findings for the full sample of regimes are reported in Table 5.2A. Statistically significant correlations are listed for each of the five opposition measures with the four independence of action variables. Several findings stand out immediately. As with commitment, not all types of opposition are significantly associated overall with independence of action. And the two types of opposition that are correlated with IOA are different: here it is political party and military opposition, both of which are less proximate to the authoritative decision processes within the regime and the ruling party. The effects underlying the correlations with mean IOA are limited to its initiative-reactive dimension; the unilateral-multilateral dimension is entirely unrelated to domestic opposition. The correlation between political party opposition and high commitment IOA is relatively weak, while the one for military opposition is stronger than that found for the general mean IOA variable. As discussed in a moment, the relative sizes of these two correlations, as compared to those for the general IOA measure, are not expected.

The dynamics of these political constraints are a bit more theoretically straightforward than the puzzling findings for commitment, even though political party and military opposition effects are in opposite directions. As indicated by the positive correlation with mean IOA, party opposition is associated with diminished independence in foreign policy, mainly with respect to the initiative-reactive dimension and indicating that regimes with strong party opposition are more reactive and passive in their foreign policy behavior. The relatively weak correlation between party opposition and the high commitment measure of IOA, however, does not conform with the logic of bargaining and controversy avoidance, where it was expected that

Table 5.2A   Significant Correlations Between Political Opposition and Independence of Action in Foreign Policy for the Full Sample of Regimes

	Mean Independence of Action	Percent Self-Initiated Behaviors	Percent Unilateral Behaviors	Mean IOA/ High Commitment
Regime Fragmentation	—	—	—	—
Intraparty Opposition	—	—	—	—
Political Party Opposition	.214*	–.233*	—	.196*
Military Opposition	-.164	.207*	—	-.284**
Regional Opposition	—	—	—	—

Significance levels: ** p < .01; * p < .05; p < .10. Table reports only those Pearson correlation coefficients that also meet significance tests (at the .10 level) for correlations using a nonparametric test and controls for nation-size and modernity.

constraints on initiatives would be stronger when they involve substantial domestic resources. In the case of military opposition, the correlations (again limited to IOA's initiative-reactive dimension) indicate that these regimes engage in greater independence in foreign policy, reflective of political legitimization dynamics. The correlation between military opposition and high commitment IOA is a bit stronger, but this runs counter to the hypothesis that the manipulation of foreign policy would not extent to making commitments abroad or substantial resource use. Once again, the linkage between domestic politics and foreign policy commitment, while present, does not conform with the theoretical logic employed.

Table 5.2B reports opposition-IOA correlations across the subsamples of regimes defined by political structure and regime properties; note that only the mean IOA and high commitment/mean IOA measures are used. Several general points stand out from this table. First, the pattern of correlations demonstrates the importance of the contextual effects of political system and regime properties, although accountability stands out as having relatively weak contextual effects. Subgroups at certain levels of

Table 5.2B   Contextual Effects of Political System and Regime Conditions on Correlations Between Domestic Opposition and Independence of Action in Foreign Policy

		Accountability (closed/open)	Institution-alization (low/mod/high)	Regime Vulnerability (low/mod/high)	Regime Fragmentation (low/mod/high)
Regime	1.	– / –	– / – / –	– / – / .389*	not applicable
Fragmentation	2.	– / –	.358* / – / –	– / – / .391*	
Intraparty	1.	– / –	– / .395* / –	– / – / .323	– / – / –
Opposition	2.	– / –	– / – / –	– / – / –	– / – / –
Political Party	1.	n.a. / –	– / .337* / –	– / – / .626**	– / .498** / .348
Opposition	2.	n.a. / –	– / – / –	– / – / .710**	– / .540** / –
Military	1.	– / –	– / –.527** / n.a.	– / – / –.296	– / –.349* / –
Opposition	2.	–.390* / –	–.380* / –.558** / n.a.	– / – / .611**	– / –.588** / –
Regional	1.	– / –	– / – / –	– / – / –	– / – / –
Opposition	2.	– / –	– / – / –	– / – / –	– / – / –

1.: correlations for mean IOA variable.
2.: correlations for mean high IOA/high commitment variable.

Significance levels: ** p < .01; * p < .05; p < .10. Table lists only those Pearson correlation coefficients that also meet significance tests (at the .10 level) using a nonparametric test and controls for nation-size and modernity.

institutionalization, vulnerability, and fragmentation have much stronger correlations, most falling solidly into the moderate range and some even approaching strong levels of greater than .500. Second, the stability of the overall findings (i.e., for the full sample) for political party and military opposition is demonstrated further by each one's enhanced correlations across the relevant regime subgroups, although in no case is the direction of these correlations altered. Third, and equally important, these contextual effects uncover sizable correlations for fragmentation and intraparty opposition, neither of which was correlated with IOA in the overall subsample. As with commitment, though, regional opposition is found to be less associated with foreign policy. Finally, the correlations for regime fragmentation and the intraparty, political party, and military opposition measures fall into common levels of the political system and regime subsamples; in other words, these precise contextual effects are consistent across different types of opposition.

These findings merit elaboration in at least two respects. The first concerns the direction of correlation coefficients and the clear evidence of opposite political dynamics. Across the subgroups of regimes, the correlations for military opposition consistently indicate greater foreign policy independence (i.e., greater initiative in all cases), although still including the unexpectedly strong tendencies for high commitment IOA. Similarly, the direction of political party correlations remains stable across levels of institutionalization, vulnerability, and fragmentation—consistently resulting in diminished independence (in all cases less initiative), yet still with decreased, not intensified, correlations when high commitment is involved. The findings for regime fragmentation and intraparty opposition parallel the diminished independence found for political parties, indicating that bargaining/controversy avoidance also dominates political decision-making in these arenas under specific political system and regime conditions.

The other striking pattern here is that correlations between opposition and IOA (except for regional opposition) occur mainly under a common set of political system and regime conditions. Once again, the contextual effects of political system accountability are limited, and the ones that do occur are not limited to the democracies; in fact, there is but a single correlation for military opposition in closed polities. As to the role of political system institutionalization, the impact of intraparty, political party, military opposition (but not regime fragmentation) on foreign policy occurs mostly for moderately institutionalized polities, as originally hypothesized.[17] The contextual effect of regime vulnerability is even clearer: the correlations for all four relevant types of opposition are limited entirely to highly vulnerable regimes. This fits with the hypothesis that greater vulnerability would increase leaders' sensitivity to all types of opposition. Finally, with regime fragmentation acting as a conditioning factor, the divergent foreign policy effects of political party and military opposition are clearly strongest for (though not limited to) the moderately fragmented group of regimes.

Affect: Direction and Intensity

Affect concerns the direction and intensity of feelings expressed by the regime toward other international actors, ranging from strong friendliness to extreme hostility. The affect variables used in the analyses here are based on a five-point scale (Hermann, Hermann, Hutchins, 1982): $(+2)$ strong positive affect, $(+1)$ mild positive affect, (0) neutral affect, (-1) mild negative affect, and (-2) strong negative affect. Whereas the other CREON measures are event based, the affect measure is dyadic. Affect scores are not computed for the single event, but instead are coded for each of the recipients in the single event. Because a single event may have multiple recipients, the direction and intensity of affect may vary across the recipients. A regime's mean affect score is computed as an average across all its total number of recipients.[18]

Seven affect measures are used in the analyses to follow, and they capture affect's direction and intensity dimensions separately and in combination. Mean affect is the most general measure, being based on the full five-point scale arraying behavior in terms of both intensity and direction. Affect direction variables, which are analogous to conflict/cooperation, are derived by distinguishing simply between hostile and friendly behaviors, and ignoring the mild and strong intensity gradations with neutral behaviors being excluded. The resulting two variables are percent positive behavior and percent negative behavior, both of which are simply the regime's total number of each type of event divided by its number of recipients. The mean affect intensity scale is created by doing just the opposite. The valences on the five-point affect scale are ignored, and the absolute values of neutral, mild, and strong affect are summed and then averaged by the regime's number of recipients. Two supplementary measures are used to tap behaviors at the extreme levels of intensity: the percentage of extreme affect behaviors (-2 or $+2$) and the percent extreme negative behaviors (-2). The former captures the most extreme of behavior of all types, while the latter allows further consideration of the interaction of direction and intensity in affect.

In this section, findings for affect direction and affect intensity are reported separately for the most part, followed by a discussion comparing the two sets of findings.[19] As argued in Chapter 3, the juxtaposition of affect direction and intensity components enables exploration of the domestic political significance of conflict in foreign policy as opposed to dramatic foreign ventures of all kinds, regardless of whether they are conflictual or cooperative. Also, the treatment of intensity as a separate dimension is reinforced by the fact that the CREON affect intensity variable is statistically independent of the other foreign policy dimensions in the regimes data set, including affect direction.

Affect direction. Friendliness and hostility in foreign policy are widely argued to be associated with the dynamics of both bargaining/controversy avoidance and political legitimization. Assuming that conflict in foreign policy is politically risky and divisive, less conflict in foreign policy would then be the result of leaders' efforts at compromise and controversy avoidance. This suggests the following hypothesis for bargaining/controversy avoidance:

> The foreign policies of politically constrained regimes have generally lower levels of negative affect.

Positive correlations are anticipated between opposition and the mean affect direction and percent positive behavior variables, as well as (especially) negative correlations for the percent negative behavior variable.[20] The logic of political legitimization asserts just the opposite. Whereas the previous hypothesis considers foreign policy conflict to be politically risky, this logic considers it to be a highly effective device for mobilizing public support by focusing attention on foreign threats and appealing to public nationalism. If anything is politically risky here, it is foreign cooperation that could make the regime appear excessively conciliatory and dependent. The political legitimization hypothesis is:

> The foreign policies of politically constrained regimes are likely to have overall higher levels of negative affect and lower levels of positive affect.

Political opposition should be negatively correlated with the mean affect and positive affect measures, with equally strong positive correlations for negative affect actions.

The findings for affect direction for the full sample of regimes are reported in Table 5.3A. Statistically significant correlations are presented for the five opposition measures with the three affect direction variables: mean affect, percent positive behaviors, and percent negative behaviors. The results parallel those found for independence of action. With the exception of a borderline correlation with regime fragmentation, the correlations again center around political party and military opposition. The magnitudes of these correlations, though, exceed those found for commitment and IOA, approaching in some respects the moderate, mid-.300 level.

As was also the case for independence of action, the direction of the correlations for political party and military opposition diverge. Political party opposition is correlated with diminished negative affect and increased levels of positive affect in foreign policy. This aversion to politically risky conflict behaviors fits with the logic of bargaining/controversy avoidance, although the equally strong propensity toward cooperation is not expected. Military opposition has opposite effects. Regimes opposed by politically active militaries show a tendency toward foreign policies marked by negative affect. Assuming this reflects a political strategy for containing the military (and not the substantive influence of a bellicose military itself), then this supports the idea that civilian leaders legitimize their policies and power in the face of military opposition by emphasizing conflict in the nation's foreign relations. There is, though, less support for the hypothesis that leaders have an equally strong aversion from cooperation in foreign policy.

The conditioning effects of political system and regime factors on the link between opposition and affect direction are reported in Table 5.3B, using only the variables for mean affect and percent negative behaviors. These effects are at least as pervasive as those found for independence of

Table 5.3A   Significant Correlations Between Opposition and Direction of Affect in Foreign Policy for the Full Sample of Regimes

	Overall Mean Affect	Percent Positive Behaviors	Percent Negative Behaviors
Regime Fragmentation	—	.158	—
Intraparty Opposition	—	—	—
Political Party Opposition	.304**	.372**	-.363**
Military Opposition	-.238**	-.189*	.300**
Regional Opposition	—	—	—

Significance levels: ** p < .01; * p < .05; p < .10. Table reports only those Pearson correlation coefficients that also meet significance tests (at the .10 level) for correlations using a nonparametric test and controls for nation-size and modernity.

action. As with IOA, the contextual effects of institutionalization, vulnerability, and fragmentation are important for most opposition variables. However, accountability also has important effects, although the influence of opposition occurs in both open and closed polities. All four contextual variables considerably increase the amount of variance in affect direction explained by opposition measures, but rarely is the direction of these effects affected by contextual political conditions.

Turning to specifics and beginning with political party opposition, the strength (but, again, not direction) of its correlations with affect direction is strongly mediated by all four political system and regime properties. Compared to those for the overall sample, the correlations between party opposition and affect direction are sharply magnified in three situations: moderately institutionalized political systems, highly vulnerable regimes, and moderately fragmented regimes. The contextual effect of accountability is far less dramatic. Not only are the party opposition–affect direction correlations much weaker than those found for the other subsamples, but they are also weaker than those found for the full regime sample. Finally, note that in all of these conditions the basic logic of bargaining/controversy

Table 5.3B　Contextual Effects of Political System and Regime Conditions on the Correlations Between Domestic Opposition and Affect Direction in Foreign Policy

		Accountability (closed/open)	Institution- alization (low/mod/high)	Regime Vulnerability (low/mod/high)	Regime Fragmentation (low/mod/high)
Regime	1.	– / –	– / – / –	– / – / .304	
Fragmentation	2.	– / –	– / – / –	– / – / –.318	not applicable
Intraparty	1.	– / –	– / .414** / –.449**	– / – / –	– / – / –
Opposition	2.	– / –	– / –.468** / .366*	– / – / –	– / – / –
Political Party	1.	n.a. / .220*	– / .478** / –	– / – / .536**	– / .444** / .331
Opposition	2.	n.a. / –.227*	– / –.542** / –	– / – / –.609**	– / –.480** / –.348
Military	1.	–.506** / –	– / –.624** / n.a.	– / – / –.365*	– / – / –
Opposition	2.	.508** / –	– / .650** / n.a.	.248 / – / .405*	– / .409* / –
Regional	1.	–.361* / –	– / – / –	– / – / –	– / – / –
Opposition	2.	.457* / –	– / – / –	– / – / –	– / .327* / –

1.: correlations for mean affect variable.
2.: correlations for percent negative behaviors.

Significance levels: ** p < .01; * p < .05; p < .10. Table lists only those Pearson correlation coefficients that also meet significance tests (at the .10 level) using a nonparametric test and controls for nation-size and modernity.

avoidance is not disputed; leaders consistently appear to respond to party opposition with less conflict and greater cooperation in foreign policy. This lends credibility to the idea that foreign policy conflict is, indeed, perceived by leaders as being very risky at home.

The linkage of military opposition to affect direction is influenced in similar ways by the political system and regime conditioning influences; in other words, the variance explained is increased while the relationship's direction is not altered. Military opposition effects are especially strong in the case of the two political system properties: accountability and institutionalization. The correlations found for closed—but not open—polities and for moderately institutionalized ones are considerably stronger than those for the overall regime sample. The role of the two regime properties is less dramatic, although they provide further evidence of especially strong constraints in highly vulnerable regimes and moderately fragmented ones. In the case of all four situations, the correlation of military opposition with mean affect is negative, while it is the reverse for negative affect actions (these last correlations are particularly strong). As with the overall findings, the evidence points consistently to the dynamic of political legitimization in which leaders respond to military opposition with a particular emphasis on foreign conflict. Although responding in a different manner than their counterparts coping with political party constraints, these leaders are as sensitive to military opposition under the same conditions of moderate institutionalization, extreme vulnerability, and moderate fragmentation.[21]

The four conditioning influences also uncover otherwise hidden correlations for the three other types of opposition: regime fragmentation, intraparty opposition, and regional opposition. Most impressive are the correlations for intraparty opposition in the cases of moderately and highly institutionalized political systems. These correlations fall within the moderate range, and they extend to both affect measures. They are, though, more complex than those found between affect and the other types of opposition; not only are the effects present at two levels of institutionalization, but also the directions of these correlations are in the opposite direction. Among moderately institutionalized polities, intraparty opposition is associated with less hostility and greater cooperation and reflects, as in the case of party opposition, the dynamics of bargaining and controversy avoidance. Just the opposite occurs in well-institutionalized polities: intraparty opposition is associated with greater conflict in foreign policy. This is, of course, surprising given that this highest level of institutionalization would otherwise seem to be associated with greater restraint in domestic and foreign affairs.

The effects of fragmentation and regional opposition are comparatively weak and more scattered. Regime fragmentation is weakly correlated with diminished conflict. Borderline correlations occur in highly vulnerable regimes, which parallels the findings for political party opposition. Regional opposition is associated with greater conflict (but unrelated to cooperation) in closed polities as well as moderately fragmented regimes. Although not strong, the evidence is that regional opposition, like military opposition, is connected with greater hostility in foreign policy and thus reflects the dynamics of political legitimization.

Affect intensity. This dimension of affect refers to the strength with which feelings are expressed, regardless of whether they are friendly or hostile. As argued in Chapter 3, there is reason to suspect that the intensity of affect—more so than its direction—is more directly associated with domestic politics. When engaging in bargaining and controversy avoidance, leaders avoid strong expressions of affect in foreign policy, either because of compromises that moderate contending preferences or because leaders seek to reduce the visibility of controversial actions. The following hypothesis is suggested by the logic of bargaining/controversy avoidance:

> The foreign policies of politically constrained regimes are characterized by milder, or less intense, levels of affect.

If this is true, negative correlations should be found between the opposition measures and the three measures of affect intensity: mean intensity, percent extreme actions, and percent extreme negative actions. As with affect direction, the dynamics of political legitimization point to opposite effects on foreign policy. Instead of posing risks to the regime, this logic holds that intense foreign policy actions can provide politically attractive drama to the public and reaffirm legitimizing themes associated with the regime. The political legitimization hypothesis is:

> The foreign policies of politically constrained regimes are characterized by generally more intense levels of affect.

Support for this hypothesis would be indicated by positive correlations between political opposition measures and the mean affect intensity, percent extreme behaviors, and percent extreme negative behaviors.

Results of the analysis for the full sample of regimes are reported in Table 5.4A. Statistically significant correlations are listed for the five opposition measures across the three affect intensity variables. Along with a relatively weak correlation between regime fragmentation and extreme behavior, political party and military opposition are once again strongly associated with foreign policy, and, as before, these correlations are in divergent directions. These overall correlations are, though, stronger than those found in the analyses of IOA, affect direction, and commitment; the almost .400 correlation between party opposition and mean intensity is the only finding for the overall sample that falls solidly in the moderate range. Political party opposition is tied to diminished intensity of affect for all three variables, further indicating that party constraints (as well as those of regime fragmentation) operate along the lines of bargaining/controversy avoidance. The impact of military opposition is also substantial, and is comparable to its impact on IOA and affect direction, although it is limited to mean intensity and extreme conflict and does not apply to extreme behavior in general. The dynamic of military opposition reflects political legitimization. Interestingly, the extreme manifestation of political legitimization centers around conflictual themes, whereas the constraining effects of fragmentation and party opposition also extend to extreme behaviors of all types.

Turning to the role of contextual influences, Table 5.4B reports correlations between the five opposition measures and two affect intensity variables (mean affect intensity and percent extreme acts) across the four regime subsamples defined by political system and regime properties. The conditioning effects of political institutionalization, regime vulnerability,

Table 5.4A   Significant Correlations Between Opposition and Intensity of Affect in Foreign Policy for the Full Sample of Regimes

	Mean Affect Intensity	Percent Extreme Behaviors	Percent Extreme Negative Behaviors
Regime Fragmentation	—	-.181*	—
Intraparty Opposition	—	—	—
Party Opposition	-.393**	-.237*	-.282**
Military Opposition	.270**	—	.250**
Regional Opposition	—	—	—

Significance levels: ** p < .01; * p < .05; p < .10. Table reports only those Pearson correlation coefficients that also meet significance tests (at the .10 level) for correlations using a nonparametric test and controls for nation-size and modernity.

and regime fragmentation are pervasive, while once again those for accountability are not. The overall correlations for regime fragmentation and political party and military opposition are enhanced under certain conditions, while the conditioning influences once again reveal correlations for intraparty and regional opposition. All of this is similar to the contextual effects found for IOA and affect direction. However, with affect intensity there is one major exception, which perhaps might be considered suggestive of the particular sensitivity of this foreign policy dimension to domestic opposition: sizable correlations (all in the same direction) appear in multiple categories of certain conditioning influences. Specifically, political party effects on affect intensity are especially pervasive. Institutionalization, vulnerability, and fragmentation each enhance the explained variance in affect intensity, while the overall correlations are actually diminished for open regimes. The enhanced effects of political party opposition occur under conditions of moderate institutionalization, moderate and high vulnerability, and low and moderate fragmentation. The findings for moderately institutionalized polities are consistent with

Table 5.4B Contextual Effects of Political System and Regime Conditions on Correlations Between Domestic Opposition and Affect Intensity in Foreign Policy

	Accountability (closed/open)	Institution- alization (low/mod/high)	Regime Vulnerability (low/mod/high)	Regime Fragmentation (low/mod/high)
Regime Fragmentation	1. –/– 2. –/–	1. –/ – / – 2. –/ – / –	1. –.293/ – / –.477* 2. –/ – / –	not applicable
Intraparty Opposition	1. –/– 2. –/–	1. –/–.317*/ – 2. –/–.429**/–.343*	1. –/–.339*/ – 2. –/ – / –	1. –/ – / – 2. –/ – / –
Political Party Opposition	1. n.a./–.196 2. n.a./–.287*	1. –.339/–.358*/ – 2. –/–.354*/ –	1. –/–.405**/–.593** 2. –/ – /–.509**	1. –.389**/–.459**/ – 2. –.290/–.404*/ –
Military Opposition	1. –/.241* 2. –/.265*	1. –/.318*/n.a. 2. –/.472**/n.a.	1. .403**/ – /.424* 2. –/.324*/.549**	1. –/.513**/ – 2. –/.405*/ –
Regional Opposition	1. –/– 2. –/–	1. –/.290/ – 2. –/.310*/ –	1. –.294/ – / – 2. –/.354*/ –	1. –/ – / – 2. –/ – / –

1.: correlations for mean intensity variable.
2.: correlations for percent extreme variable.

Significance levels: ** p < .01; * p < .05; p < .10. Table lists only those Pearson correlation coefficients that also meet significance tests (at the .10 level) using a nonparametric test and controls for nation-size and modernity.

previous findings, and those for vulnerability do not undercut the theoretical logic developed here. More perplexing are the findings for the conditioning effects of regime fragmentation. Here opposition is, unexpectedly, tied to affect intensity in cohesive regimes, as well as for moderately fragmented ones, which has previously been the case. This evidence suggests that political party constraints are widespread and consistently result in less intense behavior across different conditions.

Military opposition influences affect intensity across all four political system and regime conditions, although not quite as strongly as political party opposition. These findings are generally consistent with those found between IOA and affect direction. There are no exceptions to the basic positive direction of these correlations, which is further indication that political legitimization is closely tied to the involvement of military opposition in the foreign policy process. Furthermore, as before, the effects of military opposition are limited to moderately institutionalized polities and moderately fragmented regimes. There are, however, some complexities in the findings for accountability and regime vulnerability. First, the conditioning effects of accountability, although not resulting in stronger correlations, diverge a bit from previous findings. Whereas the effects of military opposition on IOA and affect direction are limited to closed polities, here they occur in only open regimes. Second, the conditioning effects of regime vulnerability are unusually strong. Not only are correlations increased well into the moderate range, but they are not limited to a single level of vulnerability; as happened with political party opposition, correlations occur for more than one category and, in fact, for all three levels. Mean intensity is tied to military opposition at vulnerability's highest and lowest categories; the former is expected and fits with the previous findings, but the latter does not.

The remaining correlations in the table are for the three other types of opposition, and they are generally weaker and more scattered, as would be suspected by their weak or nonexistent overall correlations with affect intensity. With controls for institutionalization and vulnerability, it is possible to identify important correlations for intraparty and regional opposition. Intraparty opposition effects occur under moderate levels of both institutionalization and vulnerability and under high levels of institutionalization, while those of regional opposition are limited mainly to the moderate levels of both conditioning influences. The effects of these two types of opposition are in divergent directions. Negative correlations for intraparty opposition reflect the constraints of bargaining/controversy avoidance, while the positive ones for regional opposition indicate political legitimization dynamics. Finally, the findings for regime fragmentation are unusual. Its admittedly weak overall correlation is mostly wiped out by control variables, and it has far fewer correlations than any of the other four opposition measures. Once again, the theorized primacy of political constraints within the regime as the most direct influence on decisionmakers is not borne out by the evidence.

Direction versus intensity in foreign policy affect. Immediately evident from these findings is that the connection between the direction and intensity of affect is not an either/or situation. Instead, both dimensions are to one degree or another connected with certain opposition measures but not others. At best the question is whether correlations are strongest for affect direction (negative and positive behaviors), affect intensity (mean intensity or extreme actions), or the two dimensions in interaction (mean affect intensity or extreme negative behaviors).

But the evidence on this matter is not simple either. Neither of the interactive measures stands out at all. In fact, correlations for the two are relatively weak compared with those for separate affect direction and intensity variables. Specifically, the correlations for the overall mean affect measure are smaller than those for the simpler negative affect variable (see Table 5.3A), and this extends to correlations across all of the subsamples (see Table 5.3B). Nor do the interactive effects outweigh those for affect intensity. The correlations for mean affect intensity are strongest for the overall sample (see Table 5.4A), while the mixed results across the political system and regime subsamples make it difficult to conclude that any interactive measure is clearly more important than intensity (see Table 5.4B). Clearly, there is little evidence that the manifestations of political opposition take the form of the interaction of the direction and intensity of affect. Instead, the evidence is that the separate dimensions of affect direction and intensity are more closely tied to domestic opposition.

This raises the question of whether one affect dimension—direction or intensity—is more strongly associated with domestic opposition than the other. A quick look back at the affect tables makes it clear that neither dimension is consistently more important. In the overall sample the differences are not great, although there is a tendency for political party opposition to be more closely tied to affect intensity, while military opposition is more associated with negative behavior. The evidence is also mixed for the four subsamples of regimes. Among closed regimes, military and regional opposition are associated with affect direction, while in the open regimes political parties are linked to both direction and intensity. The results across political institutionalization levels are the most clear-cut: significant correlations between opposition and affect direction are stronger and more pervasive. But the opposite tendency appears for vulnerability and fragmentation, where affect intensity stands out with comparatively more correlations with opposition.

Taken together, these findings suggest that the direction and intensity of affect are best treated as separate and equally important manifestations of domestic politics in foreign policy. Not only are they statistically independent (despite their common conceptual roots), but also neither one stands out as more linked to domestic politics than the other. There are numerous occurrences in which the two are equally well correlated with opposition, and if there are differences they do not take any uniform pattern. The original contention that affect intensity (alone or interactively) might be an alternative to affect direction is not supported, and domestic political opposition is linked to conflict as much as any other foreign policy dimension.

Generalizing About Political Dynamics
Across the Foreign Policy Dimensions

The results reported in this chapter picture the empirical linkage between domestic opposition and foreign policy as pervasive and yet complex. This concluding section synthesizes the findings for the four separate foreign policy dimensions. The objective is to embellish them in a way that permits generalizations about domestic politics across the multiple dimensions of foreign policy. To achieve this, I want to return to the general issues raised at the opening of the chapter. These matters concern (1) the amount of total variance explained in foreign policy by the five types of opposition (separately or combined), (2) the comparative importance of these different types of opposition, and (3) whether the conditioning effects of political system and regime properties are generalizable across opposition and foreign policy dimensions. The discussion of these questions revolves around a sequence of three sets of tables, each with an alternative summary of the findings for the four foreign policy dimensions.

Question 1: How strong are the effects of political opposition on foreign policy behavior? This implies a sequence of two issues. First, how strong are the combined effects of political opposition on the foreign policy dimensions of commitment, independence of action, affect direction, and affect intensity? Second, is the strength of these opposition effects roughly equal across the four foreign policy dimensions, or are certain dimensions more sensitive to domestic politics than others?

Multiple regression was employed to get some indication of the combined impact of the four types of opposition. Table 5.5 summarizes these multivariate statistical effects on foreign policy commitment, independence, affect direction, and affect intensity. As before, results are reported for the overall sample of regimes, as well as for the subsamples defined by political system and regime properties. The coefficients (where they are statistically significant) are reported in a way that highlights the presence of multiple opposition effects on foreign policy. Specifically, the combined effects of two or more opposition variables in a statistically significant regression equation (according to the F-value for the entire equation) are summarized by the multiple correlation coefficient (multiple R).[22] These

Table 5.5 Overall Magnitude of Opposition Effects on Foreign Policy Behaviors: Multiple Correlation Coefficients

	Overall Sample of Regimes	Political System Accountability (closed/open)	Political System Institutionalization (low/mod/high)	Regime Vulnerability (low/mod/high)	Regime Fragmentation (low/mod/high)
Commitment					
Mean Commitment	.268	– / .263	– / .352 / –	– / **663** / –	– / – / –
Intent Bhvrs	–	– / –	– / – / –	– / .389 / –	– / – / –
Deeds Bhvrs	.252	– / .315	– / .463 / –	– / .281 / –	– / – / –
Indep of Action					
Mean IOA	.214	– / –	– / .571 / –	– / – / .658	– / .507 / –
Initiatives	.278	– / .255	– / .624 / .293	– / – / .676	– / .407 / –
High Commit IOA	.312	– / –	– / .558 / –	– / – / .741	– / .644 / –
Affect Direction					
Mean Affect	.346	.518 / .220	– / .659 / .449	– / – / .536	– / .444 / –
Positive Bhvrs	.385	.470 / .220	– / .633 / .438	– / – / .642	– / .489 / –
Negative Bhvrs	**421**	.508 / –	– / .704 / .366	– / – / .612	– / .564 / –
Affect Intensity					
Mean Intensity	**430**	– / .241	– / .358 / –	.403 / **506** / .594	– / .558 / –
Extreme Bhvrs	.237	.415 / .212	– / – / –	– / .524 / –	– / – / –
Extr Neg Bhvrs	**341**	– / **350**	– / **558** / .343	– / **486** / .618	– / .405 / –

Note: Multiple correlation coefficients (multiple R) listed are significant to at least the .05 level. Underlining indicates multiple regression coefficient reflects the interaction of two or more variables (F value for entire equation). Coefficients in bold indicate that the contribution of each opposition measure is significant to the .10 level.

coefficients are underlined in the table. Furthermore, bold print is used to identify those coefficients that meet an additional, stricter statistical criterion: the separate contributions of the two or more opposition variables are each statistically significant (as indicated by the t-value of each variable's regression coefficient). Note that those coefficients without underlining are bivariate Pearson correlations, indicating that only one opposition variable in the equation had significant effects.

A look at Table 5.5, as well as a glance back at earlier tables, makes one thing quite evident: in most cases the combined statistical effects of any opposition are not dramatic. While multiple opposition effects (as indicated by underlining) are rather frequent, very few have significant and statistically independent contributions by more than one variable (as indicated by bold print). The inclusion of multiple opposition variables in most equations does little to increase the magnitude of the multiple correlation coefficient. In only about ten occurrences (as indicated by underlined correlations in bold print) are the contributions of two or more opposition variables both statistically significant. Most of these are limited to the combined effects of just two types of opposition (political parties and military actors) on just two foreign policy dimensions (affect direction and intensity). Other than this, the all-too-apparent fact from Table 5.5 is that in the vast majority of cases the interaction of opposition variables does little to increase the total amount of variance explained.

Having now considered the possibility of statistically enhanced effects in a multivariate equation, we can return to the more basic matter of the strength of the combined effects of opposition measures on the foreign policy dimensions. Overall opposition effects—those for the full sample of regimes—fall into the weak to, at best, moderate range (occasionally). The two dimensions of affect in foreign policy are influenced the most by political opposition. The combined effects of political party and military opposition on hostility and intensity in foreign policy increase multiple correlation coefficients to over the .400 level. Overall opposition effects are more limited for commitment and independence of action; these correlations are weaker (generally not exceeding .300) and do not involve any major combined effects.

Much larger multiple correlation coefficients for all four foreign policy dimensions are identified with the introduction of controls for political system and regime properties. The largest such correlations in Table 5.5 are for IOA and affect direction under conditions of moderate political system institutionalization and high regime vulnerability. These effects are arguably rather strong, with correlations well over .600 and in a few cases explaining almost 50 percent of the variance in IOA and affect direction. The impact of opposition on commitment and affect intensity is noticeably less, even under these specific political conditions. Most correlations for affect intensity are solidly in the moderate range, while opposition effects on commitment are neither as strong nor as pervasive across the cells of the table.

In sum, these findings suggest that opposition does account for all four dimensions of foreign policy, but to varying degrees and under very specific conditions. By just about all indications, foreign policy commitment (despite involving the all-too-critical authoritative resources) is the least affected, while domestic opposition is most strongly linked to IOA and affect direction. The conventional emphasis on conflict as a manifestation of domestic opposition is supported, even if the equally conventional concern for commitment is not. The attention given here to the less familiar, politically sensitive dimensions of foreign policy is also vindicated: independence and affect intensity are found to be closely linked to domestic opposition. Finally, these findings provide a basic insight into how opposition interacts to influence foreign policy. There is little evidence to suggest that opposition variables combine to affect foreign policy via multiple regression; instead, only by incorporating the contextual influences of political system and regime properties is it possible to increase the amount of variance explained in foreign policy.

Question 2: What are the relative effects of the types of political opposition across multiple dimensions of foreign policy? Thus far, the impacts of the five types of opposition have been considered separately for commitment, independence, affect direction, and affect intensity. Part of the task here is to generalize about the relative effects of different opposition across all four foreign policy dimensions. In other words, which type(s) of opposition has the strongest effects, which one(s) has the weakest impact, and is it possible to generalize about these effects across the multiple dimensions of foreign policy?

The statistically significant effects of each type of opposition on each of the four foreign policy dimensions are summarized in Table 5.6. These effects are labeled in terms of the strength of Pearson correlation coefficients: strong (greater than .500), moderate (.250–.500), and weak (less than .250). (Actual correlation coefficients are not reported because these labels summarize the opposition effects on the multiple variables of each foreign policy dimension.) This is done for each political system and regime property, a procedure that enables consideration of the strength of opposition effects and the frequency to which they occur across multiple conditions.

Glancing at the table as a whole, it is immediately evident that not all five types of opposition are equally important. Regime fragmentation has the weakest and least pervasive foreign policy effects. It is related only to affect intensity for the overall sample, and although additional correlations for it are identified at certain levels of institutionalization and vulnerability, their magnitude is moderate at best. There appears to be little support for our contention of the primacy of opposition within the regime. If anything,

Table 5.6 Summary of Each Opposition's Effects on Commitment, Independence, and Affect (Direction and Intensity) Dimensions of Foreign Policy

	Overall Sample of Regimes	Political System Accountability	Political System Institutionalization	Regime Vulnerability	Regime Fragmentation
Regime Fragmentation	COM: IOA: DIR: INT: weak	COM: IOA: DIR: INT:	COM: weak IOA: mod DIR: INT:	COM: IOA: mod DIR: weak INT: mod	not applicable
Intraparty Opposition	COM: mod IOA: DIR: INT:	COM: mod IOA: DIR: INT:	COM: mod IOA: mod DIR: mod INT: mod	COM: strg IOA: weak DIR: INT: mod	COM: mod IOA: DIR: INT:
Political Party Opposition	COM: IOA: weak DIR: mod INT: mod	COM: IOA: DIR: weak INT: mod	COM: mod IOA: mod DIR: strg INT: mod	COM: IOA: strg DIR: strg INT: strg	COM: IOA: strg DIR: mod INT: mod
Military Opposition	COM: IOA: weak DIR: weak INT: mod	COM: IOA: strg DIR: strg INT: mod	COM: mod IOA: strg DIR: strg INT: mod	COM: IOA: strg DIR: mod INT: mod	COM: IOA: mod DIR: mod INT: strg
Regional Opposition	COM: IOA: DIR: INT:	COM: IOA: DIR: mod INT:	COM: mod IOA: DIR: INT: mod	COM: mod IOA: DIR: INT: mod	COM: weak IOA: DIR: mod INT:

Note: Size of Pearson correlations is summarized in the following manner. Judgment about size of correlations for each relationship is based on the overall mean foreign policy measure; if it is relatively small, then the prevailing pattern among the other larger measures is used.
strg (strong): Pearson correlation is in excess of .500 and significant at the $p < .05$ level.
mod (moderate): Pearson correlation is between .250 and .500 and significant at the $p < .05$ level.
weak: Pearson correlation is less than .250 or not significant at the $p < .05$ level.

just the reverse seems true; the results suggest that somehow foreign policy makers are generally able to overcome these direct internal constraints. Instead, it may be that fragmentation is more significant as a conditioning influence, in which leaders in internally divided regimes are more sensitive to opposition outside the regime, when that opposition exists. Or it may be that aggregate data analysis hides complex processes within the regime, as will be considered in Chapter 6. Whatever the case, the evidence is clear that it does not have a direct impact across the aggregate behavior of a regime's foreign policy.

At the other extreme, political party and military opposition have relatively strong and pervasive effects on foreign policy. Both are significantly correlated with each foreign policy dimension, although the association with commitment is limited to only specific levels of institutionalization. In the case of IOA, affect direction, and affect intensity, though, there are significant correlations for the full sample of regimes, most of which become particularly pronounced at certain levels of institutionalization, vulnerability, and fragmentation. Also recall that many of these relationships are robust in that they extend to most, if not all, of the specific variables used for each foreign policy dimension. More generally, it may well be that the measures of political party and military opposition tap broader political scenarios—particularly as amplified by institutionalization and regime vulnerability—characteristic of highly unstable democracies and praetorian political systems.

The effects of intraparty and regional opposition fall between those of regime fragmentation and opposition from political parties and the military, and as such they are more complex. Intraparty opposition has sizable and numerous effects, but these are centered primarily around one foreign policy dimension: commitment. There is an overall relationship here, but it is considerably strengthened by the contextual influence of regime vulnerability and fragmentation. Although intraparty opposition is primarily connected to commitment, intraparty opposition is also related to IOA and affect direction and intensity at certain levels of political system institutionalization. The dynamics of these effects, and the conditions under which they occur, parallel those of political party opposition and regime fragmentation. Turning to regional opposition, its effects are as pervasive as those of intraparty opposition, but these correlations are moderate, at best, and quite scattered in that they are limited to single measures of the foreign policy dimensions. Regional opposition is the only type of opposition with no effects on any foreign policy behavior for the full sample of regimes. It does, however, have one or more significant correlations across all four of the political system and regime conditions.

In sum, the impact of the five types of opposition varies in magnitude. Political party and military opposition effects are clearly strongest and most pervasive, particularly for independence of action, affect direction, and affect intensity. Intraparty opposition has similarly strong effects, but they are associated mainly with commitment. Regional opposition has pervasive effects, but they are weaker and do not take on as clear a pattern as the other three. Regime fragmentation has an even more limited impact, and this hardly supports the theoretical centrality given it in this project.

Question 3: To what extent are the conditioning effects of political system and regime properties generalizable across dimensions of opposition and foreign policy? Addressing the previous two questions has, indirectly, demonstrated that contextual influences have an important impact on the linkage between opposition and foreign policy. The task of this section is to examine the precise dynamics of each conditioning influence: accountability, institutionalization, vulnerability, and fragmentation. Is it possible to generalize about conditioning effects across the five types of opposition and four dimensions of foreign policy behavior? In particular, do opposition effects occur only under certain levels of each conditioning influence, regardless of type of opposition or dimension of foreign policy?

Some of the summary evidence for answering these questions can be found in Tables 5.5 and 5.6. These tables, however, are not sufficiently precise to report the dynamics of political systems and regime contextual effects because they do not identify the specific level of each conditioning variable under which opposition effects on foreign policy behavior occur. Therefore, a sequence of four additional tables is used to provide this information for each conditioning variable. Each specifies the strength (strong, moderate, and weak) of statistically significant opposition–foreign policy effects at each level of the conditioning factor. This information shows if opposition effects are consistently limited to certain levels of each conditioning influence, as hypothesized in Chapter 3. Adjacent valences in parentheses are used to indicate the direction of correlations, and are indicative of the occurrence of the alternative dynamics of bargaining/controversy avoidance and political legitimization.

Turning first to political accountability, it should already be evident that its effects are not dramatic. Compared to the other three conditioning factors, the evidence in Tables 5.5 and 5.6 shows that it uncovers fewer and generally weaker opposition effects on foreign policy. There is little evidence to support the widespread idea that accountability is the primary political influence on foreign policy, even as a mediating variable. Table 5.7A further challenges the conventional wisdom about the comparative constraints in open polities and closed ones. Significant correlations are by no means limited to open regimes as widely assumed. In fact, the only strong correlations in all of Table 5.7A occur in closed political systems, and both of these indicate increased (not diminished) conflict in foreign policy. Among open regimes, the correlations between the various types of opposition and foreign policy are all relatively weak. Although the magnitude of its effects are quite limited, there is one unique and important

Table 5.7A   Summary of Significant Opposition Effects Across Open and Closed Political Systems

	Regimes in Closed Political Systems		Regimes in Open Political Systems	
Regime Fragmentation	—	—	—	—
	—	—	—	—
Intraparty Opposition	—	—	com(+)	—
	—	—	—	—
Political Party Opposition	—	—	—	—
	—	—	dir(+)	int(-)
Military	—	ioa(-)	—	—
Opposition	DIR(-)	—	—	int(+)
Regional	—	—	—	—
Opposition	DIR(-)	—	—	int(+)

Note: Statistically significant relationships at the p < .05 level are indicated in each cell. Capital letters indicate primary relationships—i.e., ones with correlations that exceed .400 and are not based on single, isolated occurrences between the opposition measure and multiple measures of the foreign policy behavior.

Valences in parentheses indicate the direction of the correlation coefficient. Positive correlations apply as follows: for commitment (COM) increased intent or deed behavior; for independence of action (IOA) decreased independence—less initiative/less unilaterism; for affect direction (DIR) decreased hostility; and for affect intensity (INT) increased intensity.

finding here: alternative political dynamics appear linked to accountability in the manner originally hypothesized. Bargaining/controversy avoidance holds mainly for opposition in open polities, and political legitimization applies to closed polities. For this reason, in particular, accountability as a conditioning influence deserves further empirical attention with a larger sample of nations and regimes.

The contextual effects of political institutionalization are far more impressive. As shown in Tables 5.5 and 5.6, this aspect of political system structure uncovers numerous correlations that were absent or weaker for the overall sample of regimes. These are mostly in the moderate to strong range and extend across most dimensions of foreign policy. The basis of these contextual dynamics is clarified in Table 5.7B, where one can see that the major effects (across all four foreign policy dimensions) of political party, military, and (in part) intraparty opposition are concentrated in

Table 5.7B   Summary of Significant Opposition Effects Across Three Levels of Political System Institutionalization

	Noninstitutionalized Polities		Moderately Institutionalized Polities		Well-Institutionalized Polities	
Regime	com(–)	ioa(+)	—	—	—	—
Fragmentation	—	—	—	—	—	—
Intraparty	—	—	com(+)	ioa(+)	com(+)	—
Opposition	—	—	DIR(+)	INT(–)	DIR(–)	int(–)
Political Party	—	—	com(+)	ioa(+)	—	—
Opposition	—	—	DIR(+)	int(-)	—	—
Military	—	ioa(-)	COM(–)	IOA(–)	n.a.	
Opposition	—	—	DIR(–)	int(+)	n.a.	
Regional	com(-)	—	—	—	—	—
Opposition	—	—	—	int(+)	—	—

Note: Statistically significant relationships at the p < .05 level are indicated in each cell. Capital letters indicate primary relationships—i.e., ones with correlations that exceed .400 and are not based on single, isolated occurrences between the opposition measure and multiple measures of the foreign policy behavior.

Valences in parentheses indicate the direction of the correlation coefficient. Positive correlations apply as follows: for commitment (COM) increased intent or deed behavior; for independence of action (IOA) decreased indepedence—less initiative/less unilaterism; for affect direction (DIR) decreased hostility; and for affect intensity (INT) increased intensity.

regimes in moderately institutionalized political systems. There is clear support for the hypothesis that opposition constraints are diminished in settings where leaders can suppress opponents (low institutionalization) or where they can depend on well-established political norms and procedures to achieve agreement with them (high institutionalization). Equally apparent, though, is that the direction of correlations does not vary across levels of institutionalization. This variable accounts for little in the occurrence of the alternative dynamics of bargaining/controversy avoidance and political legitimization in the foreign policy process.

The impact of regime vulnerability, as a conditioning influence, is almost nearly as substantial as that of political system institutionalization. Tables 5.5 and 5.6 show that this regime property uncovers strong correlations for both military and political party opposition, as well as more moderate ones for the other three types of political opposition. Table 5.7C

Table 5.7C   Summary of Significant Opposition Effects Across the Three Levels of Regime Vulnerability

	Minimally Vulnerable Regimes		Moderately Vulnerable Regimes		Highly Vulnerable Regimes	
Regime	—	—	—	—	—	ioa(+)
Fragmentation	—	—	—	—	dir(+)	int(−)
Intraparty	—	—	COM(+)	ioa(+)	—	—
Opposition	—	—	—	int(−)	—	—
Political Party	—	—	—	—	—	IOA(+)
Opposition	—	—	—	int(−)	DIR(+)	INT(−)
Military	—	—	—	—	—	IOA(+)
Opposition	—	—	—	int(+)	DIR(−)	INT(+)
Regional	—	—	com(+)	—	com(−)	—
Opposition	—	int(−)	—	int(−)		

Note: Statistically significant relationships at the p < .05 level are indicated in each cell. Capital letters indicate primary relationships—i.e., ones with correlations that exceed .400 and are not based on single, isolated occurrences between the opposition measure and multiple measures of the foreign policy behavior.

   Valences in parentheses indicate the direction of the correlation coefficient. Positive correlations apply as follows: for commitment (COM) increased intent or deed behavior; for independence of action (IOA) decreased indepedence—less initiative/less unilaterism; for affect direction (DIR) decreased hostility; and for affect intensity (INT) increased intensity.

breaks down these findings for low, moderate, and high levels of regime vulnerability. The pattern lends considerable support to our original hypothesis that highly vulnerable regimes are most sensitive to domestic opposition. The distribution of correlations is most impressive at the extremes: there are no correlations at all for the minimally vulnerable set of regimes, and the strongest correlations appear almost entirely for highly vulnerable regimes. The latter set of regimes is particularly affected by political party and military opposition, where there are strong linkages to independence of action, affect direction, and affect intensity. High regime vulnerability is also one of the few conditions in which regime fragmentation has sizable effects and ones that extend to multiple foreign policy dimensions: commitment, IOA, and intensity. Yet, like political system institutionalization, regime vulnerability does nothing to account for the alternative dynamics of these political influences; note the absence of differences in the valences listed in Table 5.7C for the moderately and highly vulnerable regimes.

The conditioning influences of regime fragmentation are also important; in fact, the findings in Tables 5.5 and 5.6 suggest that this variable serves much better as a contextual variable than as an opposition directly linked to foreign policy. Along with a strong correlation between intraparty opposition and commitment, political party and military opposition are associated with IOA, affect direction, and affect intensity at certain levels of regime fragmentation. As can be seen from the more detailed information in Table 5.7D, these effects can be traced almost entirely to the moderate level of regime fragmentation. The main exception here is, once again, the intraparty opposition connection with commitment, whose linkage is strongest for the cohesive regimes. These findings do not conform to our original hypothesis, in which it was theorized that highly fragmented regimes would be most constrained by domestic opposition. Instead, highly fragmented regimes are the ones with the fewest political effects, having only two weak correlations. Although these moderately fragmented regimes have sizable political divisions, these findings are puzzling because the most highly fragmented regimes appear unconstrained.[23] One possible explanation is that the politics within these multigroup coalitions is so intense that external actors are ignored; in other words, intense (and complex) internal political conflicts override the influence of outside actors. Finally, note that regime fragmentation does little to account for the directions of opposition effects at its different levels.

In summary, despite the puzzles for regime fragmentation, the findings reported here for the four sets of conditioning influences are striking. If the use of multiple regression and causal modeling failed (at least at this stage of research) to uncover interactions among different political oppositions as they affect foreign policy, the incorporation of conditioning influences was a useful strategy for tapping how the political context conditions the separate effects of different opposition types on foreign policy behavior. The effects of political institutionalization and both regime properties have a major mediating impact on the linkage between most opposition and most foreign policy behaviors. The general pattern of contextual effects is also consistent: opposition influences are most potent for highly vulnerable and moderately fragmented regimes, as well as ones in moderately institutionalized political systems. Equally important, the role of accountability is far more limited, which is consistent with the initial suspicion that the role of this political system property has been overemphasized.

An Overall Interpretation of Findings

While the above discussion provides theoretical insights into how political variables interact to affect multiple dimensions of foreign policy, the findings can be judged still further, from a more substantive perspective. By way of an overall summary of these findings, the following interpretation

Table 5.7D   Summary of Significant Opposition Effects Across Three Basic Levels of Regime Fragmentation

	Minimally Fragmented Regimes		Moderately Fragmented Regimes		Highly Fragmented Regimes	
Intraparty	COM(+)	—	com(+)	—	—	—
Opposition	—	—	—	—	—	—
Political Party	—	—	—	IOA(+)	—	ioa(+)
Opposition	—	int(–)	DIR(+)	INT(–)	dir(+)	—
Military	—	—	—	IOA(-)	—	—
Opposition	—	—	DIR(–)	INT(+)	—	—
Regional	—	—	com(–)	—	—	—
Opposition	—	—	dir(–)	—	—	—

Note: Statistically significant relationships at the $p < .05$ level are indicated in each cell. Capital letters indicate primary relationships—i.e., ones with correlations that exceed .400 and are not based on single, isolated occurrences between the opposition measure and multiple measures of the foreign policy behavior.

Valences in parentheses indicate the direction of the correlation coefficient. Positive correlations apply as follows: for commitment (COM) increased intent or deed behavior; for independence of action (IOA) decreased independence—less initiative/less unilaterism; for affect direction (DIR) decreased hostility; and for affect intensity (INT) increased intensity.

can be made: this broad, cross-national analysis has been able to demonstrate that domestic political conditions—in their extreme forms—account for certain overall foreign policy patterns. Even though the research design needs further elaboration (as discussed in Chapter 6), the analysis has identified particular situations in which intense domestic political pressures appear to overwhelm the usually dominant role of international pressures—ones that were particularly rigid and constraining during the Cold War of the 1960s. There is, in other words, some indication that contrary to realist approaches, in extreme domestic situations, political pressures may become a driving force behind a nation's overall foreign policy behavior. This evidence is twofold.

The first indication of such extreme political pressures comes from the correlations between political opposition and foreign policy behaviors for the full sample of regimes. The most meaningful patterns of overall correlations were found for political party opposition and military opposition as related to three dimensions of foreign policy: independence of action, affect direction, and affect intensity.[24] These correlations, though, fall into the weak to moderate range (between .200 to .350) and at most account for 10 percent of variance in the distribution of regimes. Correlations of this magnitude, as can be seen by an examination of their scatterplots (not included here), can be traced largely to a dozen or so cases at the highest points of the regression plot.[25] Thus, the negative correlations between party opposition and independence, conflict, and intensity in foreign policy can be accounted for by regimes in democratic systems facing very strong and sharply polarized party opponents in the legislature (see rankings in Table 4.5).[26] Similarly, the positive association between military opposition and the same foreign policy dimensions reflects the severe situation (in both democratic and authoritarian polities) in which military actors are contenders for power and have anti-regime or antisystemic orientations.[27] In both cases, though, the evidence is similar: the extreme levels of opposition produce patterns of equally extreme levels of foreign policy behavior, albeit in completely divergent directions.

The other way the findings capture extreme political pressures is by identifying pervasive and strong opposition effects under at least two kinds of political conditions: moderate levels of political system institutionalization and high levels of regime vulnerability. As theorized in Chapter 3, these settings represent politically extreme situations in which leaders must cope with, respectively, fluid political norms and procedures with possibly antisystemic opposition and situations in which the regime's collapse appears imminent. The findings indicate that these conditions lead leaders to be more sensitive to the full range of types of opposition with effects extending to four foreign policy dimensions, particularly independence of action and affect direction. The significance of especially the strong correlations (.500 or greater) is that they can be traced to opposition at all levels for the subsamples of highly vulnerable regimes and ones in moderately institutionalized polities.[28] In contrast to the overall correlations for the full regime sample, these findings are not dependent solely upon regimes at the highest points of the measurement scale, but rather the correspondence between opposition and foreign policy levels occurs progressively across the full range of the scatterplot. Thus, under these conditions foreign policy makers respond to moderate levels of political opposition, and so on.

The broader meaning of these two sets of findings, if taken together, can be advanced a bit further. They point to two general political scenarios where domestic pressures on foreign policy become severe in the very fluid and threatening environments of moderate institutionalization and high vulnerability. The first scenario is democratic instability, in which strong and extreme political opposition results in minimal levels of foreign policy behavior. While political party opposition is the defining feature of this democratic game, the parallel (and reinforcing) foreign policy effects of regime fragmentation and intraparty opposition suggest an interconnection among these oppositions under these conditions—all of which conforms well with the case studies of deadlocked coalitions analyzed in Chapter 2. The second scenario is one of praetorian instability, occurring in both democratic and authoritarian polities. The dominant scenario centers around intense pressure from the military, in other words, its looming intervention into the politics of the poorly established and highly vulnerable civilian regime. Its impact is distinctive from the democratic scenario—a pattern of highly assertive and hostile foreign policy behavior. The similar amplifying effects, though weaker and more scattered, of regional opposition on foreign policy suggest a possible connection with military opposition in these settings. The small size of the subsample of moderately institutionalized and highly vulnerable regimes precludes analyzing the interconnections between oppositions (as well as between the two contextual influences), but these findings point to the possibility of configurations of types of opposition in extreme political conditions with alternative effects on foreign policy. Examining them further is one of several directions for subsequent research, which are considered in Chapter 6.

Notes

1. Recall from Chapter 3 that regime fragmentation has two kinds of effects on foreign policy: first, like the other types of opposition, as an arena of opposition directly constraining decisionmakers, and, second, as a factor mediating the impact of opposition outside the regime.

2. The suspicion is that public news sources, such as the *New York Times,* provide distorted and biased coverage of different types of nations, for example, the activities of smaller, Third World states are underreported and the more dramatic aspects of their foreign policies (particularly conflict) are overemphasized. This problem received extensive attention in the 1970s, and the consensus from a variety of empirical studies was that such data should be used cautiously and draw upon multiple sources (as does the CREON data set), including both regional sources and global ones such as the *New York Times* (see original studies in Munton, 1978, as well as those summarized in the volume's annotated bibliography). Of particular importance are studies that indicate that different sources report widely different raw totals of foreign policy events, while acknowledging that the proportion of specific types of behavior (e.g., conflict) is not dramatically different (see, in particular, Salmore, 1978, and Azar, 1970). Thus, as long as data on each regime's foreign policy behavior are aggregated as a percentage of its total events, then some of the gross distortions in source reporting can be countered (see note 4). A symposium in *International Studies Quarterly* (Howell, 1983; McClelland, 1983) suggested that "the user beware," and this provides much of the rationale for the rather conservative statistical procedures and criteria employed below. I recognize that event data are not highly refined and are susceptible to distortion; thus multiple statistical procedures are used to control for certain validity problems.

3. The CREON data set also has measures of certain aspects of the decision setting that likely condition political effects (i.e., issue-area and situational variables), and they will be added to the current data set and used in further, more decision-specific analyses.

4. Raw foreign policy behavior scores for each nation are averaged across its total number of events or recipients. This procedure relates to the unit of analysis problem in making cross-national comparisons using events data, as raised by Duval and Thompson (1980: 515–518). It is critical because of the necessity of controlling for wide differences in the total activity of a nation and the fact that the more active nations do more of everything. By measuring behavior as an average (or percentage), it is possible to compare the behaviors of nations (or regimes) with sharply different levels of activity. This is also theoretically consistent, because domestic political explanations don't claim to explain amounts of behavior, but rather the propensity to engage in certain kinds of behaviors.

5. The nation-size and modernity controls would also seem to control for some of the biases in differential source coverage that would make Third World and smaller states appear more assertive in their foreign policy behavior.

6. The generous .10 level is used here in order to include correlations that would be considered, at best, to be of borderline significance. The more usual, and stricter, .05 and .01 criteria are also reported, and of course tap stronger correlations.

7. The regime dropped for Iceland was the caretaker minority cabinet under the Social Democratic Party. The regime dropped for Turkey, the second of its original seven regimes, was the first of its two CNU military juntas headed by General Gursel. Both were relatively short-lived governments that overlapped only about a month and a half of the quarterly CREON data.

8. Regimes with very short tenure—mostly highly vulnerable and fragmented ones—are far less prevalent in this data set than in an earlier one used in Hagan (1987). The number of regimes for Italy and Lebanon, in particular, are sharply reduced in this study because of revised procedures for identifying regimes that downplayed the importance of a change in the head of state.

9. The null hypothesis would also be accepted if findings were few in number and scattered across different conditioning influences. As will be seen, credible support for the role of opposition and conditioning influences requires a clear pattern of correlations.

10. Because of the complexity of reporting on multiple subsamples, economy of space precludes reporting separate correlations for all of the foreign policy variables used in the overall sample analysis.

11. Let me also point out that not all findings from the project can be presented. Not reported here are more preliminary analyses of the relationships of each opposition to each foreign policy dimension, including ones involving alternative opposition variables, alternative foreign policy measures, and various bivariate and multivariate analyses. The overriding reason for not reporting all these findings is that they do not diverge from the ones reported in the tables. Two points are worth noting. First, analyses of the strength and intensity dimensions of opposition did not suggest that either was dramatically more important than the other; nor did the interactive measures do much better, or worse. Second, alternative ways of combining the strength and intensity dimensions in creating a composite opposition measure (e.g., additively or multiplicatively, with or without simple rankings) did not seem to matter, which is another indication of a robust relationship.

12. Actually, in terms of the mean commitment measure, no correlation should be expected, assuming that positive correlations at the middle range would be canceled out by negative ones at the higher and lower ends.

13. Recall that only those Pearson correlation coefficients significant at the $p < .10$ level and that meet the same criteria using nonparametric and controls for size and modernity are reported; correlations not meeting multiple statistical criteria are marked simply by a dash.

14. The comment and intent variables are not included.

15. These are ones at the top half of the scale involving statements of intention by top policy officials as well as all kinds of deed behaviors. They are the six highest points on the eleven-point CREON commitment scale. Originally, this high commitment–IOA measure was to be based on only deed behaviors committing resources. However, that resulted in a poor distribution of data across regimes, and therefore the relatively high committal statements of intent by senior officials are also included here.

16. Remember that low independence values are at the high end of the CREON scale; thus a positive correlation indicates that opposition is increased with lower levels of independence of action.

17. The only exceptions are that intraparty and military opposition effects spill over very weakly to adjacent regime subgroups, and that the effects of fragmentation are stronger in low institutionalized regimes. The latter finding is more significant, running counter to other findings and suggesting that fragmentation has greater effects at lowest levels of institutionalization.

18. Aggregate affect scores are based on a sample of 28,477 recipients (or dyads) in the CREON data set, instead of the 12,710 events used for the commitment and IOA measures.

19. For purposes of simplifying the presentation, the interactive measures, which combine elements of intensity and direction, are incorporated into the two subsections: the results for mean affect are reported with the two measures of affect direction behavior, while extreme conflict is incorporated into the consideration of the two affect intensity variables.

20. Negative correlations should be stronger because there is not necessarily an equally powerful predisposition toward taking positive or neutral actions.

21. Recall that there are less institutionalized regimes (e.g., those in Turkey and Venezuela) with extreme opposition from both political parties and the military. Given the strength of the correlations, these cases fall at neither extreme in the regression plot, suggesting that their foreign policies reflect a mix of the countervailing effects of bargaining/controversy avoidance and political legitimization.

22. This use of the multiple correlation coefficient, instead of R^2, is unconventional. It is used here in order to facilitate the primary purpose of the table: the comparison of multiple effects to the bivariate ones reported in the previous section. The multiple correlation coefficient can be interpreted in the same manner as the bivariate correlation coefficient.

23. The moderate level of fragmentation includes regimes that are ruled by factionalized single parties as well as coalitions with multiple parties but that at least have predominant actors. These include regimes in the People's Republic of China, Japan under the Liberal Democratic Party, and Congress Party India, and if one recalls the literature review in Chapter 2, it should not be entirely surprising that this set of regimes would be politically constrained.

24. The overall association between intraparty opposition and foreign policy commitment also taps the effects of the highest levels of that kind of opposition: the extreme situation in which extraregime factions of the ruling group seek to overthrow the regime itself. But because they are in the opposite direction expected (and require further research), they will be given less emphasis at the moment. Later it will be argued that intraparty effects are associated with the bargaining and controversy avoidance dynamics of political party opposition and regime fragmentation.

25. Recall that these are not outliers, but rather fit a clear pattern at the higher levels, whereas there is a greater dispersion at the lower and middle levels. Also, there are a few sharply deviant cases in the middle range.

26. In the sample used here, these extreme cases include minority governments in Italy, Costa Rica, Norway, and Venezuela and majority governments with major party opposition in West Germany, Norway, Chile, France, India, and Italy.

27. These cases include certain of the regimes in Turkey, Venezuela, China, France, Uruguay, and the Soviet Union.

28. See Tables 4.8 and 4.9 for the regimes that fall into these categories, and note that these regimes represent a good mix of democratic and authoritarian political systems.

6

Conclusions and Directions for Further Comparative Research

At the opening of the book the claim was made that political explanations in comparative foreign policy are relatively undeveloped. What, then, has the research presented here contributed to the development of this theoretical perspective? Although this analysis is preliminary in several ways and arguably only a beginning, it provides some general theoretical insights into, as well as clear cross-national evidence of, the linkage between domestic political phenomena and foreign policy behavior. Furthermore, the outcome of this project suggests some insights to guide subsequent research on domestic politics and foreign policy. The purpose of this closing chapter is, first, to summarize these research insights and, second, to outline some specific directions for further comparative research on domestic political sources of foreign policy.

Insights for Further Research

The first, and most basic, insight is simply that it has been possible to construct a data set directly measuring political opposition groups for a sizable sample of nations. Sufficient numbers of detailed political analyses and reports by area specialists were able to provide the substantively rich information necessary to make judgments about the range of political divisions within the regime, the strength and intensity of opposition outside the regime, and various critical aspects of the political system and regime context. Employing the political regime as a unit of analysis proved conceptually useful in focusing this data collection effort. Not only did it focus attention on politics within the regime, but it also provided the conceptual means by which political opposition could be linked to the point of choice within the leadership structures of the regime. And it did so in a way that got beyond accountability by capturing the absence of constraints within certain democracies and the presence of them in some authoritarian regimes. All this is not to say that the effort was exhaustive; as noted below, the sample is not complete and certain types of opposition and political phenomena are clearly ignored. But it does suggest that large-scale data collection is possible and in a way that captures some of the complexity found in the politics of foreign policy in diverse political settings.

Second, the analysis shows that multiple types of domestic opposition are related to multiple dimensions of a regime's aggregate foreign policy behaviors. Although it was possible to identify isolated correlations between just about all opposition and all foreign policy dimensions, the effects of three types of opposition outside the regime were most pronounced. Intraparty opposition, political party opposition, and military opposition were strongest in that they were present for the overall sample, sizable under certain conditions, and linked to the different foreign policy dimensions. The same certainly cannot be said about the effects of political divisions within the regime. Contrary to original expectations, regime fragmentation was found to be generally unrelated to foreign policy and only in limited ways under different conditions. This study has done little to uncover the critical processes of coalition policymaking by which decision-makers achieve the authority to commit resources, although it has been able to show general patterns in how they respond to opposition in the broader political arena that challenges their hold on power.

Third, the findings point to the significance of alternative theoretical linkages between opposition and foreign policy, and support our opening contention that leaders respond to opposition in sharply different ways with correspondingly divergent effects on foreign policy. Military opposition and, to a lesser degree, regional opposition were shown to be associated with increased levels of independence, hostility, and intensity and lower levels of commitment in foreign policy. In contrast, the effects of regime fragmentation, intraparty opposition, and political party opposition are just the reverse: behaviors that are less hostile, generally more reactive and mild, but still with greater (perhaps more careful) commitment. In sum, political legitimization dynamics dominate in settings with military and regional opposition, while bargaining/controversy avoidance characterizes situations where regime fragmentation, intraparty opposition, and political party opposition are important.

Finally, the contextual effects of certain political system and regime conditions are striking. Incorporation of these kinds of contextual effects was a far more successful strategy for multivariate analyses than was the more direct procedure of combining the effects of the separate opposition.[1] Controls for political system and regime properties resulted in stronger correlations than those identified for the overall sample, as well as in the identification of important correlations that were otherwise hidden for the full sample of regimes. The effects of almost all types of opposition on the four foreign policy dimensions were especially pronounced in two situations:

moderately institutionalized political systems and highly vulnerable regimes. The evidence of the conditioning effects of accountability and regime fragmentation was, respectively, less apparent and more puzzling, although both certainly warrant further investigation with a larger sample of nations and regimes.

Three Directions for Further Research

Collectively these insights, as well as the specific findings, suggest that empirical cross-national studies of domestic politics and foreign policy can be executed with theoretically meaningful benefits. In doing so, they also point to specific directions for future research. Let me close by outlining three specific avenues for such research: (1) expanding upon the current research design and conceptual framework, (2) incorporating the notion of regime orientation, and (3) developing an alternative research design employing situationally based explanations centered around the concept of the ultimate decision unit.

Expanding the Current Research Design
and Conceptual Framework

The empirical validity and conceptual scope of the present study can be expanded and improved in several basic ways. As just discussed, the current analysis can be taken further to get at several persisting puzzles. As raised at the close of Chapter 5, there seem to be alternative configurations of opposition operating together under certain extreme political conditions. These need to be investigated further. Given the dominance of political party and military opposition effects, it may well be that opposition more proximate to foreign policy decisionmakers (i.e., regime fragmentation and intraparty opposition) takes on greater significance if incorporated into a broadened conceptualization of political party and military actors. Another puzzling finding concerns the question of commitment as a manifestation of domestic opposition—in other words, why greater commitment is associated with less of all types of other behaviors, or the reverse. As far as the findings go, the only final interpretation is that increased resource use is indicative of a more careful and constrained foreign policy, in which verbal behavior is precluded entirely. If true, some reworking of the idea of commitment in foreign policy is required in order to tap political constraints on the foreign use of resources and the making of binding agreements with other nations. Finally, the other puzzle here concerns the conditioning of regime fragmentation. Further thought needs to be given as to why moderately fragmented regimes are most constrained by extraregime opposition. It is not that moderately fragmented regimes should not be constrained; the question is why the most fragmented ones are not.

There are also at least three major conceptual gaps in the book's framework, but it should be possible to fill them with more elaborate comparative studies. First, the range of political opposition considered here, most of it institutionally based activity inside and outside the regime, is not comprehensive. As a result, interest groups and other issue-specific actors, as well as the more general corporatist arrangements and state-society relations, have been excluded. Nor was any direct attempt made to capture noninstitutionalized mass behavior, such as public opinion and domestic conflict. Second, there are also other types of theoretically important conditioning variables that have yet to be considered. There is good reason, in particular, to expect that properties of the situational environment (e.g., crisis versus noncrisis) and various issue-area characteristics also significantly condition the effects of domestic politics.[2] Third, the theoretical logic linking domestic opposition to foreign policy could be elaborated upon in new directions, particularly with respect to the role of a regime's support groups, as well as its opposition. There is now some evidence to suggest that leaders, when they monitor their domestic political environment, focus on avoiding the loss of their supporters as much as on facing the consequences of offending existing opposition (e.g., Ostrom and Job, 1986). Furthermore, there is a need to consider the extent to which domestic groups (especially supporters) pressure the government in ways that give them input into the substantive content of policy and even stimulate new foreign policy initiatives.[3]

Probably the most pressing need is for the findings reported here to be evaluated with a larger data set on regimes and foreign policy. The data collection effort for the thirty-eight countries in the CREON sample has demonstrated that it is possible in practical ways to construct an extensive cross-national data set on regimes and their opposition. There is no reason that such a data set could not ultimately include all nations (except very small states where source materials are probably rare) and cover the four decades since World War II.[4] This data set could then be used in connection with foreign policy events data sets with a more comprehensive sample of nations and more extended time frame, for example, the Cooperation and Peace Data Bank (COPDAB) data and the World Event Interaction Survey (WEIS) data. Although not as conceptually rich as the CREON foreign policy data, these data sets do include measures of commitment and conflict in foreign policy. The larger data set would permit the detailed analysis of opposition configurations under specific political settings, particularly instability in its democratic and praetorian forms, as just noted.

There is also no reason why this kind of aggregate research design could not be extended to other areas of cross-national, data-based research. The political variables (and their amplifying and diminishing effects on foreign policy) and research design employed here are directly relevant and compatible with research on the occurrence of war (Singer and Small,

1972; Small and Singer, 1982; Levy, 1983), militarized international disputes (Leng and Gochman, 1982; Gochman and Maoz, 1984), international
crisis behavior (Brecher, Wilkenfeld, and Moser, 1988) and foreign policy
change as evidenced by U.N. voting realignments (Moon, 1985; Hagan,
1989a). Especially important in this regard is the research on the war
proneness of different types of political systems. A regime perspective
(incorporating also the notion of regime orientation below) could provide a
more precise look at the question of the relative war proneness of democratic and authoritarian regimes. Such an effort would include developing
data on historical regimes for major powers dating back to at least 1815 to
correspond to the Correlates of War data, or even further (e.g., late 1400s)
to match Levy's data on Great Power wars.[5] Regimes and opposition could
also be usefully incorporated into studies of foreign policy change. Moon
(1985) and Hagan (1989a) have already demonstrated that Third World
voting alignments in the United Nations often vary significantly across successive regimes. Regimes classified according to opposition would provide
a further clue as to, say, precisely which new regimes are likely to seek a
realignment in foreign policy and have the internal political coherence necessary for implementing it. More generally, the types of regime changes
(e.g., revolutionary versus nonrevolutionary changes) associated with foreign policy restructuring provide important insights into the political
sources (e.g., structural versus nonstructural) of foreign policy.

Incorporating the Orientations of Political Regimes

Throughout the course of this project it has become increasingly apparent
that there is a missing element in regime-centered notions of political
explanations of foreign policy: political constraints need to be viewed within the context of the core beliefs and interests shared by the regime's leaders. This is illustrated by the case studies analyzed in Chapter 2. Certain of
these analyses are careful to place policy debates within the broader context
of the leadership's consensus about the general orientation of the nation's
foreign relations. Thus, Japanese factional disputes over, for example, the
threat of U.S.-imposed textile quotas did not call into question the LDP's
consensus over the need for close U.S.-Japan ties, but rather addressed the
narrower question of whether or not concessions should be made to the
United States on that issue (Destler et al., 1979). Similarly, Soviet leaders
agreed that the Czechoslovak reforms were dangerous and should be cur-
tailed; the prolonged debate concerned the more restrictive question of how
the Soviets should pressure the Dubcek government, either through military
force or by economic and political sanctions (Valenta, 1979). Even in such
intensely fragmented Third World regimes as Iran during Khomeini's early
days, China during the Cultural Revolution, and Indonesia prior to
Sukarno's overthrow, there was broad agreement that the superpowers were

a threat and the debates concerned just how much dependence or contact with the West could be tolerated (Stempel, 1981; Hinton, 1970; Weinstein, 1976).

As such, these kinds of studies make two important, though often implicit, points about domestic politics and foreign policy. The first is that the impact of domestic politics in all but the most extreme political situations—those captured in the analysis in Chapter 5—is likely limited because debates concern relatively narrow aspects of issues. Instead, the leadership's core shared beliefs—not domestic politics—were probably the primary motivational basis of the overall direction in the Sato cabinet's pro-Western policies, the Brezhnev Politburo's alarm over the Dubcek reforms, and the radical anti-Western policies of the Sukarno, Khomeini, and Cultural Revolution regimes. This leads to a second issue: the effects of political opposition (amplifying or constraining) are ultimately to be gauged by the extent to which leaders are able to implement their preferences. Opposition constraints restricted the Sato and Brezhnev regimes' ability to commit to a consistent course of action, while the politics of revolutionary coalitions in China, Iran, and Indonesia amplified already existing predispositions toward independence from and hostility toward the West.

There is, then, a need to develop a second property of political regimes (or whatever leadership group)—the overall orientation to foreign affairs—in a way that still permits the kind of broad cross-national analyses executed in this study. A regime's orientation reflects the ruling group's general beliefs about foreign affairs as they relate to their nation's domestic and international situation, and the coalition of societal and political interests aligned to the regime. It is, in effect, the national interest of the country as defined by the leadership group currently in power, with the assumption that different leaders may bring to power alternative views of the nation's international situation and interests. Furthermore, these overall orientations are largely shared by actors within the regime and are stable and unchanging throughout the life of the regime. Except where there are extreme political pressures, they are probably the dominant domestic political influence on a nation's foreign policy.[6]

The orientations of regimes vary with respect to the identification and relative ranking of foreign threats and problems, and the perceptions of the nature, or severity, of those threats and the appropriate strategies by which to counter them.[7] The identification and ranking of foreign threats and problems is the more familiar dimension of regime orientation, particularly alignment patterns as defined by the bipolar structure of the Cold War international system in which most nations (or actually their regimes) were either pro-Western/anti-Soviet, pro-Soviet/anti-Western, or nonaligned. This kind of scheme is undoubtably useful because it gets directly at the threats and problems that motivate governments to act.[8] However, from a domestic politics perspective, it is probably more important to focus on leaders' beliefs about the severity of foreign threats and the appropriate strategies for responding to them. This is because contending actors in a political system, although they may agree on the identification of foreign threats and problems, often disagree over how to respond to them.[9] The question of how to respond to threats and problems is arguably very much the "stuff" of politics, and the associated alternative foreign policy strategies are manifested in the same kinds of foreign policy behavior as are domestic political constraints: commitment, independence, and affect direction and intensity.

For purposes of broad, empirical cross-national analysis, it is possible (and practical for data collection) to distinguish between four basic leader orientations for classifying regimes. These are derived from a sequence of questions concerning leaders' beliefs about the character of an adversary and the nature of its foreign policy goals.[10] For purposes of illustration, these regime orientations (which are best seen as ideal types) can be summarized in a preliminary manner. Ranging from moderate to progressively more hardline, these are:

1. *Moderate or Acquiescent Regimes.* Leaders in these regimes perceive international affairs as being largely benign; they do not see any major adversaries or problems as dramatically threatening their nation's security, economic well-being, or international status. Conflicts among nations are seen as issue-specific or situation-bound in which adversaries have relatively legitimate motives and limited goals. Other nations are perceived to be more or less typical actors who are motivated by the same kinds of pressures as guide one's own nation, and this includes a recognition of significant internal economic, societal, and political constraints on their use of national power. Thus, moderate leaders tend to be restrained and flexible in their foreign policy behavior, often emphasizing a wider array of problems as they accommodate varied international problems and cooperate with other states toward their resolution. Examples approximating this kind of orientation are the United States under Carter, the Soviet Union under Gorbachev, Egypt under Sadat, Israel under Sharrett, and Jamaica under Seaga.

2. *Pragmatic Regimes.* Leaders of these regimes, as well as their counterparts in the two other relatively hardline regimes below, see the international system as an inherently threatening and dangerous environment. But these pragmatic leaders have relatively restrained and complex views of those threats as posed to their nation. Adversaries are seen to have limited goals and constrained capabilities, and thus they do not pose an immediate threat to the nation's survival and interests. This makes "room for diplomacy" (Yergin, 1977) in which bargaining, compromise, and even some limited forms of cooperation are in each other's interest; indeed, skilled diplomacy enhancing areas of mutual interest and nonmilitary tools of statecraft

are important means of containing the adversary's behavior. While not precluding confrontation entirely, these regimes show some flexibility and restraint in coping with foreign threats. Approximate examples include the détente-oriented, Cold War regimes of the early 1970s: the United States under Nixon/Kissinger, West Germany under Brandt, and the Soviet Union under Brezhnev. Among Third World nations, pragmatic regimes include China under Deng, Indonesia under Suharto, Iran under the Shah, Egypt under Mubarak, and now Israel under Rabin.

3. *Militant Regimes.* Leaders in these regimes perceive the international system to be inherently hostile in which the interaction between adversaries is an essentially zero-sum relationship. The political, economic, and social systems of adversaries are thought to drive them toward inherently aggressive foreign policies. Adversaries are viewed as having unlimited goals in that they directly threaten the security, well-being, and international status of one's own nation, and in a way that is linked across a wide variety of substantive and regional issues. The severity of these threats preclude normal diplomatic accommodation, and confrontation is ongoing in order to "contain" the threat and maintain the credibility of one's own deterrent. But this is not to say that these regimes expect unrestrained confrontation or are unable to tolerate their opponents in some ways. Two sources of restraint are that these adversaries are rational (i.e., cold and calculating) and thus capable of being deterred from confrontation, and that conflicts occur within the bounds of certain established international norms. Some approximate examples include U.S. Cold War administrations (e.g., late Truman and Kennedy), the Soviet Union under Stalin, West Germany under Adenauer, Britain under Thatcher, Israel under Ben Gurion, and Syria under Assad.

4. *Radical Regimes.* Leaders with this orientation hold the most extreme beliefs about the nature of international politics and the imperatives it poses for the nation's foreign policy. Compared to the militant orientation, foreign adversaries are thought to be even more unrelenting as they challenge the foundations of the established international and/or regional order. Adversaries are thought to be evil actors who have a non-rational aggressiveness grounded in an expansionist ideology, unrestrained nationalism, and/or severe domestic crises. Bargaining and restraint are meaningless; only clearly superior military power and a highly active foreign policy are effective in deterring aggression and advancing the national interest. There is an overriding propensity to perceive all sorts of international issues as being interconnected and linked to the aggressiveness and domination of primary adversaries. As a result, radical leaders are likely to reject the very legitimacy of the current international status quo and will, if necessary, violate international norms and domestic constraints to carry out the moral imperatives of their foreign policy. Radical regimes in the Third World likely include Castro in Cuba, Mao in China, Khomeini in Iran,

Sukarno in Indonesia, Nasser in Egypt, Sadaam in Iraq, and the unstable Ba'athist regimes in Syria during the 1960s. Possibilities among the advanced democracies that approach this category include the United States under Reagan, West Germany under Adenauer, and Israel under the Likud.[11]

In sum, across the four orientations, leaders are progressively more hardline in their beliefs about the nature of adversaries, the severity of threats they pose, and the kinds of strategies necessary to contain those threats, for example, accommodation versus confrontation. The confrontation behavior of the relatively hardline regimes is likely marked by progressively greater levels of commitment, independence of action, hostility, and intensity. Without getting too far beyond the opposition focus of the book, the concept of regime orientation could be very useful for considering the political roots of foreign policy, and particularly the matter of the relative war proneness of different political systems (Hagan, forthcoming-b).

The main point here, though, is that the concept of regime orientation is directly relevant to assessing the cross-national effects of domestic political opposition. Namely, if we assume that regime orientation constitutes the overall preferences of the core decisionmakers, then the impact of opposition can be gauged in terms of the extent to which a regime is politically able to implement its policy preferences. Except in the most extreme domestic situations (like those empirically delineated in this book), leaders are not likely to change the overall orientation of their regime simply to contain political opposition. Rather, either by bargaining/controversy avoidance or political legitimization, adjustments (in either direction) in foreign policies would still fall within the range of the regime's established orientation. Similarly, because factions and parties within a fragmented regime likely have relatively proximate orientations, it is probable that compromises between those actors will reflect a mix of those orientations. In both cases, the overall orientation of the regime sets the parameters on internal debates and reactions to external oppositions; in other words, the basic content of the foreign policy remains intact, with political effects being manifested by the level of commitment, initiative, and affect involved in implementing that orientation.

This has important implications for the kind of research design underlying the statistical analysis executed in this book, and in a way that makes some sense of the evidence of domestic pressures in politically extreme situations. Because of the centrality of regime orientation, it should not be expected that opposition effects alone could account for the full range in the distribution of regimes' foreign policy scores. Rather, regimes classified by fragmentation and opposition should distribute largely within parameters established by regime orientation scores. In other words, opposition effects account mainly for the variance remaining after the statistical effects of regime orientation have been considered. Only in cases of regimes facing the most extreme political pressures would the effects of regime orientation be overridden. Intense opposition from strong intraparty, political party, and military actors, as well as moderate levels of institutionalization and high levels of political vulnerability, are precisely such extreme political situations.

Integrating political opposition with regime orientation can also provide insight into how regimes respond to opposition, and whether domestic politics has an amplifying or diminishing effect on commitment, independence, and affect in foreign policy. In one respect, the responses of a regime's leadership are likely to reflect its foreign affairs orientation. A moderate regime facing hardline opposition will gravitate toward more assertive behavior, while a hardline regime confronting relatively moderate opposition would engage in less assertive behavior. Furthermore, it can be argued that different regime orientations are associated with the alternative political strategies. Relatively moderate regimes are, for example, less able to engage in legitimization tactics for fear of undercutting cooperative international relationships; nor do their cooperative policies usually have much appeal to public nationalism and a desire for strong leadership. In contrast, mobilizing public support with confrontational and nationalistic themes fits well with the more hardline orientations, particularly the extreme radical tendency.

A Decision Units Approach to Opposition and Foreign Policy

Another approach, based on a more situationally specific "contingency approach" to foreign policy analysis (Hagan, Hermann, and Hermann, forthcoming), could also be fruitful for further research on domestic opposition and foreign policy. Not only could it get at less extreme political situations, but it could prove especially useful in uncovering the seemingly complex political processes within the authoritative structures of the regime, which have been hidden by aggregate analyses of regime fragmentation and foreign policy. In this kind of approach, the unit of analysis is the "occasion for decision." It builds on a tradition of decisionmaking research that asserts that situational (e.g., Snyder, Bruck, and Sapin, 1962; Hermann, 1969) and issue-area (Art, 1973; Zimmerman, 1973) factors influence what type of decision body becomes involved in handling a particular problem, as well as the decision processes themselves. In contrast to the regime-centric approach used throughout this book, this approach assumes that the range of contending positions and the dispersion of policy-making authority shifts significantly across foreign policy episodes. Thus, for example, it may be that a fragmented regime can act forcefully on certain issues or in some situations, whereas a very cohesive regime will sometimes find itself internally constrained and thus unable to act.

Following the current work of the CREON project (Hagan, Hermann, and Hermann, forthcoming; Hermann and Hermann, 1989; and Hermann, Hermann, and Hagan, 1987), a useful starting point in conceptualizing political decision processes is the concept of the "ultimate decision unit." It concerns the actor or actors "at the apex of foreign policy making in all governments or ruling parties . . . who, if they agree, have both the ability to commit the resources of the government in foreign affairs and the power or authority to prevent other entities within the government from overtly reversing their position" (Hermann, Hermann, and Hagan, 1987: 311). There are three alternative types of decision units (Hermann, Hermann, and Hagan, 1991):

- *Predominant leader:* a single individual has the authority to commit the resources of a nation in response to a particular problem and others cannot reverse his or her decision (pp. 2–3).
- *Single group:* an entity of two or more people all of whose members interact directly with all other members and who collectively are able to reach a decision without consulting any outside entities, e.g., cabinets, juntas, and politburos (pp. 11–12).
- *Coalition of autonomous groups:* two or more politically autonomous groups (e.g., parties, institutions/bureaucracies) none of which alone has the ability to commit the resources of the regime without the support of all or some of the other actors; moreover, any actor may block the initiatives of others by executing a veto, threatening to terminate the ruling coalition, and/or withholding the resources necessary for action (pp. 20–21).

The occurrence of a particular type of decision unit is determined not only by the organization of a regime but also by the character of the issue and the leaders' definition of the situation. Furthermore, a full array of decision outcomes (ranging from strong agreement to deadlock) may emerge from each one of these three decision units, and in ways that are also dependent largely on aspects of the current situation and issue.

As a refinement of the concept of regime fragmentation, the value of the decision unit concept is that it identifies conditions where situational and issue-area factors, in effect, override the significance of the regime's internal political structure, and where decision unit characteristics influence how it responds to external opposition. This is true in at least three ways: (1) different types of decision units occur during a single regime, (2) within each type of decision unit conditioning factors may affect the propensity to achieve agreement, compromise, or remain deadlocked, and (3) the open or closed character of each type of decision unit influences how it responds to external opposition. The sequence of these decision-specific conditions opens the way for a wide diversity of decision outcomes to emerge from any single regime. Let me briefly summarize.

Shifting types of decision units within regimes. Turning to the first condition, the literature on decisionmaking gives good reason to expect different types of decision units across issue-areas and situations.[12] Thus, in a fragmented regime the decision unit is not always a coalition of autonomous actors, the most fragmented type of decision unit. International (or domestic) conditions may cause senior political leaders to define an issue as critical or a situation as a crisis, and thus they allow a subset of actors within the regime to operate as a single group with the authority to commit resources without referring back to the full regime.[13] Israel's decision to launch the 1967 war was taken not by the full National Unity Coalition but instead by a subset of key leaders acting as a single group (Stein, forthcoming), while in Sweden a Foreign Ministry–led ad hoc group handled the crisis of a trapped Soviet submarine in the "whisky on the rocks" crisis (Sundelius, forthcoming). Finally, Fukui's (1978a; forthcoming) analyses of Japanese decisionmaking show that the LDP factional leaders were willing to depoliticize certain critical economic issues and turn them over to the control of professional bureaucrats (although the Japanese bureaucratic environment was still quite fragmented). The point of these examples is that decision units in fragmented regimes do not necessarily involve coalition decision units composed of senior factional and party leaders.

Alternatively, decisionmaking in a politically cohesive regime can be quite fragmented with the devolution of actual authority to settings with autonomous actors. This routinely occurs because political leaders define many issues as noncritical and thus delegate authority to lower-level, interagency bureaucratic coalitions. Even on more critical issues, though, political fragmentation occurs if the senior leadership is inactive or if overarching authority is ill defined. Such was the case in the Reagan administration on arms control negotiations with the Soviet Union, in which passive leadership (by Reagan, Shultz, and Weinberger) led to decisionmaking by autonomous (and antagonistic) assistant secretaries in the State and Defense departments (Talbott, 1984). Similarly, Iranian decisionmaking on the hostage crisis could have been dominated by Khomeini, but because of his conception of his leadership role he remained aloof from the day-to-day affairs of government and left authority to an ill-defined coalition of revolutionary actors (Stempel, forthcoming). Fragmented decisionmaking also results from the political leadership having to bring in powerful bureaucratic or societal actors in a decision if it is to be successfully implemented. Even a predominant leader such as Egypt's Anwar Sadat had to share authority with his army chief of staff in planning the opening attack of the 1973 October war (Korany, 1989). Nor must such external actors be government bodies. Societal actors are often brought into the decision process, either because of corporatist decisionmaking arrangements or because they are essential to implementation of policy given the weakness of the state. These may even be extraterritorial actors, as in Third World situations where a regime formulates economic policies in coordination with international lending agencies such as the IMF and the World Bank (see Ingebedion and Shaw, forthcoming).

Shifting situational and issue-area bases for agreement and deadlock within decision units. Generalizing about the implications of regime fragmentation and coalition politics is still further complicated by the fact that any one of the three decision units can produce widely divergent political outcomes, ranging from agreement to complete deadlock. Therefore, a politically fragmented coalition of autonomous groups might arrive at a meaningful agreement, while a relatively cohesive single group could be internally deadlocked or forced to make major compromises. As with the determinants of the type of decision unit, the functioning of the decision unit depends on the contingencies of the leaders' definition of the situation, characteristics of the issue, and organization of the regime (see Hagan, Hermann, and Hermann, forthcoming). The assumption here is that these conditions vary significantly from one episode to another.[14]

A number of conditions enable a coalition decision unit to overcome its internal fragmentation and achieve meaningful agreement over foreign policy, particularly the policy positions of the decision participants and their perception of the domestic political implications of the issue, as well as whether or not the situation poses a crisis for the nation. Within a fragmented regime a leadership is likely to be polarized on certain issues but not on others. In the latter case (which may be quite frequent) the leadership will at least be able to work out a meaningful compromise, especially if the issue does not become connected to political competition between the regime's parties or factions (e.g., Fukui's cases of politically insulated bureaucratic decisionmaking in Japan). Furthermore, agreement may be possible on certain issues through various logrolling techniques in which side-payments on other matters are provided to dissenters. The presence of a pivotal actor on the issue facilitates agreement, because of its control over resources necessary for implementation or because its preferences allow it to align with either side in a policy debate. Finally, all this is conditioned by the presence of established rules for decisionmaking. Such norms preclude debates about the legitimacy of participating actors or the decision rules themselves. As shown by Swedish decisionmaking, strong consensus decisionmaking norms enable coalition governments to act relatively cohesively (Sundelius, forthcoming), while postrevolutionary Iran illustrates the complications when such rules are entirely absent (Stempel, forthcoming).

Correspondingly, the political implications of an issue or situation may undercut the ability of relatively cohesive, single-group decision units to achieve agreement. The possibility of agreement on issues, even through broad compromise, is undercut if members of the group differ over basic policy issues or if no one is willing to engage in trade-offs across issues through side-payments. This becomes especially problematic if there is a decision rule requiring unanimity in which dissenters cannot be overruled, or the absence of any strong leader or policy advocate on the issue. Finally, each of these conditions is affected by the political cohesiveness of the group as reflected by its members' loyalty to it. Where members of the group owe allegiance to outside bodies and organizations, the norms for containing disagreements are considerably weakened and debates are likely intensified as participants represent the interests of outside constituencies (see C. Hermann, 1992). The prolonged deadlock within the Soviet Politburo on the matter of military intervention against Czechoslovakia can be traced to these kinds of constraints in the early Brezhnev leadership (ones that were diminished by the time of the Afghanistan intervention decision).

Alternative decision unit responses to opposition outside the regime. With this third and final point on decision units, we shift from political processes internal to the decision unit to how the decision unit responds to opposition in the broader political environment. The decision unit concept provides insights into both if and how leaders respond to domestic opposition (particularly under less extreme political conditions), getting at whether political pressures will amplify, diminish, or insulate the decision-makers' basic predisposition to act. Consideration of the "key control variable" for each type of decision unit suggests that under some conditions a decision unit will be open to outside influences, while under others it will be driven by its internal dynamics (Hermann and Hermann, 1989; Hagan, Hermann, and Hermann, 1990). Thus, open decision units are responsive to the interests and positions of opposition actors, while in closed decision units opposition pressures will be important only in terms of the leadership's image of that opposition. Let me briefly explain the six decision unit/key control variable configurations and point out where external opposition will have an important role.

Open decision units are (1) pragmatic predominant leaders, (2) single groups without strong internal loyalty, and (3) coalitions of autonomous groups with well-established decision rules. In the latter two cases, the key control variables suggest that outside pressures will be taken into account by decisionmakers and in other ways shape their deliberations. Single groups without internal loyalty are ones in which individual members each identify with their respective bureaucratic or political group. Although these outside groups cannot block the decisions of the single authoritative group, their representative(s) in the decision unit articulates the group's particular interests in the decision process. As to the coalition decision unit, the implications of well-established decisionmaking rules are similar. Not only do such rules diminish internal conflicts over the legitimacy of the actors and processes in the decision unit, but they also guarantee access of outside interests and parties by enabling the latter to hold leaders accountable for their actions. Thus, for example, rules within the deadlocked Dutch coalition dealing with the NATO issue forced cabinet parties to be accountable to parliamentary parties, who in turn were accountable to the mass public (Everts, forthcoming). Finally, pragmatic predominant leaders are responsive to outside political actors. Their decision style predisposes them to be sensitive to pressures domestically, and when significant domestic opposition appears their pragmatism leads them to accommodate opposition pressures (e.g., Syria's Hafez Assad). In sum, in each of these cases, not only is the decision unit likely to be responsive to outside opposition, but it can also be suggested that their responses reflect bargaining/controversy avoidance dynamics and result in a more constrained foreign policy.

The situation is likely quite different in the case of closed decision units: (1) principled predominant leaders, (2) single groups with strong internal loyalty, and (3) coalitions of autonomous actors without well-established decision rules. The more principled predominant leader is less sensitive to his or her environment, and thus the leader's core beliefs and personality go a long way in defining his or her image of the political environment (even to the point of imagining nonexistent opposition). Furthermore, such leaders are unlikely to accommodate opponents, and instead they aggressively suppress or isolate them, all of which can be facilitated by projecting the legitimacy of the regime and its policies. The situation is similar with the other two decision units. Single groups with strong internal loyalty are prone toward groupthink, and a group's shared sense of alarm over domestic threats to the regime may create a siege mentality in which the group members develop a distorted image of the opposition. Where such opposition is perceived to exist, the dynamics of groupthink would point to (as it does in foreign policy) mounting internal pressure to confront the opposition. Finally, in coalition decision units in which there are no established decision rules, the decision unit is completely preoccupied with its own political games in which each actor's very existence is at stake. Therefore, it is unlikely that outside interests can effectively pressure actors in the group to represent their interests independent of the coalition's conflicts. Outside groups gain access only when they can link up to one of the contending factions, but in that case they usually end up being manipulated by the coalition factions. If anything, contending groups resort to political legitimacy themes to promote their own group and undercut the public positions of others, all of which provides an extreme amplifying effect on at least the nation's verbal foreign policy behavior. Like the other closed decision units, these internally driven dynamics sharply amplify the predispositions of leaders to act and show how domestic politics can provide a strong motivation for action.

In closing I reiterate that these three directions for further research are by no means comprehensive, nor are they set in concrete, but they should illustrate the kinds of questions and strategies that could usefully guide further research on domestic politics and foreign policy. They also make clear that the present analysis is very much a preliminary one that has rested upon fairly basic questions. In retrospect, the value of this research is not so much in that it has generated comprehensive findings, but that it has provided some evidence that, in turn, isolates in a nonspeculative way some insights for subsequent comparative research. The conceptual, operationalization, and data-gathering efforts show, I think, that it is possible to execute systematic cross-national empirical studies that move beyond basic structural variables and capture political phenomena across a wide variety of polities. In addition, certain statistical findings stand out so strongly that one could conclude that there are general patterns between opposition and foreign policy under certain, albeit extreme, contingencies. The task now is to move toward further refinement of these hypotheses, integrate them with other political phenomena missed here, and extend them to broader foreign policy analyses.

Notes

1. All this is consistent with the more significant findings on domestic politics and foreign policy in the comparative literature as discussed in Chapter 1, for example, the IBA project's findings (Wilkenfeld et al., 1980) as well as work by Hermann (1974, 1980), Moore (1974b), and Wilkenfeld (1972).

2. Not only is this evident in a number of the case studies discussed above, but it is also a prevalent theme in the decisionmaking literature considering issue-areas (e.g., Lowi, 1967; Art, 1973; Huntington, 1961; Zimmerman, 1973) and international crisis (e.g., Hermann and Brady, 1972; Snyder and Diesing, 1977).

3. The plea for this kind of analysis is effectively made in Stein's (1988) discussion of the political processes underlying U.S. Middle East policy, and is also evident in Snyder's (1991) recent theoretical explication (with case studies) of domestic political pressures favoring certain hardline interests that contribute to expansionist foreign policies.

4. See Hagan (1989a and 1989b) for reports on the construction of data sets on Third World and Western European regimes since World War II. Data collection identifying regimes and classifying types of regime changes has been completed, and will be expanded to include not only additional regimes (those of Eastern Europe and the former Soviet Union) but also data on regime fragmentation, various political opposition, and properties of the political system and regime context.

5. Despite the extended time frame involved, such an effort is quite possible because of the relatively small number of relevant powers and the rich documentation provided by historians on successive regimes of at least the major powers.

6. The concept of regime orientation also corresponds to the shared leadership properties in the various theoretical frameworks and arguments in the literature, as summarized in Chapter 1. This remains an underdeveloped area of inquiry in comparative research.

7. Another scheme that gets at regime orientation in terms of a left-right continuum is developed in Moon and Dixon (1985).

8. Comparative studies (e.g., Moon, 1985; Hagan, 1989a) show that among at least Third World nations these basic alignments, as indicated by levels of United Nations voting agreement with the United States, can shift across different political regimes.

9. This perspective rests upon the theoretical literature on leader belief systems and, in particular, threat perception (e.g., Holsti, 1976; Jervis, 1976). Another possible scheme useful for comparative foreign policy analysis is suggested by the notion of "national role conceptions" as developed by Holsti (1970) and reported in more recent works by Walker (1987) and Wish (1980). The following scheme is developed more fully in Hagan (forthcoming-c).

10. The specific questions are: What is the essential character of the adversary; is it a "typical" nation, or does it have a domestic system driven by fundamentally different (with presumably aggressive) forces? What is the range and scope of this threat; are the adversary's goals limited and legitimate, or are they unlimited in the sense of threatening the nation's very survival or well-being? Finally, to what extent must the adversary cope with other domestic and foreign constraints; are there internal limits on its ability to act internationally, or does it have exceptional power and unity of purpose?

11. Before going further, let me emphasize again that these categories are actually ideal types. Although for illustrative purposes I have attempted to place relatively familiar regimes into one category or another, this is not such a simple exercise, as indicated by the case of radical orientations. Most regimes would seem, instead, to fall between ideal types of regime orientation, although with a tendency to gravitate more closely to one of the two orientations. Note, for example, the relative positions of U.S. administrations since the 1960s. The Reagan administration (originally, at least) had a rather radical image of the Soviet Union and the U.S. strategy of containment, but certainly it was not as radical as, say, Nazi Germany or Fascist Italy. Rather, if anything, it was an essentially militant regime with radical tendencies, therefore falling between the ideal categories of militant and radical. This distinguishes it clearly from other essentially militant regimes that instead leaned in the direction of greater pragmatism (e.g., those of Kennedy and Johnson). Such subtleties are also apparent in the differentiation of the otherwise similarly prodétente administrations of Nixon/Kissinger and Carter. Both were clearly pragmatic, but if anything Carter leaned in the direction of a non–Cold War moderation while Nixon and Kissinger showed elements of militancy. This also captures shifts during the Bush administration, an essentially pragmatic regime that moved away from militant tendencies in its view of the Soviet Union to one that entertained a more moderate, post–Cold War image.

12. Along with some of the case study literature examined in Chapter 2, this is illustrated in a set of case studies applying the decision units model in diverse national settings (see Hagan, Hermann, and Hermann, forthcoming). Some of these cases are used in the illustrations that follow.

13. It is well established that power becomes centralized at the apex of the government in crisis situations and widely noted that bureaucratic actors lose their influence to the senior political leadership (Paige, 1968; Hermann and Brady, 1972).

14. These conditions, as briefly summarized in the next two paragraphs, are explained fully in Hermann, Hermann, and Hagan (1991).

Bibliography

Abboushi, W. F. (1970) *Political Systems of the Middle East in the 20th Century.* New York: Dodd, Mead.

Achen, Christopher H. (1989) "When Is a State with Bureaucratic Politics Representable as a Unitary Rational Actor?" Paper presented at the annual meeting of the International Studies Association, London, March–April.

Adomeit, Hannes (1982) *Soviet Risk-Taking and Crisis Behavior.* London: Allen and Unwin.

Ahmad, Ahmad Yousef (1984) "The Dialectics of Domestic Environment and Role Performance: The Foreign Policy of Iraq," in Bahgat Korany and Ali E. Hillal Dessouki, eds., *The Foreign Policies of Arab States.* Boulder, CO: Westview.

Ahn, Byung-joon (1976) *Chinese Politics and the Cultural Revolution: Dynamics of the Policy Process.* Seattle: University of Washington Press.

Aimer, Peter (1985) "New Zealand," in Haruhiro Fukui, ed., *Political Parties of Asia and the Pacific.* Westport, CT: Greenwood.

Ajami, Fouad (1981) *The Arab Predicament.* Cambridge: Cambridge University Press.

Akaha, Tsuneo (1991) "Japan's Comprehensive Security Policy: A New East Asian Environment," *Asian Survey* 31: 324–340.

Alexander, Robert J., ed. (1982a) *Political Parties of the Americas: Canada, Latin America, and the West Indies.* Westport, CT: Greenwood.

——— (1982b) "Chile," in Robert J. Alexander, ed., *Political Parties of the Americas: Canada, Latin America, and the West Indies.* Westport, CT: Greenwood.

———(1982c) "Venezuela," in Robert J. Alexander, ed., *Political Parties of the Americas: Canada, Latin America, and the West Indies.* Westport, CT: Greenwood.

Alisky, Marvin (1982) "Mexico," in Robert J. Alexander, ed., *Political Parties of the Americas: Canada, Latin America, and the West Indies.* Westport, CT: Greenwood.

Alleman, Fritz Rene (1967) "The Changing Scene in Germany," *The World Today* 25: 49–61.

Allison, Graham T. (1971) *Essence of Decision: Explaining the Cuban Missile Crisis.* Boston: Little, Brown.

Allison, Graham T., and Morton A. Halperin (1972) "Bureaucratic Politics: A Paradigm and Some Policy Implications," in Raymond Tanter and Richard H. Ullman, eds., *Theory and Policy in International Relations.* Princeton; NJ: Princeton University Press.

Almond, Garbriel A. and G. Bingham Powell, Jr. (1978) *Comparative Politics: Systems, Processes, and Policy.* Boston: Little, Brown.

Aluko, Olajide (1976) "Nigeria's Oil at Concessionary Prices for Africa: A Case Study in Decision Making," *African Affairs* 75: 425–443.

Ameringer, Charles D. (1982) "Costa Rica," in Robert J. Alexander, ed., *Political Parties of the Americas: Canada, Latin America, and the West Indies.* Westport, CT: Greenwood.

Anderson, Richard D., Jr. (1982) "Soviet Decision Making and Poland," *Problems of Communism* 31: 22–36.

Andrews, William G. (1966) "Change in French Politics after the 1965 Presidential Elections," in William G. Andrews, ed., *European Politics II: The Dynamics of Change.* New York: Van Nostrand.

——— (1962) *French Politics and Algeria: The Process of Policy Formation, 1954–1962.* New York: Appleton-Century-Crofts.

Andriole, Stephen J., Jonathan Wilkenfeld, and Gerald W. Hopple (1975) "A Framework for the Comparative Analysis of Foreign Policy Behavior," *International Studies Quarterly* 9: 160–198.

Angell, Alan (1967) "Castro and the Cuban Communist Party," *Government and Opposition* 2: 241–252.

Anglin, Douglas G. (1964) "Nigeria: Political Non-alignment and Economic Alignment," *Journal of Modern African Studies* 2: 247–263.

Appadorai, A. (1981) *The Domestic Roots of India's Foreign Policy, 1947–1972.* Delhi: Oxford University Press.

Arango, E. Ramon (1985) *Spain: From Repression to Renewal.* Boulder, CO: Westview.

Armstrong, John A. (1965) "The Domestic Roots of Soviet Foreign Policy," *International Affairs* 41: 37–47.

Aronoff, Myron J. (1978) "Fission and Fusion: The Politics of Factionalism in the Israel Labor Party," in *Faction Politics: Political Parties and Factionalism in Comparative Perspective.* Santa Barbara, CA: ABC-Clio.

Aronson, Shlomo (1982–83) "Israel's Leaders, Domestic Order and Foreign Policy, June 1981–June 1983," *The Jerusalem Journal of International Relations* 6:1–29.

Art, Robert J. (1973) "Bureaucratic Politics and American Foreign Policy: A Critique," *Policy Sciences* 4: 467–490.

Arter, David (1987) *Politics and Policy-Making in Finland.* New York: St. Martin's.

Ashford, Douglas (1965) "Neo-Destour Leadership and the 'Confiscated Revolution,'" *World Politics* 17: 215–231.

Aspaturian, Vernon (1976) "The Foreign Policy of the Soviet Union," in James N. Rosenau, Kenneth W. Thompson, and Gavin Boyd, eds., *World Politics: An Introduction.* New York: Free Press.

——— (1966) "Internal Politics and Foreign Policy in the Soviet System." in R. Barry Farrell, ed., *Approaches to Comparative and International Politics.* Evanston, IL: Northwestern University Press.

Austin, Dennis (1967) "Opposition in Ghana: 1947–67," *Government and Opposition* 2: 539–556.

Axelrod, Robert (1970) *Conflict of Interest.* Chicago: Markham.

Azar, Edward (1970) "Analysis of International Events," *Peace Research Reviews* 4: 28–36.

Azrael, Jeremy (1981) "The 'Nationality Problem' in the USSR: Domestic Pressures and Foreign Policy Constraints," in Seweryn Bialer, ed., *The Domestic Context of Soviet Foreign Policy.* Boulder, CO: Westview.

——— (1970) "The Internal Dynamics of the CPSU, 1917–1967," in Samuel P. Huntington and Clement H. Moore, eds., *Authoritarian Politics in Modern Society: The Dynamics of Established One-Party States.* New York: Basic Books.

Bachman, David (1989) "Domestic Sources of Chinese Foreign Policy," in Samuel K. Kim, ed., *China and the World: New Directions in Chinese Foreign Relations.* Boulder, CO: Westview.

Badgley, John H. (1969) "Two Styles of Military Rule: Thailand and Burma," *Government and Opposition* 4: 100–117.

Baerwald, Hans H. (1970) "Nikkan Kokkai: The Japan-Korea Treaty Diet," in Lucian W. Pye, ed., *Cases in Comparative Politics: Asia.* Boston: Little, Brown.

Baker, Raymond William (1978) *Egypt's Uncertain Revolution Under Nasser and Sadat.* Cambridge, MA: Harvard University Press.

Bandyopadhyaya, J. (1970) *The Making of India's Foreign Policy: Determinants, Institutions, Processes, and Personalities.* Bombay: Allied Publishers.

Banks, Arthur S. (1985) *Political Handbook of the World, 1984–1985.* Binghamton, NY: CSA Publications.

——— (1971) *Cross-Polity Time-Series Data.* Cambridge: The MIT Press.

Barghoorn, Frederick C. (1973) "Factional, Sectoral, and Subversive Opposition in Soviet Politics," in Robert A. Dahl, ed., *Regimes and Oppositions.* New Haven, CT: Yale University Press.

Barnes, Samuel H. (1966) "Italy: Oppositions on Left, Right, and Center," in Robert A. Dahl, ed., *Political Oppositions in Western Democracies.* New Haven, CT: Yale University Press.

Barnett, A. Doak (1985) *The Making of Foreign Policy in China: Structure and Process.* Boulder, CO: Westview.

Bar-Siman-Tov, Yaacov (1990) "Peace as a Significant Change in Foreign Policy: The Need for Legitimacy," *Jerusalem Journal of International Relations* 12: 13–30.

——— (1983) *Linkage Politics in the Middle East: Syria Between Domestic and External Conflict, 1961–1970.* Boulder, CO: Westview.

Baum, Richard D. (1969) "China: Year of the Mangoes," *Asian Survey* 9: 1–17.

——— (1964) "Red and Expert: The Politico-Ideological Foundations of China's Great Leap Forward," *Asian Survey* 4: 1048–1057.

Baylis, Thomas A. (1989) *Governing by Committee: Collegial Leadership in Advanced Societies.* Albany: State Univerity of New York Press.

Bebler, Anton (1973) *Military Rule in Africa: Dahomey, Ghana, Sierra Leone, and Mali.* New York: Praeger.

Beck, Carl, William A. Jarzabek, and Paul H. Hernande (1976) "Political Succession in Eastern Europe," *Studies in Comparative Communism* 9: 35–61.

Belloni, Frank P. (1978) "Factionalism, the Party System, and Italian Politics," in Frank P. Belloni and Dennis C. Beller, eds., *Faction Politics: Political Parties and Factionalism in Comparative Perspective.* Santa Barbara, CA: ABC-Clio.

Belloni, Frank P., and Dennis C. Beller, eds. (1978) *Faction Politics: Political Parties and Factionalism in Comparative Perspective.* Santa Barbara, CA: ABC-Clio.

Benes, Vaclav, Andrew Gyorgy, and George Stambuk (1966) *Eastern European Government and Politics.* New York: Harper and Row.

Benner, Jeffrey (1985) *The Indian Foreign Policy Bureaucracy.* Boulder, CO: Westview.

Bennett, George (1966) "Kenya's 'Little General Election,'" *The World Today* 22: 336–343.

——— (1963) "Political Realities in Kenya," *The World Today* 19: 294–301.

Bennett, Gordon A. (1970) "China's Continuing Revolution: Will It Be Permanent?" *Asian Survey* 10: 2–17.

Berman, Larry (1982) *Planning a Tragedy: The Americanization of the War in Vietnam.* New York: Norton.

Bernard, Jean-Pierre, Silas Cerqueira, Hugo Neira, Helene Graillot, Leslie F. Manigat, and Pierre Gilhodes (1969) *Guide to the Political Parties of South America.* Baltimore: Penguin Books.

Betts, Richard K. (1977) *Soldiers, Statesmen, and Cold War Crises.* Cambridge, MA.: Harvard University Press.

Bialer, Seweryn (1987) *The Soviet Paradox: External Expansion, Internal Decline.* New York: Alfred A. Knopf.

——— (1981) "Soviet Foreign Policy: Sources, Perceptions, Trends," in Seweryn Bialer, ed., *The Domestic Context of Soviet Foreign Policy.* Boulder, CO: Westview.

——— (1980) *Stalin's Successors: Leadership, Stability, and Change in the Soviet Union.* Cambridge: Cambridge University Press.

Biddle, William Jesse, and John D. Stephens (1989) "Dependent Development and Foreign Policy: The Case of Jamaica," *International Studies Quarterly* 33: 411–434.

Bienen, Henry (1974) *Kenya: The Politics of Participation and Control.* Princeton, NJ: Princeton University Press.

——— (1970) "One-Party Systems in Africa," in Samuel Huntington and Clement H. Moore, eds., *Authoritarian Politics in Modern Society.* New York: Basic Books.

Bill, James A., and Carl Leiden (1979) *Politics in the Middle East.* Boston: Little, Brown.

Binder, Leonard (1966) "Political Recruitment and Participation in Egypt," in Joseph LaPolombara and Myron Weiner, eds., *Political Parties and Political Development.* Princeton, NJ: Princeton University Press.

Bishop, William J. (1990) "Domestic Politics and Gorbachev's Security Policy," in George E. Hudson, ed., *Soviet National Security Policy Under Perestroika.* Boston: Unwin Hyman.

Blainey, Geoffrey (1988) *The Causes of War.* New York: Free Press.

Blank, David Eugene (1984) *Venezuela: Politics in a Petroleum Republic.* New York: Praeger.

Blondel, Jean, and Ferdinand Muller-Rommel, eds. (1988) *Cabinets in Western Europe.* London: Macmillan.

Bobrow, Davis B., Steve Chan, and John A. Kringen (1979) *Understanding Foreign Policy Decisions.* New York: Free Press.

Bogdanor, Vernon, ed. (1983) *Coalition Government in Western Europe.* London: Heinemann.

Bognetti, Giovanni (1971) "The Crisis of Parliamentary Government in Italy," in E. A. Goerner, ed., *Democracy in Crisis: New Challenges to Constitutional Democracy in the Atlantic Area.* Notre Dame, IN: University of Notre Dame Press.

Brady, Linda P. (1974) "Threat, Decision Time, and Awareness: The Impact of Situational Variables on Foreign Policy Behavior." Ph.D. Dissertation, Ohio State University.

Bray, Donald W. (1968) "Uruguay," in Ben Burnett and Kenneth Johnson, eds., *Political Forces in Latin America.* Belmont, CA: Wadsworth.

Brecher, Michael (1977) "India's Devaluation of 1966: Linkage Politics and Crisis Decision Making," *British Journal of International Studies* 3: 1–25.

—— (1974) *Decisions in Israel's Foreign Policy*. London: Oxford University Press.

—— (1972) *The Foreign Policy System of Israel: Setting, Images, Process*. New Haven, CT: Yale University Press.

—— (1968) *India and World Politics: Krishna Menon's View of the World*. New York: Praeger.

—— (1967) "Succession in India 1967: The Routinization of Political Change," *Asian Survey* 7: 423–443.

—— (1959) *Nehru: A Political Biography*. Boston: Beacon Press.

Brecher, Michael, Jonathan Wilkenfeld, and Sheila Moser (1988) *Crises in the Twentieth Century*. New York: Pergamon Press.

Brecher, Michael, Blema Steinberg, and Janice Stein (1969) "A Framework for Research on Foreign Policy Behavior," *Journal of Conflict Resolution* 8: 75–101.

Brenner, Jeffrey (1985) *The Indian Foreign Policy Bureaucracy*. Boulder, CO: Westview.

Breslauer, George W. (1982) *Khrushchev and Brezhnev as Leaders: Building Authority in Soviet Politics*. Boston: Allen and Unwin.

Bretton, Henry L. (1966) *The Rise and Fall of Kwame Nkrumah: A Study of Personal Rule in Africa*. New York: Praeger.

Brinkley, Joel (1990) "Divided Loyalties," *New York Times Magazine*. December 16.

Brown, Bernard E. (1965) "The Decision to End the Algerian War," in James B. Christoph, ed., *Cases in Comparative Politics*. Boston: Little, Brown.

Brown, Eric C., and John Dreijmanis, eds. (1982) *Government Coalitions in Western Democracies*. New York: Longman.

Brown, Robert G. (1976) "Chinese Politics and American Policy: A New Look at the Triangle." *Foreign Policy* 23: 3–23.

Brown, Seyom (1983) *The Faces of Power: Constancy and Change in United States Foreign Policy from Truman to Reagan*. New York: Columbia University Press.

Brugger, William (1969) "The Ninth National Congress of the Chinese Communist Party," *The World Today* 25: 297–305.

Brzezinski, Zbigniew K. (1967) *The Soviet Bloc: Unity and Conflict*. Cambridge, MA: Harvard University Press.

Brzezinski, Zbigniew, and Samuel P. Huntington (1964) *Political Power: USA/USSR*. New York: Viking.

Burg, Steven L. (1983) *Conflict and Cohesion in Socialist Yugoslavia: Political Decision Making Since 1966*. Princeton, NJ: Princeton University Press.

Burnett, Ben G. (1970) *Political Groups in Chile: The Dialogue Between Order and Change*. Austin: University of Texas Press.

—— (1968) "Chile," in Ben G. Burnett and Kenneth Johnson, eds., *Political Forces in Latin America*. Belmont, CA: Wadsworth.

Burnett, Ben and Kenneth Johnson (1968) *Political Forces in Latin America*. Belmont, CA: Wadsworth.

Buszynski, Leszek (1989) "New Aspirations and Old Constraints in Thailand's Foreign Policy," *Asian Survey* 29: 1057–1072.

Butler, Frederick, and Scott Taylor (1975) "Toward an Explanation of Consistency and Adaptability in Foreign Policy Behavior: The Role of Political Accountability." Paper presented at the annual meeting of the Midwest Political Science Association, Chicago, May 1–3.

Calder, Kent E. (1988) "Japanese Foreign Economic Policy Formation: Explaining the Reactive State," *World Politics* 40: 517–541.

Callahan, Patrick (1982) "Commitment," in Patrick Callahan, Linda P. Brady, and Margaret G. Hermann, eds., *Describing Foreign Policy Behavior.* Beverly Hills, CA: Sage Publications.

Callahan, Patrick, Linda P. Brady, and Margaret G. Hermann, eds. (1982) *Describing Foreign Policy Behavior.* Beverly Hills, CA: Sage Publications.

Campbell, Bruce A., and Sue Ellen M. Charlton (1978) "The Ambiguity of Faction: Fragmentation and Bipolarization in France," in Frank P. Belloni and Dennis C. Beller, eds., *Faction Politics: Political Parties and Factionalism in Comparative Perspective.* Santa Barbara, CA: ABC-Clio.

Campbell, Colin (1977) *Canadian Political Facts 1945–1976.* Toronto: Methuen.

Campbell, John C. (1972) "Yugoslavia," in Adam Bromke and Teresa Rakowska-Harmstone, eds., *The Communist States in Disarray, 1965–1971.* Minneapolis: University of Minnesota Press.

Carter, Gwendolen (1962) *African One-Party States.* Ithaca: Cornell University Press.

Cerny, Philip G. (1979) "Foreign Policy Leadership and National Integration," *British Journal of International Studies* 5: 59–85.

Chan, Steve (1984) "Mirror, Mirror on the Wall . . .: Are Freer Countries More Pacific?" *Journal of Conflict Resolution* 28: 617–648.

——— (1979) "Rationality, Bureaucratic Politics, and Belief Systems: Explaining the Chinese Policy Debate, 1964–66," *Journal of Peace Research* 16: 333–347.

Chang, Parris H. (1975) *Power and Policy in China,* 2d ed. University Park: Pennsylvania State University Press.

——— (1972) "The Changing Patterns of Military Participation in Chinese Politics," *Orbis* 16: 780–802.

Cheng, Chu-Yuan (1966) "The Power Struggle in Red China," *Asian Survey* 6: 469–483.

Chick, John D. (1970) "Uganda: The Quest for Control," *The World Today* 26: 18–28.

Christoph, James B. (1965) "The Suez Crisis," in James B. Christoph, ed., *Cases in Comparative Politics.* Boston: Little, Brown.

Christophersen, Jens A. (1968) "The Making of Foreign Policy in Norway," *Conflict and Cooperation* 4: 52–74.

Chrypinski, V. C. (1972) "Poland," in Adam Bromke and Teresa Rakowska-Harmstone, eds., *The Communist States in Disarray, 1965–1971.* Minneapolis: University of Minnesota Press.

Clapham, Christopher (1977) "Comparative Foreign Policy and Developing States," in Christopher Clapham, ed., *Foreign Policy Making in Developing States.* Westmead, England: Saxon House.

———, ed. (1977) *Foreign Policy Making in Developing States.* Westmead, England: Saxon House.

Clark, Cal (1980) "Balkan Communist Foreign Policies: A Linkage Perspective," in Ronald H. Linden, ed., *The Foreign Policies of East Europe.* New York: Praeger.

Clark, Michael (1988) "The Policy-Making Process," in Michael Smith, Steve Smith, and Brian White, eds., *British Foreign Policy: Tradition, Change and Transformation.* London: Unwin Hyman.

Clarkson, Stephen (1979) "Democracy in the Liberal Party," in Hugh Thornburn, ed., *Party Politics in Canada.* Englewood Cliffs, NJ: Prentice-Hall.

Cohen, Bernard (1977–78) "Political Systems, Public Opinion, and Foreign Policy: The United States and the Netherlands," *International Journal* 33: 195–216.

Cohen, Stephen (1988) "The Military and Indian Democracy," in Atul Kohli, ed.,

India's Democracy: An Analysis of Changing State-Society Relations. Princeton, NJ: Princeton University Press.

Cowan, L. Gray (1962) "Guinea," in Gwendolen Carter, ed., *African One-Party States*. Ithaca, NY: Cornell University Press.

Croan, Melvin (1972) "East Germany," in Adam Bromke and Teresa Rakowska-Harmstone, eds., *The Communist States in Disarray, 1965–1971*. Minneapolis: University of Minnesota Press.

Daalder, Hans, ed. (1987) *Party Systems in Denmark, Austria, Switzerland, the Netherlands, and Belgium*. New York: St. Martin's.

Daddieh, Cyril Kofie, and Timothy M. Shaw (1984) "The Political Economy of Decision Making in African Foreign Policy: Recognition of Biafra and the Popular Movement for the Liberation of Angola," in Bahgat Korany, ed., *How Foreign Policy Decisions Are Made in the Third World*. Boulder, CO: Westview.

Dahl, Robert A., ed. (1973) *Regimes and Oppositions*. New Haven, CT: Yale University Press.

———, ed. (1966) *Political Oppositions in Western Democracies*. New Haven, CT: Yale University Press.

Dallek, Robert (1983) *The American Style of Foreign Policy: Culture Politics and Foreign Affairs*. New York: Alfred A. Knopf.

——— (1977) *Franklin Roosevelt and American Foreign Policy, 1932–1945*. New York: Oxford University Press.

Dallin, Alexander (1981) "The Domestic Sources of Soviet Foreign Policy," in Seweryn Bialer, ed., *The Domestic Context of Soviet Foreign Policy*. Boulder, CO: Westview.

——— (1969) "Soviet Foreign Policy and Domestic Politics: A Framework for Analysis," in Eric Hoffmann and Frederic J. Fleron, eds., *The Conduct of Soviet Foreign Policy*. Chicago: Aldine-Atherton.

Dallin, Alexander, and Thomas B. Larson, eds., (1968) *Soviet Politics Since Khrushchev*. Englewood Cliffs, NJ: Prentice-Hall.

Daniels, R. V. (1971) "Soviet Politics Since Khrushchev," in H. W. Strong, ed., *The Soviet Union Under Brezhnev and Kosygin*. New York: Van Nostrand-Reinhold.

Darling, Frank C. (1969) "Thailand: De-Escalation and Uncertainty," *Asian Survey* 9: 115–121.

——— (1968) "Thailand: Stability and Escalation," *Asian Survey* 8: 120–126.

——— (1962) "Modern Politics in Thailand," *Review of Politics* 24: 163–182.

David, Steven R. (1991) "Explaining Third World Realignment," *World Politics* 43: 223–256.

Dawisha, Adeed (1990) "Arab Regimes: Legitimacy and Foreign Policy," in Giacomo Luciani, ed., *The Arab State*. Berkeley: University of California Press.

——— (1986) "The Politics of War: Presidential Centrality, Party Power, Political Oppositions," in Frederick W. Axelgard, ed., *Iraq in Transition*. Boulder, CO: Westview.

Dawisha, Karen (1980) "The Limits of the Bureaucratic Politics Model: Observations on the Soviet Case," *Studies in Comparative Communism* 13: 300–346.

Decalo, Samuel (1976) *Coups and Army Rule in Africa: Studies in Military Style*. New Haven, CT: Yale University Press.

Dekmejian, R. Hrair (1971) *Egypt Under Nasir: A Study in Political Dynamics*. Albany: State University of New York Press.

de Meyer, Jan (1983) "Coalition Government in Belgium," in Vernon Bogdanor, ed., *Coalition Government in Western Europe*. London: Heinemann.

Denton, Charles F. (1985) "Costa Rica: A Democratic Revolution," in Howard J. Wiarda and Harvey F. Kline, eds., *Latin American Politics and Development*. Boulder, CO: Westview.

Derbyshire, Ian (1987) *Politics in West Germany: From Schmidt to Kohl*. London: Chambers Political Spotlights.

Dessouki, Ali E. Hillal (1984) "The Primacy of Economics: The Foreign Policy of Egypt," in Bahgat Korany and Ali E. Hillal Dessouki, eds., *The Foreign Policies of Arab States*. Boulder, CO: Westview.

Dessouki, Ali E. Hillal, and Bahgat Korany (1984a) "A Literature Survey and a Framework for Analysis," in Bahgat Korany and Ali E. Hillal Dessouki, eds., *The Foreign Policies of Arab States*. Boulder, CO: Westview.

——— (1984b) "Foreign Policy Process in the Arab World: A Comparative Perspective," in Bahgat Korany and Ali E. Hillal Dessouki, eds., *The Foreign Policies of Arab States*. Boulder, CO: Westview.

Destler, I. M. (1974) *Presidents, Bureaucratic Politics, and Foreign Policy*. Princeton: Princeton University Press.

Destler, I. M., Priscilla Clapp, Hideo Sato, and Haruhiro Fukui (1976) *Managing an Alliance: The Politics of U.S.-Japanese Relations*. Washington, D.C.: Brookings.

Destler, I. M., Haruhiro Fukui, and Hideo Sato (1979) *The Textile Wrangle: Conflict in Japanese-American Relations, 1969–1971*. Ithaca, NY: Cornell University Press.

Destler, I. M., Leslie H. Gelb, and Anthony Lake (1984) *Our Own Worst Enemy: The Unmaking of American Foreign Policy*. New York: Simon and Schuster.

de Swann, Abram (1973) *Coalition Theories and Cabinet Formation*. Amsterdam: Elsevier.

de Tocqueville, Alexis (1945) *Democracy in America*, vol. 1. New York: Alfred A. Knopf.

Deutsch, Karl W., and Williman J. Foltz, eds. (1966) *Nation-Building*. New York: Atherton.

Dewachter, Wilfried (1987) "Changes in a Particratie: The Belgian Party System from 1944 to 1986," in Hans Daalder, ed., *Party Systems in Denmark, Austria, Switzerland, the Netherlands, and Belgium*. New York: St. Martin's.

Dewachter, Wilfried, and Edi Clijsters (1982) "Belgium: Political Stability Despite Coalition Crises," in Eric C. Browne and John Dreijmanis, eds., *Government Coalitions in Western Democracies*. New York: Longman.

Dinerstein, Herbert (1976) *The Making of a Missile Crisis: October 1962*. Baltimore: Johns Hopkins University Press.

Di Palma, Giuseppe (1977) *Surviving Without Governing: The Italian Parties in Parliament*. Berkeley: University of California Press.

Dixon, William J. (1989) "Political Democracy and War: A New Look at an Old Problem." Paper presented at the annual meeting of the International Studies Association, London, March–April.

Dodd, C. H. (1969) *Politics and Government in Turkey*. Berkeley: University of California Press.

Dominguez, Jorge I. (1989) *To Make a World Safe for Revolution: Cuba's Foreign Policy*. Cambridge, MA: Harvard University Press.

——— (1987) "Leadership Changes and Factionalism in the Cuban Communist Party." Paper presented at the annual meeting of the American Political Science Association, Chicago, September.

——— (1981) "Revolutionary Politics: The New Demands for Orderliness," in Jorge I. Dominguez, ed., *Cuba: Internal and International Affairs*. Beverly Hills, CA: Sage.

———— (1978) *Cuba: Order and Revolution*. Cambridge, MA: Harvard University Press.

Dominguez, Jorge I., and Juan Lindau (1986) "The Primacy of Politics: Comparing the Foreign Policies of Cuba and Mexico," in Bahgat Korany, ed., *How Foreign Policy Decisions Are Made in the Third World*. Boulder, CO: Westview.

Dowty, Alan (1984) "Israel: From Ideology to Reality," in Alvin Z. Rubinstein, ed., *The Arab-Israeli Conflict: Perspectives*. New York: Praeger.

Doyle, Michael W. (1986) "Liberalism and World Politics," *American Political Science Review* 80: 1151–1169.

Drummond, Robert J. (1972) "The Canadian Political System: An Overview," *Current History* 62: 198–202.

Duchacek, Ivo D. (1970) *Comparative Federalism: The Territorial Dimension of Politics*. New York: Holt, Reinhart, Winston.

Duignan, Peter, and Robert Jackson, eds. (1986) *The Politics and Government in African States, 1960–1985*. Stanford, CA: Hoover Institution Press.

Duval, Robert D., and William R. Thompson (1980) "Reconsidering the Aggregate Relationship Between Size, Economic Development, and Some Types of Foreign Policy Behavior," *American Journal of Political Science* 24: 511–525.

Dziewanowski, M. K. (1979) "The Communist Party of Poland," in Stephen Fisher-Galati, eds., *The Communist Parties of Eastern Europe*. New York: Columbia University Press.

East, Maurice A. (1981) "The Organizational Impact of Interdependence on Foreign Policy-Making: The Case of Norway," in Charles W. Kegley, Jr. and Pat McGowan, eds., *The Political Economy of Foreign Policy Behavior*. Beverly Hills: Sage.

———— (1973) "Foreign Policy Making in Small States: Some Theoretic Observations Based on the Study of the Uganda Ministry of Foreign Affairs," *Policy Sciences* 4: 491–508.

East, Maurice A., and Charles F. Hermann (1974) "Do Nation-Types Account for Foreign Policy Behavior?" in James N. Rosenau, ed., *Comparing Foreign Policies: Theories, Findings, and Methods*. Beverly Hills, CA: Sage.

East, Maurice A. and Philipp M. Gregg (1967) "Factors Influencing Cooperation and Conflict in the International System," *International Studies Quarterly* 11: 244–69.

East, Maurice A., Stephen A. Salmore, and Charles F. Hermann, eds. (1978) *Why Nations Act: Theoretical Perspectives for Comparative Foreign Policy Studies*. Beverly Hills, CA: Sage.

Eckstein, Harry (1975) "Case Study and Theory in Political Science," in Fred Greenstein and Nelson Polsby, eds., *Handbook of Political Science*, vol. 8. Reading, MA: Addison-Wesley.

———— (1970) "Economic Development and Political Change in Communist Systems," *World Politics* 22: 475–495.

———— (1966) *Division and Cohesion in Democracy: A Study of Norway*. Princeton, NJ: Princeton University Press.

Edinger, Lewis J. (1968) *Politics in Germany: Attitudes and Process*. Boston: Little, Brown.

Ehrmann, Henry W. (1968) *Politics in France*. Boston: Little, Brown.

Ellis, Ellen D. (1962) "Post-Revolutionary Politics in Turkey," *Current History* 42: 220–226.

Enloe, Cynthia H. (1972) *Ethnic Conflict and Political Development*. Boston: Little, Brown.

Entelis, John P. (1980) *Comparative Politics of North Africa: Algeria, Morocco, and Tunisia*. Syracuse, NY: Syracuse University Press.

Epstein, Leon D. (1964) *British Politics in the Suez Crisis.* Urbana: University of Illinois Press.

Erogul, Cem (1987) "The Establishment of Multiparty Rule: 1945–1971," in Rezan Benatar, Irvin C. Schick, and Ronnie Margulies, eds., *Turkey in Transition: New Perspectives.* New York: Oxford University Press.

Europa, Editors of (1985a) *The Far East and Australasia.* London: Europa Publications.

———— (1985b) *The Middle East and North Africa.* London: Europa Publications.

———— (1985c) *Sub-Saharan Africa.* London: Europa Publications.

Everts, Philip P. (forthcoming) "Between the Devil and the Deep Blue Sea: 48 Cruise Missiles for the Netherlands," in Joe D. Hagan, Charles F. Hermann, and Margaret G. Hermann, eds., *Leaders, Groups, and Coalitions: How Decision Units Shape Foreign Policy.*

———— (1985) "Conclusions," in Philip P. Everts, ed., *Controversies at Home: Domestic Factors in the Foreign Policy of the Netherlands.* Boston: Martinus Nijhoff.

————, ed. (1985) *Controversies at Home: Domestic Factors in the Foreign Policy of the Netherlands.* Boston: Martinus Nijhoff.

Fairbank, John King (1986) *The Great Chinese Revolution, 1800–1985.* Cambridge, MA: Harvard University Press.

Farrands, Christopher (1988) "State, Society, Culture and British Foreign Policy," in Michael Smith, Steve Smith, and Brian White, eds., *British Foreign Policy: Tradition, Change and Transformation.* London: Unwin and Hyman.

Farrell, R. Barry (1966) "Foreign Policies of Open and Closed Political Systems," in R. Barry Farrell, ed., *Approaches to Comparative and International Politics.* Evanston, IL: Northwestern University Press.

Faurby, Ib (1982) "Decision Structures and Domestic Sources of Nordic Foreign Policies," in Bengt Sundelius, ed., *Foreign Policies of Northern Europe.* Boulder, CO: Westview.

Fein, Leonard J. (1967) *Politics in Israel.* Boston: Little, Brown.

Fingar, Thomas (1980) "Domestic Policy and the Quest for Independence," in Thomas Fingar and the Stanford Journal of International Studies, eds., *China's Quest for Independence: Policy Evolution in the 1970s.* Boulder, CO: Westview.

Fischer, Georges (1963) "The Political Evolution of the Philippines," in Saul Rose, ed., *Politics in Southeast Asia.* New York: St. Martin's.

Fitzmaurice, John (1986) "Coalition Theory and Practice in Scandinavia," in Geoffrey Pridham, ed., *Coalition Behaviour in Theory and Practice.* Cambridge: Cambridge University Press.

———— (1983) *The Politics of Belgium: Crisis and Compromise in a Plural Society.* New York: St. Martin's.

Fleet, Michael (1984) *The Rise and Fall of Chilean Christian Democracy.* Princeton, NJ: Princeton University Press.

Foltz, William J. (1971) "Political Opposition in Single-Party States of Tropical Africa," in Robert A. Dahl, ed., *Regimes and Oppositions.* New Haven, CT: Yale University Press.

Fox, Annette Baker (1977) *The Politics of Attraction: Four Middle Powers and the United States.* New York: Columbia University Press.

Franeti, Paolo (1985) *The Italian Party System, 1945–1980.* New York: St. Martin's.

Frank, Thomas M., and Edward Weisband (1979) *Foreign Policy by Congress.* New York: Oxford University Press.

Frankel, Joseph (1977) "Domestic Politics of Japan's Foreign Policy: A Case Study of the Ratification of the Non-Proliferation Treaty," *British Journal of International Studies* 3: 254–268.

Freidrich, Carl J., and Zbigniew K. Brzezinski (1956) *Totalitarian Dictatorship and Autocracy*. New York: Praeger.

Friedman, Thomas L. (1990) *From Beirut to Jerusalem*. New York: Anchor Books.

Fry, Michael G., and Condoleezza Rice (1983) "The Hungarian Crisis of 1956: The Soviet Decision," *Studies in Comparative Communism* 16: 85–98.

Fukui, Haruhiro (forthcoming) "Japanese Decision Making in the 1971 Exchange Rate Crisis," in Joe D. Hagan, Charles F. Hermann, and Margaret G. Hermann, eds., *Leaders, Groups, and Coalitions: How Decision Units Shape Foreign Policy*.

——— (1985) "Japan," in Haruhiro Fukui, ed., *Political Parties of Asia and the Pacific*. Westport, CT: Greenwood.

——— (1978a) "The GATT Tokyo Round: The Bureaucratic Politics of Multilateral Diplomacy," in Michael Baker, ed., *The Politics of Trade: U.S. and Japanese Policymaking for the GATT Negotiations*. New York: Occasional Papers of the East Asian Institute.

——— (1978b) "Japan: Factionalism in a Dominant-Party System," in Frank P. Belloni and Dennis C. Beller, eds., *Faction Politics: Political Parties and Factionalism in Comparative Perspective*. Santa Barbara, CA: ABC-Clio.

——— (1977a) "Tanaka Goes to Peking: A Case Study in Foreign Policy Making," in T. J. Pempel, ed., *Policymaking in Contemporary Japan*. Ithaca, NY: Cornell University Press.

——— (1977b) "Foreign Policy Making by Improvisation: The Japanese Experience," *International Journal* 32: 791–812.

——— (1970) *Party in Power: The Japanese Liberal-Democrats and Policy Making*. Berkeley: University of California Press.

Gaddis, John Lewis (1982) *Strategies of Containment: A Critical Appraisal of Postwar American National Security Policy*. New York: Oxford University Press.

——— (1972) *The United States and the Origins of the Cold War*. New York: Columbia University Press.

Gallaher, Matthew P., and Karl F. Spielmann, Jr. (1972) *Soviet Decision Making for Defense: A Critique of U.S. Perspectives on the Arms Race*. New York: Praeger.

Gann, L. H. (1986) "Malawi, Zambia and Zimbabwe," in Peter Duignan and Robert H. Jackson, eds., *Politics and Government in African States, 1960–1985*. Stanford, CA: Hoover Institution Press.

Gardiner, C. Harvey (1966) "Costa Rica: Mighty Midget," *Current History* 50: 8–14.

Garthoff, Raymond L. (1985) *Detente and Confrontation: American-Soviet Relations from Nixon to Reagan*. Washington, D.C.: Brookings.

Geller, Daniel S., (1985) *Domestic Factors in Foreign Policy: A Cross-National Statistical Analysis*. Cambridge, MA: Schenkman.

Gellner, Marianne (1964) "Mexico: New Frontiers of Progress," *The World Today* 20: 523–532.

Gelman, Harry (1984) *The Brezhnev Politburo and the Decline of Detente*. Ithaca, NY: Cornell University Press.

George, Alexander L. (1980) "Domestic Constraints on Regime Change in U.S. Foreign Policy: The Need for Legitimacy," in Ole R. Holsti, Randolph M. Siverson, and Alexander L. George, eds., *Change in the International System*. Boulder, CO: Westview.

George, Alexander L., and Richard Smoke (1974) *Deterrence in American Foreign Policy: Theory and Practice*. New York: Columbia University Press.

Germino, Dante, and Stefano Passigli (1968) *The Government and Politics of Contemporary Italy*. New York: Harper and Row.

Gertzel, Cherry (1984) "Dissent and Authority in the Zambian One-Party State, 1973–80," in Cherry Gertzel, et al., *The Dynamics of the One-Party State in Zambia*. Dover, NH: Manchester University Press.

Gertzel, Cherry (1970) *The Politics of Independent Kenya, 1963–68*. Evanston, IL: Northwestern University Press.

Gertzel, Cherry, et al., (1984) "Introduction: The Making of the One-Party State," in Cherry Gertzel, et al., *The Dynamics of the One-Party State in Zambia*. Dover, NH: Manchester University Press.

Gilmore, David (1983) *Lebanon: The Fractured Country*. New York: St. Martin's.

Girling, John L. (1981) *Thailand: Society and Politics*. Ithaca, NY: Cornell University Press.

Gitelson, Susan A. (1977) "Policy Options for Small States: Kenya and Tanzania Reconsidered," *Studies in Comparative and International Development* 12: 29–57.

Gochman, Charles S., and Zeev Maoz (1984) "Militarized International Disputes, 1816–1976: Procedures, Patterns and Insights," *Journal of Conflict Resolution* 18: 588–615.

Godwin, Paul H. B. (1973) "Communist Systems and Modernization: Sources and Political Crises," *Studies in Comparative Communism* 6: 107–134.

Golan, Galia (1984) "Soviet Decisionmaking in the Yom Kippur War, 1973," in Jiri Valenta and William C. Potter, eds., *Soviet Decisionmaking for National Security*. London: Allen and Unwin.

Goldman, Kjell (1988) *Change and Stability in Foreign Policy: The Problems and Possibilities of Detente*. Princeton, NJ: Princeton University Press.

Goldmann, Kjell, Sten Berglund, and Gunnar Sjostedt (1986) *Democracy and Foreign Policy: The Case of Sweden*. Brookfield, VT: Gower.

Good, Robert C. (1962) "State-building as a Determinant of Foreign Policy in the New States," in Laurence W. Martin, ed., *Neutralism and Non-Alignment*. New York: Praeger.

Goodman, David S. G., ed. (1984) *Groups and Politics in the People's Republic of China*. Ithaca, NY: Cornell University Press.

Gordon, David C. (1980) *Lebanon: The Fragmented Nation*. London: Croom Helm.

Gottlieb, Thomas M. (1977) *Chinese Foreign Policy Factionalism and the Origins of the Strategic Triangle*. Santa Monica, CA: Rand Corporation.

Griffith, William E. (1964) *Communism in Europe: Continuity, Change, and the Sino-Soviet Dispute*. Cambridge: The MIT Press.

Griffiths, Franklyn (1971) "A Tendency Analysis of Soviet Policy-Making," in H. Gordon Skilling and Franklyn Griffiths, eds., *Interest Groups in Soviet Politics*. Princeton, NJ: Princeton University Press.

Grimsson, Olafur R. (1987) "Iceland: A Multilevel Coalition System," in E. Browne and J. Dreymanis, eds., *Government Coalitions in Western Democracies*. New York: Longman.

Grosser, Alfred (1966) "France: Nothing but Opposition," in Robert A. Dahl, ed., *Political Opposition in Western Democracies*. New Haven, CT: Yale University Press.

Grote, Manfred (1979) "The Socialist Unity Party of Germany," in Stephen Fisher-Galati, ed., *The Communist Parties of Eastern Europe*. New York: Columbia University Press.

Groth, Alexander J. (1972) *People's Poland: Government and Politics.* San Francisco: Chandler.

Gruner, Erich, and Kenneth J. Petterle (1983) "Switzerland's Political Parties," in Howard R. Penniman, ed., *Switzerland at the Polls: The National Elections of 1979.* Washington, D.C.: American Enterprise Institute.

Gurr, Ted Robert (1974) "Persistence and Change in Political Systems, 1800–1971," *American Political Science Review* 68: 1482–1504.

Guzman, Raul, and Mila Reforma (1988) *Government and Politics of the Philippines.* Singapore: Oxford University Press.

Hagan, Joe D. (forthcoming-a) "Governmental Decisions to Change Course in Foreign Policy: The Role of Political Regime Constraints and Domestic Opposition," in Charles F. Hermann, Margaret G. Hermann, and Richard K. Hermann, eds., *Changing Course: When Governments Choose to Redirect Foreign Policy.*

——— (forthcoming-b) "Political Systems and War," *Mershon International Studies Review.*

——— (forthcoming-c) "Political Regime Change and Foreign Policy Restructuring: A Framework for Comparative Analysis," in Jerel A. Rosati, Joe D. Hagan, and Martin W. Sampson, eds., *Foreign Policy Restructuring: How Governments Respond to Change.* Columbia: University of South Carolina Press.

———(1989a) "Domestic Political Regime Changes and Third World Voting Realignments in the United Nations," *International Organization* 43: 505–541.

——— (1989b) "Domestic Political Regime Changes and Foreign Policy Restructuring in Western Europe: A Conceptual Framework and Initial Empirical Analysis," *Cooperation and Conflict* 24: 141–163.

——— (1987) "Regimes, Political Oppositions, and the Comparative Analysis of Foreign Policy," in Charles F. Hermann, Charles W. Kegley, and James N. Rosenau, eds., *New Directions in the Study of Foreign Policy.* Boston: Allen and Unwin.

Hagan, Joe D., Charles F. Hermann, and Margaret G. Hermann, eds. (forthcoming) *Leaders, Groups, and Coalitions: How Decision Units Shape Foreign Policy.*

——— (1990) "How Decision Units Shape Foreign Policy: Insights from Comparative Case Studies." Paper presented at the annual meeting of the American Political Science Association, August–September.

Halperin, Morton H. (1974) *Bureaucratic Politics and Foreign Policy.* Washington, D.C.: Brookings.

Halpern, A. M. (1962) "Between Plenums: A Second Look at the 1962 National People's Congress in China," *Asian Survey* 2: 1–12.

Hammer, Darrell P. (1974) *USSR: The Politics of Oligarchy.* Hinsdale, IL: Dreyden.

Hampson, Fen Osler (1988) "The Divided Decision-Maker: American Domestic Politics and the Cuban Crises," in Charles W. Kegley, Jr., and Eugene R. Wittkopf, eds., *The Domestic Sources of American Foreign Policy: Insights and Evidence.* New York: St. Martin's.

Han, Sungjoo (1978) "Japan's 'PXL' Decision: The Politics of Weapons Procurement," *Asian Survey* 28: 769–784.

Handrieder, Wolfram F. (1970) *The Stable Crisis: Two Decades of German Foreign Policy.* New York: Harper and Row.

——— (1967) *West German Foreign Policy, 1949–1963: International Pressure and Domestic Response.* Stanford, CA: Stanford University Press.

Handrieder, Wolfram F., and Graeme P. Auton (1980) *The Foreign Policies of West Germany, France, Britain.* Englewood Cliffs, NJ: Prentice-Hall.

Hanson, A. H. (1968) "Factionalism and Democracy in Indian Politics," *The World Today* 24: 436–443.

———— (1967) "India after the Elections," *The World Today* 23: 188–197.

Hapgood, David (1963) "Guinea's First Five Years," *Current History* 45: 355–360.

Hardgrave, Robert L. (1970) "The Congress in India—Crisis and Split," *Asian Survey* 10: 179–195.

Harding, Harry (1980) "The Domestic Politics of China's Global Posture, 1973–79," in Thomas Fingar and the Stanford Journal of International Studies, eds., *China's Quest for Independence: Policy Evolution in the 1970s.* Boulder, CO: Westview.

Harik, Iliya (1973) "The Single Party as a Subordinate Movement: The Case of Egypt," *World Politics* 26: 80–105.

Harnhardt, Arthur M., Jr. (1984) "German Democratic Republic," in Teresa Rakowska-Harmstone, ed., *Communism in Eastern Europe.* Bloomington: Indiana University Press.

Hazelwood, Leo (1975) "Diversion Mechanisms and Encapsulation Processes: the Domestic Conflict–Foreign Conflict Hypothesis Reconsidered," in Patrick McGowan, ed., *Sage International Yearbook of Foreign Policy Studies,* vol. 3. Beverly Hills, CA: Sage.

Heeger, Gerald (1974) *The Politics of Underdevelopment.* New York: St. Martin's.

Heidenheimer, Arnold J. (1971) *The Governments of Germany.* New York: Crowell.

Hellman, Judith Adler (1983) *Mexico in Crisis.* New York: Homes and Meier.

Hellmann, Donald (1969) *Japanese Foreign Policy and Domestic Politics: The Peace Agreement with the Soviet Union.* Berkeley: University of California Press.

Henig, Stanley, and John Pinder (1969) *European Political Parties.* London: Allen and Unwin.

Hermann, Charles F. (1992) "Avoiding Pathologies in Foreign Policy Decision Groups," in Dan Caldwell and Timothy McKeown, eds., *Force, Diplomacy, and Leadership: Essays in Honor of Alexander George.* Boulder, CO: Westview.

———— (1990) "Changing Course: When Governments Choose to Redirect Foreign Policy," *International Studies Quarterly* 34: 3–21.

———— (1987) "Political Opposition as Potential Agents of Foreign Policy Change: Developing a Theory." Paper presented at the annual meeting of the International Studies Association, April.

———— (1978) "Foreign Policy Behavior: That Which Is to Be Explained," in Maurice A. East, Stephen A. Salmore, and Charles F. Hermann, eds., *Why Nations Act: Theoretical Perspectives for Comparative Foreign Policy Studies.* Beverly Hills, CA: Sage.

———— (1975) "Comparing the Foreign Policy Events of Nations," in Charles W. Kegley, Jr., Gregory A. Raymond, Robert M. Rood, and Richard A. Skinner, eds., *International Events and the Comparative Analysis of Foreign Policy.* Columbia: University of South Carolina Press.

———— (1969) "International Crisis as a Situational Variable," in James N. Rosenau, ed., *International Politics and Foreign Policy.* New York: Free Press.

Hermann, Charles F. and Linda P. Brady (1972) "Alternative Models of International Crisis Behavior," in Charles F. Hermann, ed., *International Crises: Insights from Behavioral Research.* New York: Free Press.

Hermann, Charles F., Maurice A. East, Margaret G. Hermann, Barbara G. Salmore, and Stephen A. Salmore, eds. (1973) *CREON: A Foreign Events Data Set.* Beverly Hills, CA: Sage.

Hermann, Margaret G. (1988) "Syria's Hafez al-Assad," in Barbara Kellerman and Jeffrey Rubin, eds., *Leadership and Negotiation: A New Look at the Middle East.* New York: Praeger.

—— (1982) "Indepedence/Interdependence of Action," in Patrick Callahan, Linda P. Brady, and Margaret G. Hermann, eds., *Describing Foreign Policy Behavior.* Beverly Hills, CA: Sage.

—— (1980) "Explaining Foreign Policy Behavior Using Personal Characteristics of Political Leaders," *International Studies Quarterly* 24: 7–46.

—— (1976) "When Leader Personality Will Affect Foreign Policy: Some Propositions," in James N. Rosenau, ed., *In Search of Global Patterns.* New York: Free Press.

—— (1974) "Leader Personality and Foreign Policy Behaviors," in James N. Rosenau, ed., *Comparing Foreign Policies: Theories, Findings, and Methods.* Beverly Hills, CA: Sage.

Hermann, Margaret G., and Charles F. Hermann (1989) "Who Makes Foreign Policy Decisions and How: An Empirical Inquiry," *International Studies Quarterly* 33: 361–387.

—— (1980) "A Look Inside the 'Black Box': Building on a Decade of Research," in Gerald Hopple, ed., *Biopolitics, Political Psychology, and International Politics.* New York: St. Martin's.

Hermann, Margaret G., Charles F. Hermann, and Joe D. Hagan (1991) "How Decision Units Shape Foreign Policy: Development of a Model." Paper presented at the annual meeting of the International Society of Political Psychology, Helsinki, Finland, July 1–5.

—— (1987) "How Decision Units Shape Foreign Policy Behavior," in Charles F. Hermann, Charles W. Kegley, and James N. Roseanu, eds., *New Directions in the Study of Foreign Policy.* Boston: Allen and Unwin.

Hermann, Margaret G., Charles F. Hermann, and Gerald F. Hutchins (1982) "Affect," in Patrick Callahan, Linda P. Brady, and Margaret G. Hermann, eds., *Describing Foreign Policy Behavior.* Beverly Hills, CA: Sage.

Herold, R., and S. Mahoney (1974) "Military Hardware Procurement: Some Comparative Observations on Soviet and American Processes," *Comparative Politics* 6: 571–599.

Hill, Christopher (1977) "Theories of Foreign Policy Making for the Developing Countries," in Chistopher Clapham, ed., *Foreign Policy Making in Developing States.* Westmead, England: Saxon House.

Hilsman, Roger (1971) *The Politics of Policy Making in Defense and Foreign Affairs.* New York: Harper and Row.

Hinnebusch, Raymond A. (1984) "Revisionist Dreams, Realist Strategies: The Foreign Policy of Syria," in Bahgat Korany and Ali E. Hillal Dessouki, eds., *The Foreign Policies of Arab States.* Boulder, CO: Westview.

Hinton, Harold C. (1972a) *China's Turbulent Quest: An Analysis of China's Foreign Policy Since 1949.* New York: Macmillan.

—— (1972b) "The Beginning of the Cultural Revolution," in Lucian W. Pye, ed., *Cases in Comparative Politics.* Boston: Little Brown.

—— (1972c) "Vietnam Policy, Domestic Factionalism, Regionalism, and Plotting a Coup," in Lucian W. Pye, ed., *Cases in Comparative Politics.* Boston: Little Brown.

Hodnett, Grey (1981) "The Pattern of Leadership Politics," in Seweryn Bialer, ed., *The Domestic Context of Soviet Foreign Policy.* Boulder, CO: Westview.

Holloway, David (1989–90) "State, Society, and the Military under Gorbachev," *International Security* 14: 5–24.

Holsti, Kal J. (1982) "Restructuring Foreign Policy: A Neglected Phenomenon in Foreign Policy," in Kal J. Holsti, ed., *Why Nations Realign: Foreign Policy Restructuring in a Postwar World*. London: Allen and Unwin.

———— (1970) "National Role Conception in the Study of Foreign Policy," *International Studies Quarterly* 14: 233–309.

Holsti, Ole R. (1976) "Foreign Policy Decision Makers Viewed Psychologically: 'Cognitive Process' Approaches," in James N. Rosenau, ed., *In Search of Global Patterns*. New York: Free Press.

Hopkins, Terence Kilbourne (1964) "Uganda: The Politics of Compromise," *Current History* 46: 169–181.

Horelick, Arnold L., A. Ross Johnson, and John D. Steinbruner (1975) *The Study of Soviet Foreign Policy: Decision-Theory-Related Approaches*. Sage Professional Papers in International Studies, vol. 4. Beverly Hills, CA: Sage.

Hoskyns, Catherine (1968) "Africa's Foreign Relations: The Case of Tanzania," *International Affairs* 44: 446–462.

Hosoya, Chihiro, ed. (1977) *Okinawa Reversion*. Pittsburgh: An Occasional Paper of the International Studies Association.

———— (1976) "Japan's Decision-Making System as a Determining Factor in Japan-United States Relations," in Morton A. Kaplan and Kinhide Mushakoji, eds., *Japan, America, and the Future World Order*. Chicago: Free Press.

———— (1974) "Characterisitics of Foreign Policy Decision Making Systems in Japan," *World Politics* 26: 353–369.

Hough, Jerry F. (1989) "Gorbachev's Politics," *Foreign Affairs* 68: 26–41.

———— (1980) *Soviet Leadership in Transition*. Washington, D.C.: Brookings.

Howell, Lewellyn D. (1983) "A Comparative Study of the WEIS and COPDAB Data Sets," *International Studies Quarterly* 27: 149–159.

Hsiao, Gene T. (1967) "The Background and Development of the Proletarian Cultural Revolution," *Asian Survey* 6: 389–404.

Hsieh, John Fu-sheng (1985) "The Formation of Political Coalitions in Communist China since 1949," in Yu-ming Shaw, ed., *Power and Policy in the PRC*. Boulder, CO: Westview.

Hudson, George E. (1976) "Soviet Naval Doctrine and Soviet Politics, 1953–75," *World Politics* 29: 90–113.

Hudson, Michael C. (1977) *Arab Politics: The Search for Legitimacy*. New Haven, CT: Yale University Press.

———— (1968) *The Precarious Republic: Political Modernization in Lebanon*. New York: Random House.

Hudson, Valerie M., Charles F. Hermann, and Eric Singer (1989) "The Situational Imperative: A Predictive Model of Foreign Policy Behavior," *Cooperation and Conflict* 24: 117–139.

Hudson, Valerie, and Susan M. Sims (1992) "Calculating Regime Response to Domestic Opposition: Anti-Americanism Among U.S. Allies," in David Skidmore and Valerie M. Hudson, eds., *The Limits of State Autonomy: Societal Groups and Foreign Policy Formulation*. Boulder, CO: Westview Press.

Huntington, Samuel P. (1970) "Social and Institutional Dynamics of One-Party Systems," in Samuel P. Huntington and Clement H. Moore, eds., *Authoritarian Politics in Modern Society: The Dynamics of Established One-Party Systems*. New York: Basic Books.

———— (1966) *Political Order in Changing Societies*. New Haven, CT: Yale University Press.

—— (1961) *The Common Defense: Strategic Programs in National Defense.* New York: Columbia University Press.

Huntington, Samuel P., and Clement H. Moore, eds. (1970) *Authoritarian Politics in Modern Society: The Dynamics of Established One-Party Systems.* New York: Basic Books.

Ibingira, Grace Stuart (1980) *African Upheavals since Independence.* Boulder, CO: Westview.

Ingebedion, John, and Timothy M. Shaw (forthcoming) "The Decision and Debate Concerning Nigeria's Recognition of the MPLA in Angola," in Joe D. Hagan, Charles F. Hermann, and Margaret G. Hermann, eds., *Leaders, Groups, and Coalitions: How Decision Units Shape Foreign Policy.*

Ionescu, Ghita (1967) *The Politics of the European Communist States.* New York: Praeger.

Ismael, Tareq Y., and Jacqueline S. Ismael (1986) "Domestic Sources of Middle East Foreign Policy," in Tareq Y. Ismael, ed., *International Relations of the Contemporary Middle East: A Study in World Politics.* Syracuse, NY: Syracuse University Press.

Jackson, Robert H., and Carl G. Rosberg (1986) "The States of East Africa: Tanzania, Uganda, and Kenya," in Peter Duignan and Robert Jackson, eds., *Politics and Government in African States, 1960–1985.* Stanford, CA: Hoover Institution Press.

Jackson, Robert H. and Carl G. Rosberg, eds. (1982) *Personal Rule in Black Africa: Prince, Autocrat, Prophet, Tyrant.* Berkeley: University of California Press.

James, Patrick (1988) *Crisis and War.* Kingston and Montreal: McGill-Queen's University Press.

James, Patrick, and John R. Oneal (1991) "The Influence of Domestic and International Politics on the President's Use of Force," *Journal of Conflict Resolution* 35: 307–332.

Janda, Kenneth (1980) *Political Parties: A Comparative Handbook.* New York: Free Press.

Janowitz, Morris (1964) *The Military in the Political Development of New Nations.* Chicago: University of Chicago Press.

Jervis, Robert (1990) "Models and Cases in the Study of International Conflict," *Journal of International Affairs* 44: 81–102.

—— (1976) *Perception and Misperception in International Politics.* Princeton, NJ: Princeton University Press.

Joenniemi, Pertti (1978) "Political Parties and Foreign Policy in Finland," *Cooperation and Conflict* 13: 43–60.

Joffe, Ellis (1976–77) "The Interplay of Politics and Development in the Modernization of China: An Overview," *The Jerusalem Journal of International Relations* 2: 1–14.

Johnson, Chalmers (1970) "Comparing Communist Nations," in Chalmers Johnson, ed., *Change in Communist Systems.* Stanford, CA: Stanford University Press.

Johnson, John J. (1962) *The Role of the Military in Underdeveloped Countries.* Princeton, NJ: Princeton University Press.

Johnson, Kenneth F. (1985) *Mexican Democracy: A Critical View.* New York: Praeger.

—— (1968) "Mexico," in Ben G. Burnett and Kenneth Johnson, eds., *Political Forces in Latin America.* Belmont, CA: Wadsworth.

Jonsson, Christer (1977) "Soviet Foreign Policy and Domestic Politics: A Case Study," *Cooperation and Conflict* 12: 129–148.

Juviler, Peter H., and Hannah J. Zawadzka (1978) "Detente and Soviet Domestic Politics," in Grayson Kirk and Nils Wessell, eds., *The Soviet Threat: Myth and Realities*. New York: Academy of Political Science.

Kaba, Lansine (1977) "Guinean Politics: A Critical Historical Overview," *The Journal of African Studies* 15: 25–45.

Kaminsky, Elijah B. (1975) "The French Chief Executive and Foreign Policy," in Patrick J. McGowan, ed., *Sage International Yearbook of Foreign Policy Studies*, vol. 3. Beverly Hills, CA: Sage.

Kantor, Harry (1969) *Patterns of Politics and Political Systems in Latin America*. Chicago: Rand McNally.

Karvonen, Lauri, and Bengt Sundelius (1990) "Interdependence and Foreign Policy Management in Sweden and Finland," *International Studies Quarterly* 34: 211–227.

Katzenstein, Peter J. (1976) "International Relations and Domestic Structures: Foreign Economic Politics of the Advanced Industrial States," *International Organization* 30: 1–45.

―――― (1978) "Conclusion: Domestic Structures and Strategies of Foreign Economic Policies," in Peter J. Katzenstein, ed., *Between Power and Plenty: Foreign Economic Policies of Advanced Industrialized States*. Madison: University of Wisconsin Press.

Kaufman, Edy (1979) *Uruguay in Transition: From Civilian to Military Rule*. New Brunswick, NJ: Transaction.

Kautsky, John (1969) "Revolutionary and Managerial Elites in Modernizing Regimes," *Comparative Politics* 1: 441–467.

Kegley, Charles W. (1980) "The Comparative Study of Foreign Policy: Paradigm Lost?", Institute of International Studies Essay Series, No. 10. Columbia: University of South Carolina Press.

Kegley, Charles W., and Eugene R. Wittkopf (1991) *American Foreign Policy: Pattern and Process*. New York: St. Martin's.

Keller, John (1960) "The Current German Political Scene," *Current History* 38: 30–36.

Kelley, Donald (1974) "Toward a Model of Soviet Decision Making: A Research Note," *American Political Science Review* 68: 701–706.

Kennan, George F. (1951) *American Diplomacy, 1900–1950*. Chicago: University of Chicago Press.

Kerr, Henry H. (1987) "The Swiss Party System: Steadfast and Changing," in Hans Daalder, ed., *Party Systems in Denmark, Austria, Switzerland, the Netherlands, and Belgium*. New York: St. Martin's.

Kerr, Malcolm H. (1971) *The Arab Cold War: Gamal 'Abd al-Nasir and His Rivals, 1958–1970*. London: Oxford University Press.

―――― (1968) "Egyptian Foreign Policy and the Revolution," in P. J. Vatikiotis, ed., *Egypt Since the Revolution*. New York: Praeger.

―――― (1966) "Political Decision Making in a Confessional Democracy," in Leonard Binder, ed., *Politics in Lebanon*. New York: John Wiley.

Khadra, Bashir (1985) "Leadership, Ideology, and Development in the Middle East," in Sami G. Hajjar, ed., *The Middle East: From Transition to Development*. Leiden: E. J. Brill.

Kilson, Martin (1970) "Elite Cleavages in African Politics: The Case of Ghana," *Journal of International Affairs* 24: 75–83.

Kim, Hong N. (1979) "The Fukuda Government and the Politics of the Sino-Japanese Peace Treaty," *Asian Survey* 19: 297–313.

Kim, Kwan Bong (1971) *The Korea-Japan Treaty Crisis and the Instability of the Korean Political System*. New York: Praeger.

Kim, Samuel S. (1989) "New Directions and Old Puzzles in Chinese Foreign Policy," in Samuel S. Kim, ed., *China and the World: New Directions in Chinese Foreign Relations.* Boulder, CO: Westview.

Kirchheimer, Otto (1966) "Germany: The Vanishing Opposition," in Robert A. Dahl, ed., *Political Oppositions in Western Democracies.* New Haven, CT: Yale University Press.

Kissinger, Henry K. (1966) "Domestic Structure and Foreign Policy," in Wolfram Handreider, ed., *Comparative Foreign Policy.* New York: David McKay.

Kline, Harvey F. (1985) "Cuba: The Politics of Socialist Revolution," in Howard J. Wiarda and Harvey F. Kline, eds., *Latin American Politics and Development.* Boulder, CO: Westview.

Kochanek, Stanley A. (1968) *The Congress Party of India: The Dynamics of One-Party Democracy.* Princeton, NJ: Princeton University Press.

——— (1966) "Post-Nehru India: The Emergence of the New Leadership," *Asian Survey* 6: 288–299.

Kogan, Norman (1983) *A Political History of Italy: The Postwar Years.* New York: Praeger.

——— (1963) *The Politics of Italian Foreign Policy.* New York: Praeger.

Koichi, Kishimoto (1982) *Politics in Modern Japan: Development and Organization.* Tokyo: Japan Echo.

Kolkowicz, Roman (1971) "The Military," in H. Gordon Skilling and Franklyn Griffiths, eds., *Interest Groups in Soviet Politics.* Princeton, NJ: Princeton University Press.

———(1970) "Interest Groups in Soviet Politics: The Case of the Military," in Leonard J. Cohen and Jane P. Shapiro, eds., *Communist Systems in Comparative Perspective.* Garden City, NY: Anchor.

Koo, Youngnok (1985) "Foreign Policy Decision Making," in Youngnok Koo and Sungjoo Han, eds., *The Foreign Policy of the Republic of Korea.* New York: Columbia University Press.

Korany, Bahgat (1989) "Inferior Capabilities and War Decisions: The Interaction of the Predominant Leader and Environmental Pressures in Egypt, October 1973." Paper presented at the How Decision Units Shape Foreign Policy Conference, Jackson Hole, WY, November.

——— (1986) "Foreign Policy Decision Making Theory and the Third World: Payoffs and Pitfalls," in Bahgat Korany, ed., *How Foreign Policy Decisions Are Made in the Third World.* Boulder, CO: Westview.

——— (1984a) "Defending the Faith: The Foreign Policy of Saudi Arabia," in Bahgat Korany and Ali E. Hillal Dessouki, eds., *The Foreign Policies of Arab States.* Boulder, CO: Westview.

——— (1984b) "Third Worldism and Pragmatic Radicalism: The Foreign Policy of Algeria," in Bahgat Korany and Ali E. Hillal Dessouki, eds., *The Foreign Policies of Arab States.* Boulder, CO: Westview.

——— (1983) "The Take-off of Third World Studies?: The Case of Foreign Policy," *World Politics* 35: 464–487.

Korany, Bahgat, and Ali E. Hillal Dessouki, eds. (1984) *The Foreign Policies of Arab States.* Boulder, CO: Westview.

Korbonski, Andrzej (1984) "Poland," in Teresa Rakowska-Harmstone, ed., *Communism in Eastern Europe.* Bloomington: Indiana University Press.

——— (1976) "Leadership Succession and Political Change in Eastern Europe," *Studies in Comparative Communism* 1/2: 3–22.

Kornberg, Allan, and Harold D. Clarke (1982) "Canada," in Robert J. Alexander, ed., *Political Parties of the Americas: Canada, Latin America, and the West Indies.* Westport, CT: Greenwood.

Kosaka, M. (1974) "Political Immobility and the Uncertain Future," in Pricilla Clapp and Morton H. Halperin, eds., *United States-Japanese Relations: The 1970s.* Cambridge, MA: Harvard University Press.

Kothari, Rajni (1973) "India: Oppositions in a Consensual Polity," in Robert A. Dahl, ed., *Regimes and Oppositions.* New Haven, CT: Yale University Press.

────── (1970) *Politics in India.* Boston: Little, Brown.

────── (1967) "India: The Congress System on Trial," *Asian Survey* 7: 83–96.

────── (1964) "The Congress 'System' in India," *Asian Survey* 4: 1161–1173.

Krasner, Stephen D. (1978) *Defending the National Interest: Raw Materials Investments and U.S. Foreign Policy.* Princeton, NJ: Princeton University Press.

────── (1972) "Are Bureaucracies Important? (or Allison Wonderland)," *Foreign Policy* 7: 159–179.

Kraus, Jon (1981) "Political Change, Conflict, and Development in Ghana," in Philip Foster and Aristide R. Zolberg, eds., *Ghana and the Ivory Coast: Perspectives on Modernization.* Chicago: University of Chicago Press.

Krich, Henry (1985) *The German Democratic Republic: The Search for Identity.* Boulder, CO: Westview.

Lamb, G. B. (1969) "The Political Crisis in Kenya," *The World Today* 25: 537–543.

Lamborn, Alan C. (1991) *The Price of Power: Risk and Foreign Policy in Britain, France, and Germany.* Boston: Allen and Unwin.

────── (1985) "Risk and Foreign Policy Choice," *International Studies Quarterly* 29: 385–410.

Lande, Carl (1968) "Parties and Politics in the Philippines," *Asian Survey* 8: 725–747.

Langdon, Frank C. (1968) "Japanese Liberal Democratic Factional Discord on China Policy," *Pacific Affairs* Fall: 403–415.

LaPalombara, Joseph and Myron Weiner, eds. (1966) *Political Parties and Political Development.* Princeton, NJ: Princeton University Press.

Larrabee, F. Stephen (1988) "Gorbachev and the Soviet Military," *Foreign Affairs* 66: 1002–1026.

Larrabee, F. Stephen, and Allen Lynch (1986–87) "Gorbachev: The Road to Reykjavik," *Foreign Policy* 65: 3–28.

Lawson, Fred H. (1984) "Syria's Intervention in the Lebanese Civil War, 1976: A Domestic Conflict Explanation," *International Organization* 38: 451–480.

Lawson, Stephanie (1993) "Conceptual Issues in the Comparative Study of Regime Change and Democratization," *Comparative Politics* 25: 183–205.

Lebow, Richard Ned (1981) *Between Peace and War: The Nature of International Crisis.* Baltimore: Johns Hopkins University Press.

LeFever, Ernest W. (1970) *Spear and Scepter: Army, Police, and Politics in Tropical Africa.* Washington, D.C.: Brookings.

Leff, Carol Skalnik (1988) *National Conflict in Czechoslovakia.* Princeton, NJ: Princeton University Press.

Leffler, Melvyn P. (1992) *A Preponderance of Power: National Security, the Truman Administration, and the Cold War.* Stanford, CA: Stanford University Press.

Legum, Colin (1971) *African Contemporary Survey, 1969–70.* New York: Homes and Meier.

────── (1970) *African Contemporary Survey, 1968–69.* New York: Homes and Meier.

Leiserson, Michael (1973) "Political Opposition and Political Development in Japan," in Robert A. Dahl, ed., *Regimes and Oppositions.* New Haven, CT: Yale University Press.

Lenczowski, George (1965) "The Objects and Methods of Nasserism," *Journal of International Affairs* 19: 63–76.

Leng, Russell J., and Charles S. Gochman (1982) "Dangerous Disputes: A Study of Conflict Behavior and War," *American Journal of Political Science* 26: 664–687.

Lentner, Howard H. (1976) "Foreign Policy Decision Making: The Case of Canada and Nuclear Weapons," *World Politics* 24: 28–66.

Leonard, Wolfgang (1973) "Domestic Politics of the New Soviet Foreign Policy," *Foreign Affairs* 52: 59–74.

LePrestre, Philippe G. (1984) "Lessons of Cohabitation," in Philippe G. LePrestre, ed., *French Security in a Disarming World.* Boulder, CO: Lynne Rienner.

Levi, Werner (1968) "The Elitest Nature of Foreign Policies," in Werner Levi, ed., *The Challenge of World Politics in South and Southeast Asia.* Englewood Cliffs, NJ: Prentice-Hall.

Levy, Jack S. (1989) "The Diversionary Theory of War: A Critique," in Manus I. Midlarsky, ed., *Handbook of War Studies.* Boston: Unwin Hyman.

——— (1988) "Domestic Politics and War," in Robert I. Rotberg and Theodore K. Rabb, eds., *The Origin and Prevention of Major Wars.* New York: Cambridge University Press.

——— (1983) *War in the Modern Great Power System, 1945–1975.* Lexington: University of Kentucky Press.

Levy, Jack S., and Lily Vakili (1990) "External Scapegoating by Authoritarian Regimes: Argentina in the Falklands/Malvinas Case." Unpublished manuscript, Rutgers University.

Lieberthal, Kenneth (1984) "Domestic Politics and Foreign Policy," in Harry Harding, ed., *China's Foreign Relations in the 1980s.* New Haven, CT: Yale University Press.

Lijphart, Arend (1977) *Democracy in Plural Societies.* New Haven, CT: Yale University Press.

Lincoln, Jennie K., and Elizabeth G. Ferris, eds. (1984) *The Dynamics of Latin American Foreign Policies: Challenges for the 1980s.* Boulder, CO: Westview.

Linden, Carl A. (1978) "Opposition and Faction in Communist Party Leadership," in Frank P. Belloni and Dennis C. Beller, eds., *Faction Politics: Political Parties and Factionalism in Comparative Perspective.* Santa Barbara, CA: ABC-Clio.

——— (1966) *Khrushchev and the Soviet Leadership, 1957–1964.* Baltimore: Johns Hopkins University Press.

Linz, Juan J. (1973) "Opposition to and Under an Authoritarian Regime: The Case of Spain," in Robert A. Dahl, ed., *Regimes and Oppositions.* New Haven, CT: Yale University Press.

——— (1970) "From Falange to Movimiento-Organizacion: The Spanish Single Party and the Franco Regime, 1936–1968," in Samuel P. Huntington and Clement H. Moore, eds., *Authoritarian Politics in Modern Society: The Dynamics of Established One-Party Systems.* New York: Basic Books.

Lippmann, Walter (1955) *The Public Philosophy.* New York and Toronto: New American Library.

Long, Norton (1966) "Open and Closed Systems," in R. Barry Farrell, ed., *Approaches to Comparative and International Politics.* Evanston, IL: Northwestern University Press.

Lorwin, Val R. (1966) "Belgium: Religion, Class, and Language in National Politics," in Robert A. Dahl, ed., *Political Oppositions in Western Democracies.* New Haven, CT: Yale University Press.

Lowi, Theodore J. (1967) "Making Democracy Safe for the World: National Politics and Foreign Policy," in James N. Rosenau, ed., *Domestic Sources of Foreign Policy*. New York: Free Press.

Ludz, Peter Christian (1974) "The SED Leadership in Transition," in Lenard J. Cohen and Jane P. Shapiro, eds., *Communist Systems in Comparative Perspective*. New York: Anchor.

——— (1970) *The German Democratic Republic from the Sixties to the Seventies: A Socio-Political Analysis*. Cambridge: Center for International Affairs, Harvard University.

Luebbert, Gregory M. (1986) *Comparative Democracy: Policymaking and Governing Coalitions in Europe and Israel*. New York: Columbia University Press.

Machado, K. G. (1978) "Continuity and Change in Philippine Factionalism," in Frank P. Belloni and Dennis C. Beller, eds., *Faction Politics: Political Parties and Factionalism in Comparative Perspective*. Santa Barbara, CA: ABC-Clio.

MacMaster, Carolyn (1974) *Malawi: Foreign Policy and Development*. New York: St. Martin's.

Macridis, Roy C. (1989) "French Foreign Policy: The Quest for Rank," in Roy C. Macridis, ed., *Foreign Policy in World Politics*. Englewood Cliffs, NJ: Prentice-Hall.

Macridis, Roy C., and Bernard E. Brown (1960) *The DeGaulle Republic: The Quest for Unity*. Homewood, IL: Dorsey Press.

Maessen, P.J.J. (1985) "The Introduction of the Neutron Bomb, 1977–1978," in Philip P. Everts, ed., *Controversies at Home: Domestic Factors in the Foreign Policy of the Netherlands*. Boston: Martinus Nijhoff.

Maoz, Zeev (1989) "Joining the Club of Nations: Political Development and International Conflict, 1816–1976," *International Studies Quarterly* 33: 199–231.

Maoz, Zeev, and Nasrin Abdolali (1989) "Regime Types and International Conflict, 1916–1976," *Journal of Conflict Resolution* 33: 3–35.

Marantz, Paul (1975) "Internal Politics and Soviet Foreign Policy: A Case Study," *Western Political Quarterly* 28: 130–145.

Marradi, Alberto (1987) "Italy: From 'Centrism' to Crisis of Center-Left Coalitions," in E. Browne and J. Dreymanis, eds., *Government Coalitions in Western Democracies*. New York: Longman.

Martz, John D. (1968) "Venezuela," in Ben Burnett and Kenneth Johnson, eds., *Political Forces in Latin America*. Belmont, CA: Wadsworth.

——— (1959) *Central America: The Crisis and the Challenge*. Chapel Hill: University of North Carolina Press.

Mastanduno, Michael, David A. Lake, and G. John Ikenberry (1989) "Toward a Realist Theory of State Action," *International Studies Quarterly* 33: 457–474.

Mastny, Vojtech (1982) "Kremlin Politics and the Austrian Settlement," *Problems of Communism* 31: 37-51.

Mazrui, Ali, and Michael Tidy (1984) *Nationalism and New States in Africa*. Nairobi: Heinemann.

McCauley, Martin (1983) *The German Democratic Republic Since 1945*. London: MacMillan.

——— (1979) *Marxism-Leninism in the German Democratic Republic: The Socialist Unity Party (SED)*. London: Macmillan.

McClelland, Charles D. (1983) "Let the User Beware," *International Studies Quarterly* 27: 169–177.

McDonald, Ronald H. (1982) "Uruguay," in Robert J. Alexander, ed., *Political*

Parties of the Americas: Canada, Latin America, and the West Indies. Westport, CT: Greenwood.

———— (1971) *Party Systems and Elections in Latin America.* Chicago: Markham.

McGowan, Patrick J. (1968) "Africa and Non-alignment: A Comparative Study of Foreign Policy," *International Studies Quarterly* 12: 262–295.

McLaurin, R. D., Don Peretz, and Lewis W. Snider (1982) *Middle East Foreign Policy: Issues and Processes.* New York: Praeger.

Medding, Peter Y. (1972) *Mapai in Israel: Political Organization and Government in a New Society.* Cambridge, MA: Harvard University Press.

Medhurst, Kenneth N. (1973) *Government in Spain: The Executive at Work.* Oxford: Pergamon.

Meier, Viktor (1964) "Yugoslav Communism," in William E. Griffith, ed., *Communism in Europe: Continuity, Change, and the Sino-Soviet Dispute.* Cambridge, MA: MIT Press.

Meisel, John (1967) "Recent Changes in Canadian Parties," Hugh G. Thornburn, ed., *Party Politics in Canada.* Englewood Cliffs, NJ: Prentice-Hall.

Merkl, Peter H. (1980) "West Germany," in Peter H. Merkl, ed., *Western European Party Systems: Trends and Prospects.* New York: Free Press.

———— (1978) "Factionalism: The Limits of the West German Party-State," in Frank P. Belloni and Dennis C. Beller, eds., *Faction Politics: Political Parties and Factionalism in Comparative Perspective.* Santa Barbara, CA: ABC-Clio.

———— (1974) *German Foreign Policies, West and East: On the Threshold of a New European Era.* Santa Barbara, CA: ABC-Clio.

Merritt, Richard L., and Dina A. Zinnes (n.d.) "Democracies and International Conflict." Unpublished manuscript, University of Illinois.

Midlarsky, Manus (1981) "The Revolutionary Transformation of Foreign Policy: Agrarianism and Its International Impact," in Charles W. Kegley, Jr. and Patrick McGowan, eds., *The Political Economy of Foreign Policy Behavior.* Beverly Hills, CA: Sage.

Mijeski, Kenneth J. (1977) "Costa Rica: The Shrinking of the Presidency," in Thomas V. DiBacco, ed., *Presidential Power in Latin American Politics.* New York: Praeger.

Milburn, Josephine F. (1965) *Governments of the Commonwealth.* New York: Harper and Row.

Minor, Michael (1985) "Decision Models and Japanese Foreign Policy Decision Making," *Asian Survey* 25: 1229–1241.

Mittelman, James H. (1975) *Ideology and Politics in Uganda: From Obote to Amin.* Ithaca, NY: Cornell University Press.

Moneta, Carlos J. (1984) "The Malvinas Conflict: Analyzing the Argentine Military Regime's Decision-Making Process," in Heraldo Muñoz and J. S. Tulchin, eds., *Latin American Nations in World Politics.* Boulder, CO: Westview.

Moon, Bruce E. (1985) "Consensus or Compliance? Foreign Policy Change and External Dependence," *International Organization* 39: 297–328.

Moon, Bruce E., and William J. Dixon (1985) "Politics, the State, and Basic Human Needs: A Cross-National Study," *American Journal of Political Science* 29: 661–694.

Moore, Clement Henry (1965) *Tunisia Since Independence: The Dynamics of One-Party Government.* Berkeley: University of California Press.

———— (1962) "The Neo-Destour Party of Tunisia," *World Politics* 14: 461–482.

Moore, David W. (1974a) "Governmental and Societal Influences on Foreign Policy in Open and Closed Nations," in James N. Rosenau, ed., *Comparing Foreign Policies: Theories, Findings, and Methods.* Beverly Hills, CA: Sage.

———— (1974b) "Foreign Policy and Empirical Democratic Theory," *American Political Science Review* 68: 1192–1197.

———— (1974c) "National Attributes and Nation Typologies: A Look at the Rosenau Genotypes," in James N. Rosenau, ed., *Comparing Foreign Policies: Theories, Findings, and Methods.* Beverly Hills: Sage.

Morgan, T. Clifton, and Sally Howard Campbell (1991) "Domestic Structure, Decisional Constraints, and War: So Why Kant Democracies Fight," *Journal of Conflict Resolution* 35: 187–211.

Morgan, T. Clifton, and Valerie L. Schwebach (1992) "Take Two Democracies and Call Me in the Morning: A Prescription for Peace," *International Interactions* 17: 305–320.

Morgenthau, Hans J. (1960) *Politics Among Nations.* New York: Alfred A. Knopf.

———— (1951) *In Defense of the National Interest.* New York: Alfred A. Knopf.

Morris-Jones, W. H. (1967) *The Government and Politics of India.* London: Hutchinson.

———— (1965) "India: Under New Management, Business as Usual," *Asian Survey* 5: 63–73.

Morse, Edward L. (1973) *Foreign Policy and Interdependence in Gaullist France.* Princeton, NJ: Princeton University Press.

Morton, Henry W. (1967) "The Structure of Decision-Making in the U.S.S.R.: A Comparative Introduction," in Peter H. Juviler and Henry W. Morton, eds., *Soviet Policy-Making: Studies of Communism in Transition.* New York: Praeger.

Mueller, John E. (1971) *War, Presidents, and Public Opinion.* New York: John Wiley.

Mueller, Susanne D. (1984) "Government and Opposition in Kenya, 1966–9," *The Journal of Modern African Studies* 22: 399–427.

Muñoz, Heraldo, and Joseph S. Tulchin, eds. (1984) *Latin American Nations in World Politics.* Boulder, CO: Westview Press.

Munton, Don, ed. (1978) *Measuring International Behaviour: Public Sources, Events, and Validity.* Halifax: Centre for Foreign Policy Studies, Dalhousie University.

Muramatsu, Michio and Ellis S. Krauss (1990) "The Dominant Party and Social Coalitions in Japan," in T. J. Pempel, ed., *Uncommon Democracies: The One-Party Dominant Regimes.* Ithaca, NY: Cornell University Press.

Narain, Iqbal (1985) "India," in Haruhiro Fukui, ed., *Political Parties of Asia and the Pacific.* Westport, CT: Greenwood.

Nathan, Andrew J. (1978) "An Analysis of Factionalism of Chinese Communist Party Politics," in Frank P. Belloni and Dennis C. Beller, eds., *Faction Politics: Political Parties and Factionalism in Comparative Perspective.* Santa Barbara, CA: ABC-Clio.

Nathan, James A., and James K. Oliver (1987) *Foreign Policy Making and the American Political System.* Boston: Little, Brown.

Needleman, Carolyn, and Martin Needleman (1969) "Who Rules Mexico?: A Critique of Some Current Views on the Mexican Political Process," *Journal of Politics* 31: 1011–1034.

Needler, Martin (1984) "Contemporary Mexico," in Jan Knippers Black, ed., *Latin America: Its Problems and Its Promise.* Boulder, CO: Westview.

Needler, Martin C. (1982) *Mexican Politics: The Containment of Conflict.* Stanford, CA: Hoover Institution Press.

Nef, Joseph (1978) "Factionalism and Political Stalemate: Chilean Politics, 1920–1970," in Frank P. Belloni and Dennis C. Beller, eds., *Faction Politics: Political Parties and Factionalism in Comparative Perspective.* Santa Barbara, CA: ABC-Clio.

Neustadt, Richard (1970) *Alliance Politics*. New York: Columbia University Press.

Nicholson, Norman K. (1978) "Factionalism and Public Policy in India: The Vertical Dimension," in Frank P. Belloni and Dennis C. Beller, eds., *Faction Politics: Political Parties and Factionalism in Comparative Perspective*. Santa Barbara, CA: ABC-Clio.

Nilson, Sten Sparre (1980) "Norway and Denmark," in Peter Merkel, ed., *Western European Party Systems: Trends and Prospects*. New York: Free Press.

Noble, Lela Garner (1986) "Politics in the Marcos Era," in John Bresnan, ed., *Crisis in the Philippines: The Marcos Era and Beyond*. Princeton, NJ: Princeton University Press.

Noonan, Lowell G. (1980) "France," in Peter H. Merkl, ed., *Western European Party Systems*. New York: Free Press.

—— (1970) *France: The Politics of Continuity and Change*. New York: Holt, Rinehart, Winston.

Norpoth, Helmut (1982) "The German Federal Republic: Coalition Government at the Brink of Majority Rule," in Eric C. Browne and John Dreijmanis, ed., *Government Coalitions in Western Democracies*. New York: Longman.

Nossal, Kim Richard (1989) "Bureaucratic Politics and the Westminster Model," in Robert O. Matthews, Arthur G. Rubinoff, and Janice Gross Stein, eds., *International Conflict and Conflict Management: Readings in World Politics*. Scarborough, Ontario: Prentice-Hall Canada.

—— (1979) "Allison through the (Ottawa) Looking Glass: Bureaucratic Politics and Foreign Policy in a Parliamentary System," *Canadian Public Administration* 22: 610–626.

Nuechterlein, Donald E. (1967) "Thailand: Another Vietnam?" *Asian Survey* 7: 126–130.

—— (1966) "Thailand: Year of Danger and Hope," *Asian Survey* 6: 119–124.

—— (1964) "Thailand After Sarit," *Asian Survey* 4: 842–850.

—— (1961) *Iceland: Reluctant Ally*. Ithaca, NY: Cornell University Press.

Odom, William E. (1976) "A Dissenting View on the Group Approach to Soviet Politics," *World Politics* 28: 542–567.

—— (1975) "Who Controls Whom in Moscow," *Foreign Policy* 19: 109–123.

Ogata, Sadako (1988) *Normalization with China: A Comparative Study of U.S. and Japanese Processes*. Berkeley: Institute of East Asian Studies, University of California.

Oksenberg, Michel C. (1971) "Policy Making under Mao, 1949–68: An Overview," in John M. H. Lindbeck, ed., *China: Management of a Revolutionary Society*. Seattle: University of Washington Press.

Ori, Kan (1976) "Political Factors in Postwar Japan's Foreign Policy Decisions," in Morton A. Kaplan and Kinhide Mushakoji, eds., *Japan, America, and the Future World Order*. New York: Free Press.

Ostrom, Charles W., and Brian Job (1986) "The President and the Political Use of Force," *American Political Science Review* 80: 541–566.

Ott, Marvin (1972) "Foreign Policy Formulation in Malaysia," *Asian Survey* 12: 225–241.

Paige, Glenn D. (1968) *The Korean Decision*. New York: Free Press.

Palmer, Norman (1967) "India's Fourth General Election," *Asian Survey* 7: 275–291.

—— (1965) "India Without Nehru," *Current History* 48: 69–74.

—— (1961) *The Indian Political System*. Boston: Houghton Mifflin.

Paltiel, K. Z. (1975) "The Israeli Coalition System," *Government and Opposition* 10: 397–414.

Park, Richard L. (1967) *India's Political System*. Englewood Cliffs, NJ: Prentice-Hall.

Park, Young H. (1975) "The Politics of Japan's China Decision." *Orbis* 19: 562–590.

Patterson, Thomas G. (1988) *Meeting the Communist Threat: Truman to Reagan*. New York: Oxford University Press.

——— (1979) *On Every Front: The Making of the Cold War*. New York: Norton.

Pellow, Deborah, and Naomi Chazan (1986) *Ghana: Coping with Uncertainty*. Boulder, CO: Westview.

Pempel, T. J. (1990) *Uncommon Democracies: The One-Party Dominant Regimes*. Ithaca, NY: Cornell University Press.

——— (1977) "Japanese Foreign Policy: The Domestic Bases for International Behavior," in Peter J. Katzenstein, ed., *Between Power and Plenty: Foreign Economic Policies of Advanced Industrial States*. Madison: University of Wisconsin Press.

Pendill, C. G. (1971) "'Bipartisanship' in Soviet Foreign Policy Making," in Eric Hoffmann and Frederic Fleron, eds., *The Conduct of Soviet Foreign Policy*. Chicago: Aldine-Atherton.

Peretz, Don (1986) *The Middle East Today*. New York: Praeger.

——— (1979) *The Government and Politics of Israel*. Boulder, CO: Westview.

Perlmutter, Amos (1981) *Modern Authoritarianism: A Comparative Institutional Analysis*. New Haven, CT: Yale University Press.

——— (1977) *The Military and Politics in Modern Times*. New Haven, CT: Yale University Press.

——— (1974) "The Presidential Political Center and Foreign Policy: A Critique of the Revisionist and Bureaucratic-Political Orientations," *World Politics* 27: 87–106.

Pesonen, Pertti, and Alastair H. Thomas (1983) "Coalition Formation in Scandinavia," in Vernon Bogdanor, ed., *Coalition Government in Western Europe*. London: Heinemann.

Pettman, Jan (1974a) *Zambia: Security and Conflict*. New York: St. Martin's.

——— (1974b) "Zambia's Second Republic—the Establishment of a One-Party State," *Journal of Modern African Studies* 12: 231–244.

Pikney, Robert (1972) *Ghana Under Military Rule, 1966–1969*. London: Methuen.

Porzecanski, Arturo C. (1974) "Uruguay's Continuing Dilemma," *Current History* 66: 28–30.

Posner, Alan R. (1977) "Italy: Dependence and Political Fragmentation," in Peter J. Katzenstein, ed., *Between Power and Plenty: Foreign Economic Policies of Advanced Industrial States*. Madison: University of Wisconsin Press.

Pridham, Geoffrey (1986a) "Italy's Party Democracy and Coalitional Behaviour: A Case Study in Multi-Dimensionality," in Geoffrey Pridham, ed., *Coalition Behavior in Theory and Practice*. Cambridge: Cambridge University Press.

———, ed. (1986b) *Coalition Behavior in Theory and Practice*. Cambridge: Cambridge University Press.

——— (1983) "Party Politics and Coalition Government in Italy," in Vernon Bogdanor, ed., *Coalition Government in Western Europe*. London: Heinemann.

Purcell, Susan Kaufman (1973) "Decision Making in an Authoritarian Regime: Theoretical Implications from a Mexican Case Study," *World Politics* 26: 28–54.

Putnam, Robert D. (1988) "Diplomacy and Domestic Politics: The Logic of Two-Level Games," *International Organization* 42: 427–460.

Pye, Lucian W. (1984) *China: An Introduction*. Boston: Little Brown.

—— (1981) *The Dynamics of Chinese Politics.* Cambridge: Oeleschlager, Gunn and Hain.

Quandt, William B. (1981) *Saudi Arabia in the 1980s: Foreign Policy, Security, and Oil.* Washington, D.C.: Brookings.

Quansheng, Zhao (1992) "Domestic Factors in Chinese Foreign Policy: From Vertical to Horizontal Authoritarianism," *Annals* 519: 158–175.

Ra'anan, Uri (1970) "Chinese Factionalism and Sino-Soviet Relations," *Current History* 59: 134–141.

—— (1968) "Peking's Foreign Policy 'Debate,' 1965–1966," in Tang Tsou, ed., *China in Crisis: China's Policies in Asia and America's Alternatives.* Chicago: University of Chicago Press.

—— (1973) "The U.S.S.R. and the Middle East: Some Reflections on the Soviet Decision Making Process," *Orbis* 17: 946–977.

Rabinovich, Itamar (1984) *The War for Lebanon, 1970–1983.* Ithaca, NY: Cornell University Press.

——(1972) *Syria Under the Ba'th, 1963–66: The Army-Party Symbiosis.* New Brunswick, NJ: Transaction.

Rakowska-Harmstone, Teresa (1984) *Communism in Eastern Europe.* Bloomington: Indiana University Press.

Ramet, Pedro (1984) *Nationalism and Federalism in Yugoslavia, 1963–1983.* Bloomington: Indiana University Press.

Rasmussen, Thomas (1969) "Political Competition and One-party Dominance in Zambia," *Journal of Modern African Studies* 7: 407–424.

Reed, S., III (1980) "Fin de Regime?" *Foreign Policy* 39: 176–190.

Reischauer, Edwin O. (1974) "Their Special Strengths," *Foreign Policy* 14: 142–153.

Remington, Robin Alison (1984) "Yugoslavia," in Teresa Rakowska-Harmstone, ed., *Communism in Eastern Europe.* Bloomington: Indiana University Press.

Richardson, Bradley M., and Scott C. Flanagan (1984) *Politics in Japan.* Boston: Little, Brown.

Riggs, Fred W. (1966) *Thailand: The Modernization of a Bureaucratic Polity.* Honolulu: East-West Center Press.

Rioux, Jean-Pierre (1984) *The Fourth Republic, 1944–1958.* Cambridge: Cambridge University Press.

Risse-Kappen, Thomas (1991) "Public Opinion, Domestic Structure, and Foreign Policy in Liberal Democracies," *World Politics* 43: 479–512.

Riviere, Claude (1977) *Guinea: The Mobilization of a People.* Ithaca, NY: Cornell University Press.

Robert, Jacques (1965) "Opposition and Control in Tunisia, Morocco, and Algeria," *Government and Opposition* 1: 389–404.

Robinson, Thomas W. (1982) "Restructuring Chinese Foreign Policy, 1959–76: Three Episodes," in K. J. Holsti, ed., *Why Nations Realign: Foreign Policy Restructuring in the Postwar World.* New York: Allen and Unwin.

Roca, Sergio (1982) "Cuba," in Robert J. Alexander, ed., *Political Parties of the Americas: Canada, Latin America, and the West Indies.* Westport, CT: Greenwood.

Roeder, Philip G. (1988) *Soviet Political Dynamics: Development of the First Leninist Polity.* New York: Harper and Row.

—— (1984) "Soviet Policies and Kremlin Politics," *International Studies Quarterly* 28: 171–193.

Rokkan, Stein (1966) "Norway: Numerical Democracy and Corporate Pluralism," in Robert A. Dahl, ed., *Political Oppositions in Western Democracies.* New Haven, CT: Yale University Press.

Rondot, Pierre (1966) "The Political Institutions of Lebanese Democracy," in Leonard Binder, ed., *Politics in Lebanon.* New York: John Wiley.

Rosati, Jerel A. (1993) *The Politics of United States Foreign Policy.* Fort Worth, TX: Harcourt, Brace, Jovanovich.

Rose, Saul, ed. (1963) *Politics in Southeast Asia.* New York: St. Martin's.

Rosecrance, Richard (1963) *Action and Reaction in World Politics.* Boston: Little, Brown.

Rosenau, James N. (1987) "Toward Single-Country Theories of Foreign Policy: The Case of the U.S.S.R.," in Charles F. Hermann, Charles W. Kegley, Jr., and James N. Rosenau, eds., *New Directions in the Study of Foreign Policy.* Boston: Allen and Unwin.

——— (1966) "Pre-theories and Theories and Foreign Policy," in R. Barry Farrell, ed., *Approaches to Comparative and International Politics.* Evanston, IL: Northwestern University Press.

Rosenau, James N., and Garry Hoggard (1974) "Foreign Policy Behavior in Dyadic Relationships: Testing a Pre-Theoretical Extension," in James N. Rosenau, ed., *Comparing Foreign Policies: Theories, Methods, Findings.* Beverly Hills, CA: Sage.

Rosenau, James N., and George H. Ramsey, Jr. (1975) "External and Internal Typologies of Foreign Policy Behavior: Testing the Stability of an Intriguing Set of Findings," in Patrick J. McGowan, ed., *Sage International Yearbook of Foreign Policy Studies,* vol. 3. Beverly Hills, CA: Sage.

Rosmoser, George K. (1966) "Change in West German Politics after Erhard's Fall," in William G. Andrews, ed., *European Politics II: The Dynamics of Change.* New York: Van Nostrand.

Ross, Dennis (1984) "Risk Aversion in Soviet Decisionmaking," in Jiri Valenta and William C. Potter, eds., *Soviet Decisionmaking for National Security.* London: Allen and Unwin.

——— (1980) "Coalition Maintenance in the Soviet Union," *World Politics* 32: 258–280.

Ross, Stanley Robert (1963) "Mexico: Cool Revolution and Cold War," *Current History* 44: 89–94.

——— (1960) "Mexico: Golden Anniversary of the Revolution," *Current History* 38: 150–154.

Rothstein, Robert L. (1977) *The Weak in the World of the Strong: The Developing Countries in the International System.* New York: Columbia University Press.

——— (1976) "Foreign Policy and Development Policy," *International Affairs* 52: 598–616.

Rouleau, Eric (1968) "Hawks and Doves in Israel's Foreign Policy," *The World Today* 24: 496–502.

Rudd, Chris (1986) "Coalition Formation and Maintenance in Belgium: A Case-Study of Elite Behaviour and Changing Cleavage Structure, 1965–1981," in Geoffrey Pridham, ed., *Coalition Behavior in Theory and Practice.* Cambridge: Cambridge University Press.

Rummel, Rudolph J. (1985) "Libertarian Propositions on Violence Within and Between Nations: A Test Against Published Research Results," *Journal of Conflict Resolution* 29: 419–455.

——— (1983) "Libertarianism and International Violence," *Journal of Conflict Resolution* 27: 27–71.

——— (1968) "The Relationship Between National Attributes and Foreign Conflict

Behavior," in J. David Singer, ed., *Quantitative International Politics.* New York: Free Press.

Rush, Myron (1965) *Political Succession in the USSR.* New York: Columbia University Press.

Rusinow, Dennison (1977) *The Yugoslav Experiment, 1948–1974.* Berkeley: University of California Press.

Russett, Bruce M. (1990) *Controlling the Sword: The Democratic Governance of National Security.* Cambridge, MA: Harvard University Press.

Russett, Bruce M., and R. J. Monsen (1975) "Bureaucracy and Polyarchy as Predictors of Performance: A Cross-National Examination," *Comparative Political Studies* 8: 5–31.

Safran, Nadav (1978) *Israel: The Embattled Ally.* Cambridge, MA: Harvard University Press.

——— (1975) "Egypt's Search for Ideology: The Nasser Era," in Martin Kilson, ed., *New States of Africa.* Cambridge, MA: Harvard University Press.

Salmore, Barbara G. (1978) "Regional Sources of External Behavior: A Comparison of Reporting in the World's Press," in Don Munton, ed., *Measuring International Behaviour: Public Sources, Events, and Validity.* Halifax: Centre for Foreign Policy Studies, Dalhousie University.

Salmore, Barbara G., and Stephen A. Salmore (1978) "Political Regimes and Foreign Policy," in Maurice A. East, Stephen A. Salmore, and Charles F. Hermann, eds., *Why Nations Act: Theoretical Perspectives for Comparative Foreign Policy Studies.* Beverly Hills, CA: Sage.

——— (1972) "Structure and Change in Regimes: Their Effects on Foreign Policy." Paper presented at the annual meeting of the American Political Science Association, San Francisco, September 5–9.

——— (1970) "Political Accountability and Foreign Policy." Paper presented at the annual meeting of the American Political Science Association, Los Angeles, September.

Salmore, Stephen A. (1972) "Foreign Policy and National Attributes: A Multivariate Analysis." Ph.D. Dissertation, Princeton University.

Salmore, Stephen A., and Charles F. Hermann (1969) "The Effect of Size, Development, and Accountability on Foreign Policy," *Peace Research Society Papers* 14: 15–30.

Sanger, Clyde, and John Nottingham (1964) "The Kenya General Election of 1963," *Journal of Modern African Studies* 2: 1–40.

Sarlvik, Bo (1983) "Coalition Politics and Policy Output in Scandinavia: Sweden, Denmark, and Norway," in Vernon Bogdanor, ed., *Coalition Government in Western Europe.* London: Heinemann.

Sartori, Giovanni (1976) *Parties and Party Systems: A Framework for Analysis.* Cambridge: Cambridge University Press.

——— (1966) "European Political Parties: The Case of Polarized Pluralism," in Joseph LaPalombara and Myron Weiner, eds., *Political Parties and Political Development.* Princeton, NJ: Princeton University Press.

Sayari, Sabri (1978) "The Turkish Party System in Transition," *Government and Opposition* 13: 39–57.

Scalapino, Robert A., ed. (1977) *The Foreign Policy of Modern Japan.* Berkeley: University of California Press.

Scalapino, Robert A., and Junnosuke Masumi (1962) *Parties and Politics in Contemporary Japan.* Berkeley: University of California Press.

Schandler, Herbert Y. (1977) *The Unmaking of a President: Lyndon Johnson and Vietnam.* Princeton, NJ: Princeton University Press.

Scharf, C. Bradley (1984) *Politics and Change in East Germany: An Evaluation of Socialist Democracy*. Boulder, CO: Westview.

Schmidt, Manfred (1983) "Two Logics of Coalition Policy: The West German Case," in Vernon Bogdanor, ed., *Coalition Government in Western Europe*. London: Heinemann.

Schneider, Ronald M. (1976) *Brazil: Foreign Policy of a Future World Power*. Boulder, CO: Westview.

Schulz, Eberhard (1982) "Decisive Factors in GDR Foreign Policy," in Eberhard Schulz et al., eds., *GDR Foreign Policy*. Armonk, NY: M. E. Sharpe.

Schwartz, Morton (1975) *The Foreign Policy of the U.S.S.R.: Domestic Factors*. Encino, CA: Dickenson.

Schweller, Randall L. (1992) "Domestic Structure and Preventive War: Are Democracies More Pacific?" *World Politics* 44: 235–269.

Scott, Margaret (1992) "Points of No Return," *New York Times Magazine*, September 13, pp. 38–39, 88, 96, 99.

Scott, Robert (1965) "Mexico: The Established Revolution," in Lucian Pye and Sidney Verba, eds., *Political Culture and Political Development*. Princeton, NJ: Princeton University Press.

Seale, Patrick (1988) *Asad: The Struggle for the Middle East*. Berkeley: University of California Press.

——— (1965) *The Struggle for Syria: A Study of Post-War Arab Politics, 1945–1958*. New York: Oxford University Press.

Seliktar, Ofira (1982) "Israel: Fragile Coalitions in a New Nation," in E. Browne and J. Dreymanis, eds., *Government Coalitions in Western Democracies*. New York: Longman.

Shapiro, Samuel (1972) "Uruguay's Lost Paradise," *Current History* 62: 98–103.

——— (1969) "Uruguay: A Bankrupt Welfare State," *Current History* 56: 36–42.

Shaw, Timothy (1976) *Dependence and Underdevelopment: The Development and Foreign Policies of Zambia*. Athens: Ohio University Press.

——— (1975) "The Foreign Policy System of Zambia." Paper presented at the annual meeting of the International Studies Association, Washington, D.C., February 19–23.

Shaw, Timothy M., and Olajide Aluko, eds. (1984) *The Political Economy of African Foreign Policy*. New York: St. Martin's Press.

Shirk, Susan (1990–91) "The Domestic Roots of China's Post-Tiananmen Foreign Policy," *Harvard International Review* Winter: 32–34, 61.

——— (1984) "The Domestic Political Dimensions of China's Foreign Economic Relations," in Samuel S. Kim, ed., *China and the World: Chinese Foreign Policy in the Post-Mao Era*. Boulder, CO: Westview.

Shoup, Paul (1979) "The League of Communists in Yugoslavia," in Stephen Fischer-Galati, ed., *The Communist Parties of Eastern Europe*. New York: Columbia University Press.

Sigmund, Paul E. (1977) *The Overthrow of Allende and the Politics of Chile, 1964–1976*. Pittsburgh: University of Pittsburgh Press.

Simes, Dimitri K. (1991) "Gorbachev's Time of Troubles," *Foreign Policy* 82: 97–113.

——— (1986) "The Domestic Environment of Soviet Policy Making," in Arnold L. Horelick, ed., *U.S.-Soviet Relations: The Next Phase*. Ithaca, NY: Cornell University Press.

——— (1977) *Detente and Conflict: Soviet Foreign Policy, 1972–1977*. Sage Policy Paper. Beverly Hills, CA: Sage.

——— (1975) "The Soviet Invasion of Czechoslovakia and the Limits of Kremlinology," *Studies in Comparative Communism* 8: 174–180.

Simmonds, Stuart (1963) "Thailand—A Conservative State," in Saul Rose, ed., *Politics in Southern Asia*. New York: St. Martin's.

Singer, J. David, and Melvin Small (1972) *The Wages of War, 1916–1972: A Statistical Handbook*. New York: John Wiley.

Singer, Marshall R. (1972) *Weak States in a World of Powers: The Dynamics of International Relationships*. New York: Free Press.

Skidmore, Thomas E., and Peter H. Smith (1984) *Modern Latin America*. New York: Oxford University Press.

Skilling, H. Gordon (1974) "The Fall of Novotny in Czechoslovakia," in Leonard J. Cohen and Jane P. Shapiro, eds., *Communist Systems in Comparative Perspective*. New York: Anchor.

————— (1973a) "Opposition in Communist East Europe," in Robert A. Dahl, ed., *Regimes and Oppositions*. New Haven, CT: Yale University Press.

————— (1973b) "Czechoslovakia's Interrupted Revolution," in Robert A. Dahl, ed., *Regimes and Oppositions*. New Haven, CT: Yale University Press.

————— (1972) "Czechoslovakia," in Adam Bromke and Teresa Rakowska-Harmstone, eds., *The Communist States in Disarray, 1965–1971*. Minneapolis: University of Minnesota Press.

————— (1966) "Interest Groups and Communist Politics," *World Politics* 18: 435–445.

————— (1965) "Czechoslovakia," in Adam Bromke, ed., *The Communist States at the Crossroads: Between Moscow and Peking*. New York: Praeger.

Skilling, H. Gordon, and Franklyn Griffiths, eds. (1971) *Interest Groups in Soviet Politics*. Princeton, NJ: Princeton University Press.

Skocpol, Theda (1979) *States and Social Revolutions: A Comparative Analysis of France, Russia, and China*. Cambridge: Cambridge University Press.

Skurnik, W.A.E. (1972) *The Foreign Policy of Senegal*. Evanston, IL: Northwestern University Press.

Slusser, Robert M. (1973) *The Berlin Crisis of 1961: Soviet-American Relations and the Struggle for Power in the Kremlin*. Baltimore: John Hopkins University Press.

————— (1967) "America, China, and the Hydra-Headed Opposition: The Dynamics of Soviet Foreign Policy," in Peter H. Juviler and Henry W. Morton, eds., *Soviet Policy-Making: Studies of Communism in Transition*. New York: Praeger.

Small, Melvin, and J. David Singer (1982) *Resort to Arms: International and Civil Wars, 1815–1980*. Beverly Hills, CA: Sage.

————— (1976) "The War-Proneness of Democratic Regimes, 1816–1965," *Jerusalem Journal of International Relations* 1: 50–69.

Smock, David R., and Audrey C. Smock (1975) *The Politics of Pluralism: A Comparative Study of Lebanon and Ghana*. New York: Elsevier.

Snyder, Glenn H., and Paul Diesing (1977) *Conflict Among Nations: Bargaining, Decision Making, and System Structure in International Crises*. Princeton, NJ: Princeton University Press.

Snyder, Jack (1991) *Myths of Empire: Domestic Politics and International Ambition*. Ithaca, NY: Cornell University Press.

Snyder, Richard C., H. W. Bruck, and Burt Sapin, eds. (1962) *Foreign Policy Decision Making*. Glencoe, IL: Free Press.

Socolow, Susan M. (1966) "Uruguay Today," *Current History* 51: 270–273.

Sontheimer, Kurt, and Wilhelm Bleek (1975) *The Government and Politics of East Germany*. New York: St. Martin's.

Spanier, John, and Joseph Nogee, eds. (1981) *Congress, the Presidency, and American Foreign Policy*. New York: Pergamon.

Spechler, Dina Rome (1987) "The Politics of Intervention: The Soviet Union and the Crisis in Lebanon," *Studies in Comparative Communism* 20: 115–143.

Spielmann, Karl F. (1978) *Analyzing Soviet Strategic Arms Decisions.* Boulder, CO: Westview.

Spotts, Frederic, and Theodor Wieser (1986) *Italy: A Difficult Democracy.* Cambridge: Cambridge University Press.

Starner, Frances (1963) "The Philippines: Politics of the 'New Era.'" *Asian Survey* 3: 41–47.

Starrels, John M., and Anita M. Mallinckrodt (1975) *Politics in the German Democratic Republic.* New York: Praeger.

Stehle, Hansjakob (1964) "Polish Communism," in William E. Griffith, ed., *Communism in Europe: Continuity, Change, and the Sino-Soviet Dispute.* Cambridge, MA: MIT Press.

Stein, Janice Gross (forthcoming) "Real Time and Psychological Space: Decision Units, Decisions, and Behavior in Israel, 1967," in Joe D. Hagan, Charles F. Hermann, and Margaret G. Hermann, eds., *Leaders, Groups, and Coalition: How Decision Units Shape Foreign Policy.*

———— (1988) "Domestic Politics and International Conflict Management," *International Security* 12: 203–211.

Steinbruner, John D. (1974) *The Cybernetic Theory of Decision.* Princeton, NJ: Princeton University Press.

Steiner, Jurg (1982) "Switzerland: 'Magic Formula' Coalitions," in Eric C. Browne and John Dreymanis, eds., *Government Coalitions in Western Democracies,* New York: Longman.

———— (1983) "Conclusion: Reflections on the Consociational Theme," in Howard R. Penniman, ed., *Switzerland at the Polls: The National Elections of 1979.* Washington, D.C.: American Enterprise Institute.

Stempel, John D. (forthcoming) "The Iranian Hostage Crisis: Nondecision by Coalition," in Joe D. Hagan, Charles F. Hermann, and Margaret G. Hermann, eds., *Leaders, Groups, and Coalitions: How Decision Units Shape Foreign Policy.*

———— (1981) *Inside the Iranian Revolution.* Bloomington: Indiana University Press.

Stern, Geoffrey (1974) "Soviet Foreign Policy in Theory and Practice," in F. S. Northedge, ed., *The Foreign Policies of the Powers.* New York: Free Press.

Stevens, Evelyn P. (1985) "Mexico in the 1980s: From Authoritarianism to Power Sharing," in Howard J. Wiarda and Harvey F. Kline, eds., *Latin American Politics and Development.* Boulder, CO: Westview.

Stewart, Philip D., and Margaret G. Hermann (1990) "The Soviet Debate over 'New Thinking' and the Restructuring of U.S.-Soviet Relations," in George E. Hudson, ed., *Soviet National Security Policy Under Perestroika.* Boston: Unwin Hyman.

Stockwin, J.A.A. (1975) *Japan: Divided Politics in a Growth Economy.* New York: W. W. Norton.

Stohl, Michael (1980) "The Nexus of Civil and International Conflict," in Ted Gurr, ed., *Handbook of Political Conflict.* New York: Free Press.

Storing, James A. (1963) *Norwegian Democracy.* Boston: Houghton Mifflin.

Suarez, Andres (1967) *Cuba: Castroism and Communism, 1959–1966.* Cambridge, MA: MIT Press.

Sundelius, Bengt (forthcoming) "Whiskey on the Rocks: Sweden's Response to a Trapped Soviet Submarine," in Joe D. Hagan, Charles F. Hermann, and Margaret G. Hermann, eds., *Leaders, Groups, and Coalitions: How Decision Units Shape Foreign Policy.*

———— (1989) "Das Primat der Neutralitatspolitik: Building Regimes at Home," *Cooperation and Conflict* 24: 163–178.

————, ed. (1982) *Foreign Policies of Northern Europe.* Boulder, CO: Westview.

Sutter, Robert G. (1978) *Chinese Foreign Policy After the Cultural Revolution, 1966–1977.* Boulder, CO: Westview.

Szulc, Tad (1971) *Czechoslovakia Since World War II.* New York: Viking Press.

Taborsky, Edward (1965) "Change in Czechoslovakia," *Current History* 48: 168–180.

Tachau, Frank (1984) *Turkey: The Politics of Authority, Democracy, and Development.* New York: Praeger.

Talbott, Strobe (1984) *Deadly Gambits: The Reagan Administration and the Stalemate in Arms Control.* New York: Alfred A. Knopf.

Tatu, Michel (1967) *Power in the Kremlin from Khrushchev to Kosygin.* New York: Viking.

Taylor, Alan R. (1982) *The Arab Balance of Power.* Syracuse, NY: Syracuse University Press.

Taylor, Charles Lewis, and David A. Jodice (1983) *World Handbook of Political and Social Indicators,* 3rd ed. New Haven, CT: Yale University Press.

Taylor, Philip B. (1985) "Uruguay: The Costs of Inept Political Corporatism," in Howard J. Wiarda and Harvey F. Kline, eds., *Latin American Politics and Development.* Boulder, CO: Westview.

Teiwes, Frederick C. (1984) *Leadership, Legitimacy, and Conflict in China.* Armonk, NY: Sharpe.

Terrill, Ross (1978) *The Future of China After Mao.* New York: Delta Books.

Tharoor, Shashi (1982) *Reasons of State: Political Development and India's Foreign Policy Under Indira Gandhi, 1966–1977.* New Delhi: Vikas Publishing House.

Thayer, Nathaniel B. (1969) *How the Conservatives Rule Japan.* Princeton, NJ: Princeton University Press.

Thompson, Virginia (1962) "The Ivory Coast," in Gwendolyn Carter, ed., *African One-Party States.* Ithaca, NY: Cornell University Press.

Thompson, W. Scott (1969) *Ghana's Foreign Policy, 1957–1966: Diplomacy, Ideology, and the New State.* Princeton, NJ: Princeton University Press.

Thordarson, Bruce (1972) *Trudeau and Foreign Policy: A Study in Decision Making.* New York: Oxford University Press.

Thornburn, Hugh G. (1979) *Party Politics in Canada,* 4th ed. Englewood Cliffs, NJ: Prentice-Hall.

Thomas, Hugh (1966) *Suez.* New York: Harper and Row.

Thornburn, Hugh G., ed. (1967) *Party Politics in Canada,* 2d ed. Englewood Cliffs, NJ: Prentice- Hall.

Thornton, Richard C. (1982) *China: A Political History, 1917–1980.* Boulder, CO: Westview.

———— (1972) "The Structure of Communist Politics," *World Politics* 24: 498–517.

Toma, Peter A. (1979) "The Communist Party of Czechoslovakia," in Stephen Fischer-Galati, ed., *The Communist Parties of Eastern Europe.* New York: Columbia University Press.

Tomasek, Robert D. (1968) "Costa Rica," in Ben G. Burnett and Kenneth Johnson, eds., *Political Forces in Latin America.* Belmont, CA: Wadsworth.

Trout, B. Thomas (1975) "Rhetoric Revisited: Political Legitimation and the Cold War," *International Studies Quarterly* 19: 251–284.

Tsebelis, George (1990) *Nested Games: Rational Choice in Comparative Politics.* Berkeley: University of California Press.

Tsuruntani, T. (1974) "The Causes of Paralysis," *Foreign Policy* 14, 126–141.

Tucker, Robert (1965) "The Dictator and Totalitarianism," *World Politics* 17: 55–88.

Twaddle, Michael (1973) "Order and Disorder in Uganda," *The World Today* 29: 449–454.

Ulc, Otto (1984) "Czechoslovakia," in Teresa Rakowska-Harmstone, ed., *Communism in Eastern Europe*. Bloomington: Indiana University Press.

Uzoigwe, G. N. (1983) "Uganda and Parliamentary Government," *Journal of Modern African Studies* 21: 253–271.

Valdes, Nelson P. (1984) "The Cuban Revolution," in Jan Knippers Black, ed., *Latin America: Its Problems and Its Promise*. Boulder, CO: Westeview.

Valenta, Jiri (1984a) "Soviet Decisionmaking on Czechoslovakia, 1968," in Jiri Valenta and William C. Potter, eds., *Soviet Decisionmaking for National Security*. London: Allen and Unwin.

——— (1984b) "Soviet Decisionmaking on Afghanistan, 1979," in Jiri Valenta and William C. Potter, eds., *Soviet Decisionmaking for National Security*. London: Allen and Unwin.

——— (1984c) "Soviet Decision Making and the Hungarian Revolution," in Bela K. Kiraly, Barbara Lotze, Nandor F. Dreisziger, eds., *The First War Between Socialist States: The Hungarian Revolution of 1956 and Its Impact*. New York: Brooklyn College Press (distributed by Columbia University Press).

——— (1980a) "Soviet Decision Making on the Intervention in Angola," in David E. Albright, ed., *Communism in Africa*. Bloomington: Indiana University Press.

——— (1980b) "From Prague to Kabul: The Soviet Style of Invasion," *International Security* 5: 114–141.

——— (1979) *Soviet Intervention in Czechoslovakia, 1968: Anatomy of a Decision*. Baltimore: Johns Hopkins.

——— (1978) "The Soviet-Cuban Intervention in Angola, 1975," *Studies in Comparative Communism* 11: 3–33.

——— (1975) "Soviet Decisionmaking and the Czechoslovak Crisis of 1968," *Studies in Comparative Communism* 8: 147–173.

Valenzuela, J. Samuel, and Arturo Valenzuela (1985) "Chile and the Breakdown of Democracy," in Howard J. Wiarda and Harvey F. Kline, eds., *Latin American Politics and Development*. Boulder, CO: Westview.

van Klaverin, Alberto (1984) "The Analysis of Latin American Foreign Policies: Theoretical Perspectives," in Heraldo Muñoz and Joseph S. Tulchin, eds., *Latin American Nations in World Politics*. Boulder, CO: Westview.

Vannicelli, Primo (1974) *Italy, NATO, and European Community: The Interplay of Foreign Policy and Domestic Politics*. Cambridge, MA: Center for International Affairs, Harvard University.

van Staden, Alfred (1985) "To Deploy or Not to Deploy: The Case of the Cruise Missiles," in Philip P. Everts, ed., *Controversies at Home: Domestic Factors in the Foreign Policy of the Netherlands*. Boston: Martinus Nijhoff.

Vasquez, John A. (1987) "Foreign Policy, Learning, and War," in Charles F. Hermann, Charles W. Kegley, and James N. Rosenau, eds., *New Directions in the Study of Foreign Policy*. Boston: Allen and Unwin.

———(1985) "Domestic Contention on Critical Foreign Policy Issues: The Case of the United States," *International Organization* 39: 641–666.

Vertzberger, Yaacov Y. I. (1984a) *Misperceptions in Foreign Policymaking: The Sino-Indian Conflict, 1959–1962*. Boulder, CO: Westview.

——— (1984b) "Bureaucratic-Organizational Politics and Information Processing in a Developing State," *International Studies Quarterly* 28: 69–95.

Vital, David (1968) *The Making of British Foreign Policy*. London: Allen and Unwin.

von Beyme, Klaus (1983) "Coalition Government in Western Germany," in Vernon Bogdanor, ed., *Coalition Government in Western Europe*. London: Heinemann.

Wahl, Nicholas (1959) *The Fifth Republic: France's New Political System*. Westport, CT: Greenwood.

Walker, Stephen G., ed. (1987) *Role Theory and Foreign Policy Analysis*. Durham, NC: Duke University Press.

Wallace, Paul (1969) "India: The Leadership Crisis," *Asian Survey* 9: 79–86.

——— (1968) "India: The Dispersion of Political Power," *Asian Survey* 8: 87–96.

Wallace, William (1976) *The Foreign Policy Process in Britain*. London: Allen and Unwin.

Waltz, Kenneth N. (1967) *Foreign Policy and Democratic Politics: The American and British Experience*. Boston: Little, Brown.

Warner, Edward (1974) "Soviet Strategic Force Posture," in Frank Horton, Anthony Rogerson, and Edward Warner, eds., *Comparative Defense Policy*. Baltimore: Johns Hopkins University Press.

Weede, Erich (1984) "Democracy and War Involvement," *Journal of Conflict Resolution* 28: 649–664.

Weil, Gordon (1970) *The Benelux Nations: The Politics of Small-Country Democracies*. New York: Holt, Reinhart, and Winston.

Weinberger, Naomi Joy (1986) *Syrian Intervention in Lebanon: The 1975–76 Civil War*. New York: Oxford University Press.

Weiner, Myron (1962) "India's Third General Elections," *Asian Survey* 2: 3–18.

——— (1957) *Party Politics in India: The Development of a Multi-Party System*. Princeton, NJ: Princeton University Press.

Weinstein, Franklin B. (1976) *Indonesian Foreign Policy and the Dilemma of Dependence: From Sukarno to Soeharto*. Ithaca, NY: Cornell University Press.

——— (1972) "The Uses of Foreign Policy in Indonesia: An Approach to the Analysis of Foreign Policy in the Less Developed Countries," *World Politics* 24: 356–381.

——— (1969) *Indonesia Abandons Confrontation*. Ithaca, NY: Interim Reports Series, Modern Indonesia Project, Southeast Asian Program, Cornell University.

Weinstein, Martin (1975) *Uruguay: The Politics of Failure*. Westport, CT: Greenwood.

Welfield, John (1976) "Japan, the United States, and China in the Last Decade of the Cold War: An Interpretive Essay," in Peter Jones, ed., *The International Yearbook of Foreign Policy Analysis*, vol 2. London: Croom and Helm.

Wiarda, Howard J. (1980) "Spain and Portugal," in Peter H. Merkl, ed., *Western European Political System*. New York: Free Press.

——— (1968) "Cuba," in Ben G. Burnett and Kenneth Johnson, eds., *Political Forces in Latin America*. Belmont, CA: Wadsworth.

Wiarda, Howard J., and Harvey F. Kline, eds. (1985) *Latin American Politics and Development*. Boulder, CO: Westview.

Wiarda, Ieda Siqueira (1985) "Venezuela: the Politics of Democratic Developmentalism," in Howard J. Wiarda and Harvey F. Kline, eds., *Latin American Politics and Development*. Boulder, CO: Westview.

Wilkenfeld, Jonathan (1973) "Domestic and Foreign Conflict," in Jonathan Wilkenfeld, ed., *Conflict Behavior and Linkage Politics*. New York: McKay.

——— (1972) "Models for the Analysis of Foreign Conflict Behavior of States," in Bruce M. Russett, ed., *Peace, War, and Numbers*. Beverly Hills, CA: Sage.

Wilkenfeld, Jonathan, Gerald W. Hopple, Paul J. Rossa, and Stephen J. Andriole

(1980) *Foreign Policy Behavior: The Interstate Behavior Analysis Model.*
Beverly Hills, CA: Sage.

Williams, Philip M. (1970) *French Politicians and Elections 1951–1969.*
Cambridge: Cambridge University Press.

Williams, Philip M., and Martin Harrison, eds. (1972) *Politics and Society in de
Gaulle's Republic.* New York: Doubleday.

Willis, F. Roy (1971) *Italy Chooses Europe.* New York: Oxford University Press.

Wilson, David A. (1965) "Thailand—Scandal and Progress," *Asian Survey* 5: 108–
112.

——— (1964a) "Thailand," in George M. Kahin, ed., *Government and Politics of
Southeast Asia.* Ithaca, NY: Cornell University Press.

——— (1964b) "Thailand: A New Leader," *Asian Survey* 4: 711–715.

——— (1963) "Thailand: Old Leaders and New Directions," *Asian Survey* 3: 83–
87.

——— (1962a) *Politics in Thailand.* Ithaca, NY: Cornell University Press.

——— (1962b) "The Military in Thai Politics," in John J. Johnson, ed., *The Role of
the Military in Underdeveloped Countries.* Princeton, NJ: Princeton University
Press.

Winter, David G., Margaret G. Hermann, Sidney Weinstraub, and Steven G. Walker
(1991) "The Personalities of Bush and Gorbachev Measured at a Distance:
Procedures, Portraits, and Policies," *Political Psychology* 12: 215–245.

Wish, Naomi (1980) "Foreign Policy Makers and Their National Role
Conceptions," *International Studies Quarterly* 24: 532–554.

Wit, Daniel (1968) *Thailand: Another Vietnam.* New York: Charles Scribner's.

Wriggins, W. Howard (1969) *The Ruler's Imperative: Strategies for Political
Survival in Asia and Africa.* New York: Columbia University Press.

Wright, Quincy (1942) *A Study of War.* Chicago: University of Chicago Press.

Wurfel, David (1988) *Filipino Politics: Development and Decay.* Ithaca, NY:
Cornell University Press.

——— (1964) "The Philippines," in George M. Kahin, ed., *Government and
Politics of Southeast Asia.* Ithaca, NY: Cornell University Press.

Wyatt, David K. (1984) *Thailand: A Short History,* New Haven, CT: Yale
University Press.

Wynia, Gary W. (1986) *Argentina: Illusions and Realities.* New York: Holmes &
Meier.

Yamak, Labib Zuwiyya (1966) "Party Politics in the Lebanese Political System," in
Leonard Binder, ed., *Politics in Lebanon.* New York: John Wiley.

Yaniv, Avner, and Yael Yishai (1981) "Israeli Settlements in the West Bank: The
Politics of Intransigence," *Journal of Politics* 43: 1104–1128.

Yanov, Alexander (1977) *Detente After Brezhnev: The Domestic Roots of Soviet
Foreign Policy.* Berkeley: Institute of International Studies, University of
California.

Yergin, Daniel (1977) *Shattered Peace: The Origins of the Cold War and the
National Security State.* Boston: Houghton Mifflin.

Yishai, Yael (1981) "Factionalism in Israeli Political Parties," *The Jerusalem
Quarterly* 20: 36–48.

Yu, George T. (1964) "The 1962 and 1963 Sessions of the National People's
Congress of Communist China," *Asian Survey* 4: 981–990.

Zagoria, Donald S. (1968) "The Strategic Debate in Peking," in Tang Tsou, ed.,
China in Crisis: China's Policies in Asia and America's Alternatives. Chicago:
University of Chicago Press.

——— (1967) *Vietnam Triangle: Moscow, Peking, Hanoi.* New York: Pegasus.

Zariski, Raphael (1980) "Italy," in Peter H. Merkl, ed., *Western European Party Systems: Trends and Prospects.* New York: Free Press.

Zartman, I. W. (1966) "Decision Making Among African Governments in Inter-African Affairs," *Journal of Development Studies* 2: 129–143.

——— (1963) *Government and Politics in Northern Africa.* New York: Praeger.

Zartman, I.W., and A. G. Kluge (1984) "Heroic Politics: The Foreign Policy of Libya," in Bahgat Korany and Ali E. Hillal Dessouki, eds., *The Foreign Policies of Arab States.* Boulder, CO: Westview.

Zimmerman, William (1987) *Open Borders, Nonalignment, and the Political Evolution of Yugoslavia.* Princeton, NJ: Princeton University Press.

——— (1973) "Issue Area and Foreign Policy Process: A Research Note in Search of a General Theory," *American Political Science Review* 67: 1204–1212.

Ziring, Lawrence (1978) "Pakistan and India: Politics, Personalities, and Foreign Policy," *Asian Survey* 18: 706–730.

Zolberg, Aristide (1971) "Political Development in the Ivory Coast Since Independence," in Philip J. Foster and Aristide R. Zolberg, eds., *Ghana and the Ivory Coast: Perspectives on Modernization.* Chicago: University of Chicago Press.

——— (1969) *One-Party Government in the Ivory Coast.* Princeton, NJ: Princeton University Press.

Index

About the Book and Author

Political explanations in comparative foreign policy research typically center on the assumption that foreign policy decisionmakers in democratic regimes are far more politically constrained than are their counterparts in authoritarian polities. Disputing this assumption, Professor Hagan draws on case studies of the politics of foreign policy in a variety of non-U.S. settings to develop direct measures of actual political opposition and thus to capture its pervasiveness across all types of political systems.

Hagan offers an extensive empirical analysis of the foreign policy behaviors of eighty-eight political regimes identified in a diverse set of thirty-eight national political systems. Using innovative measures of the strengths and orientations of various types of opposition, he shows that the foreign policy behaviors of highly constrained regimes are marked by distinctive levels of commitment, initiative, and hostility. The magnitude and direction of the linkages between opposition and foreign policy making are, however, conditioned in complex ways by regime vulnerability and political system accountability and institutionalization.

This analysis demonstrates the practicality of cross-national research on political influences and points to the value of incorporating regime concepts into broader examinations of such phenomena as interstate wars and foreign policy restructurings.

Joe D. Hagan is associate professor of political science at West Virginia University and associate director of the university's International Studies Program. He is also a faculty associate of the Mershon Center at Ohio State University, and, in 1993–1994, a Pew Faculty Fellow in International Affairs at the John F. Kennedy School of Government, Harvard University.